LAW FOR
THE CHRISTIAN
COUNSELOR

**CONTEMPORARY CHRISTIAN
COUNSELING**

LAW FOR THE CHRISTIAN COUNSELOR

GEORGE OHLSCHLAGER, M.S.W., J.D.
PETER MOSGOFIAN, M.A.

CONTEMPORARY CHRISTIAN COUNSELING

General Editor
GARY R. COLLINS, PH.D.

Library of Congress Cataloging-in-Publication Data:

Ohlschlager, George W., 1951–
    Law for the Christian counselor: a guidebook for clinicians and pastors/
George W. Ohlschlager, Peter T. Mosgofian
        p.   cm. — (Contemporary Christian counseling; 6)
    Includes bibliographical references and index.
    ISBN 0–8499–0889–2 :
        1. Pastoral counseling—Law and legislation—United States.
    2. Clergy—Legal status, laws, etc.—United States.   3. Christianity and
    law.   4. Law and ethics.   I. Mosgofian, Peter T., 1950–   .
    II. Title.   III. Series.
    KF4868.C44O35   1992
    253.5—dc20   92–26622
        CIP

Printed in the United States of America

    4 5 6 7 8 9 LBM 7 6 5 4 3 2

To Lorraine and Gale,
with love and thanksgiving for their
faithfulness and enduring support;

And to Noelle, Justin, and Rea,
and Summer, Isaac, Joy, and Noël,
with love and hope for their future
as citizens of church and state
in the new millennium.

Contents

Preface

Robert Barclay, in his seminal work "Apology for the Quakers" written in 1678, penned the classic statement of right relations between God, the individual, and the law of the state.

> Since God has assumed to himself the power and dominion of the conscience, who alone can rightly instruct and govern it, therefore it is not lawful for any whatsoever, by virtue of any authority or principality they bear in the government of this world, to force the consciences of others . . . provided always that no man, under the pretense of conscience, prejudice his neighbor in his life or estate; or do anything destructive to, or inconsistent with, human society; in which case the law is for the transgressor, and justice to be administered upon all, without respect of persons.[1]

We affirm, and will fiercely defend when necessary, the right of every Christian counselor to guide their helping ministry by their own God-directed consciences. The helper committed to moral purity, ethical practice, and excellence in service is governed by the God who rules over all. The state has no business—indeed, it has no right, no legitimate need—to interfere in this manner of work.

Regretfully, however, when counseling ministry strays from the Truth—when harm and not life is its outcome—the right of the state to intervene assumes legitimate power. Law is for the transgressor. Justice is rightly administered upon those who harm, whether by negligent incompetence or intentional deceit, the weak, the needy, the tormented, and the oppressed.

The time is ripe for the church to acknowledge and affirm the boundary—especially the legal boundary—between right and wrongful counseling ministry. We purpose to help Christian counselors discern and understand these boundaries and to avoid crossing them. Reversing the boundary challenge, we also hope to check, even resist undue state encroachment into the special but fragile domain of Christian conscience and Spirit-led ministry.

---

[1] Robert Barclay, "Apology for the Quakers," in *Documents of the Christian Church*, 2d ed., ed. Henry Bettenson (London: Oxford University Press, 1963), 256.

Acknowledgments

If we accomplish our goals in this book, it will be due in large measure to some wonderful people who guided and coached us on right book writing. Dr. Gary Collins, General Editor for the Contemporary Christian Counseling series, receives our strongest praise and thanksgiving. He served—as Paul did to Timothy—as a wise teacher and loving shepherd throughout these two years of labor. He believed in this project, encouraged us when our beliefs faltered, checked us when we strayed, and mediated the best of solutions when we had to scale back the length of this book to conform to series limits.

Many people at Word, Incorporated, assisted in shepherding this project to completion. Special thanks go to David Pigg, Manager of Academic and Pastoral Publishing, for his patience and kindness. Project Editor Terri Gibbs and Copy Editor Lois Stück were indispensable in transforming our manuscript into a good and useful book. Barry Kerrigan in the Desktop Publishing department was very helpful on issues regarding computerized writing and formatting.

Our Board, colleagues, and staff at The Redwood Family Institute in Eureka both supported and suffered through this project with us—thanks to each of you. Thanks, also, to the library staffs at Humboldt State University and the general, research, law, and theological libraries at Stanford University, the University of California at Berkeley, and the Graduate Theological Union in Berkeley.

Finally, our deepest thanks and appreciation is given our families, to whom this book is dedicated. To acknowledge that they persevered through thick and thin is an understatement. For the many long nights, lost weekends, and seemingly unending obsession with "the book," we are sorry. For a better and more family-focused future, we are hopeful. For your long-suffering patience with us, support for this project, and faithful love, we are truly thankful.

George & Peter
Eureka, California

PART I

The Grave New World of Christian Counseling Liability

Chapter 1

Introduction to Law for the Christian Counselor

Where there is no revelation, the people cast off restraint; but blessed is he who keeps the law.

Proverbs 29:18

As THE TWENTIETH CENTURY CLOSES AND A NEW millennium dawns, consider the evidence of the grave new world of Christian counseling liability. In California, a large church and four of its pastors were sued for clergy malpractice and outrageous conduct in a wrongful death action following the suicide of a young male congregant.[1] In Wisconsin, a number of pastors and professional counselors have been prosecuted and punished under a state statute that defines sexual relations with a counselee, in the church as well as outside it, as criminal behavior.[2] In Oklahoma, a church and its leaders were sued and faced damage claims of $435,000 for invasion of privacy and intentional infliction of emotional distress following disciplinary proceedings against an erring church member.[3] In Illinois, a student sued his Christian college and affiliated counselors for breach of confidentiality and invasion of privacy following allegations of homosexual behavior and dismissal from the school.[4]

These cases are not uncommon nor is litigation against counselors and the church an isolated occurrence. Across the United States, the Catholic church is awash in a sea of lawsuits over priestly sexual misconduct and negligent diocesan supervision.

The estimated $300 million the church and its insurers have paid in settlements to date led a Notre Dame University professor to exclaim, "We could be sued out of existence."[5] A report to national Catholic leadership *projects $1 billion paid out by the church* by the turn of the century.[6] The onslaught of litigation has even coined new terms—*litigaphobia* and *defensive counseling*—references to the fear of being sued and the impact it has on counseling practice. These are a few examples of the explosion of litigation currently being visited upon Christian counselors and the church. Join us as we explore and carefully thread our way through the minefield of this alien, litigious land.

GUIDEBOOK MISSION

May you be blessed in the best spirit of Proverbs 29:18 as you study and keep the law regarding Christian counseling ministry. Our primary mission with this book is to reveal current and developing law that impacts counseling practice, instructing you how to keep the law, prevent client harm, and avoid lawsuits. We also want to assist the professional development of Christian counseling and to challenge the field to organize and control itself under God, blocking the state from further significant legal invasion.

This book is written for Christian counselors concerned with legal boundaries and ethical guidelines to better ministry practice. These counselors will function in many, diverse roles: professional counselors and clinicians in Christian counseling clinics, agencies, and private practice; pastors, associate staff, and lay helpers in churches; and counseling staff at Christian schools, colleges, missions, and various specialized and para-church ministries. This book will also be of value as a training and policy guide to teachers, researchers, students, professional associations, lawyers, and judges.

We have written a practical and comprehensive guidebook that will help you make sense of your duties under law and guide you in the ethical practice of Christian counseling.[7] While we make reference to rich resources of clinical research, counseling theory and ethics, legal theory, and Christian theology, we have consciously emphasized the practical over the theoretical to enhance the book's usefulness to the busy practitioner or minister. You may benefit from time-limited study of a single topic or an in-depth study of the larger themes of the relationship of law to Christian counseling. The case stories we use are composite cases and do not track the facts of any one client's case history.

Though our subject matter is legal in nature, this is a book about Christian counseling practice. We write as professional Christian counselors, revealing how the law impacts your counseling ministry, where legal trends are developing, and how to shape your work in light of your legal and ethical duties. We also suggest what we believe the law should be in relation to Christian counseling and how Christian professionals can influence it according to the best interests of clients and parishioners. This is not a book on forensic practice; we address courtroom and expert testimony only as the most common forensic issues a Christian counselor may face.

We bring to this book a dedication to Christian service and a diverse and interdisciplinary background in counseling and clinical practice, pastoral ministry, law and mediation practice, church and agency administration, teaching, research, and writing. Each of us took the lead in drafting various chapters; a recently published chapter on this subject by the first author[8] was built upon, even used verbatim in some chapters. What you are reading is a product of our mutual interaction; the book is truly a joint project.

THE NATURE OF LAW

We acknowledge that for most Christians (and probably for most people), the study of law is largely a foreign and distasteful exercise. Common associations of legalism, duty, and judgment grate against our orientation toward grace, freedom in Christ, mercy, love, and justice. Furthermore, modern law is perceived to be thoroughly secularized, professionalized, and overwhelmingly complex. These perceptions, of course, are true—but they are only *partially* true.

We are aware that we must overcome some significant barriers to reach you as an interested reader. We accept this challenge because (1) such study is unavoidable in this litigious, rights-conscious age, and (2) contrary to common belief, the study of law is quite interesting; it can even be compelling and fascinating. To enhance your interest, consider the nature of law from biblical, historical, and modern perspectives.

LAW IN BIBLICAL REVELATION

Throughout Scripture, God reveals two fundamental purposes in the revelation of law to humankind. One aspect is the restraining force of the law; its positive counterpart is the revelation of law as guiding light.

Law as restraining force. The restraining force of law reveals the dark side of human nature and convicts us of sin. It is also a reality that is quickly seen in others and easily denied and minimized in ourselves. Yet, God declares this law to be good. "We know that the law is good if one uses it properly. We also know that law is made not for the righteous but for lawbreakers and rebels . . ." (1 Tim. 1:8–9a). The revelation of right and wrong and knowledge of these crucial legal boundaries is a good thing; it warns the lawbreaker in us all and gives opportunity for godly restraint.

The law of the state dynamically expresses this restraining dimension of God's law. "Everyone must submit himself to the governing authorities, for there is no authority except that which God has established. . . . he who rebels against the authority is rebelling against what God has instituted, and those who do so will bring judgment on themselves. For rulers hold no terror for those who do right, but for those who do wrong" (Rom. 13:1a, 2–3a). The power of civil government to restrain evil and punish wrongdoing is delegated directly from God, whose work is accomplished, in part, through the legal agency of the state. Christians are no more exempt from this reality than anyone else.

Law as guiding light. God also reveals in Scripture the guiding power of law that beckons every Christian to the highest good in loving service to God and others. This is the law of the new covenant that is written in the hearts and minds of regenerate believers (Jer. 31:31–34, Heb. 10:12–18). This new law—the guiding light of love in the power of the Holy Spirit—does not destroy the old, restraining law. Instead, the old is superseded and fulfilled in the new, as was taught and modeled by Jesus Christ (Matt. 5:17–20, Luke 24:44). This new covenant is law that reveals and challenges the very best of Christian service beyond a mere avoidance of wrongdoing and harmful behavior. This is the law to which the Psalmist expressed faithfulness and delight.

> Your laws endure to this day,
>   for all things serve you.
> If your law had not been my delight,
>   I would have perished in my affliction.
> I will never forget your precepts,
>   for by them you have preserved my life. . . .

Your word is a lamp to my feet
    and a light for my path.
I have taken an oath and confirmed it,
    that I will follow your righteous laws. . . .
Your statutes are my heritage forever;
    they are the joy of my heart.
My heart is set on keeping your decrees
    to the very end.
Psalm 119:91–93, 105–6, 111–12

The expression of this law is love. The counselor "who loves his fellowman has fulfilled the law. The commandments . . . are summed up in this one rule: 'Love your neighbor as yourself.' *Love does no harm* to its neighbor. Therefore love is the fulfillment of the law" (Rom. 13:8b–10, italics ours). Love that issues out of this new covenant not only avoids client harm, it fulfills the best intentions and goals pursued in the Christian counseling endeavor. Therefore, while legal study by Christian counselors is essential in this litigious age, we also recognize that mere adherence to the letter of the law is not enough. Love is our aim, sacrificial service that sets and maintains our clients' interests above our own in all our counseling work.

TENSIONS AND CURRENTS IN MODERN LAW

Most have heard the well-worn assertion, "You can't legislate morality!" This is patently false, for law, in one sense, is the codification of morality. There is an inherent moral assertion, dividing the boundary between right and wrong, in every legal act. The controversy in lawmaking is not a question of morality or not, but of which moral standard will be the basis of law and where the boundary of right and wrong will be divided. This tension in modern Anglo-American law has reflected the contending influences of natural law and legal realism, or sociological jurisprudence.

Natural law. Natural law asserts the relationship between human laws and the law of God. Alternatively, as with the ancient Greeks, the idea has been historically recognized as law grounded in some objective, transcendent other—right reason or universal understandings of moral right and wrong. Natural law proponents evaluate the rightness and justice of human law according to the objective, universal standard to which they subscribe. Christians opposed to abortion laws, for example, often do so because they recognize a higher law—a right to life ordained by God and empowered by the prohibitions against murder.

Perhaps the greatest thinker on natural law was Thomas Aquinas, the great theologian-philosopher of the thirteenth century. Consider the following excerpts from his "Treatise on Law," from *Summa Theologica:*

> Now human laws . . . do not forbid all vices, from which the virtuous abstain, but only the more grievous vices, from which it is possible for the majority to abstain; and chiefly those that are to the hurt of others, without the prohibition of which society could not be maintained. . . .
> . . . Laws framed by man are either just or unjust. If they be just, they have the power of binding in conscience, from the eternal law whence they are derived. . . . Now laws are said to be just . . . according to an equality of proportion and with a view to the common good. . . . On the other hand laws may be unjust in two ways: first, by being contrary to the human good. . . . Secondly, laws may be unjust through being opposed to the Divine good, such as the law of tyrants inducing to idolatry . . . laws of this kind must nowise be observed, because . . . we ought to obey God rather than men.[9]

Legal realism. Legal realism or legal positivism, with its roots in rationalist philosophy and empirical science, views law as a process of social control by which the power of the state is organized to enforce the political will. The relationship of law and morality is not denied, but morality is not seen as issuing from God. Instead, morality and justice are deemed a function of the dominant societal interest or power. Sociological jurisprudence studies the evolution of law in society as a socio-politico-economic process; natural law is either denied or deemed relevant only insofar as it describes one strain of influence on modern law.

The great American jurist Oliver Wendell Holmes stated the case for legal realism, and the problems he perceived in the moral view of law, in a famous *Harvard Law Review* article in 1897:

> I take it for granted that no hearer will misinterpret what I have to say as the language of cynicism. The law is the written and external deposit of our moral life. The practice of it, in spite of popular jests, tends to make good citizens and good men. When I emphasize the difference between law and morals I do so with reference to a single end, that of learning and understanding the law. . . .

> If you want to know the law and nothing else, you must look at it as a bad man, who cares only for the material consequences which such knowledge enables him to predict, not as a good one, who finds his reasons for conduct, whether inside the law or outside of it, in the vaguer sanctions of conscience. . . .
>
> Take the fundamental question, What constitutes the law? You will find some text writers telling you it is something different from what is decided by the courts of Massachusetts or England, that it is a system of reason . . . or admitted axioms. . . . But if we take the view of . . . the bad man we shall find that he does not care two straws for the axioms . . . but that he does want to know what the Massachusetts or English courts are likely to do in fact. I am much of his mind. The prophecies of what the courts will do in fact, and nothing more pretentious, are what I mean by the law.[10]

Holmes' conception of legal realism may be the best, and most benign statement of its purpose and usefulness to a society. The darker side of this philosophy—when God is rejected and moral vision extinguished—has been seen in the legal systems built to protect fascism and communism. Legal realism was perverted in Nazi Germany wherein the "Will of the Fuhrer" and law were conceived to be one and the same.[11] Similarly, Soviet legal philosophy held that the "state is an organ of class dominance—an organ whereby one class crushes another. . . . Law is a system of norms established by the state to safeguard the existing order. . . . It is the actively reflected will of the dominant class, sanctifying and perpetuating the economic and political interests of that class."[12]

THE AMERICAN LEGAL EXPERIMENT

American law is derived from several, diverse sources. The foundational source is the Constitution of the United States, which declares in Article VI, "This Constitution . . . shall be the supreme Law of the land. . . ." Our Constitution is not fixed or inerrant. It is an evolving document of governance, a principled and flexible charter with provision for amended change according to the principles and procedure prescribed in Article V.

The United States Constitution established a democratic republic with governing power separated and divided among various federal branches (the Executive, Congress, and the Judiciary), the fifty states, and key institutions (the church, the press, and commercial interests, for example). These powers are delegated to the government from the citizenry ("We the people . . ."), whose rights are enumerated in the Bill of Rights and protected through access to a free judiciary. The people's governing power is expressed by election of all executive leaders and representatives to Congress and state legislatures and by their ability to amend the constitution. Each of the fifty states also has a constitution, ultimately subject to the federal charter.

Statutes are another form of law enacted by Congress and the various state legislatures in political relationship to the executive branches. Elected representatives consider, debate, and pass resolutions that enter statutory codes. These codes are directly influenced by the United States president and governors of the various states as well as from influential citizens and special interest lobby groups. The executive branches of the federal and state governments, including regional, county, and municipal governments, also issue administrative regulations that further define and implement statutory law.

Finally, the judicial branch of the federal and state governments issues court opinions that define and advance the meaning of law when contested by affected parties. The administration of justice is delivered through an extensive trial court system in every state and in federal district courts. Each state has a supreme court and a federal appeals court stands atop each of the thirteen regional circuits that comprise the federal judiciary. The United States Supreme Court is the final court of appeal for all federal and state courts, hearing a small percentage of the thousands of cases appealed to it each year.

Weaving throughout the American legal structure are the influences of natural law and legal realism; American and Western law may well be described as a synthesis of these various influences.

> In the Constitution can be seen another vital function of our law: Protection of the citizen against excessive or unfair government power. . . . Our legal system is concerned too with protecting people against excessive or unfair private power. . . . [Recent laws] are aimed at assuring people an opportunity to enjoy the minimum decencies of life by protecting their economic and health status. . . .
>
> One other point: Is there any sense in which it is true that law has an ethical or moral function? The answer . . . is definitely yes. Most of the functions already mentioned have a

> clear ethical dimension. . . . A good deal of criminal law car-
> ries out ethical precepts of conduct—many of which are in the
> Ten Commandments. In tort law, many of the principles con-
> cerning either negligent or intentional infliction of injury may
> be traced to the Golden Rule. . . .[13]

The law that impacts Christian counseling ministry comes from all of these sources, as well as from the common law tradition we inherited from England.[14] This tradition of Anglo-American legal history had exempted church and clergy from liability based on the centuries-old doctrine of charitable immunity.[15] This religious exemption was further buttressed in America by the Religion Clauses of the First Amendment to the United States Constitution.[16]

Our approach to law. We respect both the influences of natural law and legal realism. Following Holmes, we describe to you what the law is and how it is developing. This is to apprise and help control the bad man in all of us, for we are all vulnerable to be pulled astray by our bent toward sin and wrongdoing. We recognize the great bulk of law impacting the church as honorable and worthy of respect, an instrument in God's hands to work his purposes in the land. However, not all the law can be so well evaluated. We challenge certain laws, on both biblical and natural law bases, that are unjust to either the common or the divine good.

THE LAW AND YOU

Your interest in law is warranted because you are *at risk* to be sued, prosecuted, or regulated as a Christian counselor. This is especially true if you practice as a licensed or sanctioned professional counselor; this is increasingly true if you are a pastor or lay minister counseling as part of your church ministry. The Christian counselor, the entire church in fact, can no longer remain ignorant or passive in the face of the enormous changes taking place at the boundary of ministry and law. We have little doubt that those who do remain ignorant, avoidant, or arrogant in the face of this grave new world will be the ones we will be reading about in future reports of lawsuits and regulatory action by the state.

The complex matrix of law that sets boundaries for the Christian counselor clearly expresses the cardinal rule that has guided professional liability throughout history: *do no harm* in your counseling work. The Christian counselor is held liable for his or her wrongful counseling behavior because it hurts those who have come for help. As citizen of both church and state, the Christian counselor is obliged to recognize and respect legal boundaries in counseling practice.

The presentation of law in this book, though specific at many places, is a general synthesis of current law in the United States and, to some degree, the nations associated with the British Commonwealth. Policy and practice recommendations for Christian counseling are made in accordance with settled legal principles or developing trends in law. Depending on your resident state or province, the nature of your counseling ministry, and your status as a pastor, lay minister, or counseling professional, your actual liability may be more extensive than we reveal or it may be practically nonexistent.

The wise clinician or pastor will consider all forms of potential liability and review his or her counseling ministry accordingly. The common-law heritage of our Anglo-American legal system is an active history of liberal interaction between the states, the federal system, even international review in the incremental development of law. Any Christian counselor is a potential defendant in a landmark case that sets new precedent or extends existing law to a new state or province.

This guidebook, then, will strengthen you in the face of the grave new world. We want you to be blessed and empowered by knowing and keeping the law. *Our caveat is to respect the limits of the general guidelines we offer you. Every reader with specific questions on personal and organizational liability is strongly encouraged to consult an attorney, your denomination, or state, provincial, and national professional association.* Use this book to understand issues, to form clear questions, and to consult with intelligence and wisdom. Do not rely on this book for specific answers to questions of liability and risk management that demand more specialized consultation.

NOTES

1. *Nally v. Grace Community Church of the Valley*, 47 Cal.3d 278, 763 P.2d 948, 253 Cal. Rptr. 97 (1988); cert. denied 109 S. Ct. 1644 (1989) (hereafter cited as *Nally III*).

2. Personal correspondence with John Scherpelz, M.A., staff member of The Center for Christian Counseling, Madison, Wis., December 1991.

3. *Guinn v. Church of Christ of Collinsville*, 775 P.2d 766 (Okla. S.Ct. 1989).

4. *Johnson v. Lincoln Christian College*, 501 N.E.2d 1380 (Ill. 1986).

5. Richard Ostling, "Sins of the Fathers," *Time*, 19 August 1991.

6. Rorie Sherman, "Legal Spotlight on Priests Who Are Pedophiles," *The National Law Journal* (4 April 1988): 28.

7. Other useful secular and Christian books in this area include Thomas Gutheil and P. Appelbaum, *Clinical Handbook of Psychiatry and the Law,* 2d ed. (New York: McGraw-Hill, 1991); Robert G. Meyer, E. R. Landis, and J. R. Hays, *Law for the Psychotherapist* (New York: Norton, 1988); and Steve Levicoff, *Christian Counseling and the Law* (Chicago: Moody, 1990).

8. George Ohlschlager, "Liability in Christian Counseling: Welcome to the Grave New World," in *Excellence and Ethics in Counseling,* Gary Collins (Dallas: Word, 1991).

9. Thomas Aquinas, "Treatise on Law," in *Summa Theologica* (Cambridge, England: Blackfriars, 1966).

10. Oliver Wendell Holmes, "The Path of the Law," *Harvard Law Review* 10 (1897): 459–64.

11. See Friedrich Roetter, *Might is Right* (London: Quality Press, 1939).

12. P. Yudin, "Socialism and Law," in *Soviet Legal Philosophy,* trans. Hugh Babb (Cambridge, Mass.: Harvard University Press, 1951).

13. Samuel Mermin, *Law and the Legal System: An Introduction,* 2d ed. (Boston: Little, Brown and Co., 1982), 6–8.

14. English common law, including the precedent-following principle of *stare decisis,* follows the practice of judge-made law which developed slowly and incrementally over many centuries as a dominant form of English rule. Though much changed and supplemented by all forms of lawmaking in America, this common law system retains significant influence.

15. Charitable immunity was a privilege granted the church, hospitals, and social welfare agencies that exempted them from numerous legal duties imposed by governments in recognition of their fundamental value and service to society. This doctrine has been all but abolished in twentieth-century America due to public policy favoring compensation to injured persons and the rise of the insurance industry to protect such institutions from dissolution when sued for injuries caused by their work.

16. "Congress shall make no law respecting an establishment of religion, or prohibiting the free exercise thereof." *United States Constitution,* amend. I, cl. 1 and 2.

Chapter 2

The Legal Regulation of Christian Counseling

. . . men and women need more than a religious value system. They need civic structures to prevent chaos and provide order. Religion is not intended or equipped to do this; when it has tried it has brought grief on itself and the political institutions it has attempted to control. An independent state is crucial to the commonweal.

Both the City of God and the city of man are vital to society—and they must remain in delicate balance. "All human history and culture," one historian observed, "may be viewed as the interplay of the competing values of these . . . two cities"; and whenever they are out of balance, the public good suffers.[1]

Charles Colson

WE AGREE WITH THE NEED FOR BOTH CHURCH and state and for balanced relations between them. We believe this balance is now threatened by the overzealous intrusion of the state into the realm of Christian ministry. Over the past generation the legal regulation and risk of lawsuit faced by professional counselors has grown at an exponential rate. The law that regulates medical, psychiatric, and psychotherapeutic liability is now being attached to the Christian counselor. This chapter reviews the key data and legal bases of Christian counseling liability and state regulation of counseling practice.

THE FACTS ABOUT COUNSELOR LIABILITY

Lawsuits and disciplinary actions have dramatically increased against all the major mental health professional groups. Two research projects—the Hogan study of American psychotherapy malpractice litigation and the American Psychological Association insurance trust study—reveal the data and dynamic of the current liability crisis.

THE HOGAN MALPRACTICE LITIGATION STUDY

Daniel Hogan, a social psychologist and lawyer at Harvard University, performed a valuable service to the legal and mental health professions by completing a comprehensive survey of psychotherapy malpractice litigation in the United States from the nineteenth century to 1977.[2] Three hundred cases were analyzed for their relevance to psychotherapy and mental health care. Over 80 percent of these cases were appellate decisions, coming from the courts that establish the case law foundations of our American legal system.

A key finding of the Hogan study was the dramatic rise in the incidence of malpractice litigation. Two-thirds of all decisions since 1850 were decided since 1960. One-third of all decisions were reported during the 1970–77 period.[3] Overall, plaintiffs won 31 percent of all suits, defendants won 45 percent, and 24 percent were non-final (the issue of defendant liability was not reached for various reasons). During the 1970–77 period, however, plaintiffs won 39 percent while defendants won only 42 percent. Among cases not appealed, plaintiffs won verdicts half the time.[4] Trends in case outcome clearly favor client-plaintiffs over counselor-defendants. Taken together, the above findings predict that counselors who harm clients will be sued much more frequently and will lose these lawsuits more often than in the past.

If you practice as a counselor in New York or California, you practice with a much higher risk of suit. Nearly half the cases came out of these two states. Texas, Pennsylvania, Illinois, Missouri, and Massachusetts are in a second tier of states showing a smaller but consistent incidence of suit, and the remaining states revealing from one to a few cases.[5] Plaintiffs were far more successful against private and community-based practitioners (43 percent plaintiff won vs. 14 percent defendant prevailed) than against hospitals and other institutions (32 percent plaintiff won vs. 44 percent defendant prevailed).[6] Damages recovered for the fifty-seven cases reporting recovery showed a mean figure of $45,504. New York and California also led in damage awards, with California showing the highest mean recovery of $121,250.[7]

Regarding type of harm alleged, accidental injuries in a hospital setting and often in conjunction with drug treatment, was most often cited at 20 percent. Sexual misconduct was charged in 10 percent of the suits and were the most successful of lawsuits, with plaintiffs prevailing in two-thirds (66 percent) of these actions (though sexual misconduct cases revealed a mean recovery of only $25,320). Loss of liberty involved 11 percent, and deprivation of constitutional rights was noted in 9 percent of all cases. Suicide was the issue in 9 percent of the cases, and another 9 percent noted accidental death. Some of the myriad other harms noted were self-inflicted injury, injury to reputation, economic harm, marital harm, loss of health, insanity, alienation of affection, invasion of privacy, pregnancy, and abortion.[8]

Mental health professionals were named in 32 percent of all actions. Hospitals defended 20 percent of the suits, and governments at all levels defended 33 percent. Among individual clinicians, nonpsychiatric physicians comprised half of those sued, while psychiatrists were sued 35 percent of the time. Psychologists were named in 5 percent of the suits, nurses in 4 percent, lawyers in 2 percent (primarily for hospital commitment assistance), and an amalgam of social workers, marriage and family therapists, paraprofessionals, and others comprised the remaining 3 percent of the suits.[9]

PSYCHOLOGY INSURANCE TRUST STUDY

A few years ago the Insurance Trust of the American Psychological Association analyzed malpractice suits nationwide against psychologists from 1976 to 1986.[10] The most significant finding affirms the trend of the Hogan data: malpractice suits are increasing at a geometric rate against psychologists. From an average of 44 actions filed annually from 1976 to 1981, the period from 1982 to 1986 averaged 153 suits filed per year, an increase of 347 percent! Compare this to the number of claims filed from 1955 to 1965: *zero*.[11] A total of $5.4 million was paid against claims for the years 1976 through 1983 combined; in 1985 alone, the insurers paid out $17.2 million.[12]

Sexual misconduct was the most prevalent cause of action, with 22.5 percent of all actions filed over the eleven-year period of the study. This, however, fails to reveal the major increase in these lawsuits. From roughly 9 percent of the actions filed during the early years of the study, sexual misconduct actions comprised nearly 50 percent of all suits filed at the end of the study.

In descending order of frequency, other claims were for incorrect treatment (18.5 percent), loss from evaluation (11.8 percent), client death (10.5 percent—primarily suicide), breach of confidentiality (8.5 percent), improper diagnosis (7.2 percent), fee disputes (7.2 percent), defamation (5.3 percent), civil rights violations (3.6 percent), bodily injury (3.0 percent), assault and battery (1.3 percent), and failure to warn third persons (0.6 percent).

PRINCIPLES OF CHRISTIAN COUNSELING LIABILITY

This section reviews the major bases of law that impact Christian counseling liability for the professional counselor or counseling pastor; these include tort law, constitutional law, administrative law, contract law, and criminal law.

THE MALPRACTICE TORT

The primary area of law that defines liability in counseling is tort law. A tort is a noncriminal, civil, or private wrong, independent of contract, for which the law allows money damages as redress for injuries suffered.[13] Guided by a cardinal legal principle of rule by analogy, tort liability in counseling, including Christian counseling, follows the body of law developed from medical and psychiatric liability. The field of tort law is divided into two major branches: (1) negligent tort, also known as malpractice, and (2) intentional tort. Malpractice is a less severe form of wrongdoing compared to intentional tort, while intentional tort is considered less severe than criminal wrong.

Malpractice comprises two-thirds of all psychiatric- and psychotherapy-related litigation in the United States.[14] All psychotherapists licensed or sanctioned by the state or by national professional associations are subject to malpractice liability. Every Christian counselor who practices as a licensed professional or credentialed counselor or who is publicly promoted as a counseling minister should be acquainted with the standards and procedure of psychotherapy malpractice law.

Malpractice is defined legally as an "act or omission by a professional practitioner in the treatment of a patient or client that is inconsistent with the reasonable care or skill usually demonstrated by ordinary, prudent practitioners of the same profession, similarly situated."[15] Malpractice liability exists when it can be proven that (1) a counselor owed a legal duty to his or her client, (2) the counselor breached that duty by failing to meet the requisite standard of care, (3) the client suffered some demonstrable and compensable harm, and (4) that harm was caused by the counselor's breach of duty. A lawsuit can fail at any of these four points of proof, making malpractice difficult to prove by a client-claimant in spite of its predominance as the legal basis for counseling liability.

Legal duty. The existence of a professional relationship between a counselor and a client establishes a legal duty that makes malpractice law applicable. This element of proof is the easiest one to establish, but important to assert nonetheless. *Hammer v. Polsky*[16] was dismissed in favor of the defendant physician for the simple failure of asserting the existence of the duty at the outset.

Breach of the standard of care. The next issue to prove is that the counselor somehow failed to meet the standard of care. Generally, a counselor is required to both "exercise reasonable care" in practice and possess a minimum level of "special knowledge and ability."[17] This legal standard of care is established by expert testimony according to respected standards from the profession and model of therapy one uses, taking into consideration the experience and nature of the defendant's practice. Defining the proper standard of care is the most variable and controversial element in a malpractice lawsuit.

Courts derive the standard of care from various sources: licensure statutes, professional codes of ethics, prior case law, and the principles and standards of particular models of therapy. Therapists are most protected when they can show they practice from a well-known therapy school, one with definite principles and supported by "at least a respected minority of the profession."[18] Accepted standards could be easily established for psychodynamic, Adlerian, Rogerian, cognitive, behavioral, rational-emotive, transactional analysis, family systems, and task-centered therapies, for example. The influence of the psychodynamic model is seen in the many suits that base malpractice on the mishandling of transference and countertransference dynamics.

Establishing protective standards for therapists practicing less well-known therapy models is more difficult. As Harris asserts, respected minorities "are legion in psychotherapy,"[19] so a practitioner from a newer or more radical school should have solid empirical and clinical support for his or her claims. Even so, such practitioners will not be as protected by the standard of care. Although courts recognize psychotherapy to be a progressing science with a need for innovative risk-taking, malpractice law requires that it be done without harm or detriment to the client being served.

The key here is that clinician and client are presumed to be more protected when working within an accepted model of therapy. Evidence of having exercised ordinary or reasonable skill within an accepted school of therapy allows the therapist wider latitude for mistake or error in clinical judgment. A proponent of an untested or largely unaccepted school of therapy will be held to a higher standard of care, with far less margin for error before attachment of liability. Specialists and experts are also held to a higher standard of care than generalists. Furthermore, those holding themselves out as expert or especially competent with certain kinds of problems, whether they are or not, are also held to a higher standard of care. The perception of competence and expertise that a counselor places or allows in the mind of the client is the critical factor in this determination.

Demonstrable and compensable harm. Without some demonstrable, legally provable harm, there is no award of damages. Harm for which the law allows compensation can be physical, mental, or emotional, or harm resulting from violations of civil or constitutional rights. Historically, the law was reluctant to award damages for psychological and emotional harm, considering injury only as a tangible, physical construct. Modern legal doctrine has forsaken this historic avoidance with near universal acceptance of psychological harm.

Substantial deteriorative behavior or emotional change (e.g., acute depression, suicide attempt, or therapist-induced psychotic or emotional breakdown) must be demonstrated to sustain allegations of harm. Often, these must be coupled with tangible evidence of loss—financial or job loss, divorce, or physical injury of some sort. The law attempts to separate severe loss that can lead to litigation from less severe and expected declines that are part of the therapeutic endeavor.

> This raises an important point about any injury dealt a psychiatric patient. In the myriad of psychiatric judgments, not every palpable decline in health is actionable. Perhaps only a coterie of setbacks or the kind of serious reaction that makes further improvement more difficult and costly is or should be

the occasion for successful legal recompense. There are declines of even a psychotic nature which will not and should not be compensated for, since they may be unavoidable pitfalls in working through the tangled terrain of one's mental complexion.[20]

Causation of harm. Even if the therapist breached the standard of care and the client suffered harm, the client-plaintiff must then prove that breach caused the harm they allege. Here, the law applies the well-used "but for" rule. Applied to counseling malpractice, the rule states: but for the negligence of the counselor, the client harm would not have taken place. This is not easy to prove as numerous intervening factors may influence or cause client harm. A client suffering from a physically abusive spouse or a drug addiction, for example, will have a difficult time proving that therapist negligence and not these client problems caused the harm.

The task of proving causation is easier if the therapist works from a more directive school or model of therapy. In contrast to the nondirective psychodynamic or Rogerian therapies, practitioners of behavior therapy, rational-emotive therapy, nouthetic (confrontational) Christian counseling, or directive paradoxical therapy, for example, are at greater risk for malpractice liability. Harm and causation in reliance upon therapist instructions will be much easier to prove within these models. Dawidoff notes that a crucial factual distinction—as well as a key recommendation for the directive counselor—is determination of whether therapist instructions were suggestions or prescriptions for change.[21]

Remedies. Money damages is the primary remedy for professional malpractice. The baseline standard is compensatory—intending to restore the injured plaintiff to their pre-injury status. General and special damages will be awarded to compensate for past, present, and future costs related to the injury. This includes not only direct costs such as medical and legal expenses and lost earning capacity, but also money for pain and suffering and loss of enjoyment of life.

Punitive (usually triple) damages are awarded as punishment against a defendant for willful, intentional harm. The policy behind punitive awards is that it serves as a deterrent to future actions of the same kind. These are rarely awarded in negligence cases but are increasingly attached in cases of intentional torts (see next section). Nominal damages are another remedy wherein the court awards a nominal sum to the plaintiff in cases where no serious harm exists or the breach of duty was slight.

How long will clergy remain exempt? The one group that has remained exempt from malpractice liability are ordained clergy who counsel as a function of their ministry. Every malpractice action brought against clergy over the past decade, including the landmark *Nally* case (reviewed in chapter 4), failed to establish a legal cause for clergy malpractice.[22] Though the courts declined to establish clergy malpractice for numerous reasons of law and public policy, the overarching concern was that such cause would violate First Amendment constitutional protections of ministry freedom.[23] However, the 1990 United States Supreme Court opinion in *Employment Division, Dept. of Human Resources of Oregon v. Smith*[24] (also reviewed in chapter 4), may have seriously damaged historic legal protection of Christian ministry. Its rule may pave the way for a new round of church litigation in the 1990s that could establish a legal basis for clergy malpractice.

INTENTIONAL TORT LIABILITY

Though clergy malpractice has failed to date as a basis for suit, intentional tort has at least partially succeeded as a cause by which pastoral counselors have been sued.[25] In *Hester v. Barnett*, a Baptist pastor was sued for intentionally harming a family with whom he had been counseling. After promising confidential help to the family, the minister then made repeated false accusations that the children were abused and treated cruelly. He then publicly asserted these lies in letters, in the church bulletin, and from the pulpit, and attempted to separate the family. The Missouri court held that "Pastor Barnett gained access to the Hester home through the pretense as counselor to assist in the correction of the children's behavior, when the true motive was to harm the Hesters by the disclosure of the information obtained through that guile."[26]

A unique legal paradox exists here because, due to the requirement of proving the mental state of intentionality, these torts are harder to prove than malpractice. "This general rule does not apply, however, when the wrongful conduct is committed by a clergy counselor. In that situation, the rule is clearly the converse."[27] In the case of the pastoral counselor, liability for intentional tort is easier for courts to accept than is malpractice liability. This is because the wrongful conduct of the minister is much more easily separated from the religious beliefs of the church, therefore falling outside First Amendment protection. Courts simply assert that the First Amendment is not implicated in cases of outrageous and intentionally harmful behavior, avoiding the constitutional challenge that blocks the courts from applying malpractice liability to clergy and church.

In *Destefano v. Grabrian*,[28] the plaintiff-husband sued his Catholic priest and archdiocese for a sexual affair between his wife and the priest. The affair was initiated while the couple were in marriage counseling with the priest and which allegedly led to the couple's divorce. The Colorado Court of Appeals held that the priest's conduct was not actionable under tort law. The Colorado Supreme Court reversed this rule, in part, rejecting the constitutional defense by the priest and finding tort liability, asserting that "every Catholic is well aware of the vow of celibacy required of a priest. . . . [S]exual activity by a priest is fundamentally antithetical to Catholic doctrine. [T]he conduct . . . is, by definition, not an expression of a sincerely held religious belief."[29] Since priestly sex could not be associated with religious behavior, First Amendment protection of religion did not apply to guard the priest and the church from liability.

CONSTITUTIONAL AND CIVIL RIGHTS OF MENTAL PATIENTS

Although tort law comprises the bulk of psychotherapeutic litigation, constitution-based litigation is the fastest growing type of suit over the past quarter-century.[30] A revolution in patient and client rights has reshaped mental health treatment in America. This transformation should be understood by every pastor, chaplain, and Christian counselor who works in a hospital, in residential treatment, or any form of restrictive treatment environment.

Three events in the 1960s signaled the transformation of American mental health care. Congress passed the Community Mental Health Centers Act[31] in 1963 and provided states with funding to establish a national network of community-based centers for noninstitutional mental health treatment. In 1964, the Federal Civil Rights Act was passed, attaching rights to mental patients (among other groups) and creating liabilities for those who illegally discriminate against them.[32] A federal appeals court in 1966 ruled that a mental patient could not be held involuntarily if a less restrictive alternative were available through which safe and essential treatment could be delivered.[33]

The right to treatment is an important constitutional and civil right. In a case from Alabama,[34] a federal appeals court required the state to provide treatment to its nondangerous, involuntarily confined mental patients or it must allow their release. The court applied Fourteenth Amendment due process law that barred restriction of fundamental freedoms without some quid pro quo or reciprocal obligation by the state. In this case, Alabama was duty-bound to provide treatment and decent living standards to involuntarily confined mental patients. The United States Supreme Court, in *O'Connor v. Donaldson*,[35] essentially upheld this rule and its reasoning under the Fourteenth Amendment, making the right to treatment or release applicable to mental patients in all states.

Another major constitutional right in this arena of law is the right to refuse treatment. Rooted in historic common law rights to autonomous control over one's own body and life, the right denies the application, without patient consent, of certain high-risk and invasive therapies.[36] The legally competent patient (see chapter 11) can refuse psychosurgery, electroconvulsive treatment, various kinds of drug treatments, and aversive behavior therapies.

In spite of the many benefits these legal developments have brought to mental patients, many problems have also been created. Thirty years of deinstitutionalization on a mass scale has directly contributed to our national disgrace of homelessness. Also troubling is the systemic failure to provide effective aftercare for significant populations of chronically mentally ill persons released from our nation's hospitals.[37] Psychiatrist and author Seymour Halleck echoes the concerns of many mental health professionals in decrying a "new legalism" in mental health treatment that rigidly asserts "freedom values over health values," often to the detriment of the patient.[38]

PROFESSIONAL LICENSURE

Increasingly, the most common interactions with law for the Christian counselor revolve around mental health licensure, certification, and registration statutes (see chapters 19 and 20). Every state regulates its mental health care system to some degree. Licensure of mental health practitioners—psychiatrists, psychiatric nurses, and psychologists in all states, clinical social workers in all but one state, and marriage and family therapists in nearly half the states—is a primary method of state regulation. The central justification by states for this regulatory scheme is protection of the public from incompetent and unethical clinicians and counselors.[39]

California has been a leading regulatory state in the licensure of its mental health professionals, and its model has influenced licensure laws in many states. No one, except those exempted by statute,[40] can provide counseling and mental health services for a fee without being licensed. Psychiatrists are regulated by the Medical Board, psychologists by the Board of Psychology, and clinical social workers and marriage and family therapists by the Board of Behavioral Science Examiners. Each Board defines the title, nature of practice, education and intern preparation, functions and limits, and professional requirements necessary to obtain and maintain licensure. They also define professional misconduct and the procedure by which a license may be suspended or revoked.[41]

THE LEGALIZATION OF PROFESSIONAL ETHICS

A developing and controversial issue in California is the degree to which the state incrementally incorporates professional ethics into the statutory code of professional misconduct.[42] The demand that states effectively police their erring licensees is forcing a tense marriage of ethical codes with state statutes. This process of legalizing professional ethics codes in effect transfers control of the profession from the profession itself to the state. The state, then, uses its power to revoke or deny a license to someone who fails the statutory standard of professional misconduct. For states such as California that are legislating comprehensive and mandatory licensing laws, this is a significant shift of power with major implications regarding professional self-control for all mental health professions.

CONTRACT LAW

Suits for breach of contract comprise only 3 percent of all actions in the United States.[43] These are expected to rise, however, due to increased use of contracts in counseling and therapy (see chapter 11 for guidelines to good contracts) and the relative ease, compared to the malpractice suit, of proving violations of contract. Most of these cases involve direct or implied promises of cure, treatment superiority, or lack of risk. In effect, such communication by a therapist is held to constitute a guarantee of outcome; the failure then being actionable under contract law.[44]

CRIMINAL LAW

Perhaps nothing reinforces the reality of the grave new world as much as the intrusion of criminal liability into the Christian counseling domain. A handful of states, as will be seen in the next part of this book, have attached criminal liability to sexual misconduct in counseling. Pedophilic counselors and ministers—those who sexually abuse children under the guise of counseling or ministry—have long been liable under criminal child abuse statutes.

Conclusion

Legal liability for the Christian counselor has indeed arrived and will become a familiar if unwelcome guest in the 1990s. The Christian counselor no longer ministers without some direct accountability to both church *and state*. While some will pass this off to the evil encroachment of the secular-humanist state, we acknowledge the validity of some state oversight and press instead for a correct balance in church-state relations. Church and state are both instruments in God's hands—he is sovereign over his entire creation. Throughout history, God has used or allowed the state to enact its (usually harsher) rule when the church, or Israel as his covenant people, failed at some fundamentals of spiritual life. Christian counselors and ministers who harm the people they serve and churches that do little or nothing to stop and amend this harm are failing in fundamental ways. This failure can be reversed by a church willing to act assertively to protect itself and the name of Christ. If it does not, the state is showing its complete willingness to fill the gap and regulate the church instead.

NOTES

1. Charles Colson, *Kingdoms in Conflict* (New York: Morrow/Zondervan, 1987), 47–48.
2. Daniel Hogan, *The Regulation of Psychotherapists. Vol. III: A Review of Malpractice Suits in the United States* (Cambridge, Mass.: Ballinger, 1979).
3. Ibid., Table 1, p. 373.
4. Ibid., Table 2, p. 373.
5. Ibid., Tables 3, 4, and 46, pp. 374, 416.
6. Ibid., Tables 5–10, pp. 375–78.
7. Ibid., Tables 37–40, pp. 401–9.
8. Ibid., Tables 13–22, pp. 381–90.
9. Ibid., Tables 11–12, pp. 379–80.
10. S. Fulero, "Insurance Trust Releases Malpractice Statistics," *State Psychological Association Affairs* 19, no. 1 (1987): 4–5.
11. K. Fisher, "Charges Catch Clinicians in Cycle of Shame, Slip-ups," *American Psychological Association Monitor* 16 (1985): 6–7.

12. See Kenneth Austin, Mary Moline, and George Williams, *Confronting Malpractice: Legal and Ethical Dilemmas in Psychotherapy* (Newbury Park, Calif.: Sage Publications, 1990), 16.

13. See *Black's Law Dictionary*, rev. 4th ed. (St. Paul, Minn.: West Publishing, 1968), 1660. "Three elements of every tort action are: existence of legal duty from defendant to plaintiff, breach of duty, and damage as a proximate result."

14. See Hogan, *Regulation of Psychotherapists.*

15. William L. Prosser, *Handbook of the Law of Torts*, 4th ed. (St. Paul, Minn.: West Publishing, 1971), note 43. Prosser's handbooks are considered the "bibles" of American tort law.

16. *Hammer v. Polsky*, 36 Misc.2d 482, 233 N.Y.S.2d 110 (N.Y. Sup. Ct. 1962).

17. Prosser, *Law of Torts*, 161, fn. 2.

18. Ibid., 163.

19. M. Harris, "Tort Liability of the Psychotherapist," *University of San Francisco Law Review* 8 (1973): 405–36 (quote from 419).

20. Donald J. Dawidoff, *The Malpractice of Psychiatrists: Malpractice in Psychoanalysis, Psychotherapy and Psychiatry* (Springfield, Ill.: Thomas Publishers, 1973), 75.

21. Ibid.

22. Steve Chase, "Clergy Malpractice: The Cause of Action That Never Was," *North Carolina Central Law Journal* 18 (1989): 163–85.

23. Ibid., 164–72; see also *Nally III*, 109–10.

24. 110 S. Ct. 1595 (1990) (hereafter cited as *Smith*).

25. See, for example, *Hester v. Barnett*, 723 S.W.2d 544 (Mo. Ct. App. 1987); *O'Neil v. Schuckardt*, 112 Idaho 472, 733 P.2d 693 (Idaho 1986); *Handley v. Richards*, 518 So.2d 682 (Alabama 1987); *Meroni v. Holy Spirit Association (Unification Church)*, 125 Misc.2d 1061, 480 N.Y.S.2d 706 (N.Y. 1984); and review on the controversial issue of intentional emotional distress, Lew Brooks, "Intentional Infliction of Emotional Distress by Spiritual Counselors: Can Outrageous Conduct Be 'Free Exercise'?" *Michigan Law Review* 84 (1986): 1296.

26. *Hester v. Barnett*, 563.

27. Chase, "Clergy Malpractice" 173.

28. *Destefano v. Grabrian*, 763 P.2d 275 (Colorado 1988).

29. Ibid., 284. See also *Strock v. Presnell*, 527 N.E.2d 1235, at 1238 (Ohio 1988); where the Supreme Court of Ohio used essentially the same reasoning in rejecting the First Amendment defense of a Lutheran pastor charged with a sexual affair while involved in marital counseling. The Court assertively held that this behavior was not religiously motivated but was instead a "bizarre deviation from normal spiritual counseling practices of ministers in the Lutheran church."

30. See Hogan, *Regulation of Psychotherapists.*

31. See 42 *United States Code*, sections 2681–87 (1963).

32. See 42 *United States Code*, section 1983 (1964).

33. *Lake v. Cameron*, 364 F.2d 657 (D.C. Cir. 1966); see also *Lessard v. Schmidt*, 349 F.Supp. 1078 (E.D. Wis. 1972).

34. *Wyatt v. Stickney*, 325 F.Supp. 781 (M.D. Ala. 1971), 344 F.Supp. 373 (M.D. Ala. 1972), aff'd sub nom *Wyatt v. Aderholt*, 503 F.2d 753 (5th Cir. 1974).

35. *O'Connor v. Donaldson*, 422 U.S. 563 (1975).

36. See A. Brooks, "Mental Health Law: The Right to Refuse Treatment," *Administration in Mental Health* 4, no. 2 (1977): 90–95.

37. See Phil Brown, *The Transfer of Care: Psychiatric Institutionalization and Its Aftermath* (Boston: Routledge and Kegan Paul, 1985).

38. Seymour Halleck, *Law in the Practice of Psychiatry* (New York: Plenum, 1980).

39. See J. Fischer, "State Regulation of Psychologists," *Washington University Law Quarterly* 58 (1980): 639; D. A. Hardcastle, "Certification, Licensure and Other Forms of Regulation," in *Handbook of Clinical Social Work,* ed. A Rosenblatt and D. Waldfogel (San Francisco: Jossey-Bass, 1983).

40. Those exempted by statute include members of the clergy. "Nothing in this article shall prevent qualified members of other professional groups from doing work of a psychosocial nature consistent with the standards and ethics of their respective professions. . . . These qualified members of other professional groups include, but are not limited to, the following: . . . (e) A priest, rabbi or minister of the gospel of any religious denomination." *California Business and Professions Code,* ch.14, sect. 4996.13.

41. Some of the many ways a license can be denied or revoked in California include misrepresentation of qualifications or competence, aiding and abetting unlicensed practice, any manner of sexual relations or solicitation with a client, failure to maintain confidentiality, failure to disclose fees, false advertising, intentional infliction of emotional distress, negligent supervision of staff and subordinates, failure to report child or elder abuse, and any act of gross negligence. *California Business and Professions Code,* ch. 18, sect. 1881.

42. See E. Belser, "BBSE Joint Hearing with the Board of Psychology: Public Input Sought Regarding Dual Relationships," *NASW California News* 17, no. 5 (February 1991): 6.

43. See Hogan, *Regulation of Psychotherapists.*

44. *Moxon v. County of Kern,* 233 Cal.App.2d 393, 43 Cal.Rptr. 481 (1965).

Chapter 3

Social and Systemic Trends in Legal Liability

Today there is a potentially fatal idea in circulation: that there should not be in this pluralistic society any core culture passed on from generation to generation.

To those who say we are threatened by a suffocating "hegemony" of Western civilization's classic works, I say the real danger is cultural amnesia. It is withdrawal from the challenge of finding common ground on which Americans can stand together—not the little patches of fenced-off turf for irritable groups, but the common ground of citizenship in the nation.[1]

George F. Will

IN ORDER TO PRESENT A LARGE-SCALE, or macro-social view of the regulatory problem, we will analyze trends in society, in the clinical professions, in ministry, in economics, and in the legal profession. These trends reveal the growing risk of suit for clinical professionals and pastoral counselors.

TRENDS IN AMERICAN SOCIETY

Modern American society has been described as being both psychological[2] and litigious.[3] Increasingly, many human and social problems are thought to have a psychological rather than a spiritual and moral base. Hence, the psychological practitioners have become a modern secular priesthood, and demand for psychosocial services has dramatically increased in a generation. Also, the majority of the world's lawyers practice in America and are possibly the wealthiest professional group on the planet. Americans sue one another at a per capita rate ten to thirty times more frequently than other industrialized nations. The bill, in direct and indirect costs, approaches $400 billion annually—$1,600 per year for every citizen of the United States.[4]

This secularization of American life emphasizes legal rights and individual liberty at the expense of communal values, cooperative dispute resolution, and reliance on traditional institutions such as the family, church, neighborhood, and community. Rather than own these community values and institutions as allies, American citizens too often oppose them as barriers to personal happiness and freedom.[5] More and more, religion and spiritual truth are relegated to an individualized and highly private experience in the secular society.

As a result, the Christian message is pushed to extreme, polarized roles in social and political life. On one hand, in the name of pluralistic tolerance, Christian values are allowed little or no role in informing or challenging public policy and values. On the other hand, in a self-centered culture of narcissism, private beliefs become more important and are asserted over and against traditional values and the historical institutions of society. This fundamental societal rift is fertile ground for adversarial conflict and litigation.

Finally, secular society has demanded alliance with government as the ultimate protector of rights and the only sufficient power to curb real and perceived abuses by other powerful institutions. "A new social order has evolved that [demands government protection and legal action] to mitigate almost every risk any individual might be asked to bear."[6] The church is a target that is increasingly seen as a threat against which the government must protect its citizens. Insurance executive Al Davidson is quoted as saying, "Today, people are just as quick to sue the church as a secular organization."[7] Some clergy and churches will face a hostile adversary "looking for reasons to vent their frustration and anger against such overarching authority figures [as the church]. The Grace Community Church suit startles us with this reality."[8]

TRENDS IN THE HELPING PROFESSIONS

The mental health professions are not immune from this secular drift in society. Although greatly advancing our understanding of human and social behavior, these groups have also largely cut themselves adrift from the moral and spiritual values that have guided and defined Western culture.[9] The rejection of a Christian value base disserves many seeking help since it leaves the clinical professions discomforted and confused about spiritual issues. As a result, many counselors espouse a feeble neutrality about values or open the door to counterfeit values and religion in response to client (and their own) need. "Subsequently, given their largely autonomous functioning, limited moral development, and inadequate decision-making skills, professionals are left to make judgments based upon highly subjective and frequently self-serving moral ideals."[10]

Also, unlike the scientific foundations of medicine or the common law and constitutional heritage of American law, no single theoretical or empirical base is universally accepted to guide development of counseling and psychotherapy. More than two hundred distinct forms of psychotherapy have been identified,[11] some that promote ethically questionable, even plainly harmful behavior. The counseling consumer is further confused by the multiple professions, inconsistent regulation, and myriad practitioner titles extant in the counseling industry. The five *major* professional groups—psychiatry, psychiatric nursing, clinical psychology, clinical social work, and marriage and family therapy—grant many different titles, degrees, licenses, certificates, and other professional sanctions.

Agencies, clinics, and hospitals further this consumer confusion and legal trouble by hiring substandard professionals. Pressed between exploding service demand and the political failure to fund human services, these institutions cut corners by hiring inexperienced, even nonclinical personnel who are often overwhelmed by complex clinical problems. While such therapists may have the right degrees—M.D., Ph.D., M.S.W., or M.A.—they may be social (not clinical) psychologists or physicians who have not completed a psychiatric residency. The old adage, penny wise and pound foolish, is certainly appropriate for the institutions that, by attempting to save a few dollars in salaries, end up paying enormous sums in malpractice damage claims.

Beyond these regulated and institutional groups lie a mass of unregulated counselors, helpers, consultants, and guides who offer help from extremely diverse training and personal backgrounds. Some of these helpers offer a fair service with some level of college or graduate training and counseling experience. Many more, however, hang out their shingle with little more than an ecstatic New-Age revelation and an eight-week course in mystical shamanism. "Members of the public who find their way to these 'therapists'—[some] who are, by and large, uneducated, uncredentialed and unethical—may be very displeased with the results."[12]

TRENDS IN THE MINISTRY

Many in the Christian church have been displeased with both the clinical professions and the secular drift in society. Some parts of the conservative church have led the charge of wholesale rejection of psychology and psychotherapy as part of a larger resistance to the intrusion of secularism.[13] We agree that the biblical call of separation of the church from the larger culture must be heeded (2 Cor. 6:14–7:1). Sometimes, though, this separation is pushed to extremes that genuinely risk harming people by denying church members access to helpful societal resources.

Rejecting all that the mental health professions offer, without right discernment of what is beneficial and what is not, distorts God's revelation about the church's relationship to the world. Those churches that fail to strike the divine balance—being in the world but not of it—are forced to set themselves up as expert and comprehensive providers of every kind of spiritual and emotional care. This often results in exaggerated claims of competence, spiritualized misdiagnosis that denies many medical, genetic, and psychosocial problems, and a failure to refer to and work collaboratively with clinical, even Christian, professionals. Dependent and needy Christians who rely exclusively on these insular church communities do so to their own, sometimes deadly, peril.

Compounding these difficulties is the failure of accountability for moral and ethical wrongdoing in ministry. Too many Christian ministers have allowed themselves to be seduced by the prevailing me-first culture of individualism and self-aggrandizement. A lone-ranger ministerial mentality is rampant in the American church. This dark spirit promotes pride, secretiveness, and authoritarian rule while denying humility, connectedness, and accountability within the body of Christ.

The tragic example of Jimmy Swaggart's downfall is germane. We believe the bigger tragedy was not his sexual sin, but his rejection of accountability, recovery, and restoration through the Assemblies of God, who had offered him a realistic and compassionate program for personal and ministerial healing. While this growing moral epidemic in ministry depicts only a small minority and greatly contrasts the majority of godly ministers, it shouts an invitation to secular legal regulation and redress of harm. If we Christians will not submit to one another in reverence for Christ, it seems that God cuts us loose to suffer greater loss and to be controlled by the harsher power of the state.

These troubles within segments of the church predict a difficult future. Unless challenged and transformed from within the church, this will also lead to further legal action from which the entire church will suffer. "Because of their fervent attitudes against secularization and their fear and rejection of psychology, many of these conservative churches cut their constituents off from professional help. It is the strategy of pastoral care and counseling in these churches that is most vulnerable in this age of increased charges of clergy malpractice."[14]

These difficulties for the church should not be underestimated. Lawsuits against churches outside historic Christianity and beyond its control (e.g., the Native American church, the Church of Scientology, or the Unification Church of Sun Myung Moon) are establishing the liability framework against which the Christian church shall also be judged. That is why, when there are no doctrinal grounds for fellowship, the Christian church is challenged to stand with its religious "kin" before the rule of the state, because we are all affected by that rule. However, our ability to influence these nonorthodox, even anti-Christian religions outside the legal sphere is extremely limited at best.

This is reinforced by the growing anti-Christian bias of our national media that rivets attention on the worst aspects of our fallen ministers. Frequent and one-dimensional media exposure sways its mass audience to misbelieve that what is exceptional, even rare, in Christian ministry is instead quite normative and common. When further reinforced by Elmer Gantry stereotypes in movies and on television, the secular world begins to believe a grotesque caricature of the Christian life. A societal counterreaction is unavoidable.

ECONOMIC AND INSURANCE TRENDS

The restructuring of economic priorities in America, coupled with an aggressive insurance industry's attempt to control health and mental health care costs, is also proving a significant influence in legal and regulatory trends. Societal rifts are also evident in health care policy where there exists an "unfortunate attitude of 'me-ism' as opposed to 'we-ism.' The individual often attempts to maneuver optimum personal health care, while opposing the provision of health care services at the same level for others— particularly . . . the poor." Psychologist and lawyer Robert Woody asserts that this conflicted, prevailing attitude of demanding the best health care while refusing to pay for it "is the source of many legal actions."[15]

As government support for health care and mental health care has dissipated, ever more professionals have turned to private practice as a primary mode of service delivery. The transformation of mental health care to a "private enterprise industry" has also fueled "the escalation of liability . . . [that] is definitely linked to accountability for quality."[16] Issues of professional competence and accountability are shifting to the legal system through client suit and away from agency and supervisorial control. This systemic transformation is accelerated by near-universal licensure laws and growing vendor recognition among all primary mental health professions.

"Since the entrepreneur stands to reap the financial harvest," says Woody, "society reasons that the health care professional must be monitored and made to pay the consequences for lapses in quality performance. In turn, the individual contributes to the mandate for accountability. Since the payments come directly out of [the] patient's pocket, instead of indirectly out of tax dollars, there is a more acute personal awareness of 'getting what I pay for!'"[17]

Getting paid for professional counseling in this privatized and commercial age has demanded close and familiar relations with many third-party vendors. As health and welfare services are increasingly transferred away from government to employers, concern for and accountability regarding cost issues has grown tremendously. The major restrictions the insurance industry currently impose on mental health reimbursement reflects this benefit/cost tension. Increasingly, insurance companies deny and restrict benefits by various tactics designed to control costs. Even if working, these measures may also demand significant costs to the quality of client care delivered in an environment where economics are becoming more important than the person served.

TRENDS AT BAR AND BENCH

A critical factor in our litigious society is the explosive growth in the number of lawyers and lawsuits in America. The population of lawyers has more than doubled in a generation, and litigation has nearly tripled over the past quarter-century. As legal competition steadily increases, lawyers on the economic fringe will more aggressively pursue litigation in fields that were once ignored. For example, the American Bar Association sponsored a seminar in May 1989 on how to conduct litigation against the church and religious institutions.[18] A second conference in 1990 suggests this field will receive increased and ongoing attention by the legal community in the years to come.

This aggression by lawyers is reinforced by the growth of the contingent fee arrangement that, for the legal consumer, effectively removes a traditional economic barrier to litigation. Paid only when a claimant wins and receives damages, lawyers must aggressively pursue recovery to survive professionally. This dynamic has driven a distorted pattern of contemporary litigation. Concern for the legal merits of a case has been supplanted by aggressive pursuit of cases where deep pocket money exists and the harm is most severe. "In tort theory, fault is the cornerstone of liability and then questions of causation and damages are raised, but in practice it is the reverse. The tail wags the dog—the greater the injury, the greater the chance of an adverse judgment."[19]

This trend intersects with the transformation (many would say corruption) of historic tort law into a redistributive system of victim compensation. Well-educated lawyers with "victimized" clients have become increasingly adept at convincing juries to award huge damages with less and less concern for therapist fault and causation of that harm. A rights-conscious citizenry influenced by a growing social powerlessness and adoption of a victim's mentality is very fertile soil for an explosive growth in litigation. Again, lawyers profit most from this modern dynamic; after court costs and lawyer's fees are paid, the injured plaintiff receives barely half the money awarded in damages.

These rapidly changing systemic factors also create pressure to relax traditional barriers in law that impede claimant success. Some legal theorists have attacked the protective barriers of traditional tort law, advocating simpler ways that client harm may be compensated for by professional service providers. After review of the literature on harmful outcome in psychotherapy, Furrow argues for strict liability in therapeutic malpractice, promoting a system where evidence of therapeutic harm alone would trigger damage awards.[20] The intervening requirements of showing therapist negligence and causation of harm—essential elements of proof in a malpractice action—would be forsaken.

Judges, of course, are influenced by all these changes in society, cultural values, and the professions. Although no American court has adopted the changes in American law advocated by Furrow, they have been argued in and addressed by the courts. In the confusing quagmire of law relating to third-party protection duties (see chapter 10), strict liability arguments have made inroads. Fortunately, the federal district court in Colorado rejected strict liability against the psychiatrist who had treated President Reagan's would-be assassin John Hinckley. It argued that no justification existed for such "greatly expand[ed] . . . scope of therapist's liability . . . [where] human behavior is simply too unpredictable and the field of psychotherapy presently too inexact. . . ."[21]

Traditional tort theory has always recognized the critical role that malpractice law plays as a profession-correcting mechanism when professions themselves tend to be self-protecting. This is one of many legitimate roles of law in a constitutional democracy reinforced by our modern emphasis on market-oriented professionalism. However, this legitimacy is being abused by an intrusive legal profession in need of correction and restraint. These problems in law and the legal profession should not detract us from the truth that a modern self-governing society, under rule of law and not totalitarian despots, demands an active and honorable legal profession and a free and active judiciary.

CONCLUSION

The cumulative weight of these societal trends could easily tempt us to cry, "The sky is falling!" We would rather resist that temptation and assert that God is in charge and will always provide a way out to those "who love [God and] have been called according to his purpose" (Rom. 8:28b). These trends, ominous though they be, hold no fear for the ethical and biblically faithful counselor. Even though the legal margin for error will continue to narrow, the great majority of godly ministers can and should boldly pursue their service call to counseling ministry. Our challenge is to learn better the truth of being wise as serpents while remaining harmless as doves in all our professional and ministerial relations.

NOTES

1. George F. Will, excerpt from a commencement address at Duke University, quoted in *Reader's Digest,* January 1992, 172.

2. Martin Gross, *The Psychological Society* (New York: Random House, 1978).

3. Jethro K. Lieberman, *The Litigious Society* (New York: Basic Books, 1983).

4. David Gergen, "America's Legal Mess," *U.S. News & World Report,* 19 August 1991.

5. See Charles Colson, *Kingdoms in Conflict* (New York: Morrow/Zondervan, 1987); and Christopher Lasch, *The Culture of Narcissism* (New York: Norton, 1979).

6. Yair Aharoni, *The No-Risk Society* (Chatham, N.J.: Chatham House Publishers, 1981), 1.

7. Thomas L. Needham, "Insurance Protection for Church and Clergy," in *Clergy Malpractice,* ed. H. Newton Malony, Thomas L. Needham, and Samuel Southard (Philadelphia: The Westminster Press, 1986), 127.

8. Thomas L. Needham, "Helping When the Risks Are Great," in *Clergy Malpractice,* ed. Malony, Needham, and Southard, 93.

9. See Gary Collins, *Can You Trust Psychology?* (Downers Grove, Ill.: InterVarsity, 1988); and P. Vitz, *Psychology as Religion: The Cult of Self-Worship* (Grand Rapids, Mich.: Eerdmans, 1977).

10. Thomas L. Needham, "Malpractice in the Ministry," in *Clergy Malpractice,* ed. Malony, Needham, and Southard, 13.

11. Ralph Slovenko, "Malpractice in Psychiatry and Related Fields," *Journal of Psychiatry and Law* 9, no. 2 (1981): 5.

12. Ronald J. Cohen, *Malpractice: A Guide for Mental Health Professionals* (New York: The Free Press, 1979), 21.

13. See, for example, John MacArthur, *Our Sufficiency in Christ* (Dallas: Word, 1991); Martin and Diedre Bobgan, *Psychoheresy: The Psychological Seduction of Christianity* (Santa Barbara, Calif.: Eastgate, 1987); William K. Kilpatrick, *Psychological Seduction: The Failure of Modern Psychology* (Nashville: Nelson, 1983); but compare Collins, *Can You Trust Psychology?*

14. Thomas L. Needham, "Malpractice in the Ministry," in *Clergy Malpractice,* ed. Malony, Needham, and Southard, 18.

15. Robert Woody, *Fifty Ways to Avoid Malpractice: A Guidebook for Mental Health Professionals* (Sarasota, Fla.: Professional Resource Exchange, 1988), 25.

16. Ibid., 32.

17. Ibid., 27.

18. See James Dobson and Gary Bauer, *Children At Risk: The Battle for the Hearts and Minds of Our Kids* (Dallas: Word, 1990), 23.

19. Ralph Slovenko, "The Therapist's Duty to Warn or Protect Third-Persons," *Journal of Psychiatry and Law* 16 (1988): 139–209 (quote from 150).

20. Barry Furrow, *Malpractice in Psychotherapy* (Lexington, Mass.: Lexington Books, 1980).

21. *Brady v. Hopper,* 570 F.Supp. 1333 (D. Colo. 1983), *aff'd,* 751 F.2d 329 (10th Cir. 1984).

Chapter 4

Nally and *Smith*: Lessons from Two Landmark Cases

The Fathers of the Constitution were not unaware of the varied and extreme views of religious sects, of the violence of disagreement among them, and of the lack of any one religious creed on which all men would agree. They fashioned a charter of government which envisaged the widest possible toleration of conflicting views. Man's relation to his God was made no concern to the state. He was granted the right to worship as he pleased and to answer to no man for the verity of his religious views. The religious views espoused by the respondents [nonorthodox faith-healers convicted of fraud] might seem incredible, if not preposterous, to most people. But if these doctrines are subject to trial before a jury charged with finding their truth or falsity, then the same can be done with the religious beliefs of any sect. When the triers of fact undertake the task, they enter a forbidden domain. The First Amendment does not select any one group or any one type of religion for preferred treatment. It puts them all in that position.

Justice William O. Douglas
in *United States v. Ballard*, 1944

ON APRIL FOOL'S DAY IN 1979, twenty-four-year-old Kenneth Nally, despondent and still recovering from an attempted drug overdose three weeks earlier, pressed a shotgun to his head, squeezed the trigger, and violently ended his life. One day before April Fool's in 1980, Nally's parents filed suit for wrongful death against their deceased son's church and four of his pastors alleging clergyman malpractice and outrageous conduct in failing to prevent their son's suicide.[1]

Thus began a landmark suit that ushered in the modern era of Christian counseling liability. For most of the 1980s the controversial case of *Nally v. Grace Community Church of the Valley* wound its way up and down the California judicial system. Decisions by trial, appeals, and state supreme courts alternated back and forth in support of either the aggrieved parents or the embattled church. This case and, even more, the *Smith* case to follow well represent the grave new world of Christian counseling liability. In this last chapter of part 1, we examine these landmark cases in greater depth to give readers a more personal view of the pertinent issues and relations between church and state.

REVIEW OF THE *NALLY* CASE

After a decade of tortuous litigation, Grace Community Church of the Valley, one of the largest churches in America with over four thousand members in suburban Los Angeles, did prevail and win its lawsuit. Also vindicated were its four pastor-defendants, including the well-known senior pastor and author Dr. John MacArthur, Jr. Their commitment to stay the course in the face of adversity and to persevere to a conclusion that protects fundamental Christian ministry rights gives all of us just cause for thanksgiving. On the other hand, the events that led to this suit and the behavior of the defendants that influenced the tragic course of Ken Nally's life should give pause for a sober appraisal of the role, duties, limits, and behavior of the pastoral counselor.

THE TRAGIC STORY OF KENNETH NALLY

In the early 1970s, UCLA student Ken Nally "converted to Protestantism," began attending Grace Community Church, and became involved in their extensive collegiate ministry. His conversion created much strain in his relations with his Roman Catholic parents, and he often discussed his bouts with depression and the "absurdity of life."[2] He began a counseling or "discipling"[3] relationship with Pastor Duane Rea in January 1978. Court records revealed that Pastor Rea had evaluated Nally as being distraught and depressed, stating that he could not cope and once said, "I just can't live this life."[4]

After breaking up with his girlfriend late in 1978, Nally became more despondent. He began counseling with Pastor Richard Thomson who concluded that suicide was a "vague possibility."[5] In February

1979, Nally told his mother he could not cope, and she had him consult with a general practice physician who prescribed Elavil, a strong antidepressant medicine. Neither this doctor nor the two pastors made a psychiatric referral.[6]

Ken attempted suicide by overdosing on the Elavil on March 11, 1979. Hospitalized by his parents, the family was challenged by a consulting psychiatrist to commit Ken, warning Ken and his parents that he was likely to attempt suicide again. Both Ken and his father declined, seemingly more concerned with the social stigma of suicide and psychiatric hospitalization than with receiving help.[7]

Upon release Ken stayed with Pastor MacArthur, who encouraged him to see the psychiatrist. He also had him examined by a Christian physician who was a deacon at Grace Community Church. This doctor believed Nally was a serious threat to himself and recommended psychiatric hospitalization in an Adventist facility. Ken's father telephoned the psychiatrist about this, and the doctor, convinced of the seriousness of the suicidal risk, offered to come to the Nally home to assist in rehospitalizing Ken. Tragically, the Nallys refused this offer; Mrs. Nally is reported to have stated, ". . . no, that's a crazy hospital. He's not crazy."[8]

Eleven days before his death, Ken Nally counseled with Pastor Thomson, inquiring about the salvation of Christians who commit suicide. Thomson stated that once a Christian is saved, he is always saved, but to think that eternal security justified suicide was "wrong." This pastor did not encourage hospitalization or psychiatric follow-through. Contact with other Christian counselors and psychologists was also made during that last week of his life. After a desperate plea for marriage toward his estranged girlfriend and a final family conflict, Ken Nally left home. Two days later he was found dead of self-inflicted gunshot wounds at a friend's apartment.[9]

THE LEGAL BATTLE BETWEEN PARENTS AND CHURCH

In their allegations of clergy malpractice, the Nallys asserted that Grace Community Church was negligent in the selection and training of its counselors and that they "actively . . . discouraged [Ken Nally] from seeking further professional . . . care." They charged that the church's teaching of religious doctrine disparaged Nally's Catholic upbringing and "exacerbated [Ken's] pre-existing feelings of guilt, anxiety and depression."[10] They also alleged that the church taught Nally, knowing he was suicidal, the notion that he would go to heaven even if he committed suicide.

Legal duty of care? The key legal question is one of duty: Did the church owe Ken Nally a duty of care that obligated them to act in his behalf in a way that would protect him from suicide? The trial court said no duty existed, but the court of appeals consistently answered this question in the affirmative.[11] California follows historic legal precedent that requires existence of a "special" relationship, one in which "the plaintiff is typically . . . vulnerable and dependent upon the defendant who . . . holds considerable power over the plaintiff's welfare."[12] The appeals court reasoned that this psychological dependence would be no different whether the therapist were a licensed professional or a "nontherapist [secular or religious] counselor." This court ruled against the church, holding that "the nontherapist counselor who has held himself out as competent to treat serious emotional problems and voluntarily established a counseling relationship with an emotionally disturbed person has a duty to take appropriate precautions should that person exhibit suicidal tendencies."[13]

The California Supreme Court reversed this rule in 1988, holding that the church was not liable. It held that no special relationship exists between a nontherapist counselor and his or her counselee due to the noncommercial, noncustodial, and voluntary nature of the relationship. This court looked at the question of legal duty from a structural rather than psychological perspective. Asserting that no duty to forestall suicide exists outside a medically supervised relationship,[14] it refused to extend such duty to "personal or religious counseling relationships in which one person provided nonprofessional guidance to another seeking advice and the counselor had no control over the environment of the individual being counseled."[15]

California's highest court argued that while foreseeability of harm may make referral "prudent and necessary," it is not sufficient to create a legal duty that the court thought could "stifle all gratuitous or religious counseling."[16] It noted the exemption of clergy from mental health licensure and asserted that "access to the clergy for counseling should be free from state imposed counseling standards, and that 'the secular state is not equipped to ascertain the competence of counseling when performed by those affiliated with religious organizations.'"[17] This court hedged its rule with an exception it did not apply in this case, "Our opinion does not foreclose imposing liability on nontherapist counselors, who hold themselves out as professionals, for injuries related to their counseling activities."[18]

Supreme Court Justice Marcus Kaufman (now retired) concurred with the majority's ruling but disagreed "that defendants owed no duty of care to the plaintiffs."[19] He argued that the church did owe a legal duty to Ken Nally, but that they fulfilled it through Pastor MacArthur's encouragement to Nally to follow through with psychiatric care. Kaufman believed the church owed a duty because of the way it advertised and held itself out as a major counseling ministry to the larger church and community. He reviewed facts, most of which were ignored by the majority, that showed the pastoral counseling ministry of the church to be a significant enterprise.[20] He pointedly referred to the claims that the "biblical" counselor was competent to counsel "every emotional problem," including addictions, severe depression, manic-depression, and schizophrenia.[21] Kaufman argued that a "special" relationship giving rise to the duty of care existed because the pastors "patently held themselves out as competent to counsel the mentally ill, and Nally responded to these inducements, placing his psychological and ultimately his physical well-being in defendants' care."[22]

BEHAVIOR ANALYSIS

Although the case record reveals that many people contributed to this tragedy, the inescapable truth is that Ken Nally killed himself. Along the way the church erred, Nally's parents erred, and some of the doctors and helping professionals erred in their intervention. However, had these errors not taken place, it is not at all clear that Ken Nally would be among us today—he was very serious about dying. We recognize the unique tragedy of suicide, and this knowledge tempers our critique.

Exaggeration of competence. Grace Church's biggest transgression, we believe, was its exaggeration of competence. Simply put, it misrepresented itself to the larger church and urban community in which it resides by claiming a level of expertise it simply did not have. At best, the church's claim to competently treat every kind of emotional disorder was a naive overstatement. At worst, especially if the church counseled against or even passively resisted referral to professional clinicians at the height of the crisis,[23] it was a noxious boast ripe for this kind of ministerial tragedy.

Such claims are impossible for a community service that does not have an inpatient or even partial hospitalization capability. Moreover, there was no evidence that the counselors on staff had any special training or expertise in suicide intervention. Grace did not show a commitment to refer and work closely with other professionals but (except, possibly, for MacArthur) referred reluctantly, if at all, only as a last desperate resort. Even the most comprehensive professional counseling ministries recognize the need to refer and network with other service providers to ensure the best client care.

Furthermore, claims of counseling expertise with severe depression, bipolar (manic-depressive) disorders, and schizophrenia deny a mass of accumulated psychiatric research and treatment over the past two decades that show significant genetic and biological roots to these problems.[24] Included in this psychiatric data are promising results from many new drug therapies, which are often used in conjunction with professional and pastoral counseling. We will never know whether longer-term hospitalization and psychiatric treatment would have given Ken the edge needed to live.

Grace Church failed to adhere to the most basic ethical and biblical norms. We are called to judge ourselves with sober humility, avoiding self-deceit by recognizing our limits and weaknesses, not thinking of ourselves "more highly than [we] ought" (Rom. 12:3, see 2 Cor. 10:12–18, Gal. 6:1–5). The ethical codes of every major clinical discipline speak out strongly against misrepresentation and require practice that adheres to the limits of one's competence.[25] While the church has a valid argument against being judged by professional standards or even pastoral counseling ethics it does not ascribe to (an argument it successfully pressed in court), it is a mistake to push that argument and assert that the pastor need answer only to God. The *Nally* case is hard evidence against the exaggerated argument that the pastor alone is competent to counsel everyone who seeks help.

Poor suicide intervention. The church, some of the professionals, and Ken Nally's parents all failed to provide adequate suicide intervention. The family physician who prescribed Elavil and failed to make a psychiatric referral was vulnerable to suit. Also, some of the helping professionals, including the pastors, did not communicate frequently nor work closely together as an intervention team on behalf of Nally. This was a failure of clinical networking that can be essential, even life-saving, in these types of crises.

The record also reveals a tragic picture of the plaintiffs.[26] Their failure to hospitalize their son, against the strongest medical advice and seemingly because they were more concerned about the stigma of a psychiatric disorder being attached to the family name, was a critical failure. Also, their failure to sue professionals who were, compared to the church, far more at-risk legally, and their dogged pursuit of the church suit suggests some retributive motives against the church. Such actions, faced in hindsight, often compound the grief they may still experience and was probably a factor in the level of hostility and acrimony reported about this case.[27]

Pastors Thomson and Rea failed Ken Nally in critical ways. Even conceding that they were not as expert as they claimed and that they would not be expected to competently evaluate Nally's suicidal risk, he *did* talk to them directly about depression, dying, and suicide. While it seemingly had to be pried out of them at the trial,[28] both these counselors admitted to some awareness of a suicidal risk. After the nearly successful overdose attempt, the failure to consistently encourage follow-through with hospitalization and psychiatric consultation were major errors of judgment.

Good work. A few lights shine in the darkness of this tragic story. The consulting psychiatrist accurately predicted Nally's risk and went beyond his minimal duty in offering help to the Nally family. Pastor MacArthur behaved with commendable compassion and good judgment about Nally in the final weeks of his life. Bringing Nally into his home and under his wing exemplifies the best of pastoral care; encouraging Nally to follow through with psychiatric care revealed sound judgment about the need for intensive intervention beyond the church's resources. Even Pastors Thomson and Rea, in spite of their poor counseling intervention and questionable courtroom behavior, demonstrated care and concern for Ken Nally in many ways.

Fair warning. MacArthur's blanket condemnation of psychology and psychotherapy,[29] however, is troubling. He fails to discern the good from the bad in professional counseling and may be inhibited from developing effective referral policy—a serious mistake if the church continues its exaggerated claims and misrepresentation in counseling ministry. We believe the wise biblical counselor sees God's sufficient power manifest throughout the entire Christian ministry network—not in one pastor, one church, or one particular theology or ministry policy. If MacArthur's church, and churches like it, are to avoid lawsuits in the future, a sober reappraisal of some of the theology, service policy, and practice of their counseling ministries is in order. We would advocate for a lot less of Grace Community Church's counseling policy as revealed in the *Nally* case and a lot more of Pastor MacArthur's caring and referring behavior toward Ken Nally at the end of his life.

LEGAL ANALYSIS

The California Supreme Court respected the historic boundary between church and state and was right, in our opinion, to protect Christian ministry rights by refusing to impose a broad duty upon pastoral counselors to assess and refer suicidal parishioners. It recognized the inherent limits of judicial power by agreeing that imposition of an unprecedented clergy malpractice standard would be nearly impossible for courts to manage and enforce. The court also correctly reasoned that such duty, expressed as an onerous rule of malpractice liability, would have a chilling effect by inducing a fear of suit in pastors that would inhibit rather than assist their ministry to the suicidal person.[30]

Indeed, following the court of appeals decision, the Northern California District of the Church of the Nazarene distributed a letter to their pastors from their legal counsel that cautioned the church about the opinion.[31] Since the clergy is by far the most commonly approached resource by persons in family or emotional crisis, the court rightly held that inhibiting such relations would truly be bad public policy, especially in an era of limited human services with a shrinking fiscal support base.

Though correct in refusing to create a broad legal duty, the California Supreme Court strained to exclude Grace Community Church from its own well-stated exception that liability could be found if pastoral counselors held themselves out "as professionals."[32] Exempting the church here required the high court to effectively ignore the evidence of exaggerated competence and Nally's strong psychological dependence on the church and those claims. The court may have failed to properly apply its own exception to the facts of the *Nally* case, and its holding could have declining influence in future similar cases.[33] Instead, according to a historic process where a dissent or concurrence provides the seed for future case law development, Justice Kaufman's concurring opinion along with the opinion by the court of appeals may be more convincing as future precedent. Other states reviewing *Nally* through the new constitutional standard of *Smith* (the next case we review) may well conclude a limited duty does exist and that the First Amendment will not bar its imposition on offending churches.

Justice Kaufman rightly held that the church owed Ken Nally a duty of care because they assertively held themselves out to him as competent and expert to treat severe depression and suicide. Churches will not—indeed, should never—be held accountable if they humbly recognize their limits and practice within the bounds of their competence. However, the reality of Nally's spiritual bond and psychological dependence on the church, *together with the church's exaggerated claims of competence,* justify a narrow legal duty.[34] "Where, as here, defendants have invited and engaged in an extensive and ongoing pastoral counseling relationship with an individual whom they perceive to be suicidal, both reason and sound public policy dictate that defendants be required to advise that individual seek professional . . . care."[35]

FREE EXERCISE AFTER *SMITH*

Congress shall make no law respecting an establishment of religion, or prohibiting the free exercise thereof. . . .

First Amendment Religion Clauses
United States Constitution

The First Amendment free exercise of religion clause has protected Christian ministry from government control for over two hundred years. Throughout American history this foundational rule of government between church and state has been called the First Freedom. United States Supreme Court decision-making in this arena has been historically rooted in the thesis that while freedom of belief is absolute, freedom to practice that belief is not.[36] Over a century ago the Court upheld federal antipolygamy statutes against the Mormon church, ruling that while Latter-day Saints were absolutely free to believe in polygamy, they were barred from its practice as it violated fundamental societal interests in family preservation and social stability.[37]

Over a series of cases in the twentieth century, the High Court had developed sound rules that effectively upheld societal interests while protecting core religious freedoms.[38] The Supreme Court's 1990 decision in *Smith*,[39] however, has turned its historic religious liberty analysis on its head. Ironically, considering our nation's recent celebration of the bicentennial of the Bill of Rights, the Christian church (and all religions in America) may rightly mourn the beginning loss of fundamental freedoms it has enjoyed for two centuries. Oliver Wendell Holmes's famous dictum that hard cases make bad law is most appropriate to *Smith*. The implications of this case reach far beyond *Nally* and any other case we will study in this book.

THE HISTORIC RULE SUPPLANTED

The historic rule that blocks government from prohibiting the free exercise of religion requires that *government show a compelling state interest* before any law is accepted if it has the effect of prohibiting religious liberty. Laws that interfere with legitimate religious practice will not stand unless they are essential to fundamental social order, peace, health, or safety.[40] The High Court had articulated a three-part test in analyzing free exercise disputes: (1) Is the religious activity at issue rooted in a legitimate and sincerely held religious belief? (2) Is the religious practice unduly burdened by the law in question and, if so, to what extent? (3) Does the state have such compelling interest in the regulation that the burden on religious liberty is justified? Each one of these questions has a substantial body of constitutional case law that has guided courts to resolve such controversies. In the arena of pastoral counseling, the application of this historic rule would hold that: ". . . a clergy counselor who is sued for clergy malpractice can find sanctuary in the free exercise clause if he can convince the court that his conduct was an important part of a sincere religious practice, that a finding of malpractice liability will impose a substantial burden on the exercise of his religious practices, and that such burden is not outweighed by a compelling state interest."[41]

THE NEW RULE OF SMITH

The *Smith* case involved two Native American men who were denied unemployment benefits following job loss for drug use—they had eaten the hallucinogenic peyote mushroom sacramentally in the Native American Church. The Oregon Supreme Court ruled that the men could not be denied benefits, holding that the drug practice issued from a sincere religious belief (courts do not judge whether any religious belief is right or wrong).[42] Oregon's interest in restricting this kind of drug use was judged not compelling in this case.

The United States Supreme Court reversed the Oregon court and upheld denial of unemployment benefits. It held that states could restrict religious drug use under its criminal laws so long as the law does not directly attempt to control or discriminate against religious practice. Furthermore, and most critically for the loss of religious liberty, the Court held that laws that are generally applicable and religiously neutral need not be justified under the free exercise clause. Written by Antonin Scalia, arguably the most scholarly and forceful conservative jurist on the High Court, this opinion was joined in the majority by four other conservative and moderate justices. The Court's liberal wing strongly dissented, ironically upholding historic free exercise standards by arguing that the state unjustly encroached upon the men's religious liberty.

Justice Sandra O'Connor, by far, wrote the best and most spirited opinion. She concurred with the majority holding but used historic religious liberty analysis to agree that Oregon could deny benefits. She argued that religious free exercise is burdened by general and neutral laws, requiring states to show a compelling interest to prevail. She concluded that Oregon does have a compelling state interest in restricting all peyote use by its citizens. Her analysis, restricting drug use while upholding historic First Amendment standards, was brilliant—it is a travesty her opinion did not sway the majority. She rightly reasoned that the new, unprecedented standard of the majority "is incompatible with our nation's fundamental commitment to individual religious liberty."[43]

CASE ANALYSIS OF *SMITH*

Recently, Christian attorneys and law professors have charged that the Court's decision in *Smith* was "a sweeping disaster for religious liberty."[44] The Court overturned a century of well-developed doctrine to fashion a rule that has no basis in either the original intent of the Constitution's framers nor in the Court's own free exercise precedent. "In *Smith*, the Court held that only laws specifically directed at religion were laws 'prohibiting' free exercise; no special justification is necessary if law merely has the effect of prohibiting religious exercise."[45]

The Court has effectively gutted First Amendment religious liberty and opened the door for whatever legislative or judicial burden the state may attempt to impose on the church. Christian attorneys Michael Paulsen and Rodney Smith outline a number of examples whereby "neutral" laws could restrict historic Christian practice. State laws banning alcohol at places used by minors could be used to restrict communion services. Churches refusing to ordain women might lose their tax exemption under federal laws barring discrimination against women. States might read *Smith* to allow regulation of curriculum content in Christian schools. They might also attempt to force religious hospitals to perform all lawful medical procedures, including abortion.[46]

Smith effectively removes the constitutional bar to state regulation of Christian counseling ministry. States criminalizing sexual misconduct are already including clergy in the list of counselors who may be prosecuted for this crime (see chapter 6). Arguably, no constitutional barrier now impedes the courts from developing a clergy malpractice standard, something we suspect shall be in place in some states by the year 2000. Legislatures now have a green light to regulate pastors and churches with no substantial distinction from professional regulatory standards. Not only might the clergy exemption from licensing statutes be restricted or even eliminated, but pastoral counseling standards regulated under state licensing boards is conceivable.

Although these changes in American law may be difficult to effect politically, the *Smith* decision renders them legally possible. This rule trumpets the message that 1990 was a watershed year; the rules of church and state are very different now, and the Christian counseling field cannot be ignorant or passive in the face of them. The implications of this rule are so serious that many Christian lawyers advocate amending the Constitution or pushing congressional action to restore fundamental religious freedoms that existed for two hundred years before *Smith*.[47]

How Smith *happened.* Justice Scalia and the so-called conservative wing of the Court are deferentialists—they defer to majority rule, to the power of the legislature over protection of individual rights. While done in the good name of democracy and as an antidote to a generation of judicial activism for individual rights by the High Court, the effect of such judicial deference on religious liberty is potentially devastating. What this case signals about this Court's juridical philosophy regarding church and state and how it might use *Smith* to further erode religious liberty is of primary concern to the church. In a recent cover article on church-state relations in *Christianity Today*, Kim Lawton noted that federal courts have already rendered nearly two dozen opinions using *Smith* as precedent, most going against the church and Christian ministry.[48]

Lawyers Paulsen and Smith conclude with an incisive critique of Scalia's opinion in the *Smith* case:

> The core reason given by Scalia for the majority's position was that allowing religion-specific exemptions would "permit every citizen to become a law unto himself" or involve judges in making case-by-case determinations. . . . There are at least two flaws in this view. . . . The sincere exercise of religion is not an exercise in individual autonomy or anarchy, but a claim of obligation to another, superior source of "law"—the law of God and/or the community of religious faith. This "law" is superior both to the individual will and to the state. To equate religious obligation or discipleship with radical individualism is both offensive and inaccurate. Scalia, a devout Catholic, should know better.
>
> Moreover, recognizing that the exercise of religion is an act of conscientious obedience, not anarchy, provides a limiting principle to the free exercise clause that prevents it from being the every-man-for-himself apparition that Scalia and his colleagues so feared. Only claims grounded in a sincere sense of duty to one's God—a source of duty outside and above the individual—involve the exercise of religion as the framers understood it. . . . True, there would remain many viable claims to exemption from laws adopted by democratic government and many hard cases to decide under this standard. . . . But . . . *if that is what the text of the Constitution requires, judges must yield to that command whether they think it sensible policy or not.*
>
> It is shocking, and extremely disappointing, to see Scalia author an opinion that contravenes this first principle of judicial restraint, at the expense of religious freedom. Scalia refers to this freedom as a "luxury" that "we cannot afford." That is like saying the Constitution is a luxury we cannot afford. Constitutional rights, especially provisions of the Bill of Rights, invariably have social costs. . . . Smith is a sad case of a slim majority of justices who have decided that we should no longer pay the price of religious liberty under the Constitution.[49]

IMPLICATIONS FOR THE CHURCH

The *Nally* and *Smith* cases are critically important for the church and the Christian counselor. Major change is taking place in church-state relations, and we can no longer assume that the only

standards that apply are derived from Scripture or church consti-
tutions. In many respects, the church is failing to adequately train,
supervise, and police its own ministers. This is drawing the state,
by both legislation and litigation, into this regulatory vacuum.
Sadly, Malony's prediction that litigation against the church will
increase in the future is probably accurate.[50] If this proves true, it
will be due to (1) the failure of counselors and churches to humbly
hold to biblical standards of morality and ethical competence in
ministry, and (2) the failure of the larger Christian church to hold
incompetent and harmful ministers accountable for their wrongdoing. States no longer bound by pre-*Smith* standards will show
little restraint or regret in the prosecution of erring Christian ministers and counselors.

UNIVERSAL NEEDS: HUMILITY AND ACCOUNTABILITY

Affirmatively, these two cases *challenge us to humility and accountability* in the pursuit of moral excellence and counseling
competence and in the presentation of one's ministry to the church
and larger world. Let us not presume we have arrived as Christian helpers but humbly remind ourselves that pride (and
self-deceit) goes before our own individual and ministerial fall. We
are at risk in ministry every day and need courage to say, against
our deceitful denial, "I am vulnerable." We need renewal of a
humble faith, of connectedness and sure accountability to one another, of rediscovering the truth and power in God's strength
coming alive in our weakness.

As we are renewed by God's grace through faithful humility, our
counseling ministries will also be transformed. We have recognized a
paradoxical process as this transformation advances. The public
claims made about ministry become less boastful and more circumspect, while the effectiveness of the ministry increases. God seems to
work out, at a corporate level, the truth of Philippians 2—as we
humble ourselves like Christ, he exalts and empowers us.

Even the secular world recognizes this value in the face of the
litigious threat. Psychologist-lawyer Robert Woody extols the vir-
tues of "one*down*manship" in the presentation of a counseling
practice. Modesty will not only gain collegial respect, it will be a
great virtue if you are sued.

> . . . it is apparent that a surefire way of producing nega-
> tive attitudes from laypersons and professionals alike is to

adopt a flamboyant style in clinical [and advertising] practices. . . . Provoking a negative reaction, especially from professional counterparts . . . can create enemies. When a lawsuit for malpractice is threatened, one of the last things needed is a coterie of local professionals ready to testify, "The defendant never did act like a good clinician." . . . In promoting a clinical practice, the temptation is to try to outshine the competition. . . . Such a strategy may . . . motivate . . . them to search for flaws . . . [to be] ready to speak against the defendant-practitioner. . . . Malpractice can be avoided by onedownmanship. Turning competitor-colleagues into allies makes them feel that they are important to your success—which is true.[51]

CONCLUSION

Both *Nally* and *Smith* challenge us to radical transformation in Christian ministry in the new millennium. We believe God will protect counselors against the risk of suit—counselors who take the risk of honest, sometimes painful disclosure to one another. We are vulnerable every day and apart from this level of radical accountability we might fall. As we resist the temptation to hide ourselves and instead admit our faults and temptations to one another, we are protected and empowered—indeed, we are set free to do wonderful works in his name. If we could ask one thing for the contemporary Christian counselor, it would be *sure accountability and loving connectedness to at least one other ministerial colleague.*

NOTES

1. *Nally III,* 253 Cal. Rptr., at 102.
2. Ibid., 99.
3. Ibid., 100. Compare Justice Kaufman's concurring opinion (Ibid., 115) in which he clearly saw that a counseling relationship had begun. This shows the differences by which case facts are understood and used to support the legal reasoning undergirding the judicial rule.
4. Ibid., 115. Although the majority opinion strained to distinguish these statements as referring to trouble living the Christian life (Ibid., 100, footnote 2), Nally's suicide and Pastor Rea's deposition testimony (Ibid., 115–16, footnote 3), clearly indicate that suicide was at issue.
5. Ibid., 100, footnote 3. This judgment was made in the face of strong clinical evidence of suicidal risk, including open discussion by Nally about suicide and

his past struggles with it. Apparently, Pastor Thomson adhered to a form of "biblical counseling" that led him to believe he was competent to help those with severe depression and suicide without having to consult with clinical professionals. See Ibid., 116.

6. Ibid., 100. The medical side of this tragedy begins to reveal itself here. No psychiatrist or knowledgeable general practitioner would prescribe Elavil (or would do so at very low dosage and with strictest monitoring) to a person at risk for suicide due to its lethality in overdose.

7. Ibid., 101. The record also reveals that Nally told Pastors MacArthur and Rea, while they were visiting him at the hospital, that he was sorry he did not succeed in dying and that he would try again. The pastors never informed hospital staff of these statements, presuming, it seems, that they already knew this and had taken precautions.

8. Ibid.

9. Ibid.

10. Ibid., 102.

11. *Nally v. Grace Community Church of the Valley*, 194 Cal. App. 3d 1147, 240 Cal. Rptr. 215 (Cal. App. 2 Dist. 1987) (hereafter cited as *Nally II*). In California the court of appeals is an intermediary between the trial court and the Supreme Court. It is the first appellate review court for disputed trial judgments but is always subject to the higher authority of the California Supreme Court.

12. William Prosser and W. Page Keeton, *Prosser and Keeton on the Law of Torts*, 5th ed. (St. Paul: West Publishing 1984), section 56, 374.

13. *Nally II*, 240 Cal. Rptr. at 224–26.

14. See *Meier v. Ross General Hospital*, 69 Cal.2d 420, 71 Cal. Rptr. 903, 455 p.2d 519 (1968); and *Vistica v. Presbyterian Hospital*, 67 Cal.2d 465, 62 Cal. Rptr. 577, 432 P.2d 193 (1967).

15. *Nally III*, 253 Cal. Rptr. at 106.

16. Ibid., 108.

17. Ibid., 109. See also Samuel Ericsson, "Clergyman Malpractice: Ramifications of a New Theory," *Valparaiso University Law Review* 16 (1981): 163. Ericsson, a Christian attorney and a leading constitutional scholar on church/state relations, was Grace Community Church's chief defense counsel in the *Nally* case.

18. Ibid., 110, footnote 8.

19. Ibid., 113.

20. Ibid., 114–15. The church had fifty pastoral counselors, employed a counseling appointments secretary, advertised in the Yellow Pages and served the larger church and community beyond their membership, and many counselors taught classes and published books, tapes, and various aids on biblical counseling ministry.

21. Ibid.

22. Ibid., 117–18.

23. Ibid., 102.

24. See Nancy Andreason, *The Broken Brain: The Biological Revolution in Psychiatry* (New York: Harper and Row, 1984); and Robert Ornstein and David Sobel, *The Healing Brain* (New York: Touchstone, 1987).

25. For example, the Code of Ethics of the American Association of Pastoral Counselors, which the church successfully fought as an expert witness, requires

that "Pastoral counselors accurately represent their professional qualifications . . ." and ". . . are responsible for correcting any misrepresentation of
their professional qualifications . . ." (sect. II.A.). Further on, the code states,
"Announcements of pastoral counseling services are dignified, accurate and objective, descriptive but devoid of all claims and evaluations" (sect. II.D.).

26. *Nally III*, 100–2.

27. See Thomas L. Needham, "Malpractice in the Ministry," in *Clergy Malpractice*, ed. H. Newton Malony, Thomas L. Needham, and Samuel Southard
(Philadelphia: The Westminster Press, 1986).

28. Justice Kaufman pointedly noted how Pastors Rea, especially, and Thomson
had contradicted and impeached themselves, comparing trial testimony with
depositions and counseling notes, by giving discrepant accounts of Nally's suicide risk. See *Nally III*, 115–16, footnotes 3–6.

29. See John MacArthur, *Our Sufficiency in Christ* (Dallas: Word, 1991).

30. *Nally III*, 108–9. For arguments against the chilling effect such broad duty
would have on pastoral counseling, compare Comment, "Clergy Malpractice: Bad
News for the Good Samaritan or a Blessing in Disguise?" *University of Toledo Law
Review* 17 (1985): 209.

31. James Barringer, letter to Rev. Clarence Kinzler, 23 November 1987, re:
Clergy malpractice: the Nally case.

32. *Nally III*, 110, note 8.

33. See Greg Slater, "Nally v. Grace Community Church of the Valley: Absolution for Clergy Malpractice?" *Brigham Young University Law Review* (1989): 913.

34. "With the rapid movement of fundamentalist churches into the arena of
emotional counseling comes the increased perception among parishioners of competency on the part of the clergy—a perception often fostered by the members of
the clergy themselves . . . [these] clergy have elevated themselves to a new level
of competence, skill, or knowledge, thereby making themselves susceptible to
the imposition of a duty owed to their counselees." Lawrence M. Burek, "Clergy
Malpractice: Making Clergy Accountable to a Lower Power," *Pepperdine Law Review* 14 (1986): 156–57.

35. *Nally III*, 118.

36. See *Cantwell v. Connecticut*, 310 U.S. 296, 303–4 (1940).

37. *Reynolds v. United States*, 98 U.S. 145 (1879).

38. See *Sherbert v. Verner*, 374 U.S. 398, at 398, 403 (1963); also *Wisconsin v. Yoder*,
406 U.S. 205 (1972).

39. 110 S. Ct. 1595 (1990).

40. In *Sherbert v. Verner* in 1963, the High Court overturned the denial of unemployment benefits to a Seventh-Day Adventist who was fired from her job after
refusing to work on her Saturday Sabbath. The Supreme Court held that South
Carolina did not have a compelling interest in prohibiting sincerely held Adventist
beliefs. Similarly, in the 1972 case of *Wisconsin v. Yoder*, the court ruled that the state
was not justified and reversed its prosecution under compulsory school attendance
laws of Old Order Amish families. Based on their centuries-old religious tradition,
the Order removed their children from school early (in this case after the eighth
grade) to participate fully in Amish religious and community life.

41. Steve Chase, "Clergy Malpractice: The Cause of Action that Never Was,"
North Carolina Central Law Journal 18 (1989): 163–85 (quote from 166).

42. *Employment Division, Dept. of Human Resources of Oregon v. Smith-Black*, 763 P.2d 146 (Ore. 1988).

43. See *Smith*, O'Connor concurrence.

44. Edward M. Gaffney, D. Laycock, and M. W. McConnell, "An Answer to Smith: The Religious Freedom Restoration Act," *Christian Legal Society Quarterly* 11, no. 4 (1990): 17.

45. Michael S. Paulsen and R. K. Smith, "A Luxury . . . We Cannot Afford: Religious Freedom After the Peyote Case," *Christian Legal Society Quarterly* 12, no. 2 (1990): 18.

46. Ibid.

47. Ibid.; see also Gaffney, Laycock, and McConnell.

48. Kim Lawton, "Uncle Sam v. First Church," *Christianity Today*, 7 October 1991, 38–41.

49. Paulsen and Smith, "A Luxury . . . We Cannot Afford."

50. H. Newton Malony, "The Future of Ministry in a Changing World," in *Clergy Malpractice*, ed Malony, Needham, and Southard, 146.

51. Robert Woody, *Fifty Ways to Avoid Malpractice: A Guidebook for Mental Health Professionals* (Sarasota, Fla.: Professional Resource Exchange, 1988), 99–100.

PART II

Sexual Misconduct in Christian Counseling

Chapter 5

Wrongful Sex and the Sexual Misconduct Crisis

The church still has considerable difficulty in dealing creatively and forth-rightly with sexuality. The destructive sexual dualisms, while freshly acknowl-edged, have not vanished. Anxieties, fears, and uncertainties almost paralyze us in many ways. We are often more reactive than proactive. We are unclear about the sources of our sexual theologies and about the patterns of life that should flow from them. In so many ways the church is "an uncertain trumpet" when it comes to providing sexual leadership. . . . The sexual problems experienced by clergy are one important element in this uncertainty.[1]

James Nelson

THE SEXUAL REVOLUTION HAS FINALLY COME to the church. As the ve-neer of liberation gives way to the truth, however, the destructive fruits of this revolution are being visited upon almost everyone deceived by its siren call. The church cannot escape the struggle with the values and trouble of a sex-obsessed culture. Finding God's way in the midst of multiple epidemics—adultery and mari-tal infidelity, pornography and sexual addiction, sexual violence against women and children, homosexual practice and political action, AIDS and sexual disease, promiscuity and abortion, teen-age sex and pregnancy—is neither simple nor impossible. It does require that the church honestly and humbly face its own sexual struggles and the reality of God's good sexual creation.

The church is now beginning to face the epidemic of spiritual, moral, ecclesiastical, and legal trouble due to sexual misconduct in counseling ministry. The legal response to this epidemic is also rapidly developing, and it is difficult to predict when and how this problem will abate and how much influence legal threats will have on that control. One thing is very clear: sexual misconduct has become the most troublesome issue in counseling and helping ministries. Its cases have become the most frequently seen in America's courts, before state licensing boards, professional associations, and, increasingly, before the leadership councils of the Christian church.[2]

In part 2 we will explore the crisis of sexual misconduct in counseling ministry. We define sexual misconduct in this chapter and then review the legal response to this epidemic and prevention guidelines in chapter 6.

THE SEXUAL MISCONDUCT CRISIS

The great majority of sexual misconduct in counseling is perpetrated by male therapists and pastors who victimize younger adult female counselees.[3] "The stereotypic case involves a male therapist striving to adjust to middle age and personal problems who, despite his training, misinterprets the client's overtures for purely emotional support and acceptance as efforts to establish a romantic or erotic connection. The confused client accepts the therapist's advances as a substitute for the type of caring or love she is really seeking."[4] As with all sexual misconduct, this common pattern, no matter how innocently begun or how assertively justified, almost always harms both victim and abuser in significant ways. While cases exist of female therapists abusing male clients, of homosexual misconduct, and, most tragically, of minor children sexually abused by pedophilic counselors and ministers[5] (see chapter 8), we will focus on the predominant pattern of male abuser and female victim, which comprises more than nine of every ten cases.

The various surveys on sexual misconduct done over the past twenty years indicate that between 6 to 10 percent of all psychotherapists in the United States have engaged in some form of sexual or erotic contact with their patients and clients.[6] These studies also reveal that from 40 to 80 percent of therapists who have crossed sexual boundaries with their clients have done so more than once; some of these repeat offenders have dozens of victims. While these figures are disturbing enough considering the numbers of counselors nationwide, many believe these figures are extremely conservative and do not begin to reveal the extent of this social and moral epidemic. The great discrepancies between reporting abuse by victims to authorities (very low) compared to reports to subsequent therapists (much higher) suggests the problem is far greater than the survey numbers indicate.[7]

WHAT IS SEXUAL MISCONDUCT?

Historically, sexual misconduct was defined primarily with reference to sexual intercourse between therapist and client or overt sexual foreplay that was clearly judged as intending sexual arousal. Problems of proving sexual misconduct by way of the malpractice suit required overt sexual contact if the plaintiff were to prevail.[8] Modern definitions have transformed the meaning of sexual misconduct to include any behavior or expression that may be reasonably understood to intend some kind of sexual contact, solicitation, or innuendo. This inclusive definition is driven by professional ethics codes, current case law, statutes that govern professional licensure, and, especially, by recent laws that define sexual misconduct in therapy as criminal behavior.

Psychiatrist David Rutter, in a powerful book entitled *Sex in the Forbidden Zone*, defines sexual misconduct as any "sexual behavior between a man and a woman who have a professional relationship based on trust. . . . " He declares that ". . . any sexual behavior by a man in power with what I define as the forbidden zone *is inherently exploitive of woman's trust*. Because he is keeper of that trust, it is the man's responsibility, *no matter what the level of provocation or apparent consent by the woman*, to assure that sexual behavior does not take place."[9]

Legal definitions. California statutes influence development of statutory law in many states, and its definition of sexual misconduct is becoming normative. The legislature of the Golden State has rendered illegal all sexual contact and misconduct short of contact, including asking for sex, by any licensed therapist in the state.[10] Essentially, any form of sexually expressed behavior by a therapist, whether actual sexual contact was engaged or not, is legally wrong. The statutory code for Licensed Clinical Social Workers renders liable the therapist who "has sexual relations with a client, or who solicits sexual relations with a client, or who commits an act of sexual abuse, or who commits an act of sexual misconduct, or who commits an act punishable as a sexual related crime if such act or solicitation is substantially related to [professional duties]."[11] The codes regulating psychiatrists, psychologists, and marriage and family therapists state essentially the same prohibitions.

Professional denial. These troubles are compounded by the significant numbers of professionals who deny and minimize the problem of sexual misconduct. Worse yet, some professionals still defend sex between counselor and client as beneficial. In a national study on sexual misconduct by psychiatrists, Gartrell and her colleagues found that three-fourths of the violators were motivated by "love" and "pleasure." Over half believed their patients left the sexual involvement with good feelings, and 20 percent intended to improve patient "self-esteem" as a direct result of sexual contact.[12] Contrast this with the wry and classic statement by Judd Marmor, who noted that most encounters were between male therapists and "women who are physically attractive, almost never with the aged, the infirm or the ugly; thus giving the lie to the oft-heard rationalization on the part of such therapists that they were acting in the best interests of their patients!"[13]

SEXUAL MISCONDUCT IN MINISTRY

What little data that does exist about sexual misconduct in ministry certainly denies the church any finger pointing at our secular counterparts. Many pastors and Christian leaders have anecdotes and tragic stories of clergy who have fallen under this plague.[14] The 1988 *Leadership* poll surveyed nearly a thousand pastors (with a 30 percent response rate) and an equivalent number of nonpastor subscribers to *Christianity Today* magazine. The findings reveal a pervasive and painful problem in Christian ministry, one that a pastor revealed "covers the greatest agonies of my life."[15]

Twelve percent of the pastors and 23 percent of the subscribers admitted to extramarital intercourse. Nearly a quarter (23 percent) of the pastors acknowledged some form of "sexually inappropriate" behavior while in local church ministry. In a most telling revelation, fully 39 percent of the pastors believed that sexual fantasy about women other than one's spouse was acceptable. Physical and emotional attraction was noted as the major reason for the misconduct by 78 percent of the respondent pastors, while marital dissatisfaction was noted by 41 percent. Among those people pastors were involved with sexually, 69 percent came from within their own congregations, *including 17 percent who were counselees.*[16]

Rediger, who has nineteen years experience treating clergy who fall sexually, confirms the data of the *Leadership* survey. He states that at least 10 percent of all clergy are involved in sexual misconduct, while another 15 percent are in critical danger of sexual misconduct.[17] The implications of these admissions and their pervasiveness in ministry is staggering.

The near exclusivity of male violators and female victims in clergy sexual misconduct appears to be so, not only because of the preponderance of male clergy, but also because of the "excessive genitalization of sexual feelings and meanings, a pattern much more typical of men's sexual experience than women's."[18] Our professional experience and study leads us to differentiate three types of Christian counselors who sexually violate their clients or congregants.[19] The first type is the counselor or minister who, for a variety of reasons, is at risk for sexual misconduct because of personal emotional vulnerability. The second type is the person who is essentially predatory and destructive in his behavior. The third type is the mixed or borderline counselor that shows combined characteristics of the first two types.

THE VULNERABLE (NONPREDATORY) VIOLATOR

Psychotherapy can foster a closeness between a man and a woman with moments that can be intoxicating. Yielding to temptation is a progressive process—from attraction to fantasy, fantasy to touch, to erotic touch, to sexual foreplay and intercourse. Rutter states simply, "The ordinary man, with an inclination to cross over forbidden boundaries, emerges from beneath the professional role."[20]

The profile of the typical man who becomes involved in sexual misconduct is disarmingly common.[21] One author notes that the majority of men who violate women ". . . are accomplished professionals, admired community leaders, and respectable family men whose integrity we tend to take for granted."[22] This man usually is middle-aged, often involved in an unsatisfactory marriage, with a small percent going through a divorce. He has practiced counseling over a decade, his caseload is primarily female, and he becomes sexually involved with a woman about fifteen years his junior. He often will confide his personal life to his victim, implying that he needs her, soliciting her help for his personal struggles. While often *appearing* successful, he is likely a lonely man, generally isolated from his family and peers.

While most maintain self-control, every male helper is vulnerable to sexual misconduct. Many of these men, Christian as well as non-Christian, fail to realistically evaluate their vulnerability and take the necessary precautions. So often, then, good men become trapped in a basic fault of human nature: *denial.* The common self-talk of denial, "It won't happen to me," is reinforced by the Christian helper who says, "It can't happen to me because I'm a Christian, doing God's work." Self-deceiving pride combined with denial, stressful work, and distorted priorities is truly a deadly prescription for a sexual fall.

In his drive to become someone of value through his performance, the vulnerable counselor lives out of balance, negating personal and family needs in the quest for ministry success. This serious fault leaves the minister sexually at risk for several reasons: (1) He tends to deceive himself about his relationship with Christ and allows his spiritual roots to become shallow. (2) He does not maintain intimate growth in his marriage, his second most primary relationship. (3) He generally fails to have relationships of intimacy, support, and genuine accountability with other men. (4) He is not honest with himself or others about the struggle and emptiness he feels in his work.[23] These factors, among others, foster an environment that leads a counselor to risk everything of value for a transitory intimate relationship.

THE PREDATORY (INTENTIONAL) VIOLATOR

In order to protect potential victims, the church faces a critical moral and legal challenge in its responsibility to assess and intervene in the life of a predatory minister. The predatory minister intends to violate sexually—the pursuit of sexual conquest, while denying its violative nature, is a central motivation. Numerous studies have demonstrated that the majority of women (from 40 to 80 percent) who are sexually exploited are hurt by counselors who tend to victimize more than one woman. This behavioral characteristic—the number of different victims and overall sexual incidence—is a key factor that is easily assessed. As incidents and victims increase, so does the judgment of predatory behavior.

Most of the same characteristics that lead a vulnerable helper to violate exist in the predatory counselor, except that they stem from a more pathological base. The intentional violator often comes from a dysfunctional family-of-origin, with higher incidence of child (including sexual) abuse, parental drug abuse, divorce, or parental neglect and abandonment. The predator's history usually includes drug abuse and promiscuous sexual behavior. Outwardly well liked, even respected and admired in church and community, his lust remains hidden to most people but is largely uncontrolled and tends to lead to affairs with a variety of women. These men may abuse drugs and maintain an addiction to pornography or other compulsions well into midlife. Psychodynamically, his predatory behavior masks a marked distrust, even a hatred of women.[24]

Clinically, the predatory counselor is often diagnosed as a person with a sociopathic or narcissistic personality disorder. Predators are often quite intelligent with assertive, charismatic personalities and a charming though superficial social grace. They are frequently controlling, manipulative, and given to excessive power demands, though the power plays are subtle early in relationships. The predator has a strong denial system in place, frequently lying to himself and others to maintain his image of goodness and success. He usually has poor impulse control, has a very low tolerance for frustration, is often abusive and explosively angry, and resists even caring authority.

This counselor differs from the vulnerable violator in that he has an erotic focus, rarely experiences guilt or remorse, and rarely becomes positively emotionally involved with his counselee. His goal is to gain power over women and have sexual relations with as many women as possible.

THE BORDERLINE SEXUAL VIOLATOR

We suggest you think of this distinction we have portrayed between vulnerable and predatory ministers as a continuum from purely vulnerable to purely predatory. The majority of sexually abusing ministers will show characteristics of both. They can be massed in the middle of the scale in a category we might call the zone of the borderline violator. The vulnerable violator becomes more and more predatory as he maintains the incidence and secretiveness of his sexual abuse. This distinction we propose not only describes differences in violative attitude and behavior but is significant in the likelihood of successful restoration in life and ministry. Restoration of the sexual predator is rare, while the vulnerable violator shows a much greater likelihood of change.

SEXUAL CONTROL IN THE MINISTRY

The church could and should lead the fight to maintain sexual self-control in counseling ministry and psychotherapy.[25] Throughout the church there is near unanimous condemnation of sexual exploitation. It might be easy to conclude that, like the poor, the sex-offending counselor will always be with us. Instead, we would rather proclaim that every Christian counselor has the power through Christ Jesus to resist the pervasive sexual temptation in counseling. There should be no doubt that if the church will not proclaim sexual self-control and take authority over its erring ministers, it will be done for us and to us by the state. As regretable as it is to say, we must admit that we will deserve the state's control in this arena if the church cannot control itself. We are not willing or ready to concede such control to the state. Instead, we pray the church will yield this epidemic to God and be powerfully transformed as a result.

NOTES

1. James Nelson, "Foreword," in *Ministry and Sexuality: Cases, Counseling and Care,* G. Lloyd Rediger (Minneapolis: Fortress Press, 1990), x.

2. See, for excellent reviews on these subjects, John F. Shackelford, "Affairs in the Consulting Room: A Review of the Literature on Therapist-Patient Sexual Intimacy," *Journal of Psychology and Christianity* 8, no. 4 (1989): 26–43; Peter L. Steinke, "Clergy Affairs," *Journal of Psychology and Christianity* 8, no. 4 (1989): 56–62; Terry Muck, ed., *Sins of the Body: Ministry in a Sexual Society* (Dallas: Christianity Today Institute and Word, 1988).

3. A compilation of the available research data on the incidence of sexual misconduct reveals this male perpetrator/female victim pattern in nearly 90 percent of all cases.

4. Robert G. Meyer, E. R. Landis, and J. R. Hays, *Law for the Psychotherapist* (New York: Norton, 1988), 24–25.

5. For an excellent review of this problem in the church, see Raymond C. O'Brien, "Pedophilia: The Legal Predicament of Clergy," *Journal of Contemporary Health Law and Policy* 4 (1988): 91–154.

6. See Nanette Gartrell et al., "Psychiatrist-Patient Sexual Contact: Results of a National Survey, I: Prevalence," *American Journal of Psychiatry* 143, no. 9 (1986): 1126–31 (the most extensive survey that showed 6.4 percent of psychiatrists have engaged in sexual misconduct); Kenneth S. Pope, P. Keith-Spiegel, and B. G. Tabachnick, "Sexual Attraction to Clients: The Human Therapist and the (Sometimes) Inhuman Training System," *American Psychologist* 41, no. 2 (1986): 147–58 (revealed that 9.4 percent of all psychologists had engaged in some form of erotic contact with clients).

7. See Nanette Gartrell et al., "Reporting Practices of Psychiatrists Who Knew of Sexual Misconduct of Colleagues," *American Journal of Orthopsychiatry* 57 (1987): 287.

8. See *Zipkin v. Freeman,* 436 S.W.2d 753 (Missouri 1968). This leading precedent-setting case was finally won by the plaintiff who eventually received just $5,000 in damages. This was for behavior in which the psychiatrist induced his patient to leave her husband and move into an apartment above his practice, file

lawsuits against and burglarize her husband's home, give the doctor money for speculative business ventures, engage in nude swimming parties, and have frequent sex, including when she escorted him on weekend conferences.

9. Peter Rutter, *Sex in the Forbidden Zone* (Los Angeles: Jeremy P. Tharcher, 1989), 22 (italics in original).

10. See *California Business and Professions Code*, sections 726, 728 and 4982(k).

11. Ibid., at section 1881(f).

12. Gartrell et al., "Reporting Practices."

13. Judd Marmor, "Some Psychodynamic Aspects of the Seduction of Patients in Psychotherapy," *The American Journal of Psychoanalysis* 36 (1976): 320–21.

14. See Tim LaHaye, *If Ministers Fall, Can They Be Restored?* (Grand Rapids, Mich.: Zondervan, 1990), chapter 1. Through our own clinical and mediation practice with The Redwood Family Institute, we serve a Northern California region of approximately 125,000 people with 120 churches. We are aware of seven men in church leadership—pastors, church staff, and key lay leaders from conservative, evangelical, or charismatic churches—who have recently fallen prey to ruinous sexual misconduct within and outside the church.

15. "Special Report: How Common Is Pastoral Indiscretion? Results of a Leadership Survey," *Leadership* 9, no. 1 (1988): 12–13, (hereafter referred to as *Leadership* survey).

16. Ibid., 12.

17. G. Lloyd Rediger. His data and observations are primarily based on the Protestant clergy population of the Midwest United States.

18. Ibid., from the foreword by James B. Nelson, xii.

19. For an excellent review of the problem and how to respond to this issue, see Gary Schoener et al., *Psychotherapists' Sexual Involvement With Clients: Intervention and Prevention* (Minneapolis: Walk-in Counseling Center, 1989).

20. Rutter, *Forbidden Zone*, 22.

21. See Janet Sonne and Kenneth Pope, "Treating Victims of Therapist-Patient Sexual Involvement,"*Psychotherapy* 28, no. 1 (1991): 183, table 2. Our profile is not meant to convey the idea that there is but one type of abuser—Pope reveals ten different abuse orientations around the themes of power, anger, and sadism.

22. Rutter, *Forbidden Zone*, 2.

23. Jim Conway, *Men in Mid-Life Crisis* (Elgin, Ill.: David C. Cook, 1978).

24. See Margaret Rinck, *Christian Men Who Hate Women: Healing Hurting Relationships* (Grand Rapids, Mich.: Zondervan, 1990).

25. See, however, *Leadership* survey, 13. One of the disturbing findings that raises legitimate questions about the church's control of this problem was the number of pastors who thought sexual fantasy about other women (not one's spouse) was okay (39 percent). Gary Collins noted how temptation begins in the mind and asserted that while behavior may be effectively controlled by personal accountability, "we need to be even more careful what we let our minds dwell on, because there can be no outside accountability there. Only the person knows what he's thinking." The failure of accountability and fear of loss of confidentiality was reflected by nearly half the pastors who stated they talk to no one, not even their wives about this problem. Larry Crabb noted that pastors are not allowed to admit their struggles and temptations, "Most churches require their pastors to live in denial."

Chapter 6

Legal Liability for Sexual Misconduct in Counseling

Can a man scoop fire into his lap without his clothes being burned? Can a man walk on hot coals without his feet being scorched? So is he who sleeps with another man's wife; no one who touches her will go unpunished. But a man who commits adultery lacks judgment; whoever does so destroys himself. Blows and disgrace are his lot, and his shame will never be wiped away.

Proverbs 6: 27–29, 32–33

THE CRIMINALIZATION OF SEXUAL MISCONDUCT HAS BEGUN, and some who read these words who are engaged sexually with a counselee will one day be imprisoned for this wrong. The law at all levels is rapidly changing, and though we cannot predict how far it will go, it is now clear that the sex-offending counselor will be severely affected by any victim who takes action against this behavior.

THE HARM SUFFERED

Significant personal, marital, social, and financial harm is suffered by most people who are involved sexually through a helping relationship. This is true for both victim and abuser, though the frequency and degree of victim's harm is usually much greater. One writer reviewed the empirical research and concluded that "serious harm result[ed] to almost all patients sexually involved with their therapists."[1] A study of California psychologists who worked with clients who had been involved sexually with former therapists reported that 90 percent of these victims had suffered adverse effects. Eleven percent required hospitalization, and 1 percent had committed suicide. Suicidal ideation is common, as is loss of spousal or support networks, often because of divorce, shame, self-blame, or even the suicide of a spouse.[2]

Other studies reinforce the evidence of significant personal and social harm. This harm includes depression, emotional disturbance, sexual dysfunction, guilt, shame, impaired social adjustment, increased drug and alcohol abuse, major weight gain or loss, marital conflict, divorce, and the inability to use therapy.[3] In addition, many of these victims suffer from posttraumatic stress disorder (PTSD). They experience great difficulty in talking about the trauma because they are afraid of being blamed or they fear that their self-blaming judgments will be validated. It has been suggested that, "Nearly all victims of sexual abuse by professionals report experiences of shock, suppression of the memory, guilt about their own falsely presumed responsibility, and worry that no one would believe their report of abuse."[4] Women sexually abused in therapy have significantly more mistrust and anger toward men, including problems of mistrust and aversion toward their husbands.

We agree that ". . . most women who have had exploitive sexual relationships experience a deep wound to their most inner, sacred sense of self. This psychological injury—often felt as the death of hope itself—remains the greatest casualty of sex in the forbidden zone."[5] This betrayal of hope lies at the heart of the crushing impact of sexual misconduct with a Christian professional. The woman, who already felt so needy, hopeless, and defeated, has her worst fears confirmed by a pastor or professional Christian helper: she is valued only as a sexual object. Because of the sexual violation, the woman concludes in her heart that she is worthless to God and to others. Her "good" Christian helper confirms for her the worst lies that she is to be used and abused, beyond hope of healing.

SERIOUS HARM—SUCCESSFUL SUIT

After reviewing the limited evidence on harm that existed fifteen years ago, Masters and Johnson asserted that therapeutic sexual misconduct should be viewed and prosecuted as a form of rape.[6] Feminist analysis also recognizes the rape (as well as an incest) analogy and decries the sexist standards in the predominant male abuser/female victim typology. They also forcefully challenge the ineffectual systemic response to sexual misconduct by the mental health professions. The charge of a "conspiracy of silence" that works to deny, minimize, and ultimately protect male-dominated professions is indeed strong.[7] Considering the manifold evidence regarding this epidemic, however, the church cannot and should not dismiss this charge.

The failure of the professions and the church to control its harmful members, especially its sex-abusing members, invites the legal control it detests. Currently, *over half the lawsuits and legal actions against all counselors are for some form of sexual misconduct.* Hogan's research (see chapter 2) also showed sexual misconduct suits were the most successful actions by plaintiffs. No doubt the evidence of serious harm to victims of therapeutic sexual abuse is a key reason for both the incidence and growing success of victim action.

Contrast this with the evidence that only 1 to 5 percent of therapeutic sexual abuse is reported.[8] If these dismal reporting rates were merely doubled—if just one victim in ten took action against her abuser—the courts and licensing boards would be flooded with suits and disciplinary actions. A sleeping giant of sexually victimized women is awakening from slumber. When it is fully awake and acts, it will bring just retribution on sexual violators and forever change the social fabric of our culture.

THE LEGAL RESPONSE TO SEXUAL MISCONDUCT

By legislative mandate, all licensed mental health professionals in California have available a small booklet for clients entitled *Professional Therapy Never Includes Sex.*[9] As a consumer-oriented response to the sexual misconduct epidemic, the state hopes to educate and embolden victims to overcome the dismal reporting rate of such abuse and get the help they need. This booklet provides a convenient outline of four options for victim action that, taken together, constitute the sum of legal and ethical response to this problem.

LIABILITY UNDER PROFESSIONAL ETHICS CODES

Every major mental health professional group, including those that regulate pastoral and Christian counseling, condemn sexual activities with clients as unethical.[10] The National Association of Social Workers (NASW) Code of Ethics condemns any form of client exploitation and asserts, "The social worker should under no circumstances engage in sexual activities with clients."[11] Commenting on the language used in this prohibition, the NASW Task Force on Ethics stated that it "deliberately used the strongest language of absolute prohibition, 'under no circumstances' found any place in the code" in view of the "great damage" done to sexually exploited clients.[12]

The American Association of Pastoral Counselors (AAPC) indicated record numbers of claims and losses against their liability insurance during the 1991–92 policy year.[13] Eight of the twelve claims reported were for sexual misconduct; male subscribers faced a significant increase in their malpractice premiums due to this trouble. The recently amended (1991) Code of Ethics of the AAPC—reflecting the trends in law and ethics and pushing it to the next level—states the strongest prohibition against sexual misconduct we have encountered.

PRINCIPLE III—CLIENT RELATIONSHIPS

G. All forms of sexual behavior or harassment with clients are unethical, even when a client invites or consents to such behavior or involvement. Sexual behavior is defined as, but not limited to, all forms of overt and covert seductive speech, gestures and behavior as well as physical contact of a sexual nature; harassment is defined as, but not limited to, repeated comments, gestures or physical contacts of a sexual nature.
H. We recognize that the therapist/client relationship involves a power imbalance, the residual effects of which are operative following the termination of the therapy relationship. Therefore, all sexual behavior or harassment as defined in Principle III. G. with former clients is unethical.[14]

Many, but not all therapists and counselors belong to these professional associations that exist to advance the profession, set standards for membership and conduct, and discipline its erring members. A victim can file a complaint with the association which may, based on evidence of violation against its ethical code, take various disciplinary actions, including removal of the offending member from the association. This is not the same as license revocation;

the erring therapist might still practice even if removed from professional association. This option is recognized as the weakest in terms of punishment and protection of the public from further harm.

LICENSE REVOCATION UNDER ADMINISTRATIVE LAW

As states increasingly license and regulate mental health professionals, the threat of license revocation becomes a more powerful tool for compliance with statutory standards of professional conduct. Courts have uniformly upheld the power of licensure boards to deny or revoke license under administrative law.[15] The problems of proving sexual misconduct in this arena are easier for a victim since there is often no statute of limitation, and the standards of proof are less stringent than those required in a courtroom. Proof of sexual misconduct by a licensed professional almost certainly leads to loss of that license and an inability to practice in a growing number of states.

Numerous problems exist in the use of license revocation as a regulatory device for control of sexual misconduct. The most significant problem is the lack of comprehensive mental health licensure. "While psychiatrists, psychologists, and . . . social workers are licensed, other therapists go unregulated. [In some states] virtually any person, qualified or unqualified, can hang out a shingle and put an ad in the yellow pages describing services as that of 'counselor.' . . . While most states license hairdressers, [etc.], a significant portion of this critical industry of therapy providers goes totally unregulated."[16]

Even when licensure boards function, the discrepancy between the high incidence of abuse and the very low numbers of disciplinary actions raises serious questions about their effectiveness. The assertion that licensure means competence, though a widely disputed assumption, is a problem for both clients and referring professional colleagues. Benetin and Wilder argue:

> Though licensure statutes serve a purpose in protecting patients from illegitimate and incompetent treatment in the medical profession, they do not accomplish the same purpose in the mental health industry. Their success depends on requiring licensing of the entire mental health industry, providing adequate enforcement mechanisms against those who abuse the privilege they have been granted, and educating the public as to the requirements for and meaning of a

license. By licensing some but not all of the industry, the state places the burden of selecting a competent, ethical therapist on the patient—often with little information about the ramifications of selecting an unlicensed therapist.[17]

CIVIL LAWSUITS UNDER TORT AND RELATED LAW

More and more victims are filing and winning lawsuits against sexually abusing counselors, including pastoral counselors. The victim who prevails in a civil suit is the recipient of money damages, and this fact makes such lawsuits the most restorative legal action for the victim. The growing success of these suits against therapists is also reflected by the widespread insurance industry refusal to cover liability for sexual misconduct, a fact that makes winning damages an increasingly hollow victory.

Other problems for victims in civil lawsuits revolve around proof. In the case of *Roy v. Hartogs*,[18] the defendant psychiatrist was nearly successful in denying sexual contact and blaming the victim for her own distress. The case was won by the plaintiff-victim only after three former sexual abuse victims of the psychiatrist came forward and testified against him. Not only must the victim prove each element required under malpractice—duty, breach of duty, harm and causation—they must also prove they did not consent to sexual relations. Some courts and legislatures have limited this defense,[19] but the consent defense remains a formidable barrier to claimant relief. We should anticipate more states legislating easier ways for sexual abuse victims to sue violators in the 1990s. Furthermore, due to the *Smith* decision, it is probable that legislatures will also include pastors and church-based counselors as defendants in these actions.

Finally, courts are beginning to accept liability for sexual misconduct under legal theories other than tort. The *Destafano* case discussed in chapter 2 is significant in this regard. As you may recall, a man who came to his priest for marital counseling sued the priest and his diocese following an affair between his wife and the priest. While no malpractice liability attached, the Colorado court found liability under fiduciary trust—the sexual misconduct of the priest violated his fiduciary duty to advance the best interests of the couple's marriage. Fiduciary law (see chapter 24) is and will be increasingly accepted by America's courts in cases of sexual misconduct. The message is growing loud and clear: if you violate sexually and your client sues you, you will be found liable.

CRIMINAL LIABILITY: THE FUTURE IS FAST ARRIVING

Through 1991 seven states had criminalized sexual misconduct between counselors and clients. These include Wisconsin, the first to make this conduct criminal in 1983, Minnesota, Colorado, North Dakota, California, Maine, and Florida.[20] Numerous other states are considering the passage of similar legislation, likely making this behavior criminal throughout the United States by the new millennium.

California's law makes it a crime for a licensed therapist to have sexual contact with a client during therapy and for two years after the close of therapy. This two-year post-termination bar of sexual contact was passed as a legislative compromise to forestall ending therapy for the purpose of engaging in sex that was perceived by participants to be legally safe. A first offense in California is punished as a misdemeanor, and second and subsequent offenses may be felonies with fines up to $5,000 and a year in state prison.

The criminal laws and penalties in the other states mentioned are much more stringent than California's. Colorado law, for example, applies to anyone doing psychotherapy and defines therapy so broadly that pastoral counselors would easily come under this rule.[21] Wisconsin's statute explicitly includes any "physician, psychologist, social worker, nurse, chemical dependency counselor, *member of the clergy* or other person, whether or not licensed by the state who performs or purports to perform psychotherapy"[22] (italics ours). All these states regard sexual contact as felonious behavior and have prosecuted offending therapists, some of whom are now imprisoned. In Colorado sexual penetration is aggravated sexual assault and can lead to an eight-year prison sentence.[23] The same act in Minnesota, criminal sexual conduct in the third degree, is punishable by up to ten years in prison with fines up to $20,000.[24]

The mixed blessing of criminalization. Criminalizing sexual misconduct is truly a mixed blessing for victim and violator.[25] Positively, it communicates a powerful warning that could deter the vulnerable or borderline violator (review chapter 5) from engaging in wrongful sex. Though deterrence is not likely in the case of the sexual predator, retribution through criminal punishment is certainly just desserts for such intentional exploitation. Theoretically, money through state victim assistance programs will also be available for the therapy of sexual abuse victims.

Negatively, criminalizing this behavior may paradoxically deter desired reporting. Victims and subsequent therapists may be inhibited by the thought that criminal penalties are too severe a response. Rehabilitation of offenders who can genuinely change, but will refuse to come forward for fear of retribution, will also be hampered. The criminal process itself removes effective control of the process from the victim, countering the therapeutic and spiritual need for personal empowerment.

Criminalizing sexual misconduct may also hamper the process of license revocation and civil suit, which may have to wait until a criminal trial is ended. Insurance companies are strengthened in their drive to exclude this behavior from coverage, making financial recovery for victims all the harder (see chapter 23). Some states are making insurers indemnify sexual abuse claims even though the behavior is criminal. A Minnesota appellate court upheld a suit against an insurance company to collect damages by holding that the sexual misconduct was the "incidental outgrowth of the primary malpractice"—the mishandling of client transference.[26]

Criminal sanction is a harsh response by the state to the sexual misconduct epidemic. In spite of the problems with this legislation, more and more states will criminalize this behavior as the epidemic continues into the new millennium. For the offending counselor or at-risk minister, the criminalization of this behavior may be the shower of cold water needed to maintain sexual control. If Christian counselors will reprogram their thinking against the intoxication of sexual attraction, there is hope for escape. The abuser should soberly think that "my sexual misconduct is a crime that will severely hurt my victim, cause me to lose my family and ministry, land me in prison with a massive fine, and expose me to hostile convicts with AIDS who sexually abuse sexual abusers . . . HELP ME, GOD!"

HANDLING TEMPTATION WITHOUT A FALL

Your flesh will always serve the law of sin. And God never tries to fix it. It is dead. So Paul said his flesh was serving sin; he could not fix his flesh anymore than you can.[27]

A transformed man can see the true woman. The problem of sexual exploitation of women must be resolved from two perspectives: inner transformation and outer control. The ideal constraint is by the transformation of the inner man's view of a woman. In Christ, a man is able to see a woman as one to be valued and not exploited. The female client, indeed all women, can be prized and enjoyed in a mutual sharing of genuine Christian love. From this eternal and spiritual view, the greatest loss the woman suffers is not the sexual violation per se, as traumatic as that is, but the loss of dignity and personhood through the violation. She has also lost a man who could have helped heal her woundedness within and celebrate her as a unique person before God.

Assessing and respecting sexual vulnerability. The counselor must learn how to set and keep appropriate sexual boundaries within the professional context. A key to clear boundaries is assessment and respect of one's own vulnerability to sexual misconduct. This evaluation should be an essential and regular part of good self-care for all helpers. Paul warned us that he who thinks he is strong should "be careful that you don't fall! No temptation has seized you except what is common to man. And God is faithful; he will not let you be tempted beyond what you can bear. But when you are tempted, he will also provide a way out so you can stand up under it" (1 Cor. 10:12b–13).

Stop the fantasy. What often fuels sexual misconduct is self-permission to develop and expand sexual fantasies about clients or congregants. By themselves, sexual fantasies about clients are extremely common—between 80 to 90 percent of male therapists experience them on occasion.[28] What is dangerous is not the fantasy, but maintaining and painting the fantasy further in the mind's eye. This reinforces the denial process by desensitizing you to the trouble of fantasy while increasing your justification of inappropriate sexual activities. This also corrupts right judgment, substituting the misbelief that falling in love with another is a passion you cannot control. Rather than fuel sexual fantasy, helpers must learn to deliberately stop and take control of this dangerous bridge to wrongful behavior.

Temptation too hot? Flee immorality! The true test of one's success at preparing to avoid sexual misconduct occurs at the point of stepping into the encounter. This focuses the absolute necessity to flee from sexual temptation, much as Joseph did from Potiphar's wife. If you have temptation thrown in your face, drop everything and run, *run, RUN!* Rutter reveals, even in the midst of passionate temptation, the healing power of sexual restraint:

> When a forbidden-zone relationship becomes erotically charged, several moments of decision inevitably occur that determine whether the sexuality will be contained psychologically

or acted upon physically. Whenever a man relinquishes his sexual agenda toward his protégée in order to preserve her right to a non-sexual relationship, a healing moment occurs.

Because so many women have been previously injured by the uncontained sexuality of men who have had power over them, the potential healing power of restraint is enormous. Not only is the woman made safe from being exploited by this particular man, but the moment kindles the promise that she can be valued as a woman entirely apart from her sexual value to other men.[29]

Committing to accountability. Every Christian helper should evaluate his or her vulnerability with someone who is in a position to help without the threat of disclosure or termination—someone to whom he or she can confess personal sins and fantasies. We advocate a quarterly tune-up; such accountability to another believer should be foundational to Christian counseling in the 1990s. The days of lone ranger ministry independence and unaccountable behavior are over.

CONCLUSION

Good sex is so sweet—God created it to be so. It stays sweet and grows sweeter and richer when confined to one man and one woman in a healthy and growing marriage. Outside of this—in every way outside of this—sweet sex eventually sours, ultimately becoming toxic and deadly. Wrongful sex in the forbidden zone of Christian ministry is proving the high cost of deadly wages. The delusional intoxication of sexual lust and unrestrained fantasy quickly gives way to reveal the bitter onslaught of betrayal, horrific pain, and broken life. The future will bring not just disgrace, shame, and loss of family life, it will also bring imprisonment. Even so, it is not too late to pull back from the moral precipice. The church can creatively show the way out of the new sexual slavery to an exhausted and sex-saturated culture.

NOTES

1. Kenneth Pope and Jacqueline Bouhoutos, *Sexual Intimacy Between Therapists and Patients* (New York: Praeger, 1986), 63.

2. Jacqueline C. Bouhoutos et al., "Sexual Intimacy Between Psychotherapists and Patients," *Professional Psychology: Research and Practice* 14, no. 2 (1983): 185–96.

3. Shirley Feldman-Summers and G. Jones, "Psychological Impact of Sexual Contact Between Therapists or Other Health Care Practitioners and Their Clients," *Journal of Consulting and Clinical Psychology* 52, no. 6 (1984): 1054; see also Phyllis Chesler, *Women and Madness* (Garden City, N.Y.: Doubleday, 1972), 136–57.

4. G. Lloyd Rediger, *Ministry and Sexuality: Cases, Counseling and Care* (Minneapolis: Fortress Press, 1990), 24.

5. Peter Rutter, *Sex in the Forbidden Zone* (Los Angeles: Jeremy P. Tharcher, 1989), 44.

6. William H. Masters and Virginia E. Johnson, "Principles of the New Sex Therapy," *American Journal of Psychiatry* 133 (1976): 548–54.

7. Juanita Benetin and M. Wilder, "Sexual Exploitation and Psychotherapy," *Women's Rights Law Reporter* 11, no. 2 (1989): 121–35; Denise LeBoeuf, "Psychiatric Malpractice: Exploitation of Women Patients," *Harvard Women's Law Journal* 11 (1988): 83–116. See Jonas Robitscher, *The Powers of Psychiatry* (Boston: Houghton-Mifflin, 1980), 417.

8. A compilation of the data from various studies indicates that victims report the incidence of sexual misconduct by therapists only 1 to 5 percent of the time. Considering that sexual misconduct cases are now the most prevalent and successful legal actions for plaintiffs, it is easy to conclude that even a small increase in the barely existent reporting rate will influence a major increase in legal actions of all types against sexually abusing therapists.

9. Available through the California Department of Consumer Affairs, 400 R Street, Suite 3150, Sacramento, Calif. 95814-6240.

10. See American Psychiatric Association, "The Principles of Medical Ethics with Annotations Especially Applicable to Psychiatry," *American Journal of Psychiatry* 130 (1985): 1057; American Psychological Association, *Ethical Standards of Psychologists* (Washington, D.C., 1979); National Association of Social Workers, *NASW Code of Ethics* (Washington, D.C., 1980); American Association of Pastoral Counselors, *Code of Ethics* (1991), in *AAPC Handbook*, Fairfax, Va.; American Association for Marriage and Family Therapy, *Ethical Principles for Family Therapists* (1982), p. 149, and Christian Assiciation for Psychological Studies, *Proposed Code of Ethics* (1985), p. 163 in *Clergy Malpractice*, ed. H. Newton Malony, Thomas L. Needham, and Samuel Southard (Philadelphia: The Westminister Press, 1986).

11. National Association of Social Workers, *NASW Code of Ethics* (Washington, D. C., 1980), II. R. 5.

12. NASW Task Force on Ethics, "Ethics Analysis—Conduct and Responsibility to Clients," *NASW News* (May 1980): 12.

13. "Malpractice Claims Against Pastoral Counselors Continue to Mount—Premium Adjustment Inevitable," *AAPC Newsletter* 30, no. 2 (Spring 1992): 3.

14. *AAPC Handbook*, Principle III. G. and H., 22–23.

15. Juanita Benetin and M. Wilder, "Sexual Exploitation and Psychotherapy," *Women's Rights Law Reporter* 11, no. 2 (1989): 121.

16. Ibid.

17. Ibid., 133.

18. *Roy v. Hartogs*, 85 Misc.2d 891, 381 N.Y.S.2d 587 (Sup.Ct. 1976).

19. In *Cotton v. Kambly*, 101 Mich.App. 537, 300 N.W.2d 627 (1980), the Michigan court ruled that psychiatrist's sexual actions were "under the guise of

psychiatric treatment" and therefore the patient could not consent to sex related to therapy.

20. *Wisconsin Statutes Annotated,* section 940.22 (1983); *Minnesota Statutes,* section 609.341 et seq; *Colorado Revised Statutes,* section 18-3-405.5 (Supp. 1988); *North Dakota Revised Statutes Annotated,* section 12.1-20-06.1 (Michie Supp. 1989); *California Business and Professions Code,* section 729 (Supp 1989); *Maine Revised Statutes,* title 17-A, section 253(2) (Supp 1989); *Florida Statutes Annotated,* section X (West 1990).

21. Ibid., *Colorado,* section 18-3-405.5(b) and (c).

22. Ibid., *Wisconsin,* section 940.22(1)(i).

23. Ibid., *Colorado.*

24. Ibid., *Minnesota.*

25. Larry Strasburger, Linda Jorgenson, and Rebecca Randles, "Criminalization of Psychotherapist-Patient Sex," *American Journal of Psychiatry* 148, no. 7 (1991): 859–63.

26. *St. Paul Fire and Marine Insurance Co. v. Love,* 447 N.W.2d 5 (Minn. Ct. App. 1989).

27. Jeff Harkin, *Grace Plus Nothing* (Wheaton, Ill.: Tyndale House, 1991), 72.

28. See Janet Sonne and Kenneth Pope, "Treating Victims of Therapist-Patient Sexual Involvement," *Psychotherapy* 28, no. 1 (1991): 180.

29. Rutter, *Forbidden Zone,* 215.

PART III

_____

Confidentiality and Its Many Exceptions

Chapter 7

Confidentiality and Privileged Communication

A gossip betrays a confidence, but a trustworthy man keeps a secret.
Proverbs 11:13

Helen was tense, sitting at the edge of her chair, furtively glancing around the room. She fixed her gaze on the door as if mentally noting the way of quick escape. It was her first appointment, and she wasted no time getting to her primary concern. "You *have* to keep what I tell you in confidence, right?!" Her question was also an assertive demand. I affirmed to her my legal and ethical duty to maintain confidentiality, which could only be broached by a number of situations in which the law compels or allows me to disclose information. "What kind of situations?" she shot back. I began to recount them, and as I was explaining my duties under *Tarasoff* (see chapter 10), she interrupted with a nervous laugh, "I'm not going to kill anybody . . . unless it's my husband and my pastor!"

Now I was concerned and compelled to pursue this statement. Her anger and hurt had clearly surfaced, and I asked what happened. She had been counseling with her pastor for a number of sessions about her marital separation. Her husband had left her after she had confronted him about an affair that he denied. While separated they had been sexually intimate, and she contracted a sexual disease. Then the truth spilled out, and she was enraged at her husband for his lying denial of the affair and for being the source of her disease.

The husband's affair had gone sour, and he wanted to return home. She refused, and he was now blaming her for her angry resistance. Her pastor had also encouraged her to allow her husband to return home. He asserted that her anger showed an unforgiving spirit that would block reconciliation. Then, without her consent or knowledge, the pastor shared all this with the church's ministry council. She was shocked when the council invited her to a meeting to discuss this with the whole group.

Helen was enraged at the betrayal of her trust, first by her husband and then by her pastor. She was caught in the dilemma of blaming the victim, as her church group reacted as if her anger was unfounded. Instead it confirmed to them the pastor's concern for her resistance, and they began to pray for her repentance. Helen had not been back to church since this and told me she was never going back. She had come to see me only at a friend's insistence but stated that coming was probably a waste of time because she expected me to violate her trust.

The sting of betrayal. Helen suffered the bitter fruit of betrayed confidence. Some in the church would easily fault Helen for her anger and avoidance. However, God understands her response: "A gossip betrays a confidence, so avoid a man who talks too much" (Prov. 20:19). Jesus instructed his disciples to respect confidentiality in the resolution of disputes. "If your brother sins against you, go and show him his fault, *just between the two of you* . . ." (Matt. 18:15a, italics ours). The loose-mouthed counselor loses possibly the most important thing he or she must maintain as a helper—the moral respect and social influence of client trust—by disclosing those secrets that harm the most vulnerable parts of a person's life.

THE RULE AND ROLE OF CONFIDENTIALITY

The Christian counselor owes a broad duty to a client or parishioner not to disclose the communications from their counseling relationship. This duty to maintain confidentiality is rooted in many ancient cultures, including the Old Testament and Greek civilization, having been part of the Hippocratic oath for more than two millennia.[1] Modern rules governing confidentiality, however, have become highly complex. The legal trend over the past half-century shows a

consistent erosion of the right of confidentiality and a corresponding expansion of disclosure exceptions driven by law, new
information technologies, and third-party fee payment. There are
now so many ways that confidential communications can be legally compelled and excepted that some consider it valid to
question whether the exceptions have overtaken the rule.[2]

> The average clinician must now consider the impact of
> many different factors in order to comply with confidentiality
> principles: state and federal laws, court rulings on specific
> cases . . . regulations mandated by licensing and accredita-
> tion bodies, [professional ethics codes], disclosure demands
> of third-party payers, specific agency policies (which may be
> vague or non-existent), the data-hungry computer, client
> rights (including access to public records), the litigious con-
> sumer, and old-fashioned common sense. These various
> factors often conflict with one another in their philosophy and
> demands, leaving the practitioner in the uneasy position of
> being "damned if he does and damned if he doesn't."[3]

The right to confidentiality is grounded in a twofold rationale.
First, every client has a fundamental moral and legal right to privacy, to be left alone, to have personal thoughts, opinions, beliefs,
and behavior protected from public knowledge . Second, in pastoral counseling and professional therapy, confidentiality is
considered essential to facilitate client self-disclosure and fully
engage the therapeutic alliance to bring about the most enduring
client change. Failure, then, to maintain confidential communications violates both the client's fundamental privacy right and the
therapeutic trust essential to maintain hope and fulfill the goal of
lasting change. The recognition of the unique nature of therapeutic communication and the policy justification for legally
protecting it was probably best articulated by a federal court in
Taylor v. United States:

> The psychiatric patient confides more utterly than anyone else
> in the world. He exposes to the therapist not only what his
> words directly express; he lays bare his entire self, his dreams,
> his fantasies, his sins, and his shame. Most patients who un-
> dergo psychotherapy know that this is what will be expected
> of them, and that they cannot get help except on that
> condition. . . . It would be too much to expect them to do so
> if they knew that all they say—and all the psychiatrist learns

from what they say—may be revealed to the whole world from a witness stand.[4]

LIABILITY FOR BREACH OF CONFIDENTIALITY

Confidentiality and privilege share many common elements, but they are not the same. Privilege statutes narrowly protect confidential information in a legal proceeding only. Confidentiality refers to the ethical and legal duty to protect client information against every other source outside the judicial arena. Breach of either confidentiality or privilege outside a legally defined exception to the rule creates liability for which clergy or counselor can be sued. Both the right and its exercise are almost always with the client or his or her representative, not with the counselor or pastor, who cannot disclose information without client consent or a legally compelling exception to the rule.

Any invasion of the client's privacy right or nonconsenting breach of confidentiality creates liability risk for the counselor. Contrary to Levicoff's assertion,[5] the duty to maintain client confidence has legal ramifications apart from its statutory expression as privileged communication. Lawsuits and license revocation actions for breach of client confidentiality are steadily rising and becoming common legal actions. This risk is greatly reduced when disclosure is legally mandated, but unless a counselor is granted immunity from suit by statute (as in the case in child abuse reporting statutes), the risk is not altogether eliminated.

The counselor's bind. Recent studies have shown that most counseling clients presume confidentiality to be absolute, and even those who know it is not, believe that it should be absolute.[6] Hence, owing to client resistance to even mandated disclosures, counselors are placed in a difficult ethical bind. The at-risk counselor is one who, by principle[7] or ignorance, reinforces these perceptions by communicating or implying that confidentiality is absolute. Too often the counselor fails to disclose the limits and exceptions to confidentiality at the beginning of therapy. Courts have ruled against counselors who promised or implied that confidentiality is absolute or who did not challenge a client's presumptions of absolute confidence at the outset of therapy.[8]

There are many ways that counselors violate client privacy and confidentiality rights. Disclosure without client consent to third parties (i.e., vendors, employers, spouses, family members, or close friends) is a common breach of confidential relations. Pastors and

Christian counselors in churches often breach confidence in this way, usually with some justification on behalf of the church or parishioner. Many counselors, presuming their communications about clients would never get back to them, have been surprised and embarrassed when their presumptions have proven wrong.

Breach of privacy suits for slander and libel are increasing where counselors use case material in books and publications that fail to adequately conceal client identity. Pastors are facing this dilemma more commonly when using counseling data in writing and sermons or when disclosure is made in pursuit of church disciplinary actions (see chapter 19). Counseling trainees and interns often fail to inform clients that their sessions are reviewed with a supervisor or in staff consultation. Even with consent in these situations, counselors may be liable for disclosing more information than is necessary.

Client remedies. Clients have essentially three means of redress for violation of privacy rights and confidentiality. These include civil lawsuits, license revocation actions, or professional disciplinary proceedings. Civil suits are increasing for breach of confidentiality and invasion of privacy, and plaintiffs are winning them more consistently. Some of these suits are against pastors and churches, actions that will become more common in the years to come.

The legalization of confidentiality is also seen in mental health licensure statutes. Failure to maintain confidentiality is professional misconduct and can lead to license revocation. In California, disciplinary guidelines of the Board of Behavioral Science Examiners calls for an immediate penalty of license suspension for sixty to ninety days with a probation of three to five years. During this time, any further violations will lead to automatic license revocation. One probationary requirement is that the offending therapist retake both written and oral licensure exams that are required of all new licensees. A worst case scenario in California can lead to criminal prosecution.[9] While no cases yet exist, intentional breach of confidentiality showing malice on the part of an offending therapist can lead to six months in jail and a $2,500 fine. These are indeed harsh penalties for failure to maintain confidentiality.

More commonly, the same evidence used in license discipline may also be used by a professional association in disciplinary proceedings. Breach of confidentiality, as a violation of professional ethics, can lead to various sanctions, including removal from membership in the association. All of these actions are increasingly publicized in professional journals and lead to significant loss by a counselor. The counselor who violates confidentiality can suffer loss of practice, income, professional identity, and collegial esteem, even criminal sanction in the worst case.

PRIVILEGED COMMUNICATION

Recall that privilege statutes are designed to protect confidential communications from disclosure in court and other legal proceedings only. The public policy justification for all privilege statutes is that the benefit to justice by compelling disclosure in court is outweighed by the benefit to society by keeping communications secret. Considered first is the clergy-penitent privilege; then more recent statutes creating a psychotherapist-client privilege will be examined.

CLERGY-PENITENT PRIVILEGE

Penance, the public act of sin confession, forgiveness, and recompense, was an integral part of the early apostolic church. As the Roman Catholic church matured, the act became a sacrament and was transformed into a private event between priest and penitent. The clergy-penitent privilege developed out of the ancient Seal of Confession of the Catholic church. The Seal, entrenched in Church Canon Law for more than a millennia, was absolute, and severe penalties were imposed on priests for its violation. Strong sentiment remains to this day in favor of the absolute nature of the privilege; a popular legal manual for clergy published in 1962 asserted that

> *Every communication* made by a person professing religious faith, or seeking spiritual comfort, to any Protestant minister, or to any priest, or to any Jewish rabbi . . . shall be privileged. No such minister, priest, or rabbi shall disclose *any communication* made to him by any person professing religious faith or seeking spiritual guidance, or be competent or compellable to testify with reference to *any such communication* in court.[10]

The modern reality is that the privilege is not absolute.[11] This reflects the logical corollary to the policy justifying the privilege—courts limit the privilege when the demands of justice outweigh the benefits of maintaining privacy. The trouble with this reality is defining clearly where privilege ends and the right or duty to disclose these communications begins. Leo Pfeffer, a law professor and attorney for the American Jewish Congress, believes two principled exceptions exist to the privilege. One is ongoing evil that can be stopped (e.g., continuing child abuse). The other is where a grave injustice would be made or compounded (e.g., the execution of an innocent person by the state when the guilty party reveals their guilt to a minister).[12]

The trend in current law reflects an expansive/restrictive tension—every state except Alaska has legislated a clergy privilege, something nonexistent in common law, but courts have generally ruled to limit its scope. Nearly all states restrict protected communications to those heard by a cleric while in his or her pastoral (as opposed to personal or family) role. Furthermore, privilege is valid only in those cases where the penitent is genuinely seeking spiritual help. Courts have consistently denied the privilege when things are heard outside a ministerial role or, even when they are heard in the ministerial role but the communicant has revealed no intent to receive absolution or spiritual help.[13]

Tougher questions surround the nature of the communication itself—whether privilege covers narrower confessional communications only or a broader range of information that would include almost anything revealed in the course of pastoral counseling. The states vary greatly in this area when defining the boundaries of privilege. It is incumbent that ministers know the specific boundaries in their resident states. California, by statute and court rule, represents a minority of states that have defined a narrower confessional privilege, one that does not protect many things heard in the course of pastoral counseling.[14] Many more states, in contrast, define the privilege more broadly to protect communications heard beyond the confessional role.

A final question concerns who holds the privilege. Every state recognizes the penitent as the holder, with most also recognizing a guardian, executor, or other legal representative on behalf of the penitent. Some states, in deference to First Amendment religious freedom, also grant the privilege to clergy independent of the penitent, allowing assertion of the privilege by the minister even if waived by the penitent. Most states define *clergy* as those duly ordained or licensed by a reputable church body. A few states also extend the privilege to elders (in the Presbyterian church) and deacons (in the Catholic church) in churches where these functions have been historically recognized. Unique applications are the Florida statute that extends privilege to a lay person the penitent believes to be a minister[15] and the Mississippi code that extends protection to a clergy's secretary or clerk.[16]

PSYCHOTHERAPIST-CLIENT PRIVILEGE

Privilege statutes protecting psychotherapist-client communications are a recent legislative phenomena. These statutes follow the precedent of attorney-client and clergy-penitent privilege and are similar to those protecting communications to doctors, journalists, accountants, and political leaders. (Recall President Nixon's unsuccessful assertion of executive privilege to protect, ostensibly for national security reasons, his White House tapes in the Watergate affair.) As with all others, psychotherapist-client privilege is not absolute in its protection of confidential information. Not every state grants therapeutic privilege, especially those states without a history of mental health licensure.

California reveals the trend in psychotherapist-client privilege into the twenty-first century. A privilege statute exists for all licensed mental health professionals—psychologists, clinical social workers, and marriage and family therapists as well as psychiatrists, who historically have been covered under medical privilege.[17] Recent legislation has amended the Evidence Code to include those registered with state licensing boards and working under prelicense supervision—psychological assistants, associate clinical social workers, and marriage and family therapy interns. Apart from being enumerated under a protected professional designation, no privilege exists.

California has codified the historic rule to assert privilege upon receipt of a subpoena. All psychotherapists shall claim the privilege as a first response, with liability by civil suit or license board discipline possible if he or she does not assert privilege. Refusal to release records under privilege, which must be formally asserted by the clinician, does not violate the subpoena as long as the intent is client protection and not to never disclose records to the court. Absolute refusal to release records is not covered under privilege and makes one liable for contempt of court and a possible jail sentence. Protecting client communications as the first step to disclosure gives the client, the lawyers, and the court needed time to decide what information, if any, is necessary to resolve the legal dispute.

The client or his or her legal guardian or representative is the holder of the privilege. Generally in the case of a minor, the parent, as legal guardian, controls the privilege. This rule is not absolute, however, as a California appellate court recently ruled that a child's attorney held privilege on behalf of the child, not the father, who was accused of molestation and was seeking to gain access to records of the child's therapist regarding communications about the molestation.[18] The court stated that this was an exception to the general rule that the parent exercises privilege on behalf of their minor children.

EXCEPTIONS TO CONFIDENTIALITY AND PRIVILEGE

The law on exceptions to confidentiality is arguably the murkiest and most conflicted area of legal doctrine the Christian counselor will face. There are five general categories under which the duty to maintain client confidence may be legally compelled or excepted. Not every state allows or mandates all five, and each state has distinctive rules, by both statute and judicial opinion, that define the boundary between confidence and disclosure. Again, *it is imperative that the Christian counselor study the rules of your resident state to know your specific duties under law.* Your state may not agree with these exceptions nor have ruled clearly on their applicability to your counseling ministry.

1. *Client consent to disclosure.* The most common exception to confidentiality is when the client voluntarily consents to disclose information by written release of information.
   a. *Consent for third-party reimbursement.* An increasingly problematic exception is consent given for the purpose of receiving payment for counseling services by insurance and other third-party vendors.
2. *Child and elder abuse reporting.* Child and elder abuse reporting requirements (see chapter 8) serve as a significant statutory exception to the rule of confidentiality and privilege.
3. *Danger to self or others.* A counselor with a client who is a danger to himself or herself (see suicide risk, chapter 9) or to someone else (see risk of homicide or assault, chapter 10), may be legally compelled to breach therapeutic confidence and take action to protect threatened persons.
   a. *Involuntary hospital commitment.* Clients who are a danger to themselves or others may be committed to a hospital against

their will for time-limited inpatient psychiatric evaluation based on evidence of the risk obtained in therapy.

   b. *Duty to warn or protect.* Following the landmark *Tarasoff* decision in California (see chapter 10), a growing number of states have established duties to warn or protect third parties at risk due to the homicidal and assaultive threats of clients.

4. *Emergencies.* Common law tradition, statutes, and courts have defined various emergency exceptions to the rule of confidentiality. These include but are not limited to abuse reporting or dangers to self or others. Section 1027 of the California Evidence Code, for example, creates an exception to privilege when a minor under age sixteen has been the victim of a crime.

5. *Judicial order and court action.* Courts often compel disclosure by subpoena for a variety of legal actions by clients. While privilege statutes protect penitent and clergy or client and therapist in most states, these rules are not absolute. We encourage every reader to obtain information on the specific boundaries of privilege statutes as they apply to you in your state.

   a. *When your client sues you.* Last and, by desirability, most certainly least is the partial waiver of privilege and confidentiality by clients if they sue you for malpractice. Such action gives you the right to use confidential case notes to defend yourself. Guidelines for defense and maintenance of your ministry and sanity will be addressed in chapter 24.

PRACTICE AND POLICY RECOMMENDATIONS

The following recommendations for policy and practice guidance are geared to the general duty to maintain confidentiality and protect privileged communication.

1. *Develop clear organizational policies for confidentiality.* Your church, clinic, or agency should have clear, written policies that honor confidentiality and its limits under law. Courts highly respect such policies, especially when cognizant of your state's particular laws, and their existence strengthens your defense against charges of breach of confidentiality. Be sure such policies include intake and clinical practice disclosure guidelines with clients and third parties. Also outline rules for keeping records under lock and key, for training support personnel in the rules about confidentiality, and for procedures for staff or supervisory consultation when records are requested.

a. *Protect computer and electronic data.* Computers and electronic data storage and transmission are creating a revolution in the nature and provision of professional services. Maintaining confidentiality with these tools is a formidable challenge. The English Data Protection Act requires registration of all British users of patient electronic data storage and imposes criminal penalties for the lack of protecting confidentiality.[19] We encourage clinicians to use, at minimum, password entry systems with CPU hard disk drives and to keep portable disks physically secure in locked cabinets. Greater security may require data encryption programs and copy protection devices.

2. *Explain confidentiality and clarify its limits at the start of counseling.* During your counseling intake, explain and discuss your commitment to confidentiality and its limits with respect to legally mandated disclosure situations. Describe your policy in writing and include written questions about abuse, suicidal, homicidal, or assaultive thinking or behavior on your intake form (see appendix D). You then have justification to thoroughly discuss and explore these issues with your client, including their clinical and legal significance, at the outset of counseling.

3. *Always favor confidentiality over disclosure.* Mandated disclosure is very clear in a few cases. In most cases the question is far less clear and, in these, it is preferable to constantly err in favor of confidentiality over disclosure. As stated by Richard Leslie, legal counsel to the California Association of Marriage and Family Therapists, "I don't know of any therapists who have gotten into trouble for claiming confidentiality under the good faith belief that it was their duty to do so. I do know of many therapists who have gotten into trouble who, in good faith, released information they believed they were authorized to release."[20]

4. *Always seek client waiver.* Get your client's written permission to release confidential communication in every case that you can, whether disclosure is permissive or mandatory.

a. *Mandatory disclosure.* Even in mandatory disclosure situations (e.g., child abuse reporting), it is best to review your duty with your client and seek a waiver even if you will report anyway. This allows you to explain the procedure to your client in the hope of maintaining his or her clinical trust. Such action reinforces your commitment to him or her as a client and reduces the chance that you will be sued. These cases also reinforce the value of explaining the limits of confidentiality at the outset of the counseling relationship.

b. *Permissive disclosure.* It is imperative that you gain your client's written release in all situations of permissive disclosure. While mandatory disclosure grants you immunity from liability, permissive disclosures do not. It is a good practice to talk with and get permission from your client as the first step in all requests for information. The apparently valid, even clinically supportable situations where a spouse, parent, or pastor seeks information for the good of the client can backfire if such information ends up in a divorce or a child custody or church discipline dispute.

c. *When pursuing public ministry.* Get your client's release when you use counseling examples at professional conferences, in writing and publication, in staff consultation and training, and in sermons. Increasingly, a popular tactic (one that we use in this book) is to develop a composite case that represents the problem but cannot be tied to any one person's identity. This is commendable and should be done to protect the identity of all congregants or clients in books, articles, presentations, and sermons. Unfortunately, this may not be sufficient to avoid suit by an aggrieved subject who identified with the case example. In all public ministry using case examples, even composite ones, it is best to seek written waiver. A composite case is less threatening because you do not use one person's life in all its detail, and a client may even support use of his or her case when presented for the purpose of helping others in the church.

5. *Always assert privilege to courts and lawyers.* In any case of subpoena, deposition, or lawyer request of information, it is recommended that the counselor assert privileged communication. Immediate compliance with a subpoena or other request may expose the counselor to subsequent liability for breach of privilege or confidentiality. This is because (1) the client or penitent wanted the privilege protected and did not waive it, or (2) the counselor divulged all communications, including information that was not necessary to resolve the particular court dispute. Subpoenas usually sweep too broadly in their demand for information, often without legal justification.

a. *Consult with your client and disclose only what is necessary.* Once confidentiality or privilege is asserted, it may then be waived in consultation with a client and his or her lawyer. In some cases it is resolved by judicial rule that addresses this question separately. Asserting confidentiality protects your client's privacy and the integrity of the counseling relationship. This also gives the counselor time, if you choose to do so separately, to consult with legal counsel and to disclose only that carefully circumscribed information necessary to resolve the dispute at hand.

Christian counselors must tend carefully to the boundary between protected communication and overdisclosure of information. It is easy and quite common to disclose too much confidential communication. Like subpoenas that sweep too broad in their demands for information, we increasingly see insurance companies demanding far more information (e.g., confidential session notes) than is necessary to pay a subscriber's claim. To protect against excessive disclosure in compliance with a subpoena or other request for information, it is always better that it come by specific direction from your client's lawyer or by court order.

6. *Contract for confidentiality in the gray zones.* Numerous clinical situations and therapeutic modes are gray zones without clear rules regarding confidentiality. Some common examples are counseling with a troubled adolescent with intrusive parents or family and group therapy. In these cases, we recommend having the participants negotiate, agree to, and sign a confidentiality contract (see appendix C). A contract gives the counselor opportunity to discuss the importance of confidentiality both clinically and legally and protects him or her in case breach does occur. Again, attorney Richard Leslie notes, with respect to group therapy agreements:

> By obtaining a group therapy confidentiality agreement, the therapist accomplishes several things. First, the therapist has informed each of the group therapy participants of the seriousness of the group therapy process and is actually facilitating the free flow of information. Secondly, the therapist is arguably creating a cause of action (breach of contract/breach of confidentiality) by getting the group participants to sign this agreement. It is reasonable to assume that a court would rule that such an agreement, because of the quid pro quo, the mutual promises constitute an enforceable contract. Lastly, but nevertheless important, the

therapist has protected himself/herself from allegations of negligence for failure to inform group members about confidentiality and for failure to protect group members from each other.[21]

Conclusion

Confidentiality—the protection of client communications to maintain their trust—is critical to successful counseling. As a legal and ethical principle, however, confidentiality is not absolute, and it is imperative that Christian counselors know the boundaries of its protection and how best to manage the risks of disclosure. Lawsuits and disciplinary actions regarding this principle are rising dramatically, many from sheer ignorance or a well-meaning but misplaced value attached to the fiction that confidentiality and privacy rights should be absolute.

Even among those who acknowledge its limitations and agree that exceptions to the general rule should exist, there is much concern that the exceptions are too many and too intrusive. Excessive power is being exercised by government, courts, and insurance companies, combined with information technologies that can access and distribute data with incredible speed and range. This makes essential the need for strong legal protection of the most intimate personal information disclosed in counseling and psychotherapy. While respecting the limits of confidentiality, Christian counselors must also be diligent and assertive in their protective defense, both in client relations and in legislative advocacy.

NOTES

1. "Whatever I see or hear in the life of men, which ought not to be spoken of abroad, I will not divulge, as reckoning that all such should be kept secret." Quoted, in part, from the Oath of Hippocrates, in R. Smith, *Privacy* (Garden City, N.Y.: Anchor Press, 1979).

2. See Ralph Slovenko, "Psychotherapist-Patient Testimonial Privilege: A Picture of Misguided Hope," *Catholic University Law Review* 23 (1974): 649–73.

3. Susan J. Wilson, "Confidentiality," in *Handbook of Clinical Social Work*, ed. A. Rosenblatt and D. Waldfogel (San Francisco: Jossey-Bass, 1983).

4. *Taylor v. United States,* 222 F.2d 398, at 401 (D.C. Cir. 1955).

5. Steve Levicoff erroneously asserts that "Confidentiality is traditional in nature and, while it enjoys historical protection, it has no legal protection." In *Christian Counseling and the Law* (Chicago: Moody, 1990), 73.

6. See D. J. Miller and M. H. Thelan, "Knowledge and Beliefs About Confidentiality in Psychotherapy," *Professional Psychology* 17 (1986): 12–19.

7. The argument for absolute confidentiality and privilege holds that conditional or limited confidence always blocks complete client disclosure and, therefore, inhibits the therapeutic process at a fundamental level. Countering this argument is recognition that client disclosure is blocked by many things, including unconscious defenses and resistance by the client directly and by the recognition of a fundamental societal interest and protective duty that, in the classic statement by the *Tarasoff* court, asserts that "the privilege ends where the public peril begins."

8. See, for example, *Cutter v. Brownbridge*, 228 Cal. Rptr. 545 (Cal. Ct. App. 1986).

9. See *California Business and Professions Code*, section 4983.

10. George Joslin, *The Minister's Law Handbook* (Manhasset, N.Y.: Channel Press, 1962), 116 (italics added).

11. For an excellent review of the history and modern status of privileged communication, see Jacob Yellin, "The History and Current Status of the Clergy-Penitent Privilege," *Santa Clara Law Review* 23 (1983): 95.

12. See C. Menendez, "Clergy Confidential," *Church and State* 39 (1986): 128.

13. Nearly one hundred years ago, the Iowa Supreme Court ruled against privilege where a criminal defendant who confided in a minister did not do so for the purpose of spiritual assistance; see *State v. Brown*, 95 Iowa 381, 384-85, 64 N.W. 277, 278 (1895).

14. See *California Evidence Code*, sect.1033 (West Supp. 1989); also in *Simrin v. Simrin*, 233 Cal.App.2d 90, 43 Cal.Rptr. 376 (1965), a California appellate court refused to protect the communications of a couple in marital counseling with their rabbi.

15. *Florida Statutes Annotated*, sect. 90.505(1),(2).

16. *Mississippi Code Annotated*, sect. 13-1-22(4).

17. *California Evidence Code*, sect. 1010.

18. *In re Daniel v. Daniel*, 269 Cal. App.3d. 624 (Cal. App. 6 Dist. 1990).

19. See Bruce Bongar, "Clinicians, Microcomputers, and Confidentiality," *Professional Psychology: Research and Practice* 19, no. 3 (1988): 286–89.

20. Richard Leslie, "Confidentiality," *The California Therapist* 1, no. 4 (1989): 35–42.

21. Ibid., 41.

Chapter 8

Child and Elder Abuse Reporting and Intervention

I tell you the truth, unless you change and become like little children, you will never enter the kingdom of heaven. Therefore, whoever humbles himself like this child is the greatest in the kingdom of heaven. And whoever welcomes a little child like this in my name welcomes me. But if anyone causes one of these little ones who believe in me to sin, it would be better for him to have a large millstone hung around his neck and to be drowned in the depths of the sea.

Matthew 18:3–6

CHILD ABUSE AND THE EXPLOITATION OF THE powerless and oppressed is as old as recorded history. Child sexual abuse along with homosexuality was commonly practiced in ancient Sodom (Gen. 19:5–8). Baal worship was common in ancient Palestine, including the fiery sacrifice of children to Molech. At times the Israelites became so depraved that they too worshipped Baal and sacrificed their children (2 Kings 17:16–17). Even Manasseh, King of Judah for fifty-five years, "sacrificed his own son in the fire, practiced sorcery and divination, and consulted mediums and spiritists . . ." (2 Kings 21:6).

God's laws, as revealed to Abraham's descendants, forbade exploitation of the weak, the powerless, and the oppressed (Exod. 22:21–27; Lev. 19:33–34; 25:35–36). Child sacrifice and sexual abuse through incestuous relations were strictly forbidden (Lev. 18:6–16; 20:1–5). In Leviticus 19:29, a father is instructed: "Do not degrade your daughter by making her a prostitute. . . ." Toward the elderly, God commands respect for one's mother and father, and instructs the people to "Rise in the presence of the aged, show respect for the elderly and revere your God. I am the Lord" (Lev. 19:32).

These rules and concerns are reflected by Jesus Christ in Matthew 18:1–6, quoted above. Jesus pictures a child as the model of a genuine Christian, the example of how we are to relate to God. He reveals the severe consequences that will fall upon those who violate the vulnerable members of his realm. Jesus was very clear—his followers are to adhere to radical standards of protection for the vulnerable, with severe consequences, both individually and as a culture, if we do not.

Contemporary rules. The modern law of abuse reporting and intervention has developed only over the last thirty years. Two studies conducted in the mid 1980's indicated that between 22 and 38 percent of adult Americans were abused as children.[1] The *Los Angeles Times* poll, conducted nationwide in 1985, revealed that 27 percent of the women and 16 percent of the men in America are sexual and/or physical abuse victims—a staggering 38 million people. This data indicated that abuse was prevalent through all levels of society—rich and poor, white and minority, educated and uneducated, and religious or nonreligious.

Since the late 1800s, child welfare advocates and social workers used moral persuasion and laws against animal cruelty to protect children. The political will to legally protect children from abuse was empowered by physicians who began to document and publicize abuse through the 1950s. The United States Children's Bureau proposed a model child abuse statute in 1963. Since that time all states have legislated child abuse protection laws under the legal doctrine of *parens patriae* or the state assuming parental power to protect the powerless and disabled.

Laws to protect elders and dependent adults from abuse are even more recent, having been legislated only over the past decade. America is getting older—the median age is steadily rising with baby boomers entering midlife and the number of people over age sixty-five increasing. Though living longer, the quality of life for many older people is declining. A growing number of elderly men and women are left to live their remaining years in settings where they are abused and neglected on a regular basis.

CHILD AND ELDER ABUSE REPORTING LAWS

Abuse reporting laws are intended to protect, preserve, punish, and prevent. The primary purpose of these laws is to protect victims

from further victimization. In addition, provision is made to preserve family units and move them toward restoration. The laws
intend that offenders are treated as criminals who should be punished for their crimes against persons. Finally, the laws intend
to prevent further abuse by providing treatment and by removing
the offender to an environment where he or she cannot abuse other
persons. Unlike the conflicts with confidentiality seen in suicide and
third-person protection law, there is a strong national consensus that
child abuse prevention far outweighs the cost of maintaining client
confidentiality.

ESSENTIAL ELEMENTS OF CHILD ABUSE REPORTING LAW

The statutes for child abuse law cover the following aspects: reportable conditions of abuse and neglect; who must report; reporter's
immunity; penalties for failure to report; and the abrogation or application of certain privileges. Unlike the law regarding suicide or
third-person protection, child abuse standards have developed with significant uniformity throughout the United States and Canada. It is vital
for pastors and Christian counselors to be familiar with the statutes of
their own state or province in order to know what to report and what
procedures to follow.

Reportable conditions for child abuse generally include physical
abuse, sexual abuse, physical neglect, and emotional maltreatment
of a minor seventeen years or younger. Each state has slightly different language to describe these categories and their specific
elements. The California Penal Code, which includes detailed definitions of each of the categories noted, defines child abuse as
". . . a physical injury which is inflicted by other than accidental
means on a child by another person . . . the sexual abuse of a
child . . . willful cruelty or unjustifiable punishment of a child
. . . unlawful corporal punishment or injury . . . neglect of a
child . . . abuse in out-of-home care. . . ."[2]

Every state has two classes of reporters, mandatory and permissive, with extensive listing of classes of mandatory reporters. These
lists are sweeping in their scope and usually include teachers and
school personnel, social workers and child welfare personnel, child
care providers, health and mental health practitioners, and, increasingly, commercial film processors (processing film that might
show child abuse). Only four states define clergy as mandatory
reporters by statute. In many states it is not clear whether or not
mandatory reporting is required of clergy.[3] The longstanding

precedent for clergy privilege in counseling and penitential communication is limited by these laws.

The legal power behind mandatory reporting is the liability that attaches for failure to report. The California statute is representative: "Any [mandatory reporter] who fails to report an instance of child abuse he or she knows to exist or reasonably should know to exist, is guilty of a misdemeanor and is punishable by confinement in the county jail for a term not to exceed six months or by a fine of not more than $1,000, or by both."[4] In order to protect the mandatory reporter, every state grants these reporters immunity from civil suit, and the courts have held that this immunity is absolute.[5] For permissive reporters, immunity is granted so long as the person does not make a report that "was false or was made with reckless disregard for the truth."[6]

ESSENTIAL ELEMENTS OF ELDER ABUSE REPORTING LAW

Legislatures have recognized that elderly and physically or mentally impaired adults are key at-risk populations. *Adult protective services* have been created to provide caretakers, social service providers, and law enforcement with guidelines to adult standards of care and procedures for reporting, protection, and prosecution when these standards are not met. Legally, an *elder* is anyone sixty-five years or older, and a *dependent adult* is anyone from age eighteen to sixty-four who has physical or mental limitations that restrict his or her ability to carry out normal activities or protect his or her rights. This includes any person from eighteen to sixty-four admitted as an inpatient to a twenty-four-hour health facility.

The list of elder abuse conditions is quite extensive. In California, for example, elder or dependent abuse means physical or sexual abuse, neglect, intimidation, cruel punishment, prolonged or unreasonable physical restraint, fiduciary abuse (improper use of money or property by a trustee), abandonment, or treatment with physical pain or mental suffering. Also forbidden is the deprivation by a care custodian of nutrition, medical and mental health care, and other goods or services that are necessary to maintain adequate health and function and avoid physical harm or mental suffering.

Elder abuse statutes also distinguish mandatory and permissive reporters and, similar to child abuse report procedures, define the manner, time, and other details that guide a reporter to action.

Four vocational groups (with nearly fifty distinct categories and titles among these groups) are defined as mandatory reporters. These include adult care custodians, health (including mental health) practitioners, adult protective service agencies, and law enforcement personnel.

LEGAL AND ETHICAL ISSUES AND DILEMMAS

There are many dilemmas facing the Christian counselor who becomes aware of abuse. It behooves all Christian counselors to learn the law and expect that legal consequences will only increase in civil and criminal penalties. One author has noted that " . . . there is every indication that society shall react to abuse statistics with more extensive reporting requirements, more severe criminal penalties, higher civil awards for negligent or intentional torts associated with abuse, and great laxity in the rules of evidence associated with privilege or children."[7]

CHILD ABUSE AND THE CHRISTIAN COUNSELING PROFESSIONAL

While abuse reporting statutes are clear for counseling professionals, there are numerous ethical judgments and moral dilemmas that are not easily resolved for the Christian counselor. What is the difference between legitimate corporal punishment and child abuse? How do we reconcile the biblical support for corporal punishment with the opposition of many Child Protective Service (CPS) workers to any form of spanking? How easily do we report a Christian for child abuse investigation by the secular state? Many Christian professionals working with CPS units know of the unequal treatment of people, often promoting values that are at odds with Christian values. These cases make it difficult to trust the state to treat victims and their families well.

The professional who does not report will be penalized, however, especially if the abuse gets worse while the family is under the care of the treating professional. Clinical trust and client gain may suffer some loss by breaking confidence and reporting child abuse. Such loss, however, is not inevitable—a recent study on the impact of mandated reporting on therapeutic trust showed that, contrary to negative expectations, over three-fourths of sixty-five reporting cases in a child guidance clinic either did not change or therapy actually improved.[8] It takes a skilled and dedicated professional to support and adhere to the law while retaining the client and going forward in counseling or therapy. Even if clients are lost due to mandatory reporting, we encourage Christian counselors to advocate their best interests to the state, demanding that state personnel respect their beliefs and values.

Many Christian professionals also get caught between the law and the church. More than a few churches presume that the state is evil and corrupt and, therefore, should not be engaged in any church problem. Child abuse, then, becomes viewed as a family matter to be addressed entirely within the confines of the church. We have noted the trouble, both biblically and legally, with this hyperseparatist view (see chapter 3). The Christian counselor who must report abuse and work with the state may be perceived by such churches as untrustworthy for colluding with the enemy.

This is a significant dilemma for the church at this time. Not only does this attitude make it extremely difficult for Christian professionals to serve these separatist congregations, but much litigation against the church is arising out of these insular communities. Christian counseling professionals cannot rightly hold to the false dichotomy that rigidly separates church and state. Though difficult, we believe that it is possible to serve Christ and his ideals while also adhering to the rules and reason of the state in its policy against child abuse. We do confess, however, that we are frustrated by the lack of response by some churches to this possibility.

CLERGY LIABILITY FOR FAILURE TO REPORT

A related and thorny moral and legal issue is the pastor who chooses not to report a known abuse situation, and further abuse takes place causing physical and emotional harm.[9] Because of *Smith* (see chapter 4), which potentially weakens the clergy privilege, clergy are far more at risk legally when they know of abuse but choose not to report. This action may result in liability for civil damages, though many questions regarding liability remain unanswered. Does the liability attach if the cleric learned of the abuse while in the confessional or in counseling? Does liability still exist if the cleric learned of the abuse indirectly or outside the clergy role?

Clergy will increasingly be held liable for not exercising due care and failing to report reasonably suspicious abusive behavior. However, since most clergy are not mandatory reporters, the lack of immunity from suit provides good reason for them to avoid reporting abuse. This dilemma must be resolved or the clergy will be the victims of ever more lawsuits. The law here is asserting a clear message to clergy: have and enforce clear church policies for child abuse reporting that follow the lead of your state statutes.

Child abuse vs. clergy privilege. The current shift in public policy favoring child protection makes it unclear in many states what is more important—the confidential privilege or the duty to report abuse. Also, many pastors do not know if they would be immune if a report were made. One author noted, "Only a few states have *expressly* retained the privilege: Kentucky, Oregon and South Carolina; a few more are silent as to the priest-penitent privilege, thus implying that it is still in effect. But silence still connotes potential conflict and presents a significant predicament for the cleric, caught among the criminal offense, the responsibility to his or her religious duties, the personal abhorrence of child abuse and consideration of the medical needs of the penitent."[10]

The dilemma here is a values-based conflict between the privacy of the privilege and the need to identify child abusers. American law has historically sided with the clergy privilege under free exercise of religion, but current social policy favoring child protection indicates increased pressure to harness the clergy to the same laws as the professional therapists. Although clergy privilege statutes will remain in force, it is reasonable to expect that the courts will narrow the scope of the privilege—especially in the context of child abuse.[11]

The legal question is whether the state, in the face of the clergy-penitent privilege, has created a reporting exception that limits the privilege in cases of abuse. Recent court opinions indicate that clergy who find out about child abuse outside the confessional role will be required to report the abuse and would lack defense for not reporting. In a recent California case, the court upheld liability against a church and two pastors who failed to report a young girl who told them that her stepfather, who had been involved in the church's lay ministry, was abusing her sexually. The court held for liability because the girl was a Christian school student under the church's ministry, and the pastors, as school administrators, came under reporting rules. The court also held that privilege did not apply, because the abuse was reported by the victim and came to light in a nonconfessional role.[12]

CLERGY WHO ABUSE CHILDREN

A tragic concern of the modern church is the pastor who abuses children. It is a grievous commentary on our culture that so many

Christian ministers are falling to sexual sin, including the crime of pedophilia and child sexual abuse. Clergy who abuse children are not only liable for criminal consequences, they also are vulnerable to civil litigation by victims for the serious emotional distress caused by these offenses. Considering the destructive costs to victim, to family, to the church, and to the name of Christ, it is little wonder that Jesus revealed that it would be better to hang a millstone around one's neck and be drowned than to be the perpetrator of such destruction.

Expect an explosion of litigation. Child sexual abuse by clergy is per se violative of the clergy's fiduciary responsiblity to a child and his or her family. Under tort law, the abused person is likely to recover damages, especially in cases where the violator has a history of misconduct and the denomination knew it, by proving that:

(1) The abuser either intended to cause emotional distress or knew or should have known that the abuse would result in serious emotional distress to the child (this element is currently becoming a given presumption in child sexual abuse cases).

(2) The abuser's conduct was extreme and outrageous, going beyond all possible bounds of decency, and it can be considered as utterly intolerable in a civilized community.

(3) The abuser's actions were the legal cause of the person's psychic and emotional injury.

(4) The mental anguish suffered by the person is serious and of a nature that no reasonable person could be expected to endure.[13]

Every faith and denomination is bedeviled by this tragedy; it is vital for church leadership to realize that they are not immune from suit. The Catholic church, especially, is facing an avalanche of litigation around this behavior that will constrain its ministry well into the twenty-first century. For them and their Protestant brethren, gaining control of the pedophilic priest and pastor is a critical moral and legal issue. It is distressing to us how many churches are so defensive and secretive on this issue; this can only serve the enemies of Christ. Many clergy, through the actions of their superiors, have been protected from punishment or treatment for their abusive behavior or transferred to new assignments where, tragically, they abuse again. This has compounded the betrayal and anguish suffered by victims and their families and has resulted in harsh legal response. We would rather see leaders across all denominations convene a national Christian conference that addresses and forms clear policy to control the sexual abuse epidemic in the church in all its forms.

THE DILEMMA OF SEXUAL DEVIANCE

Another facet of this dilemma concerns individuals who confess pedophilic (a desire for sexual relations with children) or other sexually deviant behavior to a minister. What are we to do with those who chronically engage in pedophilic behavior and seek pastoral help to deal with the problem? If mandatory reporting is required, might we not miss out on an opportunity for spiritual healing and behavior change? In reality, how many pedophiles are transformed because of imprisonment or counseling through the mandatory of-fenders programs? The data reveals that few of these programs are successful and that pedophilic relapse rates are quite high.[14]

If the state requires pastors to report, this will hinder some who recognize their need to change from voluntarily seeking help. The intent of these laws, including their immunity clauses, is to foster reporting so that the crime of child abuse will abate. Logically, it follows that making clergy mandatory reporters and granting them immunity from suit will also serve the purpose of slowing down abuse. In reality, it could increase abuse by stopping offenders from disclosing to clergy whom they know must report to the state. The healing of offenders is minimal because they maintain tremen-dous denial and resist the treatment process. They rarely change because they do not want to change and are often angry about be-ing branded as criminals and forced into coercive treatment.

Of course, child abuse is criminal behavior and should be de-fined as such. The issue here is not whether to redefine the crime as less offensive, but rather whether punishment or rehabilitation is the best societal response to the criminal. Research and clinical evidence demonstrate that those who voluntarily seek help, rec-ognizing their need and wanting to change, are the ones with the greatest potential for transformation. If we require clergy to re-port, we may be defeating the opportunity to help heal a person who might not otherwise seek transformation through spiritual means.

Law and the nature of human change. Fundamental to this struggle between church and state are the differences about human change and transformation. The predominant theory in the secular arena, for example, is that gender-identity or sexual orientation change is not possible. The homosexual, it is asserted, is at root a biological or identity dynamic that is not changeable. Similarly, secular theory offers little or no hope for root transformation in those who are pedophiles.

Christian counselors, while respecting the tremendous difficulties of this change, need to advocate and demonstrate that, in Christ, real change is possible for homosexuals and pedophiles.[15] At the same time, we must not let the truth of Christ's power to transform the pedophile cloud the fact that few are actually transformed. While advocating for Christ-centered rehabilitation, the church must also act and support all means, including sure imprisonment, to protect the children of our society from the abuse of the pedophile.

In the conflict between client confidentiality and reporting child abuse, we believe it is better for churches and counselors to err on the side of child protection. There are too many tragic stories of known but unreported abuse in the church. Under cover of right confessions and apparent commitment to counseling help, the abuse has gone on secretly and destructively. Pedophiles are notorious con artists, and they continue to deceive even the wisest professionals. Pastors are not trained to deal with all the behavior and roots of pedophilia, and the cost of continued child abuse when it can be stopped is far too high—neither church nor society can tolerate its continuation.

ELDER ABUSE AND THE CHURCH

The church is actively involved in ministry and service provision to the elderly. A great deal of the housing and care facilities used by the elderly in America are built and sponsored by the Christian church. Pastors, administrators, and direct care providers within these facilities are increasingly being included as mandatory reporters in elder abuse laws. As in child abuse reporting, numerous dilemmas exist between compelled reporting and doing good ministry on behalf of the elderly and their families.

Elder abuse statutes tend to be more complex than child abuse laws; there are many more and subtle ways in which an elderly person may suffer abuse. A big challenge is learning both the variety and severity of abuses that the law requires to be reported. Elder and dependent adult abuse laws include, by comparison with the policies of most care institutions, a much broader scope of behavior within their definition of abuse. Reeducation and renewal of commitment to the protection of the elderly are essential tasks for Christian care providers.

It is not unusual for an elderly person being abused to suffer in silence, passively acquiescing to the abuse because he or she fears losing the care, attention, or help that the abuser may also provide. Hence, a minister required to report may face a terrible dilemma. The abused person, when confronted with disclosure of their abuse, may choose to allow the abuse to continue in order to avoid the loss of the caregiver, who is often an adult child or other close relative.

The law resolves this dilemma by making reporting mandatory among adult care personnel and granting them immunity from liability in their reporting. This is as it should be to achieve the societal aim of stopping this abuse. The law, however, does not deal with the emotional and relational loss that can follow the report and prosecution of a caregiver. It is a disturbing paradox to assist an older person who, though no longer abused, sinks into hopeless depression, listlessness, and illness because the bond with his or her abusive caregiver is broken and may never be restored.

POLICY AND PRACTICE RECOMMENDATIONS

1. *Establish policies favoring child and elder protection.* Churches and Christian agencies should develop clear policies in favor of the protection of children and the elderly from abuse. The key to these policies is specific criteria under which abusive behavior will be reported. Even if not a mandatory reporter, churches need policy guidelines about their discretionary right to report abuse.

   The church must be informed about child and elder abuse reporting laws to protect against the risks involved in our current litigious society. In a civil suit, the church's defense will be greatly enhanced by clear, written policies and procedures that show an intent to protect children and all vulnerable citizens, even while maintaining the confidence and privacy of ministry.

2. *Commit to child and elder abuse education.* Christian professionals should educate those in the church with reporting requirements, whether by statute or church policy. These professionals can also help define workable policies about the nature, definitions, and symptoms of abuse as well as the procedures for reporting and protection of an abused person.

a. *Maintain ongoing education and supervision.* Proper training of staff and their subsequent supervision is essential (see chapter 19). The church is held liable for the conduct of those who perform services on their behalf, including volunteers and independent contractors. The accountability of supervision and training not only satisfies the law but more importantly helps to prevent trouble by enhancing early detection of abuse problems. This also helps to control the quality of the ministry provided by nonlicensed, nonordained counselors. Such action will reduce the risk of suit and help to establish a good defense in the event of a suit.

3. *Establish clear reporting procedures.* Clergy must have clear procedures in place describing reportable abuse and when and how to respond to abuse situations. These should include:

a. *Establish guidelines to reportable conditions.* State reporting statutes should be distributed to all clergy and those employed by the church in key childcare and elder ministry roles. Boundaries for discretionary reporting should be clear and should be outlined in view of state statutes. Clear lines of communication must be established that direct lay ministers and caregivers to report suspected abuse to pastors and supervisors.

b. *Distinguish pastoral counseling from confession.* Clear guidelines are essential for reporting abuse discovered in pastoral counseling versus the confessional arena. Not all counseling is protected under clergy-penitent privilege, exposing the minister to greater liability in the face of abusive situations. Also, knowing that the confessional privilege does not fully protect, clarify the situations that would ethically and morally compel disclosure of abuse. The one who hears confessions should be prepared to help the penitent find resources for dealing with his or her sinful behavior without turning the confessional into a counseling session.

c. *Provide guidelines for volunteers and support staff.* Define how church and agency support staff and volunteers are to deal with abuse situations. Sunday school teachers and visitation helpers who see the elderly in their homes, for example, need direction on how to address the evidence of and the reporting of suspicious behavior to a pastor.

4. *Maintain compassion and commitment to abusers.* Provide for the fair and prompt treatment of the alleged abuser pending the

determination of the complaint. Removal of the person from all child or elder care ministry is imperative until resolution of the matter. Even so, it is also crucial to maintain contact and ministerial support for the person and his or her family during this difficult time. Discerning truth from error and quashing gossip and rumor is difficult but extremely important for the sake of the integrity of the entire church.

5. *Know how to intervene on behalf of abuser and abused.* Clergy and professional clinicians should have policies that outline an intervention strategy in response to abusive situations. A two-track policy that directs both short-term crisis action and longer-term help is needed. Churches should have referral resources of Christian professionals who can help a family defuse abusive stressors and address and change the roots of abusive behavior. Referral to emergency shelter care may be necessary to avoid immediate threats of violence.

   Pastors can be key players, in collaboration with the courts, counseling professionals, and social service providers, in service provision to abused families. They often assume liason, mediating, and coordinating roles between the family and service providers as well as between the abuser and the abused. The demands of an abuse crisis can easily overwhelm a pastor's time and resources, and, therefore, we encourage pastors and churches to form ad hoc service committees, pulling key family, friends, and lay ministers together following an abuse incident. These ministry groups should be able to commit to serving the family needs for a time-limited period during and following an abuse crisis.

6. *Maintain strict staff accountability.* Clergy and denominations must apply strict accountability in the arena of sexual behavior and *not assume* that clergy and Christian workers are always faithful to their vows or without problems in the call to maintain sexual purity.

   a. *Identify, offer help, and heal or remove abusers from ministry.* The prevention of pedophilic and abusive behavior in clergy and Christian workers must begin by identification of those with sexual control problems, especially among those preparing for ministry. Intensive treatment and reorientation should be offered those who abuse or reveal the risk, with the church taking the lead and showing the world that offender rehabilitation is possible in Christ.

When necessary to protect parishioners, offending clergy must be removed from all ministry and helping endeavors until transformation and restoration to ministry can be successfully achieved. If full restoration is unattainable, such ministers should be barred from ministry and a national network developed to communicate such action to the church universal. Such persons should be helped in retraining and securing new kinds of work. The church should spare no cost in the development of such a program. Compared to the stain on Christ's name, the effects on victims, and the money otherwise paid in damages following lawsuit, any price is a pittance.

b. *Know your staff and protect your people.* Be strict in the hiring of employees, especially those who work with children and elders. Thorough background checks, including inquiries beyond the references given you by a prospective employee, and periodic review and evaluation on these issues is a must in this day and age. Talk to children and parents, letting them know you favor abuse protection and want to know of suspicious behavior. Offer instruction to families on what to look for, and be sensitive about communications with children on these issues.

7. *Contract with abuse response staff.* Many child abuse and elder/dependent abuse statutes require that an agency that employs mandatory reporters must have them sign a specific agreement that they are familiar with the reporting requirements and will comply. We encourage all agencies and churches to do this as a method of compliance with abuse response policy and as a protection in defense of your ministry in case of suit.

Developing, writing down, and revising abuse response policies among key staff is essential both for proper and helpful response and for legal protection. Having key church or agency staff sign statements of their knowledge and participation in abuse response procedures will carry significant weight in court. It also communicates to service providers that you are well prepared to assist in the effort to protect the abused, rehabilitate the abuser, and reconcile the family.

CONCLUSION

Child and elder abuse laws are essential in a society that inflicts so much violence on its vulnerable citizens. Mandatory reporting of abuse is beneficial to victims, has saved many lives, and has protected thousands of children, especially, from lifelong traumatic harm. However, for clergy and all Christian counselors there are dilemmas with many of these laws that do not yield simple solutions. We have identified some of the main issues and offered suggestions as to how one can act in the face of these demands and dilemmas as a Christian counselor.

Child and elder abuse are serious social, family, and ministerial problems. Society does have a legitimate interest in these problems beyond the sphere of the church, and the church must find ways to work in conjunction with the many systems that intervene in these affairs. A hyperseparatist mentality will only block constructive work and frustrate both service providers and the church. Churches who are willing to serve collaboratively will best help their families caught in this tragedy and will communicate the best witness for Christ. God controls the whole of his creation, and he will use all resources to protect the weak and oppressed— even those resources of the state that do not honor his name.

NOTES

1. Diana Russell, "The Incidence and Prevalence of Intrafamilial and Extrafamilial Sexual Abuse of Female Children," *International Journal of Child Abuse and Neglect* 7 (1983): 133–39; see the nationwide poll data on child sexual abuse conducted by and summarized in the *Los Angeles Times,* 25 and 26 August 1985.

2. *California Penal Code,* section 11165.6.

3. Raymond C. O'Brien, "Pedophilia: The Legal Predicament of Clergy," *Journal of Contemporary Health Law and Policy* 4 (1988): 91–154.

4. *California Penal Code,* section 11172(e).

5. *Krikorian v. Barry,* 196 Cal. App. 3d, 1211 (Cal. App. 2 Dist. 1987).

6. *California Penal Code,* section 11172(a).

7. O'Brien, "Pedophilia," 94.

8. Holly Watson and Murray Levine, "Psychotherapy and Mandated Reporting of Child Abuse," *American Journal of Orthopsychiatry* 59, no. 2 (1989): 246–56.

9. A somewhat related problem occurs when the client is no longer a child and the clergy has reasonable suspicion to believe that other minor children are at risk. The pastor probably should report in order to protect any child still at risk from this perpetrator.

10. O'Brien, "Pedophilia," 135 (italics in original).

11. Mary Mitchell, "Must Clergy Tell? Child Abuse Reporting Requirements Versus the Clergy Privilege and Free Exercise of Religion," *Minnesota Law Review* 71 (1986): 723.

12. *People v. Hodges,* case no. 614153 (Cal. Superior Crt., 1989).

13. O'Brien, "Pedophilia," 140.

14. Ibid.

15. See Judith A. Reisman et al., *Kinsey, Sex and Fraud: The Indoctrination of a People* (Lafayette, La.: Lochinvar-Huntington House, 1990); where they challenge the Kinsey Institute research, which asserts a supposed 10 percent of the total United States population with homosexual orientation. Also consider the successes of such ex-gay ministries as Desert Stream, Leanne Payne, and Exodus International.

Chapter 9

The Duty and Practice of Suicide Intervention

As pastor and mother, I have witnessed the tragic death of my youngest son by suicide. . . . Eighteen, a freshman in college, [Andrew] was home for the weekend when he died of a self-inflicted wound to his head. . . . It happened about 3 a.m. . . . Sleeping in our bedroom, buffered from the sound, . . . we slept through the shot which would forever change our lives.

It was our Sunday off. We had planned a leisurely breakfast, worship with Andrew, brunch at a restaurant. . . . Those well-made plans suddenly turned into chaos, finding his room empty, lights and TV on, and his note by the phone . . . his words grabbed us with panic. We rushed to the basement. . . .

Herb was first to the landing. As if he had been grabbed, he stopped short, gasping, "Oh, my God!" White as a sheet, he held me back, saying, "Don't look." All I saw was Andrew's legs. Favorite old khaki pants and black high top canvas shoes.

There are no words to describe the fright of finding him. Or the stumbling up the stairs. Or the frenzy to make those first calls for help. Or what followed. Police. Coroner. Sisters and friends coming on the run. Getting our children home. Crying with his friends. Choosing a casket. Facing the fact of family suicide. Missing him. Wanting him. Becoming suicide survivors.[1]

Corrine Chilstrom

THE GRIPPING STORY OF HER SON'S SUICIDE by Corrine Chilstrom, a pastoral consultant in the Evangelical Lutheran Church of America, reveals the unique tragedy of suicide. A client or parishioner who kills himself or herself also tragically impacts the counselor long after the event.[2] We explore this tragedy and the legal, moral, pastoral, and clinical aspects of suicide in this chapter.

THE DATA AND DYNAMICS OF SUICIDE

Friedrich Nietzsche, the famous nineteenth-century German philosopher, held that "the thought of suicide is a great consolation: by means of it one gets successfully through many a bad night."[3] This statement reveals a number of reasons why suicide has a complex and controversial history in America and Western culture. Suicidal thinking in time of crisis is fairly common, yet there exists great fear and a seeming cultural taboo that bars open acknowledgement of its attraction and familiarity.

This attraction, the tragic choice of death over life, is what so greatly confounds us and strikes us with fear. It makes no sense to the healthy-minded how suicide could be such great consolation. To the person who has lost all hope of relieving intense and unending pain, whether physical or psychological, suicide can easily become an obsessive consolation, a final solution when nothing else beckons. In the distorted and pain-dominated judgment of the sufferer, suicide can become the most logical and effective choice to resolve an impossible problem.

We must pull back, however, and not let our empathy that helps understand the suicidal mind push us to accept suicide as a right to be exercised by all those wishing it. The euthanasia movement that asserts a right to die and to assist those wanting to die is a growing and powerful assault against our moral and legal prohibition that forbids suicide assistance. In our current culture of moral relativism, legally allowing assisted suicide may be a slippery slope by which we lose the ability to define any boundaries that protect life.

Approximately 200,000 suicide attempts take place in America every year; nearly 30,000 of those succeed.[4] Roughly 40 percent of these deaths are by persons over sixty-five years of age, most suffering in pain from terminal and/or debilitating diseases. A quarter of these suicides are by young people between the ages of fifteen and twenty-four, a threefold increase in the rate of suicide within this age group in a quarter-century. "Even more alarming is the number of children younger than fifteen who kill themselves. In 1950, forty committed suicide; in 1985, three hundred did."[5]

The dynamics of suicide are highly complex; simplistic reasons and easy solutions are nonexistent. It is not just a matter of acute and severe depression, although the National Institute of Mental Health considers depression the leading cause. Suicide prevention requires more than restraining or avoiding lethal behavior, although individuals must act aggressively to succeed in killing themselves. Finally, it is not just a problem of meaningless and existential despair, although a pastor and Christian psychologist cogently argue that "suicide is primarily, although not entirely, a spiritual problem. Persons who are suicidal are asking, either explicitly or implicitly, such critical existential questions as: Does my life have meaning or purpose? Do I have any worth? Is forgiveness possible? Is there any hope for a new life beyond this current mess?"[6]

LEGAL DUTIES IN SUIDICE INTERVENTION

The Christian counselor has a general duty to intervene in the life of the suicidal person to give that person a fair chance to live. This statement of duty is a synthesis of biblical morality, current law, and counseling ethics from the various counseling professions.

Professional clinicians are increasingly at legal risk for the suicide of their clients and patients. Indeed, the clinician working in an inpatient or restrictive treatment setting has a strong duty to intervene in the life of someone judged to be a substantial risk for suicide. In contrast, a pastor in a church setting may be ethically and morally but not legally bound to a duty of suicide intervention.

There is no pure legal duty to *prevent* suicide—the duty is to *intervene appropriately.* The law recognizes limits in the ability to stop a determined person from killing himself or herself. The duty to intervene is determined by the degree of suicidal risk exhibited by a client and the counselor's ability to accurately assess and control that risk. The counselor's liability increases as the risk of suicide increases and the counselor is able to foresee and control the client's actions. Since the clinician in an inpatient facility can control the patient's behavior far more than in an outpatient setting, liability is greater when suicide occurs in that setting.

Lawsuits following suicide have risen dramatically over the past decade. Messinger and Taub noted suicide risk at the top of their list of litigation fears of psychiatrists.[7] In the APA Insurance Trust study (chapter 2), client death, predominantly from suicide, made up 10 percent of the cases against psychologists. Of the thirty-eight cases of suicide in Hogan's study (also in chapter 2), twenty cases were resolved in favor of plaintiffs and eighteen in favor of defendant-clinicians.

Lawsuits in this field are rising not because the law itself is changing—apart from clinicians working in inpatient facilities there is no substantial legal duty to prevent suicide. Instead it is the seriousness of the harm—the unexpected death of a client that shocks the family—that is driving suit in this field. One commentator revealed this connection between emotions and lawsuit very well:

> Wrongful death (to compensate survivors for monetary loss) and malpractice suits for the suicide of a patient are more frequent than other causes of death for two reasons that are peculiar to suicide. Unlike other types of serious illness, there is usually no expectation that mental illness will be terminal. It is assumed that given proper medical care the patient will survive. Premature death, the likely outcome of some maladies, is felt to be preventable for the depressed patient. Hence, the outcome of suicide is per se unreasonable, bizarre, unexpected, and often irrational.
>
> Prior to the suicide, the relationships between the deceased and close family members are bound to be emotionally charged and at the same time ambivalent. Typically, relatives who love him and have his best interests at heart become angered and frustrated by his helpless and despondent behavior. His suicide may be perceived as a personal attack, for it "represents the ultimate in undiluted hostility." Family members are plunged into a morass of contradictory feelings: sadness, shame, guilt, shock, bewilderment, and hostility toward the deceased. They alternately blame themselves and the deceased. To resolve this apparent contradiction, the bereaved may displace their hostility on to the treating psychiatrist or psychologist. The resulting malpractice suit absolves the family of both guilt and helplessness and gives them a reasonable outlet for their anger by blaming the psychotherapist for the suicide.[8]

THE LEGAL DILEMMA FOR THE CHURCH

There is no legal duty for pastors, churches, or counselors working under church supervision to assess and intervene effectively to prevent suicide. But in practice, churches should disregard this apparent protection and act as if liability does exist, because they are likely to be sued anyway. Following *Smith*, lawyers will continue to seek a judicial forum that will accept a cause of action against the church for suicide. The church, then, must intervene effectively with the suicidal person, not so much because of legal duty, but rather to fulfill the call of love and to avoid suit and the massive costs of legal defense.

Should clergy counsel the suicidal? Following *Nally*, there has been increasing debate as to whether clergy should even counsel suicidal persons.[9] The arguments against such clergy counseling assert growing legal liability, the lack of effective training, the demands of a suicidal crisis, the lack of time and energy to address it, and the failure of many pastoral counselors to recognize and respect these limitations. Those making these arguments assert that clergy not engage in this counseling, but instead refer the suicidal person on to psychiatrists or other professional helpers.

On the other side of this argument is the thoughtful analysis of Sullender and Malony, who support the role of the clergy counselor in work with suicidal persons.

> To treat suicide or suicidal depression as just a psychiatric problem—a problem to be treated primarily through medication or hospitalization—is to miss the complexity of the dynamics and do sufferers a disservice. And to argue from the false premise that pastors should never work with suicidal persons and always refer them elsewhere for "real" professional help is to belittle the expertise of clergy and the contribution that the religious community can make to the healing of persons. There are clear religious and spiritual dimensions to most, if not all, suicidal dynamics, and therefore religious professionals have a definite and significant contribution to make in the overall treatment of depressed and suicidal persons.[10]

These writers, while cautioning against attempts to evangelize everyone who comes in crisis, assert that "suicidal persons really need to hear and experience anew . . . the 'good news' of God's forgiveness and new life."[11] To experience this life afresh many times requires pastoral intervention. "Often, the average parishioner perceives a pastor to be more available and more trustworthy than most mental health professionals. Furthermore, many people see their problems primarily as spiritual and moral in nature and specifically want the counsel of their pastor regarding their troubling situation."[12] The question, then, needs to be reframed—not *should* clergy counsel the suicidal, but how best to do it. At the end of this chapter we outline practice recommendations for clergy and clinicians.

SUICIDE LIABILITY AND THE COUNSELING PROFESSIONAL

Professional liability for suicide cuts across two issues—the setting in which the crisis arises and the nature of the alleged harm, whether it involved failure to take preventive action to avoid suicide or whether the clinical behavior caused the suicide.

Liability for suicide in an inpatient setting. The clinical professional who works in a hospital or other restrictive treatment setting has a duty to *take reasonable precautions* to prevent suicidal persons from killing themselves.[13] If proper precautions are taken, the inpatient therapist will not be held liable even if a patient succeeds in killing himself or herself. The law recognizes that some are determined to die and will not hold another responsible for that death in every circumstance. In *Baker v. United States,* a federal court in Iowa held that a Veterans Administration psychiatrist was not liable following the suicidal death of a patient because both the doctor and the hospital had taken good precautions.

> It is particularly recognized in the treatment of mental patients that diagnosis is not an exact science. Diagnosis with absolute precision and certainty is impossible. Further the objective is treatment, not merely incarceration. . . . [T]he court finds that Dr. Kennedy exercised the proper standard of care under the circumstances. Calculated risks of necessity must be taken if the modern and enlightened treatment of the mentally ill is to be pursued intelligently and rationally. Neither the hospital nor the doctors are the insurers of the patient's health and safety. They can only be required to use that degree of knowledge, skill, care, and attention exercised by others in like circumstances.[14]

Of course, there is much litigation concerning the question of proper precautions. Treatment plans must reflect individualized care that respects the degree of risk shown by different patients. General suicide precautions will not be adequate for someone hospitalized following a serious suicide attempt and still showing acute risk. The hospital practitioner also has a duty to exhibit skill in suicidal diagnosis. *Meier v. Ross General Hospital* held staff and hospital liable where clinical evidence was missed due to poor assessment that resulted in inadequate suicide precaution.[15]

Liability for failing to prevent suicide in an outpatient setting. For the outpatient counselor, the historic right to intervene to prevent suicide is currently being transformed to a limited duty to take preventive action. When suicide becomes foreseeable, the counselor has a duty to take preventive action on behalf of the person at risk. This usually involves increasing clinical intervention, consulting with and referring to other professionals, or hospitalizing the suicidal person. Even if suicide is accomplished, *you will not be found liable if you behaved appropriately*, within the clinical guidelines that would define a reasonable standard of care.[16]

In *Bellah v. Greenson*,[17] a California appellate court affirmed that therapists can be held liable for outpatient suicide if it could be reasonably foreseen and preventive measures were not taken. No court in America has yet enunciated what these measures are, but current standards in the clinical literature would be used to establish a standard of care. A critical concern is the level of training and experience of the counselor to foresee suicide. An experienced clinician with training in suicide assessment and intervention would obviously be held to a much higher standard of care than the new clinician still working under supervision.

Liability for causing suicide in an outpatient setting. Allegations of therapist causation of suicide are numerous, though rarely proven in court. The cases across the country reveal four patterns of alleged causation:

- Intentional, harmful breach of the therapeutic boundary that results in suicide. This is especially the case in sexual misconduct and willful and defamatory breaches of confidentiality.
- Therapeutic directives that backfire. The directive therapies and techniques (e.g., rational-emotive therapy, behavior therapy, paradoxical instruction and symptom prescription, and nouthetic counseling) are all modes of higher risk for suicide-causing assertions.
- Abandonment or abrupt termination of a codependent, symbiotic therapeutic relationship. The rejection experienced by an extremely dependent client, especially if the termination followed harmful therapy (e.g., sexual relations), can easily promote a suicidal crisis for the victim.
- Physicians who prescribe lethal quantities of medicine to a person at risk for suicide.

Suicide following sexual relations between client and therapist, including the suicide of the client's spouse who finds out about the infidelity, are the most successful wrongful death actions.[18] Cases on other grounds, even against physicians prescribing lethal quantities of medicine,[19] are very difficult to prove under malpractice law. The plaintiff must show an unbroken chain of events tied to gross therapeutic negligence that inevitably pushed the victim to deadly action.

> To be liable, the therapist's negligent act must bring about insanity in the patient which prevents him from realizing the nature and risk of the act, or which creates an irresistible impulse, thus rendering the patient irresponsible. Implicit here is the notion that the suicide must be irrational or involuntary, for there cannot be negligent liability for voluntary suicide. The difficulty with causation is obvious when one considers that a patient under psychiatric care is likely to be seriously disturbed to begin with, and it must be shown that the therapy itself is what tips the balance completely out of control. Clearly only the most blatant and shocking examples of therapeutic negligence or recklessness will be held to show this subtle change in causation.[20]

PREVENTIVE HOSPITALIZATION AND THE LAW

Most civil commitment statutes give therapists a *right* to initiate hospitalization proceedings when clients with mental disturbances become a serious danger to others *or to themselves*. Section 1024 of the California Evidence Code, however, states that no privilege exists when a suicidal threat confronts a therapist and "disclosure of the [confidential] communication *is necessary to prevent the threatened danger*." Commentary by the state Law Revision Commission, indicating how the right to intervention is becoming a limited duty, held that "it is essential that appropriate action be taken if . . . the patient is a menace to himself or others and . . . refuses to permit the psychotherapist to make the disclosure necessary to prevent the threatened danger."[21]

In the case of the suicidal client who resists voluntary admission, however, most states' involuntary commitment procedures are so strict and onerous that some persons at risk will not be hospitalized. As the duty to intervene with suicidal persons gains strength, this barrier will become more and more problematic for the counseling professional. Two law reform remedies could be pursued here. One is to grant therapists immunity from liability for good-faith initiation of hospitalization, whether or not the act succeeds in hospitalizing the client. Second, the law could presume the suicidal person to be seriously mentally ill for purposes of statutory commitment.

POLICY AND PRACTICE RECOMMENDATIONS

Guidelines for assessment and intervention with the suicidal person are made with both the counseling professional and pastor in mind. It is assumed that pastors and churches will adapt policies from these recommendations that incorporate some, if not all, of the suggestions offered.

GENERAL GUIDELINES

1. *Work from a written policy.* Develop and follow clear step-by-step procedures for yourself and your staff that will guide decision-making throughout a suicidal crisis. Clearly written policies help guide you through moral and ethical dilemmas and provide a reference or common language for consultation and referral. A well-written policy also communicates favorably to courts and lawyers that you are a thoughtful and serious professional, not one prone to negligence, foolishness, or exaggeration in your decision-making about people in your care. This evidence will carry great weight in the event you are sued or have to defend yourself in any forum.
2. *Set clear limits on yourself, then consult and refer.* Every clinician and pastor must be able to define clear limits of competence and the level of intervention beyond which he or she will not work. *Working within your competence is the first line of malpractice defense, a safety zone within which the court will not intrude to find you liable if you stay inside its shelter.* When events push beyond the limits of your competence, then consult and refer. Sullender and Malony strongly challenge clergy—a challenge appropriate to all Christian counselors—to "not work in isolation." There will be trouble for those who do not respect this key requirement of risk-avoidant ministry.

> The clergyperson's own needs and self-deceptions are common barriers to effective referrals. Clergy must be mature enough and professional enough to know their limits when it comes to counseling troubled persons. These limits may

involve training, available time, conflict of interest, or just
available energy.[22]

a. *Consult first, then refer.* The clinical professional and committed pastoral counselor should first consult with a respected
   and knowledgeable colleague when dealing with suicidal
   crises. Referral may not be necessary with close consultation
   to confirm and add to clinical decision-making on behalf of
   the person in crisis. This not only improves and advances the
   professional's clinical skills, it also serves the client who may
   be confused and mistrusting by having to face referral to a
   probable stranger. If referral is indicated, however, by all
   means do it. It is far better to refer to an expert stranger than
   to carry on a case that may lead to suicide.
b. *Work with your own flock.* We agree with Sullender and Malony
   that pastors and churches should not counsel with those
   outside their own flock. The inherent moral and legal protection of the clergy-congregant relationship is lost to a pastor
   counseling someone outside his church. Other than in short-
   term crisis situations that would lead to early referral, pastors
   should limit their counseling help to their own parishioners.
   Beyond the time and energy that such work demands in lieu
   of service to one's own church, there are simply too many
   legal, ethical, and moral risks to the counseling pastor in
   working with persons outside the local church or parish.

SUICIDE ASSESSMENT

Assessment of suicidal risk[23] involves gathering information
from multiple sources across a number of key variables. The essential two-part question of suicide assessment is: Is this person at
risk for committing suicide, and, if so, how serious is the risk? The
competent counselor will assess this risk according to trait, history, and situational factors.

1. *Begin counseling with assessment of suicide risk.* The easiest way to
   get information about suicide risk is to ask questions at the beginning of counseling. We incorporate questions about suicide
   (and homicidal and assaultive behavior) in our clinical intake
   forms (see appendix D). This gives us direct access to these issues at the start of professional relations and allows us to
   intervene early in cases where these issues are pressing. Struc-

turing assessment this way and addressing these questions at the initial interview puts clients more at ease as they see it as part of the routine we follow with all new clients.

2. *Evaluate risk across seven key variables.* Assess risk for suicide according to:

    a.   *Past suicide attempts.* Clinically and empirically, past behavior is the best predictor of future behavior. Careful assessment of both the incidence and seriousness of past suicide attempts is a significant factor in assessing current risk. Assessment of the seriousness—the degree of lethality of past attempts— can give important clues distinguishing whether the client has an intent to die or is using suicide to manipulate others. Superficial wrist slashing or overdosing on aspirin may yield a different hypothesis about client intent compared to the person hospitalized in intensive care following a failed gunshot wound or massive overdose of sleeping or pain medications.

    b.   *Communication of intent/denial of intent.* A second factor is a client who communicates suicidal intent or, following a serious attempt, denies any intent to further harm himself or herself. This information is rarely offered by the person at risk. You must ask directly and matter-of-factly about suicidal thoughts and intent. Incorporating these questions into your intake (section 1 above) will serve this interest well.

    c.   *Assessing the violent/angry person.* Clinical researchers have identified two constellations of violence and mood that correlate with suicide risk.[24] One is the person revealing a history of violence and unmanaged anger, which empowers suicidal action. The second type (next section) shows a history of depression without violence. The violent/angry person will:

- show a history of violent behavior—assault, hitting others, destroying or damaging property, and injury to self for such action;
- reveal anger or rage that is explosively triggered by various people or events—the person gets quickly out of control and destructive to things or relationships;
- show a tendency to hurt others and vengefully react when angry—using cutting, harmful words or hiding or destroying things special to the person who is the focus of the client's anger;

- project blame onto others—is critical and condemning of others while being unable to receive and react against any criticism from others;
- justify anger and harmful expression and show an inability to forgive, tending to hold grudges and resentments over a long period of time;
- suppress anger, denying anger in the face of obvious evidence—flushed face, clenched teeth and muscles, harsh and loud tone of voice, threatening posture;
- repress anger, denying anger problems (contrary to history) without obvious anger signals—passive-aggressive, aloof, sarcastic, cynical, conflict-avoidant;
- show associated physical complaints and symptoms—gastric-intestinal distress, ulcers, spastic colon, headache, hypertension, and cardiac irregularities.

d. *Assessing the nonviolent/depressed person.* The other key pattern in assessment of suicide risk is the person showing depression with little or no history of violence. Clinical depression is not just a bad case of the blues. A variety of mental, emotional, behavioral, and environmental indicators exist for depression, including:

- recurrent, hard-to-control, sometimes obsessive thoughts of worthlessness, hopelessness, helplessness, death, or suicide;
- problems in mental function: inability to concentrate, short-term memory lapses, and difficulty with reasoning, decision-making, and problem-solving abilities;
- mood disorders: sad, flat, numb feelings, or strong anxiety, agitation, or quick-tempered irritability, or swings between these moods;
- crying easily and frequently, or an inability to cry at all;
- sleep disturbance: sleeping too much but not feeling rested, or not getting enough sleep, awakening often in the night and sleeping fitfully;
- appetite disturbance: overeating and weight gain or undereating with resultant weight loss;
- disinterest in people and self: increased social withdrawal and isolation, poor diet, and/or increased neglect of personal appearance and hygiene;

- loss of interest in sex, hobbies, and things that have been pleasurable;
- various physical complaints: chronically fatigued and tired, headaches, floating aches and pains, gastric distress, constipation, and fast heartbeat in some.

e. *Other changes in personality and behavior.* Other changes that correlate with suicidal risk include:

- increased alcohol and drug abuse: combining drugs with depression and suicidal threats is serious as the last internal barriers to suicidal action may be relaxed by the drug;
- giving away favorite or treasured possessions and putting one's affairs in order may precede deadly action that has been secretly decided upon by the person;
- failed or declining performance: school grades plunge, work performance falters, or a high level of absenteeism may precede an attempt;
- trivial things become important, and important things are trivialized.

f. *Environmental stressors.* A key correlate with suicide is the sudden, massive experience of recent loss. The tragic death of a spouse, child, or best friend may precipitate suicidal crisis, especially if one is left living alone after the death. Loss of physical or mental ability following an accident or medical crisis is a risk, especially if one is left with chronic, intractable pain. Major financial or job loss can also be critical, especially if criminal behavior is involved. Suicide risk begins to decline, however, two or three months following such loss.

g. *Demographic factors.* Increased risk of suicide is indicated for: men over women (though women attempt suicide at over twice the male rate), whites over people of color, nonbelievers over religious believers, Protestants over Catholics and Jews, higher incomes over lower incomes, homosexuals over heterosexuals, men between the ages of fifteen to thirty-five, and women between the ages of twenty-five to seventy-five. Singles commit suicide at twice the rate of married persons, and the rate of divorced and widowed persons who commit suicide is four to five times that of the married. Suicide is also a higher risk for those who have a family history of suicide, especially suicide by the same-sex parent.

SUICIDE INTERVENTION

1. *Discuss suicide openly and matter-of-factly.* Contrary to seemingly popular opinion, talking about suicide does not make it happen. Keeping it secret and not hearing the cry for help are far more likely to facilitate a tragic death. Getting the issue out in the open robs it of some of its mystique and power, including Satan's power to tempt the at-risk person with deadly thoughts. Questioning about suicide openly and discussing it matter-of-factly helps the one in crisis see it more normally and easily. Communicating that suicidal thinking and feelings are common in crisis also helps people evaluate themselves more soberly and realistically. They are much more able to conclude they are not going crazy, even though they are struggling with or attracted to suicidal ideas.

    a. *Expand alternate thinking and options to suicide.* The suicidal person's thinking often tunnels and fixates on suicide to the exclusion of alternate ways to deal with the crisis. Explore, reinforce, and gain client commitment to alternate courses of action. Often, the client will protest that he or she has tried your suggestions or is convinced that nothing will work. Help the client focus on the least offensive option or refocus something that has been tried in the past that was partially successful. Assist the client to develop and work simple behavior plans, reporting frequently to you about progress and revision of the plan. A client who will explore and work options to suicide is resolving his or her suicidal crisis.

    b. *Respect and use the fears that block suicide.* Discuss and constructively use the things that block the person from further suicidal thinking or action. Many things stop people from suicide: fear of death and going to hell (believing there is no chance to repent), failing to die and being left an invalid, the pain of dying, being found by spouse or family, leaving children to be raised by spouse or parents, or leaving children a suicidal legacy. These things are important internal boundaries that are better nurtured than challenged when suicide is at issue.

2. *Increase clinical or counseling intervention.* Key ways to intensify the level of intervention to increase protection against suicidal risk include:

a. *Increase frequency of sessions.* Meeting more frequently should always be considered in suicidal crisis, with daily contact justifiable in high-risk cases. Setting limits here and respecting referral needs is critical, especially if the person is manipulative or overly dependent.

b. *Use the telephone wisely.* Meeting more frequently without major schedule disruptions or excessive use of time can be facilitated by brief telephone contacts. Daily five-to-ten-minute calls may be far more helpful and protective than the weekly one-hour session. Again, some can abuse the telephone, and clear limits need to be set here as well.

c. *Get friends and family involved.* With consent from your client or congregant, disclose the risk to family or friends who can make a commitment to assist the person through the crisis. Surrounding the suicidal person with caring, praying, supportive, nonjudgmental, and available people can greatly reduce the risk of isolated, deadly action. Temporary helping networks can be powerful channels through which God's power can flow mightily to the needy person. We frequently rely on this means of suicide intervention because it is so effective.

3. *Act assertively to protect in crisis situations.* In a serious suicidal crisis, referral should be made to a hospital emergency center, acute psychiatric care facility, suicide prevention center, or even the police. Connect the person in crisis with resources able to handle emergencies, and act quickly to intervene to protect life. Less serious or acute crises widen the range of potential referral sources. Sending the suicidal parishioner to a trusted Christian mental health professional is a valuable resource for the busy pastor. If none exist in your area, make referral to an honorable professional who respects and will not denigrate Christian values. Also important is referral to a psychiatrist or competent family physician who can evaluate depression and respond medically, either to facilitate hospitalization or to prescribe antidepressant medications.

a. *Make good referrals to people you know and trust.* Let your client know that you trust the person to whom you refer him or her. Your client will then carry your trust to the other professional, which will assist in the crisis. If you are new in an area, ask your colleagues to list their referral sources, and develop a list of trusted people as one of your first professional tasks.

Make an effort to meet and discuss referral situations with community professionals if you do not have a good referral network. Maintain contact with these referral sources during the crisis and afterwards for a time until the client or parishioner is resettled into a normal life routine.

4. *Contract for no suicide.* When nonacute risk exists, negotiate and contract with your client or congregant against suicide. Help him or her agree with you not to take suicidal action for a time-limited period that is as long as possible—months preferably, session to session at the very least. Let him know you realize he can kill himself if he chooses, but that if he contracts with you, he will be counted on to maintain his agreement with integrity. If possible, get him to agree to call you or someone else before taking deadly action. Formalize the agreement, and reinforce its power by putting it in writing and having both of you sign and date it.

Contracting against suicide is an effective and flexible procedure that increases protection and aids the clinical process through the crisis period. This helps clients realize they have more control than they often perceive they have when in crisis. It can also serve to distract the one whose obsession with suicide is creating a clearer mental picture of how suicide would take place.

5. *Remove access to lethal weapons and means of death.* Having the client or family remove or reduce easy access to the means of death can be critical to suicide prevention. Help the client agree to give up or lock away guns or ammunition, allowing a third party to control access. This can also be necessary for drugs, prescription medications, and car keys as well. Increasing the difficulty of killing oneself can be a crucial factor at the height of a crisis when, if easy means were available, tragedy might well occur.

CASE MANAGEMENT

1. *Help hospitalize the suicidal person.* Again, hospitalizing a suicidal person may be necessary to save his or her life. Seek agreement to admit himself to a hospital voluntarily and refer him, even take him, to the nearest Christian or other inpatient facility. If he will not agree to admit voluntarily, seek involuntary admission for crisis assessment and intervention. If admission criteria is met—serious mental illness and danger to self—most states

allow a person to be held for forty-eight to seventy-two hours initially. If the risk is serious and protracted, a hearing will be held to prove the need for longer detention, which may last for a number of weeks. This often is all that is necessary to help a person get beyond the acute and deadly phase of a suicidal crisis.

2. *Monitor your client closely.* Staying with your client or congregant through a suicidal crisis is essential. Even if you refer, they will likely return to you, so your legal duty does not end with referral. It is usually necessary to walk a second mile with them, sacrificing some time and energy to ensure their safe passage through the valley of the shadow of death. Since suicidal risk is transient, and the great majority of people live through the crisis, you will gain significant influence in their lives if you have walked with them. Your ability to assist them to grow in Christ and to maturity may be keyed to your crisis commitment to the person.

CONCLUSION

If Nietzsche is right and suicide is great consolation, it could only be so to a very pained and desperate few. For most, especially for those who loved the deceased, it is much more a tragic and painful heartache carried throughout life. Even though never fully washed away, the grief of suicide can be redeemed by the crucified and risen Savior, the man of sorrows who was and is well acquainted with grief. Counselors who lose a client or congregant to suicide will have their grief compounded if they are also subsequently sued for the death. Even if liability is not found—and it likely will not be found if one follows the steps we have outlined above—Christian counselors must still go on in the work of ministry. To go on without great sorrow, or fear that it will happen again, or without anger and repressed hostility toward the deceased and his or her family requires great faith in response to unyielding grace from God.

NOTES

1. Corrine Chilstrom, "Suicide and Pastoral Care," *The Journal of Pastoral Care* 43, no. 3 (1989): 199–208.

2. See Claude Chemtob et al.,"Patient Suicide: Occupational Hazard for Psychologists and Psychiatrists," *Professional Psychology: Research and Practice* 20, no. 5 (1989): 294–300.

3. Fredrick Nietzsche, *Beyond Good and Evil* (New York: Vintage Books, 1966).

4. Reported in *Medical Essays* (Rochester, Minn.: Mayo Clinic Health Letters, September 1985).

5. Jolene Roehlkepartain, "Saving the Suicidal," *Leadership* 13, no. 1 (1987): 53.

6. R. Scott Sullender and H. Newton Malony, "Should Clergy Counsel Suicidal Persons?" *The Journal of Pastoral Care* 44, no. 3 (1990): 203–11 (quote from 204).

7. See Steve Messinger, "Malpractice Suits—The Psychiatrist's Turn," *Journal of Legal Medicine* 3, no. 4 (1975): 21; Sheila Taub, "Psychiatric Malpractice in the 1980s: A Look at Some Areas of Concern," *Law, Medicine and Health Care* 11(June 1983): 97–103 (quote from 97).

8. Elizabeth V. Swenson, "Legal Liability for a Patient's Suicide," *Journal of Psychiatry and Law* 15 (1986): 409–34 (quote from 411–12).

9. See Sullender and Malony, "Should Clergy Counsel."

10. Ibid., 205.

11. Ibid.

12. Ibid., 204.

13. *Abille v. United States*, 482 F.Supp. 703 (N.D. Cal. 1980).

14. *Baker v. United States*, 226 F.Supp. 129 (S.D. Iowa 1964).

15. *Meier v. Ross General Hospital*, 69 Cal.2d 420, 71 Cal.Rptr. 903, 445 P.2d 519 (1968).

16. See *Baker v. United States*.

17. *Bellah v. Greenson*, 146 Cal.Rptr. 535, 81 Cal.App.3d 614 (1978).

18. See *Roy v. Hartogs*, 85 Misc.2d 891, 3812 N.Y.S.2d 587 (Sup.Ct. 1976); and *Anclote Manor Foundation v. Wilkinson*, 263 So.2d 256 (Fla.Dist. Ct.App. 1972).

19. *Runyon v. Reid*, 510 P.2d 943 (Okla. 1973).

20. Swenson, "Legal Liability," 419.

21. Richard Leslie, "The Dangerous Patient: Tarasoff Revisited," *The California Therapist* 2, no. 2 (1990): 11–14.

22. Sullender and Malony, "Should Clergy Counsel,"206.

23. For examples of some of the better suicide assessment scales, see "Hopelessness Scale," in Aaron Beck et al., "Relationship Between Hopelessnes and Ultimate Suicide," *American Journal of Psychiatry* 147 (1990): 190–95; "Suicide Probability Scale," in J. G. Cull and W. S. Gill, *Suicide Probability Scale Manual* (Los Angeles: Western Psychological Services, 1982); and "Los Angeles Suicide Prevention Center Scale," in Aaron Beck, H. Resnik, and D. Lettieri, eds., *The Prediction of Suicide* (Bowie, Md.: Charles Press, 1974).

24. See Alan Apter et al., "Correlates of Risk of Suicide in Violent and Nonviolent Psychiatric Patients," *American Journal of Psychiatry* 148, no. 7 (1991): 883–87.

Chapter 10

Protecting Third Persons from Client Violence

. . . therapists in jurisdictions where a duty [to protect] is owed . . . may think about putting a sign in the office, "Please don't identify people you are threatening." In these jurisdictions the therapist would have incentive for the patient to withhold information, since it would produce no duty. It is no wonder that the formula "two and two make five" has its attractions.[1]

Ralph Slovenko

IMAGINE FACING THIS CLINICAL NIGHTMARE. A man and his wife come to you in crisis because he has been in a full manic episode for over a month. He is an emergency-room physician with a ten-year history of bipolar (manic-depressive) disorder. They have been on vacation for two months, during which he had refused to take his Lithium, reporting that he has had the most "enlightened and creative time" of his life. She, ragged and angry from his sleepless nights, renewed substance abuse, and spending spree for various unfinished creative projects, is only happy he came to counseling and will be returning to work the next week.

He then informs you and his wife that he is going back to work without restarting his medicine. As you and his wife listen incredulously, he asserts his conviction that he can work twenty-four-hour shifts and perform medical miracles on everyone who comes in the door. Of course, he is not going to inform the hospital or medical director of his situation, even though he has agreed to work only while medicated. The risk of harm to patients treated by this doctor under his condition—a delusional state of great energy that he so much enjoys—is clearly very high.

Your mind races for answers to your clinical, moral, and legal dilemma. Should you maintain the confidence of this couple who clearly need counseling help, or are you compelled by law to take protective action on behalf of probably dozens of emergency-room patients? You decide to engage them in a discussion about your dilemma. While she shrinks back in mute and pained silence, he explodes with indignant anger, appalled that you even question his power and competence, threatening you with a lawsuit if you take any action that puts his job or reputation at risk. Suddenly you realize the irony of Slovenko's paradox—two and two just may be five in this no-win world!

A Surreal Realm of Law

Welcome to the surreal and contradictory world of third-person protection law. Following the landmark 1976 California Supreme Court decision in *Tarasoff v. Regents of the University of California*,[2] the controversy, confusion, and diversity of opinion about this field of law has only increased. In the 1990s, lawsuits are steadily increasing against all kinds of counselors facing this quandary. No area of law faced by the Christian (or any) counselor is fraught with more difficulty in discerning what the law requires and how to accomplish it in the best clinical interests of clients.

The principle undergirding *Tarasoff* is admirable: it is more important to protect life than to maintain therapeutic confidence when the two values clash. As eloquently stated by the California Supreme Court, the "protective [confidential] privilege ends where the public peril begins." The simplicity of this balanced boundary statement belies the complexity of its application. Legal standards across the country are notorious for the vagueness and conflict in their direction to counselors about this rule. As one commentator who sees a bad situation getting worse noted, "Aiming for a prudential 'Better safe than sorry,' [lawmakers] achieve a perverse 'Guess the truth, or pay the consequences.'"[3]

Worse yet, some states have not accepted this balanced principle, issuing judicial and legislative rules to either extreme of a confidentiality/disclosure continuum. Some states have abandoned the *Tarasoff* principle altogether by affirming either the primacy of confidentiality or denigrating it in favor of protection duties. While a rough consensus is developing among states accepting *Tarasoff* in principle, other states that reject the rule sabotage any hope of legal clarity and nationwide uniformity of law.

In this chapter we will inform you about *Tarasoff* law and its contradictory development nationwide. We will offer a proposal for legislative reform and make practical recommendations for counselors facing this dilemma. We follow the predominant legal doctrine of *Tarasoff* in the development of our recommendations for counseling policy and practice because (1) we believe the *Tarasoff* principle is biblically defensible, grounded in the right to and protection of human life, and (2) most states are following California's lead in this regard.

Our most important counsel to you may come now: CONSULT WITH YOUR LAWYER, DENOMINATION, OR PROFESSIONAL ASSOCIATION TO KNOW YOUR STATE LAW REGARDING THIRD-PERSON PROTECTION DUTIES. Our recommendations in this chapter may directly contravene the law in your state. Even states following *Tarasoff* have not done so uniformly, *so specific legal direction is imperative here.*

TARASOFF AND ITS PROGENY

Tarasoff is probably the most well-known mental health law case in the world. Commentary on the case, its ruling, and its progeny (the string of cases following it that use it as precedent or reference) fills many volumes.[4] We will outline the case and its rule, including the trends in development of *Tarasoff* law across the country.

TARASOFF AND ITS PROGENY IN CALIFORNIA

This case is rooted in the murder of Tatiana Tarasoff by her obsessive, jealous boyfriend Prosenjit Poddar. Poddar had disclosed his violent intentions prior to acting on them to a psychologist at the psychiatric outpatient clinic of the University of California at Berkeley. The psychologist took these threats seriously and contacted university police to assist in what became a failed attempt at hospitalization. The police contacted Poddar, questioned him, but did not detain him because he convinced the police he intended no harm. Meanwhile, the clinic's supervising psychiatrist castigated the psychologist for the breach of confidentiality, blocked further intervention, and the victim was never warned. Poddar never returned to therapy, and a few months later he stabbed Tarasoff to death.

Tarasoff's parents sued the university, its clinic, and the various staff having contact with this case for wrongful death. After trial and appellate courts held for the defendants, the California Supreme Court reversed in 1974, holding that psychotherapists have a duty to warn potential third-party victims of the serious homicidal threats made by clients.[5] The decision created a nationwide storm of protest that, in part, led the court to grant an unusual rehearing to clarify and refine its rule. In 1976 the court issued its revised rule that remains precedent in California and has become a legal benchmark for lawmakers and clinicians across the nation. Vacating its rigid 1974 rule, the court reconstructed a more flexible standard—more rightly known as the duty to protect.

> When a therapist determines, or pursuant to the standards of his profession should determine, that his patient presents a serious danger of violence to another, he incurs an obligation to use reasonable care to protect the intended victim against such danger. The discharge of this duty may require the therapist to take one or more of various steps, depending upon the nature of the case. Thus it may call for him to warn the intended victim or others likely to apprise the victim of the danger, to notify the police, or to take whatever other steps are reasonably necessary under the circumstances.[6]

Subsequent cases in California. Cases in California since *Tarasoff* have, on the whole, confused rather than clarified the rule. Two earlier cases narrowed and clarified the scope of the rule. In *Bellah v. Greenson* in 1978, the state appeals court refused to extend the duty to warn family members in the case of suicide.[7] In 1980 in *Thompson v. County of Alameda,*[8] the court limited the scope of the duty to situations where a specific, identifiable victim was at risk.

Any clarity *Bellah* and *Thompson* brought to the turbulent waters of *Tarasoff* law, however, was muddied by two later cases in California. *Hedlund v. Superior Court of Orange County,* in 1983, extended liability for failure to warn those "in close relationships with the object of a patient's threat."[9] A therapist was held liable for the trauma of a young son sitting next to his mother while she was shot and severely wounded. Even though the boy was not directly threatened or shot, his mother was, and failure to warn her also made the therapist liable for the son's harm.

That same year in *Jablonski v. United States,*[10] a case that arose in a veterans hospital in central California, a federal court found liability even though no threats had been made against any individual. A patient's hospitalization records that indicated threats and incidents of violence toward women close to the patient were held to render the patient's girlfriend "readily identifiable," creating a duty to protect the murdered mother of the girlfriend. The judge found malpractice for failing to obtain these records, infer imminent violence, warn the police, and protect the victim.

Legislative relief. The growing problems of *Tarasoff* law in California influenced the state legislature to enact the nation's first duty to protect statute in 1986. This law states in part:

> (a) There shall be no monetary liability on the part of, and no cause of action shall arise against any . . . [licensed] psychotherapist . . . in failing to warn of and protect from a patient's threatened violent behavior or failing to predict and warn of and protect from a patient's violent behavior except where the patient has communicated to the psychotherapist a serious threat of physical violence against a reasonably identifiable victim or victims.
> (b) If there is a duty to warn and protect under the limited circumstances specified above, the duty shall be discharged by the psychotherapist making reasonable efforts to communicate the threat to the victim or victims and to a law enforcement agency.[11]

The statute both helps and hurts the quest for clear and flexible counseling guidelines. Positively, it codifies the rule of *Thompson* in the requirement for a "reasonably identifiable victim," someone who can realistically be warned or protected. Better still, it removes the untenable requirement of predicting violence short of serious, stated intent by requiring clear communication of a threat. Under the statute, the therapist must actually know a threat exists against someone identifiable by direct patient communication.

The problem with the statute is the response requirements for counselors. If a legitimate threat exists, subsection (b) requires "reasonable" communication of the client's threat both to the intended victim and to police. While both actions make the therapist immune from legal and monetary liability, it formalizes a rigid legal standard that denies the clinical benefits of a flexible counselor response that was allowed in the *Tarasoff* decision. In order for the counselor to be immune from suit, the statute requires dual warnings that may not be necessary or clinically desirable.

Tarasoff Trends in Other States

Every state addressing third-person protection refers to the lodestar of *Tarasoff*, with most states following its lead in principle, if not in detail. Colorado relied on *Tarasoff* and *Thompson* to deny liability against the psychiatrist who treated John Hinckley, Jr., prior to his assassination attempt of President Reagan in 1981. Even though evidence showed Hinckley's interest in guns and obsession with the movie "Taxi Driver," with its assassination theme, the Court ruled in *Brady v. Hopper* that "Unless a patient makes specific threats, the possibility that he may inflict injury on another is vague, speculative and a matter of conjecture."[12] Nearly half the states now have case law or legislation that essentially follows the *Tarasoff* principle.

Protection duties over confidentiality. As noted before, some states go their own unique way in this field of law. Cases from Nebraska and Wisconsin and the Indiana statute represent the denigration of confidentiality in favor of a dominant third-party protection duty. The Nebraska case of *Lipari v. Sears, Roebuck & Co.* rejected the requirement of a readily identifiable victim.[13] A federal court ruled instead that therapists, without specific threats, have an affirmative duty in accordance with professional standards to know a patient's dangerous propensities and take whatever action is necessary to protect unforeseen victims. Similarly, Indiana's statute requires protective action, without specific threats or identifiable victim(s), according to a vague showing of conduct or statements ". . . indicating an imminent danger [that the client may] cause serious personal injury or death to others."[14]

The most troubling case in this line of reasoning is a Wisconsin Supreme Court decision, *Schuster v. Altenberg.*[15] The court held a psychiatrist liable for failure to warn the family of a bipolar (manic-depressive) patient who was killed in a car accident in which her daughter was also severely injured. There was no issue or allegation of homicidal threats; indeed, there was no inclination to harm anyone. The court reasoned that negligence attached because of the doctor's failure to recognize and warn the family of the dangerous implications of the patient's manic-depression. In rejecting *Tarasoff* and *Thompson*, the court held that "the duty to warn or to institute commitment proceedings is not limited by a requirement that threats made be directed to an identifiable target."[16] It attaches liability, without any imminent threat or even suggestion of harm, when potential harm becomes possible.

This is law run amuck—no court in America goes so far to define almost unlimited liability for protection of third persons. *Schuster* is a worst-case nightmare that places an intolerable burden on Wisconsin counselors. The Wisconsin Supreme Court was persuaded that therapists are much more able to predict dangerousness than is widely shown by most empirical evidence.[17] It relied on and quoted liberally from a study, published in the Wisconsin Law Review,[18] that surveyed therapists across the country who self-reported confident levels of prediction of danger in clients. One commentator, in barely concealed sarcasm, noted:

> . . . psychotherapists' confidence in themselves, though undeniably self-flattering, is sorely misplaced. One wonders why society would trust psychotherapists to accurately diagnose dangerous propensities in their patients when they are demonstrably unable to accurately perceive themselves.
> For psychotherapists, the importance of all this lies in the expertise and knowledge the judiciary stands poised to impute to them. If psychotherapists are seen as expert predictors of violence, then courts are likely to find therapists negligent in more instances for failing to foresee the violent acts of their patients. It is this trend [as shown in *Schuster*] that threatens to destroy the "broad range of reasonable practice" buffer zone that *Tarasoff* first conceded to psychotherapists.[19]

Confidentiality over protection duties. A few states have ruled to the opposite extreme—upholding client confidentiality at the expense of protecting third parties from client harm. A Maryland appellate court upheld confidentiality by way of statutory privilege in a case where the plaintiff was shot by the husband of his married lover who caught them nude and in bed together.[20] The enraged husband did not reveal to his psychiatrist any intentions to harm the plaintiff. Furthermore, the court held that the plaintiff assumed the risk by going to bed with a married woman.

Ohio has codified the primacy of confidentiality over third-person protection. The relevant portion of its recent statute states that "No person shall be liable for any harm that results to any other person as a result of failing to disclose any confidential information about a mental health client, or failing to otherwise attempt to protect such other person from harm by such client."[21] It will be interesting to see what Ohio courts do with this statute and the *Tarasoff* rule when someone who could have been protected is killed in that state.

Though this rule is undeniably simpler, more supportive of the therapeutic endeavor, and avoids the police role of therapists demanded by the *Schuster* line of cases, upholding confidentiality to the exclusion of societal protection is still unjustified. The rejection of some limited duty to protect ultimately weakens the commitment to the sanctity of life already under societal assault. We believe the *Tarasoff* standard—balancing client confidentiality with third-person protection—is preferred law.

TARASOFF IN THE NEW MILLENNIUM

Tarasoff has grown out of its infancy and childhood and is entering, in the developmental metaphor, a stormy adolescence. The storm rages as we consider numerous applications of *Tarasoff* to new problems.[22] The rule applied to AIDS cases is considered in chapter 18.

A DUTY TO HOSPITALIZE?

An issue rapidly developing in this field is whether hospitalization of a dangerous client is a mandatory duty or a discretionary choice. The trouble of *Schuster* is further reinforced by its duty to hospitalize a risky patient in a legal regime where it is extremely difficult to hospitalize someone involuntarily. Wisconsin's involuntary commitment law, like the law in most states, requires a finding of dangerousness *and* mental illness before the commitment passes legal muster. "Needless to say, not all patients of psychotherapists which have the potential for violence are mentally ill . . . mere anger, . . . a strong propensity for violence, . . . [or] seeing a psychotherapist will not provide a finding of mental illness . . . [however]because therapists will fear liability where a duty to commit is imposed, more patients . . . will be involuntarily committed."[23]

The dilemma that commitment law places on therapists—imposing a duty to commit when it is nearly impossible to do so legally—was addressed in *Currie v. United States*.[24] An IBM employee in North Carolina suffered rage attacks and made threats against other employees he eventually killed and wounded. The treating psychiatrist warned both IBM and law enforcement, but in staff review with other psychiatrists held the man not committable under North Carolina statute. The federal district court in *Currie* ruled that a duty to hospitalize exists when random violence is reasonably foreseeable—even though there is no readily identifiable victim.

The court also held that no liability should be found if a decision not to commit is made in good faith with proper professional diligence. A psychotherapist judgment rule (PJR) was proffered as a test for the soundness of commitment decisions. Key factors of this test include whether (a) the evaluation was made "in light of the proper legal standards," (b) other opinion was sought on a commitment decision, (c) reviewing therapists were competent and properly trained, and (d) relevant documents were adequately and promptly reviewed. The court found the defendants not liable due to their thorough, professional staff review.

SHOULD PASTORS PROTECT THIRD PERSONS?

Most clergy would agree that the protection of life is an inseparable part of their call to pastoral ministry. Many ministers would act to protect someone seriously threatened by a client or parishioner. This moral and ethical duty, however, arising from a root of biblical commitment, should not be incorporated into a legal duty that exposes those in church or parish ministry to risk of suit. As with the issue of suicide intervention, we argue against a broad legal duty of church and clergy to protect third persons.

We do not believe clergy, even those with seminary degrees and graduate courses in pastoral counseling, are adequately trained to work with dangerous persons. Such a legal duty, generally imposed, would also violate historic (pre-*Smith*) religious free exercise. As the California Supreme Court reasoned in *Nally*, such duty would inhibit clergy ability to help dangerous people in need of Christ and godly help. Limited legal duty might attach only in those cases of gross negligence compounded by clergy communication of special skill or competence in this area.

We would rather promote a legally protected *right* of clergy to intervene to protect third persons threatened by parishioner or counselee harm. We think it best that clergy have a well-defined right to protect, the proper exercise of the right granting clergy immunity from suit by either a victim of violence or a counselee or congregant whose confidence has been breached. Again, granting a protected right instead of imposing an onerous duty best honors First Amendment religious freedom. It also fulfills affirmative public policy that recognizes and supports church and clergy as significant helpers in the entire web of societal resources available to troubled persons.

Toward Enlightened Law Reform

We encourage the church—pastors, leaders, and Christian counselors of all persuasions—to support law reform and legislative advocacy that will lead to rational and uniform *Tarasoff* standards across the country. We propose a statute that integrates third-person protection with maximum therapist choice in response to client need—a counselor's *Tarasoff* statute.

Law Reform Proposal: The Counselor's *Tarasoff* Statute

Legislative Purpose: This statute shall define and regulate the law regarding third-person protection duties in the practice of professional counseling and psychotherapy. It defines required professional behavior and grants immunity to mental health professionals who face patients or clients threatening violence or serious harm to another person or persons. This statute shall supersede—incorporate or rescind—all prior statutory and/or case law rendered in this state on this issue.

A. Competent Assessment of the Risk of Violence
   No liability or cause of action shall arise against a licensed, registered, or certified mental health professional for failing to predict, warn, or protect others from a patient's or client's violent or violence-threatening behavior *if*:
   1. the clinician has conducted a competent professional assessment of the possibility of violent behavior against a third person by the patient/client,
   2. *and* such assessment fails to yield reasonable evidence
      a. of a communicated threat of violence
      b. that indicates serious and imminent danger
      c. against an identified or reasonably identifiable victim(s).
B. Therapist Discharge of a Duty to Protect
   No liability or cause of action shall arise against a licensed, registered, or certified mental health professional for confidential communications disclosed to third persons appropriate to the discharge of a duty to protect others from client harm. The duty to protect others from a client's violence or threats of violence shall be done with the least possible harm to the client's confidential privacy interest.
      The duty to protect may be discharged by competent and timely professional action that includes one or more of the following actions:

1. Communication of the dangerous threat to
   a. the identified victim(s),
   b. *or* the victim's family or significant other persons,
   c. *and* appropriate law enforcement.
2. Hospitalize the dangerous patient/client by
   a. securing client decision for voluntary admission,
   b. *or* a good-faith attempt at involuntary commitment.
3. Application of a clinically competent treatment plan that
   a. addresses the risk of violence
   b. *and* demonstrates a reasonable likelihood of preventing the threatened harm.

This proposal is not new law but clarifies and develops the *Tarasoff* duty in its last clause "to take whatever other steps are reasonably necessary under the circumstances." Colorado's statute also accepts "other appropriate action including, but not limited to, hospitalizing the patient."[25] The Council on Psychiatry and Law of the American Psychiatric Association has drafted a *Model Statute on the Physician's Duty to Take Precautions Against Patient Violence*. The drafters of this model code also support resorting to other clinical means of intervention "as would be taken by a reasonably prudent [physician] under the same circumstances."[26]

Preferred assessment. This proposal affirms the foundations of *Tarasoff* and codifies numerous duties critical to good *Tarasoff* law. It requires an assessment of the risk of violence that must show a quantum of three pieces of evidence to trigger a duty to protect. First is the clearer, more narrow standard of a threat actually communicated—in other words, if no stated threat exists, there is no duty to protect. Second, the statute distinguishes threats that are serious from those that are not or are not feasible. Many clients in therapy vent their anger and exclaim, "I could kill so-and-so!" or "I wish he [or she] was dead." These events are to be distinguished from those where such threat is serious and likely to be carried out in the foreseeable future. Third, the threat must be against an identified or identifiable third person or group of persons.

Requiring an overt, serious, and imminent threat against identifiable victims increases the predictive reliability of assessment in an area of law notorious for its vagueness and unpredictability. A standard of care that reflects these elements could be defended as rational, workable, and worthy of respect by clinicians, researchers, lawyers, and judges. This is preferred law, fulfilling a fundamental rule that law be understood and give clear direction to those upon whom it imposes a duty.

Preferred action. The proposed statute attempts to maximize therapist choice by allowing three types of professional response to the duty to protect. In cases of the most severe and imminent danger, the therapist would be duty bound to warn the intended victim or persons close to him or her and the appropriate law enforcement agency. The option of hospitalization, as an alternative to warning threatened victims and police, is legitimate in many cases where risk exists but is less imminent or severe. A preference may exist for persuading the threatening client to voluntarily admit himself or herself for observation and treatment. For those resisting this option, the therapist may attempt an involuntary commitment. Recognizing the difficulty of involuntary hospitalization, the statute grants immunity to good-faith initiation of commitment proceedings as a way to discharge one's duty. Therapists are legally protected when they seek hospitalization but, by reason of stringent commitment standards beyond their control, are not successful in getting their client hospitalized.

Many situations of third-person risk can be adequately managed solely in the context of therapy. Even hospitalization may not be necessary, the pursuit of which can damage client trust and derail clinical progress. We advocate inclusion of a third option as a valid response to the duty—intensive clinical intervention short of hospitalization or warning. Actions here might include increasing the frequency of counseling meetings; incorporating the client's family, pastor, or key friends into a network of support and accountability; mediating conflict between the client and intended victim; or short-term marital separations, leaves of absence from work, or vacations to give time to resolve crises and reduce the risk of harm.

Immunity would be granted to the therapist who develops and applies a clear treatment plan designed to manage the risk in a way that protects others. Such a plan should include contingencies for hospitalization or warning in case clinical intervention is insufficient. As in *Currie,* courts may be more inclined to accept those plans that show consultation with a colleague or supervisor about treatment decisions. By adding hospitalization and intensified treatment as options to warning for therapist action, the next, more mature generation of *Tarasoff* law can best serve both societal protection and clinical service values.

POLICY AND PRACTICE RECOMMENDATIONS

We outline policy and clinical practice recommendations according to accepted *Tarasoff* law—baseline rules we believe should be adopted as uniform national standards of practice.[27]

GENERAL RECOMMENDATIONS

1. *KNOW THE LAW.* Knowledge of your state's specific legal requirements is essential in this field. Counselors in the few states that have rejected or deviated from the *Tarasoff* standard will want to review these recommendations very carefully to discern what applies and what does not.
2. *Work from a written policy.* Develop a clear, well-written, step-by-step policy statement to guide clinical decision making by you and your staff or colleagues. Use and incorporate your state's law as a minimal standard, careful that you do not violate its basic provisions. You must go beyond the law of your state, however, and define clinically useful guidelines that will assist you in ongoing practice and case management. Consult with a knowledgeable attorney, your denomination, or professional association and revise your policy accordingly.

    A well-conceived policy will afford significant legal protection, especially in the many gray areas and dilemmas of counseling judgment not specifically addressed by the law. Even if your intervention does not avoid tragedy, evidence that you followed church, agency, or practice guidelines in good faith will serve to protect you from charges of negligent practice.

    a. *Church direction.* Clergy are encouraged to develop reputable professional referral resources to assist you in helping dangerous persons. Then, set your referral trigger points at places in this outline where the skills required are beyond your training and expertise. Drafting an outline of risk assessment questions and a list of referral resources that will be consistently used by all church staff will go far as policy protection for clergy and church.

ASSESSMENT OF DANGEROUSNESS

Assessment must help answer a two-part question: Is this a dangerous person who is currently at risk to violently harm someone, and, if so, what must I do in response to this threat?

1. *Begin counseling with assessment of dangerousness.* Incorporate questions about violent and assaultive thoughts, feelings, and behavior into your client intake form. Then probe, ask questions, and discuss both suicidal and homicidal/assaultive issues as part of your normal assessment routine in the initial interview.
2. *Review prior records and document carefully.* Obtain client release and pursue all former records, reviewing them for past evidence of dangerous behavior or propensities. Carefully document, including incorporation of past incidents into your records, all *Tarasoff* issues, disclosures, and collateral contacts made during the course of assessment and therapy.
3. *Evaluate risk across six key variables.* Assess risk of acting out dangerous behavior by gathering and evaluating evidence on these key criteria:
   a. *Current assessment.* Assess the current level and seriousness of violent thinking, planning, and behavior. Is violent thinking intrusive and obsessional or more sporadic and controllable? Does the client counter or deflect such thinking or has he or she begun to imagine or plan how to carry out an attack on someone? Is there an identifiable victim? If so, who is it, what is the nature of their relationship, and what feelings are associated with this person or group of people? Has the client rehearsed an attack or simulated the violent behavior to be engaged in if opportunity arose? Does the client have easy access to the threatened victim and the means to carry out an attack? Accurate evaluation of this dimension is foundational to risk assessment.
   b. *Past violent behavior.* Considered by many the most reliable factor in predicting violence, the likelihood of future violence increases with evidence that past violent behavior has been varied and frequent. Other correlative factors include whether the client has been jailed or prosecuted for assault or abuse, general criminal history, and violence in association with gangs.
   c. *Past victim of violence.* Violent adults were often physically and/or sexually abused as children. Growing up in a family system where violence was normal and used as a primary tool to resolve conflict predisposes the adult to this same pattern of conflict resolution.
   d. *Drug and alcohol abuse.* Over half of all violent crime is committed while intoxicated. Drugs more commonly associated

with violent behavior are alcohol, cocaine, methamphet-
amine ("crank") and other stimulants, and PCP, LSD, and
other hallucinogens. Drug use can facilitate violent behavior
when interacting with neurological and physiological im-
pairments—learning disabilities, mental retardation, chronic
pain, or hypothyroidism. A thorough substance abuse evaluation is important to assessment of dangerousness.

e. *Psychological disorders and personality factors.* Though the cor-
relations are weaker, certain psychological and personality
traits have been associated with violence. The paranoid personality, of course, has historically been known for the
risk of violent behavior. The sociopath, especially with a
history of crime and drug abuse, has been shown to have
some violent tendencies. Some introverted, socially withdrawn persons have been shown to be at risk. A few psychotics
susceptible to hostile delusions and fantasies or command
hallucinations may act out in violent ways. Violent behavior
has also been associated with major depression and a history
of chronic depression.

f. *Demographic and situational factors.* Nearly 90 percent of those
arrested for violent crimes in America are men, the great
majority of these being young adult males. Many of these
men are unemployed or underemployed, poorly educated,
and lacking good job skills. Marital and family stress, especially if chronic and unresolved, correlates strongly with
violence. Easy access to victims and to lethal weapons, especially guns, is another critical situational factor. Since one's
spouse, children, or extended family members tend to be the
most prevalent victims and are often shot or stabbed, this
assessment should not be overlooked.

INTERVENTION WITH VIOLENT PERSONS

1. *Engage the client in all interventions.* Engage your client in all action
discussions and seek client consent in all intervention. Ask your
client's permission even when you are obligated to warn others or
to hospitalize. Even if he or she denies you permission, he will respect your pursuit of it and be less likely to mistrust or sue you
following mandatory response behavior. If permission is not given,
inform him of your course of action and affirm your commitment
to him as a counselor. The only exception to this is when your (pre-

sumptively sociopathic) client lies in such a way that prior disclosure would only lead to evasion and increase the risk of dangerous action.

2. *Least restrictive intervention.* Always consider first the least restrictive means of intervention, but do not avoid the need to take more intrusive action as state law may prescribe. These protection duties are always exceptions to your primary duty, your fiduciary trust to your client. You should work to take effective protective action on behalf of third persons in ways that maintain your client's confidentiality and best clinical interests. Therefore, even though many *Tarasoff* states require or give immunity only by a duty to warn, we recommend that such be done as a last step in a chain of clinical decision making that first considers intensive clinical intervention and hospitalization.

3. *Increase and intensify clinical intervention.* Consider a more intensive outpatient regimen as the first step of intervention. Contract with your client regarding the following procedures:

   a. *More frequent sessions.* Meet as frequently as possible for a short time, even on a daily basis if necessary, focusing on crisis intervention, anger management, and close monitoring of violent thinking and behavior.

   b. *Defuse explosive situations.* Assist your client to manage crises, including consideration of time off from work, family, or an oppressive routine in order to rest and regain personal control. Adopt the very short time frame of crisis intervention—preferably day-by-day. Contract to remove access to lethal weapons and close proximity to the intended victim. Help your client plan, contract, and focus on priority behavioral tasks, letting go of chronic problems, long-term resentments, and things that may be disturbing and overwhelming.

   c. *Facilitate a network from the client's social system.* With your client's permission, seek to develop a network of accountability, protection, and support from key people within the client's social system. Use this systems therapy as an adjunct to your continuing clinical intervention for the time corresponding to the risk of violence. Networks typically involve two to eight people from a client's family, church, and friendship circles. An outpatient substitute for inpatient intervention and often the first warning step taken, the best networks will commit to ongoing availability to and frequent contact with the client to help maintain control of anger and impulsive rage.

    d. *Referral to another professional.* Refer to a psychiatrist or other mental health professional for further, more intensive intervention. Consider psychiatric referral for possible medication intervention to deal with out-of-control behavior. Use another professional as frequently as you can as a trusted consulting and decision-making resource. Referral and consultation also strongly communicates professional responsibility to the court.

4. *Hospitalize your dangerous client.* The logical extension of intensive clinical intervention is hospitalization. We applaud those states that are mandating or allowing this action as a viable clinical option to warning potential victims and others.

    a. *First, seek voluntary hospitalization.* Try to persuade your client to voluntarily enter the mental health unit of a good hospital. Know the resources in your area, especially Christian inpatient programs, and serve as a broker and mediator between your client and the hospital.

    b. *Next, initiate involuntary commitment.* Even if your client is not admitted involuntarily, a good-faith attempt may be essential to the discharge of your legal duty. Always discuss and explain your action to your client in advance, unless secrecy is necessary to protect.

5. *Warn appropriate persons of the danger.* Warning necessary people of imminent danger to a third person is the final step in the chain of intervention/protection action. We recommend this step be taken only in a serious emergency or when action under the prior steps has failed. When a warning is delivered, only that information necessary to take effective protective action should be disclosed. Client confidence must be respected even when the therapist is under a duty to warn.

    a. *Warning the victim and his or her social network.* With high-risk threats, the counselor must warn or attempt to warn the intended victim. Direct, matter-of-fact communication of the client's threat is all that is necessary to discharge the duty. Also, as in systems intervention with your client, warning the victim's family or spouse may be essential and can add important protection that warning the victim alone may not provide. Again, care must be exercised here as the victim's network may respond to a threat by preemptively attacking your client.

b. *Warning police and protective services.* A duty to warn the potential victim nearly always is accompanied by a warning to local law enforcement. Police should be notified in emergencies and in case quick response is needed to intervene in imminent danger. Other protective social and medical services may be notified—women's abuse shelters, rape crisis services, child welfare and protective services, acute psychiatric facilities, and the like—to assist you in protecting victims and maintaining your commitment to help your client.

c. *Warning as therapy.* If possible, warn the intended victim in the presence of your client, mediating and monitoring a no-contact agreement between them. This brings the duty to warn into the therapeutic regime in an attempt to protect without harming clinical goals. Care must be taken here as this action often does not work and will not always be safe for some victims. When it does work, however, both clinical and protection goals are served.

CASE MANAGEMENT

1. *Monitor the client closely for increased or reduced risk.* Continue a crisis intervention mode that maintains, for a time-limited period, close and frequent monitoring of the client and the risk of dangerous behavior. Be prepared to assess increased risk that may require hospitalization or warning police and the intended victim if that was not your initial response. Be ready, also, to evaluate reduced risk that leads to relaxed intervention and a return to a more normal routine of counseling or clinical intervention.

2. *Protect yourself.* Last, but hardly least, is the necessity of self-protective action in the face of violent threats. Especially with drug-induced or psychotic paranoia, a client in severe crisis may perceive the therapist as a threatening person and attack him or her. Counselors should carefully attend to safety factors in their intervention with dangerous clients. See such clients only at your office and when others are present; if necessary, see the client only with a colleague or supervisor in attendance. Talk to the client directly and assertively about your threat perceptions, demanding and prescribing ways to control the threat and manage anger. Do not let your client sit between you and your office

door if the threat is significant. Also, do not hesitate to call the police and have your client detained or hospitalized. No counselor has to maintain his or her client's interest and remain passive in the face of assaultive or threatening behavior.

CONCLUSION

Dangerous clients tax all your energy and challenge your knowledge and skill as a clinician to the maximum. Experienced counselors can attest to sleepless nights and ragged nerves that seem unavoidable when working with a violent client. The counselor who has a client kill himself or herself or someone else can carry the tragic effects of this violence for years. Knowing Christ and seeking his divine wisdom and power is essential in these crises.

Serving your client's best clinical interests while under a duty to protect those threatened may seem an untenable contradiction. We believe the contradictions exist more in the poorly conceived legal regime regarding this problem than in the principle itself. Most clients will suffer a lifetime of loss, guilt, and shame if they do kill or severely harm someone. Doing all you can to prevent such tragedy really does serve the client's best interests. If Christian counselors can join, even lead enlightened law reform that integrates the best in client service and societal protection values, there is hope that someday two plus two will once again make four in this surreal and contradictory world.

NOTES

1. Ralph Slovenko, "The Therapist's Duty to Warn or Protect Third Persons," *Journal of Psychiatry and Law* 16 (Spring 1988): 139–209 (quote from 189).

2. *Tarasoff v. Regents of the University of California*, 17 Cal.3d 425, 131 Cal. Rptr. 13, 551 P.2d 334 (1976) (hereafter cited as *Tarasoff*).

3. C. J. Meyers, "Hard Cases: The 'Duty to Warn' As a Felt Necessity of Our Time," *Journal of Psychiatry and Law* 15 (Summer 1987): 189–204 (quote from 189–90).

4. For possibly the most comprehensive legal and clinical work on *Tarasoff*, see James C. Beck, ed., *The Potentially Violent Patient and the Tarasoff Decision in Psychiatric Practice* (Washington: American Psychiatric Press, 1985).

5. *Tarasoff v. Regents of the University of California*, 13 Cal.3d 117, 118 Cal. Rptr. 129, 529 P.2d 551 (1974).

6. *Tarasoff*, 551 P.2d at 340.

7. *Bellah v. Greenson*, 146 Cal.Rptr. 535, 81 Cal.App.3d 614 (1978).

8. *Thompson v. Alameda County*, 27 Cal.3d 741 (1980).

9. *Hedlund v. Superior Court of Orange County,* 34 Cal.3d 695, 194 Cal.Rptr. 805, 669 P.2d 41 (1983).

10. *Jablonski v. United States,* 712 F.2d 391 (9th Cir. 1983).

11. *California Civil Code,* section 43.92 (West Supp. 1989).

12. *Brady v. Hopper,* 570 F.Supp.1333 (D. Colo. 1983)

13. *Lipari v. Sears, Roebuck & Co.,* 497 F.Supp. 185 (D. Neb. 1980).

14. See *Indiana Statutes Annotated Code,* section 34-4-12.4.

15. *Schuster v. Altenberg,* 144 Wis.2d 223, 424 N.W.2d 159 (1988).

16. Ibid., 144 Wis.2d at 234.

17. See John Monahan, *The Clinical Prediction of Violent Behavior* (DHHS Publication, No. [ADM] 81-921, 1981); and Bernard Diamond, "The Psychiatric Prediction of Dangerousness," *University of Pennsylvania Law Review* 123 (1974): 439.

18. David Givelber, W. Bowers, and D. Blitch, "Tarasoff, Myth and Reality: An Empirical Study of Private Law in Action," *Wisconsin Law Review* (1984): 443–97.

19. Steve Bednar, "The Psychotherapist's Calamity: Emerging Trends in the *Tarasoff* Doctrine," *Brigham Young University Law Review* (1989): 261–81.

20. *Shaw v. Glickman,* 45 Md.App. 718, 415 A.2d. 625 (1980).

21. *Ohio Revised Code Annotated,* section 5122.34 (Anderson 1989).

22. For legal applications of *Tarasoff* to property destruction, see *Peck v. Counseling Service of Addison County,* 146 Vt. 61, 499 A.2d 422 (1985); and speculating on application to the academic or clinical researcher, P. Appelbaum and A. Rosenbaum, "Tarasoff and the Researcher: Does the Duty to Protect Apply in the Research Setting?" *American Psychologist* 44, no. 6 (1989): 885–94.

23. Bednar, "Psychotherapist's Calamity," 277–78.

24. *Currie v. United States,* 644 F.Supp. 1074 (N.C. 1986).

25. See *Colorado Revised Statutes,* section 13-21-117.

26. Paul Appelbaum et al., "Statutory Approaches to Limiting Psychiatrists' Liability for Their Patients' Violent Acts," *American Journal of Psychiatry* 146, no. 7 (1989): 821–28, appendix 1; and for examples of the better statutory proposals in this arena, see James Beck, "The Psychotherapist's Duty to Protect Third Parties from Harm," *Mental Disability Law Reporter* 11 (1987): 141–48; and Samuel Knapp, L. Vandecreek, and D. Shapiro, "Statutory Remedies to the Duty to Protect: A Reconsideration," *Psychotherapy* 27, no. 2 (1990): 291–96.

27. See also John Monahan, "Limiting Therapist Exposure to Tarasoff Liability: Guidelines for Risk Containment," *American Psychologist* (in press).

PART IV

The Counseling Process: Managing Liability Risk

Chapter 11

A Good Start:
Informed Consent and
Counseling Agreements

You never get a second chance to make a first impression.

A GOOD BEGINNING IN THE COUNSELING RELATIONSHIP can greatly influence a successful outcome. A large body of research data supports the proposition that communicating confident knowledge and expert skill to clients engenders hope and good working relations.[1] Clients who perceive you as trustworthy, able to help, and honestly supportive of them will grant you legal and psychological permission to enter their lives in a significant way in the helping endeavor.

Legal issues in successful beginnings revolve around informed consent and counseling contracts. Clients and patients must consent and agree to engage in counseling relations. In this chapter we review the law of informed consent and then outline good contract procedures. We want to help the Christian counselor make the best beginning possible, both therapeutically and legally.

THE LAW OF INFORMED CONSENT

Like the rule of confidentiality, the complexity and controversies of the modern doctrine of informed consent belie the simplicity of

153

its origins. Informed consent applies primarily to three areas of professional practice: clinical treatment, clinical research, and release of confidential information. The duty to obtain client consent to treatment was stated, in the context of medical practice, in comprehensive form in *Sard v. Hardy:*

> Simply stated, the doctrine of informed consent imposes on a physician, before he subjects his patient to medical treatment, the duty to explain the procedure to the patient and to warn him of any material risks or dangers inherent in or collateral to the therapy, so as to enable the patient to make an intelligent and informed choice about whether or not to undergo such treatment. . . .
> This duty to disclose is said to require a physician to reveal to this patient the nature of the ailment, the nature of the proposed treatment, the probability of success of the contemplated therapy and its alternatives, and the risk of unfortunate consequences associated with such treatment. . . . The law does not allow a physician to substitute his judgment for that of the patient in the matter of consent to treatment.[2]

THE ELEMENTS OF INFORMED CONSENT

Informed consent consists of three elements: disclosure, competence, and voluntariness. The Christian counselor has a duty to (1) fully and fairly disclose the expected benefits, risks, and alternatives to treatment (2) to a competent client so that he or she can (3) make a voluntary decision to engage in treatment.

Adequacy of disclosure is judged by what a reasonable person would want to know to make an informed decision. Every conceivable risk and alternative is not necessary to disclose—such is a practical impossibility. Discussion of risk and alternatives to treatment is especially important in an inpatient setting and with a variety of psychiatric treatments such as electro-convulsive or drug treatment. In outpatient counseling, discussion and agreement concerning goals, the likelihood (and not) of obtaining them, and the time and cost to reach them would be sufficient disclosure in the majority of cases. It is critical to avoid any exaggerated claim of benefit; clients believing you have guaranteed an outcome are more likely to sue if that outcome is not realized.

Competency is a legal judgment that requires the client have sufficient mental capacity to make an informed, voluntary decision. Since competency is not a clinical diagnosis, it is important to keep in mind that a mental disorder does not presume that the disordered person is incompetent.[3] Competency decisions focus on whether or not the person is able to adequately conduct his or her personal affairs (i.e., self-care, financial management, maintenance of shelter, health, and safety) in a rational and independent manner. Incompetent persons often include the severely mentally retarded, organically impaired, psychotic patients in acute phase, minor children (although, as discussed in chapter 16, some children can consent to treatment), and certain elder persons. The counselor must obtain consent to treatment from the legal representative—parent, spouse, child, guardian, conservator, or attorney—of an incompetent client.

Breach of voluntariness occurs when the counselor's disclosure and application of treatment is manipulative or coercive. This risk increases significantly in restrictive treatment settings—hospitals, residential treatment, and involuntary commitments. A Michigan case in 1973 went so far as to rule that voluntary consent to treatment in an acute psychiatric facility was impossible due to an institutional environment that was "inherently coercive."[4] Psychiatrists working in public mental health frequently confront the dilemma of the involuntary patient who is legally competent to refuse drug treatment (see chapter 17). There is limited evidence that lawmakers are beginning to pull back from extreme rulings and better balance freedom and treatment values in this regard.[5]

Also like the law of confidentiality, numerous exceptions to the consent requirement exist. Any counselor claiming an exception has the burden of proving it so. Three general exceptions exist: (1) an emergency in which the client is temporarily precluded from making an informed judgment about treatment; (2) disclosure that would unduly alarm the client or reasonably result in a refusal to undergo needed treatment; and (3) the client voluntarily waives his or her right to be informed about a particular treatment. Even if a valid exception exists, it is often true that consent will be required from a close relative or guardian.[6]

INFORMED CONSENT LIABILITY

Legal liability focuses on both the sufficiency and elements of informed consent. The therapist who fails to gain informed consent altogether can be liable for an intentional tort. Negligence can be proven against the clinician who obtains inadequate consent. The sufficiency of the consent requirement corresponds to the degree of risk associated with the nature, goal, setting, and dynamic of the counseling work. The degree of consent-related disclosure increases in relation to the restrictiveness of the setting and the invasive/directive nature of the procedure or counseling intervention. Informed consent for a voluntary client in an outpatient setting engaged in nondirective therapy would be wholly insufficient for the involuntary patient in a hospital emergency situation.

Simon suggested there is no duty to obtain informed consent for psychotherapy due to the relative absence of risk to clients engaged in the talking therapies.[7] We disagree. Some therapies (i.e., directive techniques in marital and family therapy, behavior rehearsal, and anger ventilation) involve an active, physical component that can be injurious. Also, Simon presents far too narrow a conception of harm, inferring that it is significant only with respect to the physical harm associated with medical and psychiatric treatment. Modern law clearly respects a broad conception of client harm, including mental, emotional, familial, and constitutional factors.

Simon is correct in his observation that the risk of harm in the verbal therapies is comparatively lower than the risks attendant to medical treatment. Rather than dispensing with consent altogether, however, the duty is instead reduced in scope and detail to correspond to the risks that are present.[8] It is this calibration of the scope of the consent requirement to correspond with the degree of risk in psychotherapy that makes this issue more difficult. For the agency or church-based counselor, a thorough discussion of goals, fees, work expectations, limits of confidentiality, and a reasonable time frame for the duration of counseling will be sufficient to meet the consent requirement.

One final note—a caveat to the counselor. No client can consent to negligent or harmful treatment. An informed consent, even expressly given to a harmful treatment, will not shield the counselor from breach of professional duty. Growing numbers of states, for example, are removing the consent defense in cases of sexual misconduct in counseling (see chapter 6).

CLIENT INTAKE AND COUNSELING AGREEMENTS

In this section, we outline good intake procedures, including the development of a counseling contract that establishes proper professional relations, protects counselor and client legally, and directs the clinical effort toward successful resolution.

POSITIVE CLIENT INTAKE

The first contact between counselor and counselee is usually charged with some anxiety over issues of needing help and asking for it. Even the pastor, who knows the one asking for help, should be sensitive that it is not an easy thing to do. The client who contacts the professional counselor may often talk first with a receptionist on the telephone. Receptionists must be well trained to be sensitive, informative, helpful, and encouraging in their communication and tone. A disinterested, insensitive, or annoyed tone conveyed in the first contact can kill any further counseling relations.

The counselor should call back the one making a counseling inquiry as soon as possible. He or she should inquire about problem concerns, severity or level of emergency, who intends to come to counseling, and when an initial appointment might be scheduled. Fees and insurance issues should be discussed and may be agreed upon if prospective clients know their finances well. If the counselor and inquiree agree to meet for a first session, *a verbal contract exists that the counselor must fulfill.* This agreement will expire and be superseded by a formal written service agreement or by referral elsewhere. The helper must realize that an agreement to meet creates a legal duty which, if breached without justification, makes the helper liable to the person they have yet to meet face-to-face.

The first session. The first counseling session has three objectives: (1) put the client at ease and develop trust and rapport in the relationship; (2) help the client tell his or her story in a way that gains useful information about problems, goals, and resources; and (3) if you can help, enter into an agreement that commits both you and your client to work together. Counselor and client should arrive at an initial definition of problems and goals to be addressed in counseling, including an appropriate and estimated time frame for their resolution. Fees and initial appointment schedules should also be agreed upon, with a clear understanding of procedures for fee payment, cancelled appointments, and changes in schedules. Concluding the first session with encouragement and hope-building praise for taking action will bear fruit in the struggle of change to come.

THE COUNSELING AGREEMENT

The Christian counselor, whether pastor or professional clinician, should use written contracts as a basis for professional relations and to define the counseling work (see appendices A, B, and C for examples of useable contracts). The benefits of a well-executed agreement far outweigh any risks associated with contract liabilities. A good contract will reduce liability risk by structuring discussion, negotiation, and agreement of those critical issues that often lead to suit.[9]

The counseling contract should be written in clear, nontechnical language. It should be structured logically according to the key elements of risk and clinical service. Most elements should be addressed with specificity and precision, *yet there must not be any statements, direct or implied, that promise or guarantee a specific outcome in a rigid time frame.* A good contract balances specific language about client services and mutual behavior with open-ended statements about goals and outcomes. A comprehensive service agreement should include all or most of the following elements (not necessarily in this order):

1. *Comprehensive scope of coverage.* Begin with a statement that this contract "shall govern *all* professional relations" between the counselor and client. It is important that all issues of import that can be contracted be brought under written agreement. (Remember that tort duties and constitutional rights exist independent of contract.)

2. *An agreement regarding dispute resolution procedures.* We recommend stating that it "is agreed that any disputes or modifications of agreement shall be negotiated directly between the parties; if negotiations are not satisfactory, then the parties *agree to mediate any differences with a mutually acceptable third-party mediator.*" (See appendix A.) Such statement does not contract away the client's right to litigate; instead, it binds the client contractually to litigate only as a last resort. A commitment to negotiate and mediate in good faith can avoid a great many lawsuits.

3. *A clear statement of counselor title and licensure or certification status.* Clients should know and consent to work with counselors who are unlicensed or in a prelicense intern training status. More and more insurers and third-party vendors are requiring licensure for reimbursement. Clients may be quite upset and consider suit if they believed an unlicensed counselor was licensed and eligible for reimbursement that an insurer subsequently refuses to grant.

4. *A statement on fee and insurance policy and agreement about fee rates.* This statement should indicate the requirements and limits of client payment, whether session-by-session or by billing agreement. The expectations of copayment by clients with insurance

should be spelled out specifically. The limits of accounts receivable—how many sessions without payment you will allow before suspending counseling—should be exactly stated. Finally, make it clear that clients are fully responsible for all fees if insurance or other vendors do not pay.

5. *A statement about cancellation policy.* The conditions and time for cancellation without payment should be very explicitly stated. In our agency, we require payment for sessions if the client does not show or cancels without emergency after 6:00 PM on the day prior to the appointment.

6. *The rule and limits of confidentiality must be clearly outlined.* A general statement of commitment by the counselor and any support staff to keep all therapeutic communications in confidence should introduce this section. Then a clear outline of the situations and procedure requiring disclosure (see chapter 7) should be included, in accordance with the dictates of your resident state law. It is a good policy, barring emergencies, to apprise clients before mandated disclosure, and a statement of this intent is useful.

7. *A statement of the goal-directed work of counseling.* Space should be allowed to write in one to four specific goal statements that reflect the key problem issues revealed by the client. The contract should state clearly that these issues will be *addressed* in counseling—not solved or accomplished in a way that expresses a guarantee. This section should also note that revision of goals is likely as counseling advances.

   Also, especially for the male therapist working individually with a female, it is imperative to contract in a clear and explicit way for any sexual therapy. State in your contract goals that sexual dysfunctions or issues will be addressed in a goal-directed manner. Make sure your client is fully informed and agreeable to this work. Since wrongful sex in the therapeutic relationship now includes sexual speech without touch, it is important to discriminate correct therapeutic speech concerning sexual problems. Contracting these issues clearly in writing will help protect the therapist who works in this field.

8. *Any other limiting factors in the counseling relationship.* Pastors, especially respecting other pastoral duties, may have policies that limit the time, number of sessions, and type and severity of parishioner problems. We recommend inclusion of any other limiting factors in the counseling agreement.

9. *Concluding materials.* The final section includes both a consent statement and lines for the counselor and the client or congregant to sign and date the agreement. This should state that the client has read, discussed, and fully understands the policies, limits, and agreements that he or she is about to enter. We include an agreement to negotiate and mediate disputes and a statement that we have agreed to fees and an initial definition of the work to be done in counseling. The contract should be signed and dated by the therapist and the client or the client's legally responsible representative (the parent of a minor receiving services). A copy of the completed agreement should be given to the client for his or her records.

Conclusion

Contracting for counseling explicitly defines clear expectations that otherwise are left to speculation and fantasy. Such an instrument guides mutual and ethical decision-making by both counselor and client. It also reinforces the professional nature of the relationship and the seriousness of the counseling task. Revision of the agreement is inevitable as goals and problem issues change and demand greater clarity as counseling progresses. Some clients also experience changes in their life and income that require fee and session revisions as well. A good contract will anticipate and make provision for such changes, greatly protecting the counselor from the problems that lead to suit.

NOTES

1. See chapter 3, "Building the Helping Relationship," and particularly the section on "Helping as a Social Influence Process," 75–80, in Gerard Egan, *The Skilled Helper: A Systematic Approach to Effective Helping,* 4th ed. (Pacific Grove, Calif.: Brooks/Cole, 1990).

2. *Sard v. Hardy,* 281 Md. 432, 379 A.2d 1014 (1977).

3. See *Mitchell v. Robinson,* 334 S.W.2d 11 (Mo. 1960).

4. *Kaimowitz v. Michigan Department of Mental Health,* Case No. 73-19434-AW (Mich. Cir. Ct., July 10, 1973).

5. See Paul Appelbaum, "The Right to Refuse Treatment with Antipsychotic Medications: Retrospect and Prospect," *American Journal of Psychiatry* 145, no. 4 (1988): 413–19.

6. See *Canterbury v. Spence,* 464 F.2d 772 (D.C. Cir. 1972).

7. Robert I. Simon, *Psychiatric Interventions and Malpractice: A Primer for Liability Prevention* (Springfield, Ill.: Thomas Publishers, 1982).

8. Patrick S. Cassidy, "The Liability of Psychiatrists for Malpractice," *University of Pittsburgh Law Review* 36 (1974): 108–37.

9. See Thomas Gutheil and Paul Appelbaum, *Clinical Handbook of Psychiatry and the Law* (New York: McGraw-Hill, 1982); and the contracts in the appendix of Robert Schwitzgebel and R. Kirkland Schwitzgebel, *Law and Psychological Practice* (New York: Wiley, 1980).

Chapter 12

Improper Treatment and High-Risk Counseling Practices

In September 1987 the longest, costliest and most complex psychotherapy malpractice case in California history came to an end when the [Board of Psychology] . . . revoked the licenses of Joseph Hart and Richard Corriere, former heads of the Center for Feeling Therapy. . . .

Since 1980 when the Center closed, complaints from former patients . . . were so nightmarish and bizarre that at first investigators found them hard to believe. . . . Patient after patient recounted instances of sex with therapists, of being hit, kicked, punched, ordered to strip, called "dead," "insane," of being told how often to have sex and with whom, where to live and work, how much to weigh, what to eat, what to think, what to feel.

Through two years of state hearing and several civil suits that resulted in a reported $6 million in settlements to former patients, a portrait of Center life emerged that was not silly, but ugly, brutal and frightening. Perhaps by 1987 it should not have been hard to be shocked by the existence of a wierd, cultish group. But this had not been some hidden, far-out sect. The men who had run the Center held Ph.D.s from Stanford and the University of California. They had written three books published by the mainstream press. . . . They had given lectures across the country and . . . had been regulars on the talk-show circuit. . . .

What had happened? . . . most people saw a new psychotherapy promising happiness, fulfillment and utopian community. In reality there were 350 people who had spent up to ten years of their lives in what administrative law judge Robert A. Neher called an "almost gothic maelstrom."[1]

Carol Mithers

CAROL MITHERS'S RIVETING ACCOUNT OF THE Center for Feeling Therapy in the August 1988 issue of *California* magazine reveals the worst of therapeutic malfeasance. While it might be tempting to pass this off as just another crazed California story, lawsuits for improper, high-risk, even dangerous and abusive treatment are steadily increasing throughout the country. In this chapter we address problems in recordkeeping, fraud, battery, false imprisonment, and defamation. Liability for these practices can be negligence; the majority of suits in these realms are for more serious intentional torts and even criminal prosecutions by the state. Licensed therapists engaging in these practices can also expect action by state boards that will result in license revocation.

PROPER RECORDKEEPING

The Christian counselor should keep sufficient and well-managed records of all counseling interactions. Inadequate recordkeeping, by itself, has been judged negligent malpractice,[2] and most state licensing statutes have deemed negligent recordkeeping to be grounds for professional misconduct. Slawson asserted in the *American Journal of Psychiatry* that "good clinical records" are the key to a defendant's case and that at trial, "sloppy and incomplete records count heavily against the litigant who relies upon them."[3] Beyond the legal necessities of proper recordkeeping, a good clinical record is an invaluable asset as a guide to the definition and attainment of counseling goals.

RECORDS-BASED LIABILITY

All counselors should meditate on this fundamental fact: *every lawsuit ending favorably for the counselor-defendant is a primary, oftentimes exclusive result of a good client record.* The sobering corollary to this truth is that a poor record can sabotage a good case—a defendant likely will be found liable if the record cannot substantiate proper practice. The notion that one will be better protected if there is no record of wrong is certainly fallacious, as "an inadequate record of itself is taken to be indicative of poor care,"[4] and can be a basis for malpractice. The first and foremost rule of recordkeeping, then, is maintenance of an adequate record—a clear, comprehensive, and current client file.

Two studies by Siegel and Fischer[5] noted that one-fourth of the mental health professionals studied (psychiatrists, psychiatric nurses, psychologists, and clinical social workers) kept inadequate records. Psychologists invested the least amount of time and work on records. Lack of treatment plans and medication assessment notes were the most frequently missing items of legal import. Poor and inadequate documentation is also a problem in client emergencies and decisions with significant legal or malpractice risk (e.g., suicide crises or hospitalization decisions).[6]

The management of client records also intersects a wide range of confidentiality issues. Unauthorized release of client information contained in records is a serious breach of the client's confidence. Poor records management, especially the failure to secure and protect records from inadvertent disclosure to others, is also a basis for legal action. Care must always be exercised in maintaining records secrecy to protect client confidentiality, even when disclosure is mandated.

GUIDELINES TO PROPER RECORDKEEPING

A client's record should be clearly written and factual, with concrete descriptions of problems tied to client behavior, verbal statements, and emotional expression. All relevant and important issues discussed should be noted in the record. Willful exclusion of material to protect a client can backfire and expose the counselor to liability. If the client fears eventual disclosure of sensitive or embarrassing material, better they not discuss it than for the helper to yield to the client's request to exclude it from the record.

Speculation about internal dynamics should be kept to a minimum, and reference to derogatory and judgmental opinions should be strictly avoided. Avoid communication of commands or instructions in a prescriptive sense. Respect for client decision-making should guide the therapist to act and record instructions as suggestions and recommendations, noting whether the client adheres to them or not. Finally, all records should be kept secure in locked file cabinets with access only by the therapist and supervisor. Computer or electronic storage should use software that requires passwords or a coded message for file entry.

A range of opinion exists about what should be contained in a client's record. Some argue that "no amount of documentation is too much and no detail too small."[7] We agree with those who subscribe to the notion of adequacy—meeting standards of sound clinical and risk-managed practice without obsessive documentation.[8] A good clinical record by the Christian counseling professional—one that is adequate and comprehensive for both treatment and legal purposes—should include:

1. *Professional services contract.* See the previous chapter for information about this instrument.
2. *Intake materials.* This includes your intake form, which elicits essential client information including previous therapy and data on family and other current care providers. Financial and insurance information may be included or be held separately within your billing system (see appendix D).
3. *Initial evaluation and treatment plan.* This should include client identification, presenting complaint or problem, recent medical history, and current drug use profile (prescription and illicit), psychosocial and family history, mental status, diagnosis (both narrative description and DSM-III-R code), and treatment plan. This plan should outline goals and subgoals in a clear, objective, and specific manner, and an initial time frame for work together if that has been agreed upon. This statement is a critical professional document and should be typed in good outline form as it is often the key clinical reference used in third-party professional communications.
   a. *Treatment plan updates.* The client treatment plan should be revised and updated every three to six months. Modifications of diagnosis and treatment goals should be reviewed and revised, with changes written and included in the record. These updates should also include a statement of treatment prognosis, indicating the degree to which the therapist expects goals to be reached and the problems that block goal attainment.
4. *Prior records and releases.* Copies of prior records or summaries of previous therapy or mental hospitalizations should be included in the record file. Also include written forms signed and dated by the client showing permission for all transmissions of client information. *Counselors should not use the service contract or a blanket consent form but rather gain written permission for each disclosure or series of disclosures with a particular person.* All insurance clients should have a written referral note from their current physician regarding counseling or therapy.
5. *Progress notes.* Each session and contact with the client should be indicated by a progress note. This includes both in-person and telephone contacts to address issues other than appointment changes. These notes should indicate the date of contact and time of session and be signed by the therapist. They should be written in clear, factual, objective form, with an expectation that the client or others may someday read them. Again, abusive,

derogatory, sarcastic, or harshly judgmental references should be strictly avoided in these notes. These notes should include reference to significant issues discussed, changes in mood, progress toward goals (both positive and negative), and suggestions or recommendations for therapeutic change.

a. *Critical judgment notes.* Progress notes should be expanded for those sessions that address crises and situations of heightened risk requiring critical judgment by the therapist. Issues addressing suicide, homicide or assault, hospitalization, and client crises should be documented more carefully. Careful attention to therapist suggestions and instructions, including the reasoning for them, is essential here, including how and when the client follows your suggestions. Also note any third parties (i.e., family members and other professionals) contacted and consulted.

b. *Process notes.* Some therapists work with a second set of notes— process notes are taken in session or alongside progress notes. These are used for more impressionistic reference wherein the therapist records his or her own emotional and other responses during therapy. These can be clinically useful, and there is certainly no legal bar to their existence. While these notes rarely come to light (they are almost always known by and used by the therapist only), those who use them should always remember that they are discoverable and can be subpoenaed.

6. *Correspondence and third party consultations.* All letters on behalf of and received about your client should be in the record. Consultations about your client with third parties (parents, guardians, family members, and other professionals) should also be noted. A key principle in all correspondence about clients is the necessity to remain objective, communicating strengths as well as problem issues. Also, unless specifically at issue and the client has given you permission to disclose, avoid reference to highly personal and embarrassing material in the client's life. As much as possible, make it your policy to have clients review and assist you in editing letters sent about them.

7. *Termination and discharge.* A discharge summary should be included, noting the reasons for discharge and any referrals to other helpers (see chapter 14).

PASTORAL COUNSELING RECORDS

The counseling pastor should also keep brief notes of counseling sessions and maintain appropriate security regarding them.

Maintaining confidence in church settings is a significant challenge, and pastors and church leaders must set a consistent example and require their staff and secretaries to do likewise. Pastors should disclose the limits of congregant confidentiality up front and contract with their counselee on these issues. Junior staff and lay helpers should inform congregants about pastoral supervision and knowledge of the client's problems.

The file maintained by the pastor need not be as extensive as that of the counseling professional. A contract (see appendix B) and intake information are valuable and should be a part of the pastoral counseling process. An initial evaluation should be included but in briefer form. Psychiatric diagnosis and mental status exams should be avoided as the pastor is not trained in them and could be liable for their inclusion. A treatment plan that states clear goals and a time frame is important. Consultations and referrals to other helpers and professionals should be noted. Brief progress notes should be kept as stated above, and a summary note at the conclusion of counseling should detail goal attainment.

High-Risk Practices to Avoid

The Christian counselor must also take care to avoid a variety of high-risk practices that correlate with heightened legal risk. These include fraud, battery, false imprisonment, and defamation.

Fraudulent Practice

There are essentially two types of fraudulent practice. One relates to insurance and third-party billing and is addressed in chapter 15. The second type is fraudulent misrepresentation of title, credentials, or ability to deliver more than one can in counseling. Fraud that intends to deceive and gain materially by that deception is a crime in most states. Victims of such fraud may also sue under intentional tort and receive damages. Damages may also be won by proving negligent misrepresentation—fraud done more out of ignorance or arrogance than clear intention to deceive.

Fraudulent counseling practice of the worst sort—those intending to deceive—usually is done by persons lying about their title, degrees, and license status in order to earn fee payments. The most blatant are those who pass off phony degrees and licenses to promote themselves as professionals to dupe the consumer. More common is the intern or practitioner under suspension who fails to disclose his or her licensure status or even advertises as a licensed professional in good standing.

The church is facing a growing problem with the unlicensed pastor or minister under disciplinary suspension who then sets himself or herself up as an independent counselor. Misrepresentation of this type has been condoned or denied as problematic due to the relative lack of legal sanction, but in this litigious age it should no longer be ignored. Counseling ministers should practice under accountable authority that does not allow the counselor to be called a psychologist or psychotherapist. Some counselors have been sued for calling themselves *psychotherapists* in states where psychologists have gained title protection for the prefix *psych*.[9]

Another way fraud arises is through misrepresentation of ability and curative powers. Again, the lessons of the *Nally* case are instructive. Had professional counselors made the exaggerated claims of the pastors at Grace Community Church, there is little doubt the lawsuit would have been lost and their licenses revoked. Being a minister and pleading ignorance, lack of training, or First Amendment protection will be a very flimsy defense against fraud and misrepresentation in the future.

Humility is the antidote to fraud and misrepresentation. Strict adherence to the limits of one's title, professional status, credentials, and competence is essential. Woody's challenge of practicing one*down*-manship (see chapter 3) is fine advice. Working against our natural bent to exaggerated self-promotion and humbly communicating our ministry in understated ways is excellent legal protection. Paul, in defending his ministry to the Corinthian church, asserted that:

> We do not dare to classify or compare ourselves with some who commend themselves. When they measure themselves by themselves and compare themselves with themselves, they are not wise. We, however, will not boast beyond proper limits, but will confine our boasting to the field God has assigned to us. . . . Neither do we go beyond our limits by boasting of work done by others. Our hope is that, as your faith continues to grow, our area of activity among you will greatly expand. . . . But "Let him who boasts boast in the Lord." For it is not the one who commends himself who is approved, but the one whom the Lord commends (2 Cor. 10:12–18).

Such humility will also reduce practice stress, increase confidence, and promote better client outcome by focusing on those areas of genuine strength in your practice. Your reputation as an effective professional can only grow when working honestly within the boundaries of your competence.

BATTERY AND FALSE IMPRISONMENT

Consider the case of *Abraham v. Zaslow*.[10] Dr. Zaslow developed his "Z therapy" to reduce and free the client of primal rage. Client resisitance was overcome by application of tactile stimuli—tickling, poking, and slapping clients while being forcibly held if they were not fully open and honest. One client recovered $170,000 after being restrained for ten hours and severely bruised on her upper body, suffering kidney failure shortly after this therapy.

Any procedure that involves physical contact or restraint of any kind creates heightened risk. Counselors applying active family, child, and adolescent procedures should carefully explain the procedure and its potential risks, gaining informed consent for their application. Hospital and residential ministries that use restraint and time-out for patient management should have written policies that clearly outline the rationale, supporting research, and limits of use of these procedures. It is then essential to carefully disclose and obtain consent from patients or guardians for their use.

Policies that advocate reasoned and limited use of physical procedures will protect counselors when these are vital to ministry operations in restrictive settings. It is critical that inpatient and residential ministries adhere to these policies, however. While it may be tempting to apply more of the same and exceed limits with manipulative and abusive patients or residents, such action may only lead to suit for battery, false imprisonment, and civil rights violations. Far better to admit that your program cannot manage difficult patients, referring them to more structured programs.

DEFAMATION

Defamation refers to the spreading of false, distorted, and misleading information about another in a way that harms one's person or reputation. Defamation can be either slander or libel. *Slander* refers to verbally spreading defamatory information, while *libel* is a more lasting form of defamation—written, taped, or filmed communications. While proving the truth of one's allegations is an absolute defense, the rarity of successful defenses here suggests that lies and distortions of the truth more often creep into and corrupt the process.

The law of defamation challenges the counselor against public disclosure or the fallacious or harshly judgmental communication of client material. The Christian church has recently been hit with a variety of suits regarding defamation in a way that must challenge us to a sober appraisal of our care and respect for one another. Marvin Gorman's successful defamation suit against Jimmy Swaggart is only the most well-publicized example of the way the church is *not* to treat one another.[11] Other suits have pressed defamation in cases of church discipline, counseling disagreements, and communications made from the pulpit that have been harmful.[12]

Research on libel litigation against the press and news media was conducted by the first author while in law school.[13] This data showed that plaintiffs sued not so much because of the libel itself, but because of the arrogant or malicious way the press defended, even pressed their libelous allegations further following complaint. Similar dynamics are revealed in those cases of defamation in the church. In the Swaggart case and others, the revelation of hostility, vindictiveness, and intent to slanderously harm in the case record is disturbing and shameful. If for no other reason than to avoid a destructive defamation suit, the call to love one another and bless those who persecute us is revelation we need to respect as we approach the twenty-first century (see Luke 6:27–36; Rom. 12:9–21).

In the professional sphere, suits for defamation are becoming common among professional colleagues. In some ways, it is much easier to slander colleagues who perform poorly by discussing their faults and failures within our own professional circles. We must learn to be very careful about whom we talk and the things we say about them. We are not barred from warning others or communicating our concerns about others. We must be circumspect, however, and refer to specific behavior and instances that are true or reported with a high degree of veracity.

The law of defamation is a terrible way to learn how firey is the tongue and how important it is to control it (James 3:5–10). It is one thing to tell a few key people that a professional colleague did not respect your client's spiritual values by saying or doing this or that when seeing your client. It is quite another to widely disseminate your conclusion that this person must be an anti-Christian reprobate who is opposed to all things of God and the church. Such a conclusion may easily be deemed slander and lead to a defamation suit; professional reputations tend to be jealously guarded both within and outside the church.

Counselors are protected from defamation when testifying in legal proceedings or communicating professionally by a grant of privilege. Absolute privilege from defamatory liability is granted in legal or legislative testimony, because the threat of perjury is incentive to communicate what the testifier believes to be true. A qualified privilege exists in cases of professional communications between referring professionals or with insurance companies and certain family members. In these cases, liability is waived when the professional can make good-faith demonstration that the information conveyed about the client is believed to be true.

The most important strategy a counselor can adopt when challenged with charges of defamation is to humbly admit any wrongdoing that can be admitted and carefully explain and support the truthfulness of allegations made. The human tendency to defend oneself and press claims against another will increasingly lead to a high price paid in a war of harmful charges or in court. Apology, retraction, and restitution are sadly becoming lost arts in modern society; hopefully the Western church will not follow this blind, selfish precedent.

CONCLUSION

Improper and high-risk treatments attract the highest concentration of lawsuits against counselors within and outside the church. The problems of the poorly trained, marginally ethical (PTME) counselor are most serious in this regard. This behavior, often judged under intentional tort law or criminal statutes, is not covered by malpractice insurance, exposing counselor and church to uninsured liability. The lack of effective control of this behavior foreshadows increased legal trouble and shame brought on the name and witness of Christ. The church and the professions must concentrate resources now to gain control here; the alternatives are just too harmful and costly to wait any longer for major corrective action.

NOTES

1. Carol Mithers, "When Therapists Drive Their Patients Crazy" *California* 13, no. 8 (1988): 76–85, 135–37.

2. *Whitree v. State of New York*, 56 Misc. 2d 693, 290 N.Y.S.2d 486 (N.Y. Ct. Cl. 1968).

3. P. F. Slawson, "Psychiatric Malpractice: A Regional Incidence Study," *American Journal of Psychiatry* 126 (1970): 1302–5.

4. Ralph Slovenko, "On the Need for Record-keeping in the Practice of Psychiatry," *Journal of Psychiatry and Law* 7 (1979): 339–440.

5. Carole Siegel and S. Fischer, "A National Questionnaire Survey of Mental Health Professionals on Their Use and Attitudes Toward Psychiatric Records," 87–120, and "A Field Study of the Clinical Uses of Psychiatric Records," 120–205, in *Psychiatric Records in Mental Health Care,* ed. C. Siegel and S. Fischer (New York: Brunner/Mazel, 1981).

6. Thomas Gutheil and Paul Appelbaum, *Clinical Handbook of Psychiatry and the Law* (New York: McGraw-Hill, 1982).

7. See "Physician Team Studies OB Claims," *Malpractice Digest* 12 (June 1985): 2; and H. Hirsh, "Will Your Medical Records Get You Into Trouble?" *Legal Aspects of Medical Practice* 6 (1978): 46–51.

8. Richard Leslie, "Should I Keep Clinical Records?" *The California Therapist* 1, no. 5 (1989): 19–20.

9. See "Association, Chapter Submit Briefs Supporting Clinical Practice Rights," *NASW News* (April 1981): 12.

10. *Abraham v. Zaslow,* Case No. 245862 (Cal. Super. Crt. June 30, 1972).

11. See Mark Hansen, "$10 Million Dollar Defamation Award: Evangelist Claimed His Exploits Exaggerated by Rival Preacher," *ABA Journal* 77, no. 2 (November 1991): 28.

12. For examples of cases where defamation is claimed when ministers publicly disclose false or embarrassing facts, see *Hester v. Barnett,* 723 S.W.2d 544 (Mo. Ct. App. 1987); and *Guinn v. Church of Christ of Collinsville,* 775 P.2d 766 (Okla. 1979).

13. See data and conclusions on the Iowa Libel Research Project, reported in Randall Bezanson, Gilbert Cranberg, and John Soloski, *Libel Law and the Press: Myth and Reality* (New York: Free Press, 1987).

Chapter 13

Dual Relationships, Undue Influence, and Conflict of Interest

Do nothing out of selfish ambition or vain conceit, but in humility consider others better than yourselves. Each of you should look not only to your own interests, but also to the interests of others. Your attitude should be the same as that of Christ Jesus: Who, being in very nature God, did not consider equality with God something to be grasped, but made himself nothing, taking the very nature of a servant, being made in human likeness. And being found in appearance as a man, he humbled himself and became obedient to death—even death on a cross!

Philippians 2:3-8

BILL BURNSIDES HAS A WELL-ESTABLISHED CHRISTIAN counseling practice in a small town. He knows most of the pastors and Christian professionals personally since their referrals are his bread and butter. Several years ago, Bill had an opportunity to help a client by becoming a distributor for Aceway, a direct-marketing corporation that the client represented. The matter came up as an aside in the counseling process, and the opportunity pricked Bill's interest.

Bill liked the products and decided to become a distributor to supplement his income and to serve people. Bill was an enthusiastic salesman and built up his distributorship with some success. He occasionally presented clients with products, initially as gifts, but was soon selling products to a number of his clients. He was always careful not to pressure clients to buy his products but only offered them as people seemed to have the need. Unfortunately, a colleague in his small town complained, and now Bill's counseling license is in jeopardy. He stands before his state's licensing board defending charges of violating the dual relationship clause in the license regulations.

Illegal practice? There is increasing state scrutiny designed to protect clients from undue influence and dual relationships with counselors. This is considered necessary to protect client well-being and maintain the client's interest as top priority. It may also be a trend, due to the rigidly legalistic approach to this area by many, that needs balance so that we do not become extreme in our interpretation of dual relationships. Indeed, there are some settings where the attempt to eliminate all dual relationships may not be possible and may even be detrimental.

DUAL RELATIONSHIPS

The dilemma of dual relationships will challenge the helping person throughout his or her career. Our goal is to assist you in understanding this law and to advocate for a clinically humane and biblically ethical approach. The pastor and professional Christian counselor must guard the counseling relationship boundaries with great care. The issue of boundaries is at the core of our considerations of dual relationships, including undue influence and conflict of interest.

BOUNDARY VIOLATIONS

Every dual relationship involves a breakdown of *professional boundaries* between counselor and client. A dual relationship is the mixing of two or more levels of relationship—therapy plus personal, business, political, or romantic relations—that can harm the therapeutic endeavor. A key goal of therapy is to keep the therapeutic milieu a safe place for client expression. When this sense of safety or trust is harmed, the client will not gain all the benefits of therapy. Sexual misconduct, for example, is a dual relationship and serves to give the concept sharp meaning as a violation of boundaries.

In dual relationships, the emphasis in the law is upon the therapist's impaired judgment, though the client's judgment often becomes impaired as well. During periods of conflict and difficult change, an otherwise safe dual relationship can adversely affect the clinical progress. An innocent action on the part of the therapist may be easily misinterpreted, and the client might react negatively. Even though some dual relationships may not be unethical in and of themselves, they have the potential to disrupt or destroy the therapist-patient relationship.

Undue influence and conflict of interest. Whenever a counselor utilizes the power of the therapeutic relationship for personal gain, the court is likely to find that undue influence was exercised. Similarly, whenever a counselor seeks or accepts gain from the client beyond their agreed fee, there may be a legal conflict of interest. Some of the common situations that result in charges of conflict of interest or undue influence include accepting gifts from clients, advising a client to divorce or make some major life change, evangelizing, and providing advice to a minor against his or her parents' wishes.

A recent case against the church litigated under undue influence is *In re The Bible Speaks.*[1] An heiress who ended up in bankruptcy court had given over $6 million to a broadcast ministry. Arguing undue influence, she was allowed to recover her donations. The donor was influenced by counsel and pleas from the minister that were judged to be fabrications. This case received nationwide attention due to the monies involved and the fraudulent way they were obtained.

EVANGELISM IN PROFESSIONAL COUNSELING MINISTRY

It is easy to agree that the Christian counselor can share his or her beliefs with someone who desires this help. What is more ethically difficult and legally problematic—by way of undue influence concerns—is evangelism or promotion of Christian values with non-Christians or with Christians who do not want to address these issues. Those who do not want us to share our values in counseling often judge that the only way for a Christian to share his or her values is to impose them unethically, even forcibly on the client or patient. Unfortunately, some do force their values, and this is wrong. It is also wrong to presume that any sharing of the faith is to be avoided in counseling.

These issues should be clarified as soon as possible in the counseling process. We have found that this information is often readily shared by people on an initial telephone contact. Regardless of how the values information is gained, it is important to discuss the client's views and contract to deal with issues in light of those views. If, for example, a person wanted you to support a lifestyle that you found difficult or unbiblical, then it is important to resolve that by a referral as soon as possible. We suggest that there are three possible ways for the Christian counselor to approach sharing his or her faith—imposition, no position, and exposition.

Imposition. All counselors, whether Christian or not, are ethically bound to not impose their beliefs on another person. However, some therapists may be primarily concerned with their client's spiritual well-being and find it imperative to push their religious beliefs on them. The imposition of this agenda readily puts the counselor in the position of being an ineffective listener, creates a coercive dynamic, and actually hinders the helping process. Some clients may comply with the imposition because they are compliant people, while others will terminate therapy.

No position. Some Christian therapists assert that the only proper position is not to evangelize clients. One reason for this is the influence of secular psychology graduate programs which often stress a pathological view of religion and the vital import of not imposing one's beliefs. Also, some therapists feel uncomfortable sharing one of the most personal aspects of life. Some have tried to share their faith but have been rejected by resistant or angry clients. The resulting embarrassment may lead the counselor to decide to avoid that uncomfortable aspect of counseling.

The idea that counseling does not and should not involve values is a fiction. Bergin has consistently shown how professional counselors cannot and do not practice a valueless therapy. In his latest study he demonstrated that "clinicians value certain attributes and attempt to develop them in their clients."[2] Many others have also shown that personal values are constantly at play in counseling.

Exposition. The real challenge is how to expose clients to Christian values without manipulating the client or abusing the therapeutic trust. Bergin states, "The therapy process can best be compared with that of good parenting: Trust is established; guided growth is stimulated; values are conveyed in a respectful way; the person being influenced becomes stronger, more assertive, and independent; the person learns ways of clarifying and testing value choices; the influencer decreases dependency nurturance and external advice; and the person experiments with new behaviors and ideas until he or she becomes more mature and autonomous."[3]

We believe it is important to help clients explore their belief systems without imposing our own beliefs. When counseling people, it is vitally important to respect their belief systems, affirm what is godly, and gently challenge that which is not. This approach fosters an exposition of beliefs—the careful exposure of the client to the ways and love of Christ. The effective helper can lead the client into a careful evaluation of beliefs, both those that are helpful and those that are destructive. Even if you disagree with what the client believes, it is unethical to ignore what they believe since beliefs form the heart of what a person will or will not do. Exposition of the Gospel communicates the challenge of life to be found in Christ while respecting the client's values, including the right to decline the Gospel call.

LEGAL ISSUES IN DUAL RELATIONSHIPS

Actions regarding dual relationships arise in three contexts: a lawsuit; a disciplinary action by a state licensing board; or a disciplinary action by a professional association due to ethics violation. In California, for example, the law for Marriage, Family, and Child Counselors "includes but is not limited to" twenty different types of misconduct that could lead to disciplinary action.[4] Dual relationships are expressed in the prohibition against client sexual relations. Furthermore, the law leaves room to search elsewhere to establish added standards of dual relationships.

Professional ethics codes have generally been more specific about dual relationships. For example, the California Association for Marriage and Family Therapists' (CAMFT) *Ethical Standards for Marriage and Family Therapists,* Section 1.2 reads: "Marriage and family therapists are cognizant of their potentially influential position with respect to patients, and they avoid exploiting the trust and dependency of such persons. Marriage and family therapists avoid dual relationships with patients that could impair their professional judgment or increase the risk of exploitation. Sexual intercourse, sexual contact or sexual intimacy with patients or a patient's spouse or partner is unethical."[5]

The ethics code of the American Association of Marriage and Family Therapists (AAMFT)[6] expands the definition further. It states, "examples of such dual relationships include, but are not limited to, business or close relationships with clients . . . sexual intimacy with former clients for two years following the termination of therapy is prohibited."

These sections do not prohibit all dual relationships, but only those that could impair professional judgment or increase the risk of exploitation. The key word here is *could* and means "likely to," not "any possibility of" exploitation or impaired judgment. Each case must be evaluated on a case-by-case basis to determine if such exploitation actually happened or was very likely to happen given the dynamics of the situation.

DUAL RELATIONSHIPS: BE VERY CAREFUL

When dual relationships break down, the client begins to see himself or herself as victimized by the therapist. Problematic dual relationships include: socializing with patients, hiring clients to provide secretarial or other services, borrowing money from patients, business and barter agreements and associations, sexual involvement, and engaging in similar acts with ex-patients. Several areas in particular deserve special attention in order to be clear and safe about the legal dilemmas involved.

Barter and business relations. Barter involves trading clinical services for services the client provides. Barter avoids most or all exchange of cash and is appealing because of the possibility of providing services that the client may not otherwise be able to afford. Some barterers simply want to exchange goods and services of value in order to avoid taxation. Opinions vary regarding barter; some consider it acceptable if the barter is "fair and reasonable and not likely to exploit or impair judgment."[7] Current legal and ethical realities, however, strongly suggest that counselors should avoid all business and barter relations with clients.

While barter and business relations are not necessarily bad in themselves, it is an arrangement that can easily go awry along the way. In one incident "a client who bartered bookkeeping services for sessions became dissatisfied with the agreement when she saw the amount of the therapist's earnings. When the therapist refused to change the terms of the agreement, the client angrily threatened to file a complaint and quit therapy."[8] Dual relationships that involve money and barter tempt clients to act out negative transference— easily venting their anger or hostility onto the therapist.

Termination. Some counselors recognize that certain activities practiced during the course of counseling (e.g., business relations or a romance) could lead to charges of undue influence or conflict of interest. Therefore, they may be tempted to terminate the counseling relationship in order to pursue the conflicted activity. Ethical counselors will only terminate a client for sound clinical reasons in the best interests of the client, not for the purpose of engaging in the questionable conduct. In order to safeguard yourself from lawsuit or ethical actions, it is wise to terminate in good faith and to carefully document the causes for termination.

In addition, some say never have any relationship after termination, while others say a relationship is valid within a reasonable time after concluding therapy.[9] We suggest that any involvement with clients after termination is dependent on other factors besides time. These include the basis for termination, the mental and emotional health of the individual(s), and the degree of dependency and personal freedom of the client (are you and your former client really mutually consenting adults?). These termination issues will be addressed more fully in the next chapter.

Supervision. Dual relationships in supervision, while not yet leading to many lawsuits, is another important area to consider. California law prohibits gaining hours toward licensure under supervision by one's spouse or relative by blood or marriage.[10] This law also prohibits supervision by one with whom the supervisee has a personal relationship, presuming that it could undermine the authority or effectiveness of the supervisor. In addition, some licensing laws prohibit gaining clinical hours toward licensure if they are gained while receiving individual or group counseling from one's supervisor. The minimal consequence would be to lose supervised hours toward licensure; such loss is actionable harm and grounds for a suit. Section 4.1 of CAMFT's Ethical Standards states: "Marriage and family therapists are cognizant of their potentially influential position with respect to students and supervisees, and they avoid exploiting the trust and dependency of such persons. Marriage and family therapists therefore avoid dual relationships that impair their professional judgment or increase the risk of exploitation. Sexual intimacy and/or harassment of any kind with students or supervisees is prohibited."[11]

Pastoral counseling. The pastor's role is fraught with dual relationships since his or her parishioners also sit on leadership boards, serve as deacons, and are Sunday school teachers. Especially in smaller communities, some congregants are small business owners who serve the pastor as a customer or client. It may be quite easy for the pastor to get into a counseling situation where he or she is unable to remain objective enough to be helpful to the parishioner being counseled. Pastors will almost always have some level of or potential for dual relationships; avoidance of this is neither possible nor, in some cases, desirable. From our perspective, the trouble with dual relationships remains one of the key reasons why the pastor must be cognizant of his or her counseling limits and aware of when to make appropriate referrals.

RIGID TRENDS IN DUAL RELATIONSHIP LAW

In 1988, the California Psychology Examining Committee [now Board of Psychology] recommended that all psychologists in the state be barred from any and all dual relationships. The Office of the Attorney General responded, in part, that the recommendation was too broad and prohibited conduct "which either should not be prohibited or cannot be avoided in many instances."[12] The state attorney general wisely recognized that in some cultural or community situations, and especially in rural areas, this type of prohibition would do much more harm than good.

The California Board of Behavioral Science Examiners (BBSE), however, has consistently refuted this realistic advice from the attorney general's office. In a recent four-and-one-half year period, every one of their investigations into complaints about dual relationships resulted in charges of unprofessional conduct![13] The board believes that any professional takes an enormous risk in entering any dual relationship because if a complaint is filed, much explanation is required to defend the actions as professionally appropriate.

These trends reveal a harsh judgment against dual relationships in order, it is argued, to provide the best client protection. The results may do more harm than good; this is an example where an increasingly rigid legalism regarding dual relationships can threaten the effective practice of therapy.

RURAL VS. URBAN PRACTICE

A rigid prohibition of dual relationships is nearly impossible in a rural or small-town practice. Our counseling agency, for example, is located in a beautiful but isolated county on California's north coast. The over 100,000 people living within a twenty-five mile radius of our central offices represents just one-third of 1 percent of California's 30 million people. In this setting, it is virtually impossible to have a counseling practice without some dual relationships, because key helpers and service providers are few in number. Urban rule makers may never face such issues and should not be allowed to impose urban rules on rural communities. We ought to view some legal and ethical rules as guidelines, not as rigid absolutes. These guidelines ought to enable the clinician to have some flexibility in decision-making, including considering the dynamics of the rural environment.

This small-town social environment gives rise to a unique set of legal and ethical issues. If the counseling professional takes part at all in community life, then he or she runs the risk of dual relationships. This may be especially true if the professional provides excellent clinical services, as he or she then becomes even more vital and well respected within the community service network. In rural areas one must often practice as a generalist because of the limited resources available. Service availability is a major issue—professionals must be accessible in ways that challenge the boundaries of both competence and dual relationships. This may mean, at times, that the clinician is providing services simply because he or she is the only helper available. While taking care not to harm someone, it may be that some treatment is better than no treatment at all. The professional must "look at the resources of the rural environment for solutions to problems that result from that environment."[14]

CROSS-CULTURAL DYNAMICS

There are also cross-cultural situations that challenge the strict interpretation of dual relationship laws. We have grown up thinking of the United States as a great melting pot, but this concept has its limits. In some American cultural groups the strict application of a WASP (White Anglo-Saxon Protestant) dual relationship statute would severely hinder therapy. This may be complicated by the fact that one's ethnicity or other cultural dynamics further limit service access. Even in large urban centers, ethnic and culture-specific practices exist that mirror the dynamics and relations of the rural practitioner. The strict limits demanded by the legalists would be interpreted as negative judgments about the culture rather than as necessary and appropriate counseling limits.

One minority group that could be damaged by the strict legalist view is the evangelical Christian culture. For good reasons this group holds a significant mistrust of the humanistic psychological mainstream. More than a few clients reveal to us stories of being ridiculed for their faith and having their values blamed as the basis of their psychopathology. While there are extreme reactions to this dynamic by some Christians,[15] it is wise for Christians to be cautious in seeking advice from those who are potentially hostile to the Christian worldview.[16]

As more Christian professionals serve the Christian community, the chances of dual relationships are enhanced considerably. We confess that the combination of working in a small town with a

Christian culture makes avoidance of all dual relationships nearly impossible. Naturally there are boundaries that must be adhered to strictly such as those dealing with sexuality and business partnerships. However, there are other dual relationships that cannot be avoided. Treating a physician for marital and family counseling while also consulting with that physician because he or she may be the only specialist in town is one example of an unavoidable dual relationship. Also, serving someone in counseling who attends the same church as you do may be justifiable.

Creativity in Counseling and Life

We must challenge a rigid state legalism that will chill our willingness to be creative in therapy and, ultimately, harm our clients and patients. One author laments that all this "standardization throughout the field of therapy makes it a minefield, scattered with hidden pitfalls and snares and icky slimes, and thereby greatly diminishes creativity and responsive good work."[17] We must guard against becoming too legalistic in our attempts to protect the client—carefully balancing the demands of client protection with the need for creative risk-taking that ultimately advances our ability to better serve others.

It is difficult enough to battle the spiritual legalism of many in the Christian church without adding a layer of unjust state legalism and rigid interpretation of law that doubly hampers our cause. Why should someone be excluded from choosing a fellow Bible study group member as a therapist during a personal crisis? Having come to trust this person and his or her ability to understand, why must clients be forced to go to one who is safe—no dual relationship risk—but is not known or trusted?

We do not question that it is good to know and respect our limits—this book attempts to reveal and divide the proper boundary between right and wrong practice. We do question where the boundaries are drawn and assert that it is important to not be overly controlled by them. The rigid view barring all dual relationships oversteps the boundary of right practice and should be resisted. Serving the client's best interest does not necessarily mean no other forms of relationship can take place.

Recommendations

It is vital to remain clear and circumspect about professional boundaries. The following recommendations are important considerations in order to avoid conflict of interest, dual relationships, and undue influence.

POLICY ISSUES IN LAW AND ETHICS

We are opposed to the interpretation of law that absolutely bars all dual relationships. We ask all professional counselors to join with us in this resistance. While this may be attainable in an urban environment, it is not possible in rural settings, even if it were altogether desirable. Even in an urban environment, it may not be possible due to the geographic and cultural community a counselor lives and works within. Under the guise of consumer protection, such rigid standards may instead foster, in effect if not in principle, social isolation, alienation, and the breakdown of community.

Strict statutes against dual relations would also bar working with friends, because a friend is one who will "impair your judgment." This concept stands in contradiction to the ideal that Christ promoted in the book of John when he told his disciples, "I no longer call you servants. . . . Instead I have called you friends" (John 15:15). The wisest man who ever lived did not convey the impression that his friendship with his brothers necessarily impaired his ability to judge accurately. While you may wisely (and should seriously consider the decision to) decline to counsel your friends, a friend may come to you and seek help because it can be found in no other.

AVOID ALMOST ALL DUAL RELATIONS

In spite of our assertion that legislation should not forbid *all* dual relationships, because of the risks we have outlined, we recommend that Christian counselors avoid dual relations whenever possible. We suggest that any dual relationship be presumed troublesome and to be avoided if at all feasible. This presumption might be rebutted and work engaged with potential dual relationship problems in only a few select situations. There may be only two situations in which this might be allowed: (1) the counselee provides an indispensable service to you or your family (i.e., specialized medical or legal services that cannot be obtained elsewhere), or (2) the counselee is a member of the same organization (i.e., church or service club), but a close personal relationship does not exist. The following guidelines will help to clarify the issue of dual relationships.

1. *Avoid all dual relations involving the exchange of money.* Business and barter relations should be avoided scrupulously. Paying for costly clinical services and the transferent expression of client troubles through resistant and delinquent payment is struggle enough in counseling relations. Adding a layer of financial dual relationship trouble is clinically unwise and legally stupid.

2. *Avoid personal, especially all romantic and sexual, relations.* We have addressed sex and romance problems in part 2. Avoidance of personal relations while in counseling means no socializing nor meeting together outside of therapy for mutually enjoyed activities. Whether one should engage in such relations when therapy is terminated depends on making a good-faith termination, not for the purpose of being in another relationship together. Also, the therapist must reasonably determine that the client will never pursue therapy with him or her in the future. Since this is nearly impossible to predict, one might best avoid personal relations after counseling. If allowed to develop, it should be made clear that any future counseling should be with someone else.

3. *Avoid counseling with family or friends.* It is wise to refer close family (some would assert all family), friends, associates, and colleagues for counseling with a trusted associate or colleague. Counseling someone already close to you is fraught with all manner of clinical problems and, legally, is becoming impossible to defend. You might justify working with an acquaintance or distant family member, but even this is becoming hard to defend. It is wise to be cautious and refer them to others, explaining to your (possibly annoyed) friends that law and ethics bar professional relations.

4. *Contract clear relations in questionable cases.* If you work with someone with a limited or potential dual relationship, document closely, even contract the relationship on this point. Notes of agreement that you and your client have thoroughly discussed and consent to this arrangement will help greatly if you must defend yourself. Such documentation should include acknowledgement of potential dual relationship problems, justification for it, client consent to it, and agreement about terminating relations and referral if the problem becomes unmanageable.

This last element, while important, is a two-edged sword for the therapist. Those who believe the relationship should have been avoided altogether will argue that the fiscal and emotional costs of termination and referral did not have to be paid by the client. Therefore, while agreement concerning dual relations will be helpful, it may not completely protect against liability. If the absolute bar against any dual relations becomes the law, there will be no defense.

CONCLUSION

The argument against dual relationships—that therapy is contaminated and the risk of negative outcome increases—is valid and must be respected by maintaining a presumption against such relations. The argument is not absolute, however, and in some settings and situations, unavoidable dual relations are manageable. If our society goes the way of increased conflict and obsessive legalization, the margin for acceptable relations will regrettably close. If societal renewal regarding godly and honorable values takes place instead, there is hope that flexibility and rationality may be maintained in these boundary rules.

NOTES

1. *In re The Bible Speaks*, 73 Bankrup. 848 (D. Mass. 1987).

2. Allen E. Bergin, "Values and Religious Issues in Psychotherapy and Mental Health," *American Psychologist* 46, no. 4 (1991): 394–403 (quote from 394).

3. Ibid, 397.

4. See *California Business and Professions Code*, section 4982 (Unprofessional Conduct).

5. California Association for Marriage and Family Therapists, "Ethical Standards for Marriage and Family Therapists," in *The California Therapist* 3, no. 5 (1991): 31–39.

6. The American Association of Marriage and Family Therapists, *Code of Ethical Principles for Marriage and Family Therapists*, section 1.2.

7. Richard Leslie, "Dual Relationships: The Legal View," *The California Therapist* 1, no. 5 (1989): 12.

8. Jane Vinson, "Reflections on Dual Relationships: Therapist Beware," *The California Therapist* 1, no. 5 (1989): 17.

9. Consider the AAMFT's ethical code, for example, which states that "Sexual intimacy with former clients for two years following termination of therapy is prohibited." Section 1.2.

10. See *California Business and Professions Code*, Title 16, section 1833.

11. See "Ethical Standards for Marriage and Family Therapists."

12. Leslie, "Dual Relationships," 12.

13. The California Board of Behavioral Science Examiners (BBSE) oversees the licensing of and disciplinary actions toward Marriage, Family, and Child

Counselors, Clinical Social Workers, and Educational Psychologists.

14. David S. Hargrove, "Ethical Issues in Rural Mental Health Practice," *Professional Psychology: Practice and Research* 17, no. 1 (1986): 23.

15. In our opinion the Bobgans, David Hunt, and Jay Adams overreact and represent extreme responses to the problems of dealing with a humanistic psychological culture that does not understand or respect true Christian values.

16. See Psalm 1:1–6 as a basic challenge on the value of carefully evaluating the ways and wisdom of this world.

17. Bruce Bryant, "Red Flags and the Bureaucratization of Therapy," *The California Therapist* 2, no. 4 (1990): 42.

Chapter 14

Failure to Consult or Refer, Abandonment, and Wrongful Termination

Though I walk in the midst of trouble, you preserve my life; you stretch out your hand against the anger of my foes, with your right hand you save me. The Lord will fulfill his purpose for me; your love, O Lord, endures forever—do not abandon the works of your hands.

Psalm 138:7-8

TODAY YOU ARE WONDERING WHY YOU EVER CHOSE this line of work (or, to avoid the overgeneralizing you so often challenge in your clients, you wonder why you ever accepted this client!). You have received the third phone message in an hour from Cynthia, a deeply troubled woman in her late twenties, who is very angry that you have not returned her call yet. With guilt and frustration, you admit to yourself that you wish that she would just disappear rather than have to deal with her anymore, especially since this is the third day in a row that she has called at least three times.

You have consulted with her psychiatrist several times, and he has confirmed your worst fears. She is as bad off as you surmised, but not so bad off that she can be hospitalized in a public facility, nor does she have the money or insurance to cover private hospitalization. In either case, she has not cooperated with the suggestion that hospitalization might help her.

You are feeling trapped with this client. She is certainly a borderline personality, who also reads like a textbook case of self-defeating personality disorder. She is not, however, so bad off that you can say with certainty that her only child is at risk for abuse or neglect. She is isolated within her church because of her abnormal behavior, and her husband left her a year ago for similar reasons.

Finally, she has made allegations to her pastor and other Christians about your incompetence and inadequacy as a helper, basically lying about your treatment methods. Even when she terminates because of your incompetence, she always manages to reschedule an appointment for one reason or another. She will not improve, nor will she leave; the two of you are stuck in a very messy impasse. No matter how you try to help her, as soon as progress seems to occur in one area, a different crisis overwhelms her, and she imposes a new demand. You think about ways to escape her clutches, and abandonment begins to look very attractive.

Boundaries, again. Each counselor has limits, must know and respect those limits, and must deal with the consequences of these limitations in counseling practice. If these boundaries are not honored, then the counselor is at greater risk of lawsuit. This chapter will inform you about consultation, referral, client abandonment, and proper termination of counseling relationships.

DUTY AND LIABILITY

FAILURE TO CONSULT OR REFER

The Christian counselor has a moral and, increasingly, a legal and ethical duty to consult or refer to other professionals when faced with situations beyond his or her competence or discipline. Failure to do so for the clinical professional can lead to malpractice suits and license revocation action. The pastor's liability is not legal (not yet anyway) but moral and reputational in nature. Consultation and referral duties are outlined in every professional ethics code; generally, such help should be pursued whenever it "is in the best interest of the client."[1]

Two types of violative behavior are most common. The first type is impasse or lack of gain in counseling that reflects client demand beyond the competence or ability of the counselor. This is especially common with a novice helper, who should have supervisory consultation built into his or her practice. Every therapist will encounter such situations, however, and everyone should have some form of collegial consultation opportunities.

A second violation involves the counselor who crosses professional boundaries and becomes at risk for unauthorized practice of medicine, law, or psychology. Referral to other professionals is essential when encountering cross-disciplinary issues. Christian counselors who work in medical or psychiatric settings, in criminal justice settings, or as divorce counselors and mediators should be especially sensitized to the duty to consult and refer.

Client Abandonment

The Christian counselor must be careful not to abandon his or her clients or congregants. The duty of care operates continuously until counseling relations are validly terminated. Abandonment is the unjust and harmful termination of helping relations that can lead to malpractice suit, license revocation, or loss of congregant membership. The worst case is the counselor who summarily or abruptly terminates counseling without warning the client. The possibility for client harm here is significant, and suits for abandonment and wrongful termination are on the rise.[2]

"There are many instances when the [counselor] is not available to the client. [Counselors] leave town, are transferred, and give up [counseling] practice. Further, they become ill, take vacations, sabbaticals and, occasionally, just do not go to work. At such times, the [counselor] must take precautions so that his or her behavior will not be construed as abandonment."[3]

Abandonment often occurs with clients who become threatening, fail to pay their bill, or need help when the counselor is unavailable. While counselors are not required to continue services to threatening or nonpaying clients, neither can they abandon them for these reasons. At the very least, referral to another helper is called for. Counselors must also be careful about the lack of services to needy clients during long-term absences (i.e., vacations and illnesses). Provision should be made for consistent coverage during these absences by referral or collegial care for key clients.

Finally, some clients are highly resistant to change or are just not liked by the counselor. Disliked clients are a reality; the helper who says, Will Rogers fashion, "I never met a client I didn't like," is probably in denial. In both these situations, counselors can be trapped in an uneasy paradox. Valid and ethically suggested attempts at referral can instead be perceived and reacted to by the client as abandonment. No matter what evidence you might present at trial showing impasse and the need for referral, the client may undercut your testimony by asserting that they were helped simply "by seeing my therapist faithfully every week."

WRONGFUL TERMINATION

Liability for wrongful termination is closely related to both abandonment and duties to consult and refer. Termination is called for when continued therapy would no longer produce any substantial benefits. The ideal case, of course, is termination by mutual agreement because the client has achieved his or her therapeutic goals. Some counseling relationships, unfortunately, end far short of this ideal.

Liability risks increase in cases of prolonged therapeutic stalemate, lack of client improvement, and unresolved tension or conflict between counselor and client. The counselor's incentive is increased to abandon the client or withdraw psychologically and make himself or herself unavailable for appointments. Clients may stop therapy prematurely and then become angry about the time and money spent with no appreciable gain. Dependent clients, however, may resist termination or referral, riding out a stalemate in denial or in hope of eventual improvement.

Another dilemma is the tension between long-term supportive therapy and short-term problem-solving intervention. Clients with quick-fix expectations, consumer advocates, client employers, and insurance companies are all pressing short-term treatment as a normative model. There is no empirical validation for the idea that short-term treatment can be applied successfully to everyone. The drive of multiple client, social, and financial forces in this direction, however, is creating its own ethic—one that will deliver unpleasant consequences if violated. Simon recognized this dilemma a decade ago:

> It is often very difficult to distinguish between the patient who requires years of maintenance and supportive therapy to function at a job or stay out of an institution from the patient who is stalemated in a non-therapeutic relationship with the therapist. The stalemated patient tends to resist any efforts at making internal or external changes [living] his life in and for the therapy. Should the therapist attempt to terminate such a relationship, he may fear that the patient will undergo a severe emotional crisis or a psychotic episode. Nevertheless, if the patient is truly stalemated and a sustained therapeutic effort has been made, the patient should be referred. . . .[4]

MANAGING COUNSELING IMPASSE

Managing client impasse in counseling will yield better outcomes for the client and reduced risk of suit for the counselor. Learn to ask yourself this key question: Can I effectively help this person with the problem he or she presents, or should I refer him or her to more competent help? Since we conceptualize therapy as a three-stage process, we will consider this question in the context of each stage.

BEGINNING STAGE: AM I COMPETENT ENOUGH?

In the beginning stage of counseling, a careful diagnostic evaluation of the client is in order to determine whether or not you are competent to treat this particular problem with this particular client. Part of the diagnostic process must include a treatment plan that not only defines the problem but also considers the resources that may be necessary to help properly treat this client. The importance of accuracy in client assessment and *competency-based self-assessment* at this phase cannot be overlooked. If the client is beyond the scope of your practice, not only will proper referral best help him or her, but it will be easiest to make early in the counseling relationship.

The quality of the referral is critically important as it is properly presumed that referral is made to *someone better equipped to help* this person. Counselors may be held liable for a referral that turned sour because they did not properly evaluate the quality or appropriateness of the referral. Clients may easily be left feeling hopeless and angry if they were referred and could not be helped either by the counselor they approached or the person to whom the counselor referred them. Careful evaluation, including in-depth questioning and references on referral people, is a must.

Referral by Christian counselors. Christian counselors need to be especially careful about referrals, not only for the competency of the referral but also for spiritual values. A referral to a skilled specialist can be sabotaged if that person denigrates your client's faith or perceives it as part of his or her pathology. The client, and often the client's pastor, will blame you for making the referral. A sour referral, though legally risky, may not result in a lawsuit; more likely it will cause real harm to one's professional reputation as a reliable helper within the Christian community.

The ideal, of course, is to make referral to Christian professionals who are competent in the problem area and committed to faith in Christ. Short of this ideal, we encourage network relations with competent professionals who, even though they may not be Christians, will respect your client's Christian values. We advocate for respect of our clients' faith and spiritual values with those trusted, competent professionals to whom we refer them. We have found many professional colleagues who, though they are not believers, will respect our clients' values and provide a good service.

We do not agree with the judgment that a non-Christian helper can never help but only harm the Christian. Christian counselors and pastors should guard against this false generalization—a real temptation when one experiences a nonbeliever who attacks or ridicules faith in Christ. This attitude creates legal risk for the pastor or counselor who hopelessly hangs on to a client or parishioner, creating an impasse that increases the risk that the client will be abandoned.

MIDDLE STAGE OF COUNSELING

The middle phase of counseling normally is the longest period during which most treatment occurs. Once involved in this phase, it can be difficult for the client *and* the counselor to disengage from it and refer the client. In previous chapters we have outlined steps that need to be taken in order to properly consult or refer in cases of potential suicide or homicide.[5] One of the tragedies of the *Nally* case is how Grace Community Church's pastoral staff, insisting on their competence, waited until the last minute to consult and refer. This, combined with the fact that Nally had become quite dependent on their intervention, no doubt contributed to his success in committing suicide.[6]

Client dependencies are normative in the middle stage of counseling; consultation and referral must be done carefully, with consideration of the adverse impact on the client. Emergency help, psychiatric consultation, even hospitalization may be advised as some clients work through repressed traumas and buried pain. For the sake of legal protection, if nothing else, it is very important to carefully *document* all steps you take to manage an impasse in this phase of the counseling process.

Middle-stage consultation. It is vital to consult with one or more colleagues in order to evaluate the care needed and to brainstorm about potential options for treatment. This kind of consultation will keep the counselor from being discouraged and overwhelmed, better able to plan continuing service provision. It can also be a form of continuing education by the way it delivers new knowledge and skill in the face of the clinical challenge. If the consultation leads to a confirmation that this client is beyond your professional help, then the next steps must be seriously considered.

Middle-stage referral. It is critically important to prepare to refer the client to other competent counselors. For some clients referral can feel like rejection and they may use the process to further label themselves as beyond help. This will be especially true with clients who are passive, codependent, or at least moderately borderline. Poor and abrupt referral may anger the client, who may then sabotage the referral process and threaten charges of abandonment or lawsuit. So, do not abruptly terminate a client with whom you have reached an impasse. Rather, thoroughly discuss referral with the client in at least one appointment prior to making the referral(s). When referring, if at all possible, give the client several names to choose from.

Referral follow-up. Follow up your client when you have referred him or her to another professional. This should be done to determine whether or not the client has seen the helper and to determine the usefulness of the helper to the client. When appropriate, it can be beneficial to affirm to clients that you will see them again once this specific aspect of their treatment process is resolved. Ongoing professional relations are common even when referral must be made. If the client does not go to the referral(s), call or write to him or her about the risks incurred when he or she does not follow through. Again, keep a copy of all written correspondence and document all contacts and procedures in your case notes. Chart your rationale for referring or terminating the client at this time.

FINAL STAGE OF COUNSELING

In the final phase of counseling, the client and counselor prepare to conclude treatment and bring successful closure to counseling. Ideally this is a smooth process, with counselor and client(s) agreeing on the time and manner in which to finalize the treatment process. In many situations, for a variety of reasons, the final phase of counseling may not draw to a smooth conclusion.

Working toward good termination. Maintenance of treatment gains is a key goal in the concluding phase of counseling. As you near conclusion, it is helpful to summarize together what has happened in a way that best benefits the client. It can be useful to brainstorm numerous ideas for helping the client keep the gains he or she has so diligently worked to achieve. Discuss what worked and what did not work for them in terms of what you had to give as a therapist. A written summary can be quite helpful because it assists clients in remembering what was covered in therapy. Ask your clients to call in six to eight weeks to schedule an appointment to update on gains and possibly deal with any unresolved or newly discovered issues. Lastly, finalize any financial arrangements and return any books or other materials exchanged.

Managing difficult terminations. Should counseling head toward a premature conclusion, four steps will safeguard you legally and provide the best care for your client(s). These are: (1) consult, (2) prepare referrals, (3) discuss premature termination, and (4) make and follow up referrals. If your client decides to terminate counseling prematurely, it is important to advise the client(s) of the potential risks of his or her choice. Respect the client's right to terminate treatment, but give suggestions you may have for continued assistance, including names of other helpers. Within a short time after termination, write a follow-up letter to your client including suggestions and referral sources.

The concept of open termination may be advised with some difficult or chronic clients. This refers to termination with an explicit invitation to return to counseling if needed in the future. It is premised on the idea that "once a client, always a client." In some ways this is implicit with most counseling terminations. Some clients need to take this thought with them to blunt concerns about rejection and to deal with the anxiety of never seeing their counselor again. Others may abuse this, and boundaries may need to be carefully drawn to protect yourself.

Clients who resist termination must be carefully evaluated as to the reasons for this resistance. You may take an entirely different approach with a highly dependent client versus one with separation anxiety and little support network outside of counseling. Sometimes inviting family members, friends, or the client's pastor to one or more termination sessions can be helpful in this transition. With many, tapering back the frequency of sessions to eventual extinction is recommended. Switch from active therapy to a maintenance mode, noting this transition in your notes, and stretch out the time between sessions. Another year of therapy may be manageable and defensible for both counselor and client if the client is seen every three to six months.

Preference for Group Practice

We strongly recommend that Christian counselors affiliate themselves with other practitioners. This facilitates the ongoing need for consultation and referral that exists throughout professional life. This also protects against malpractice suits by planning proper coverage for clients' emergencies and when therapists are on vacations and days off. Group practice may be done in a variety of ways. Pastors in multistaff churches have a built-in support network; pastors in small churches should explore ministerial associations and seek others to join in voluntary support and consultation groups.

Professional counselors and clinicians may work in hospitals, clinics, or agency settings with peer consultation and support built in. Private practitioners may affiliate in office-sharing or more informal ways that serve mutual consultation and client coverage needs. While care must be taken about consultative and other liabilities among private practitioners (see chapter 21), the risks of group practice are far reduced vis-à-vis the solo counselor. Cohen states:

> Psychologists, psychiatrists and other mental health professionals engaged in applied work would do well to join together in group practice if they are unaffiliated with teaching or service institutions. The opportunity for formal and informal meeting with colleagues to discuss treatment approaches is indispensable and is to be much preferred to sequestering oneself professionally.
>
> Group practice also facilitates the provision of twenty-four-hours-a-day, seven-days-a-week coverage for the patient who may have an emergency or a crisis. Another advantage of group practice is the advantage it offers if a malpractice action does arise. The competent professional whose work is respected by colleagues will have no difficulty in finding sympathetic expert witnesses should that need arise.[7]

Counseling and psychotherapy is not a job for one person working in an isolated manner. It is at best a practice that incorporates many members (see 1 Cor.12:14–21) to be of the greatest help to those who are in need. Much harm has ensued for individuals who have been abandoned or wrongfully terminated because of a failure to recognize and utilize these practices.[8]

Conclusion

In our clinical experience, we recognize three categories of therapeutic challenge. These are clients who are (1) easy to treat because they readily fall within our range of skill and interest; (2) difficult to treat because they challenge our present skill levels; and (3) not proper to treat because they fall out of our skill range. In the first instance, the counselor can serve well and with confidence. In the second, the helper must learn and consult to be effective, always prepared to refer if needed. In order to avoid charges of counseling impasse and the attendant risks of suit, referral should always be made in the third instance. The wise and humble counselor will admit to and respect these limits, taking specialized training if he or she chooses to become competent in a new area.

NOTES

1. See National Association of Social Workers, *NASW Code of Ethics* (section II. F. 8.) (Washington, D.C.: NASW, 1980).

2. Daniel Hogan, *A Review of Malpractice Suits in the United States,* vol. 3, *The Regulation of Psychotherapists* (Cambridge, Mass.: Ballinger, 1979).

3. Barton E. Bernstein, "Malpractice: Future Shock of the 1980s," *Social Casework* 62 (1981): 179.

4. Robert I. Simon, *Psychiatric Interventions and Malpractice: A Primer for Liability Prevention* (Springfield, Ill.: Thomas Publishers, 1982), 80.

5. See chapters 9 and 10.

6. Review chapter 4.

7. Ronald J. Cohen, *Malpractice: A Guide for Mental Health Professionals* (New York: The Free Press, 1979), 270.

8. For an excellent discussion of the impact of these behaviors on clients, see Uriel Last and Zipora Schutz, "Patients' Reported Initial Reactions to Abrupt Disruption of Psychotherapy: The Aftermath of a Doctors' Strike," *Psychotherapy* 27, no. 3 (1990): 436–44.

Chapter 15

God or Mammon? Fees and Money Issues in Christian Counseling

Be shepherds of God's flock that is under your care, serving . . . not because you must, but because you are willing, as God wants you to be; not greedy for money, but eager to serve; not lording it over those entrusted to you, but being examples to the flock. And when the Chief Shepherd appears, you will receive the crown of glory that will never fade away.

1 Peter 5:2–4

As any professional counselor can attest, the issues surrounding money and fees in counseling are fraught with trouble. The call to ministry is soberly balanced by the need to earn an income from counseling. Yet there exists sharp awareness of some clients' unwillingness, even resistance to payment and the inequities in many clients' ability to pay for counseling services. As young men in college preparing for seminary, graduate school, and professional counseling practice, we envisioned helping money-poor clients in exchange for food or other services that they could provide. Though that vision remains with us as professionals in midlife, the process is filled with demands and complications that our twenty-something minds had not even conceived.

While many of these complications are common to all counselors, the Gospel presents challenges which secular therapists do not consider deeply, if at all. For example, Jesus intends for the poor to receive help in their troubles, yet counseling is an expensive enterprise. While many of these issues are not legal matters per se, conflicts concerning these issues are increasingly leading to lawsuits. We will clarify the law and suggest ways for Christian counselors to honorably arrange their financial relations with clients to both earn a living and fulfill their ministry call.

GOD OR MAMMON?

As with many other topics considered so far, honorable client fee relations require setting and maintaining right boundaries. These boundaries should adhere to biblical standards, ethical guidelines, and the demands of the law. Also, as we have shown with respect to other legal issues that impact the counseling process, financial matters generate resistance that sometimes become therapeutic issues.

WHY PAY FOR CHRISTIAN COUNSELING?

Payment for professional services within a Christian context often raises the question of why people must pay for ministry.[1] Let's consider the words of Jesus as he sent out the disciples, commissioning them for ministry: "Freely you have received, freely give. Do not take along any gold or silver or copper in your belts; take no bag for the journey, or extra tunic, or sandals or a staff; for the worker is worth his keep" (Matt. 10:8b–10). Two statements here are central to our consideration: *"freely you have received, freely give,"* and *"the worker is worth his keep."*

Most people who question having to pay for Christian counseling seem to have the first statement in mind. There is a strong expectation by many that Christian counselors should not charge (*freely give*) because they have received freely from the Lord. However, if we consider the entire passage, it is apparent that Jesus does not expect ministers to live on nothing. He challenged the disciples to rely on God to move in the lives of people, and the receivers' response to the Gospel would include provision for the disciple's physical needs, "for the workman is worth his keep."

There is no charge for sharing the Gospel message, but those who toil to help the saved grow to maturity are to be cared for by financial provision. It has long been accepted in Christian church history to pay ministers for those tasks that the laity do not have the time, training, or expertise to do themselves. Even pastors who provide counseling without cost do not give *free* counseling—their time is paid for by the church, and they must use the time and energy they give to counseling wisely.

The worthiness of the Christian counselor. Is the professional Christian counselor worth his or her keep? Preparation to minister as a professional counselor requires a very significant investment of time, energy, and money. The professional therapist will study for six to ten years in college, seminary, and graduate school in order to earn master's and doctor's degrees, credentials necessary for professional counseling. In a growing number of states the counselor must also gain thousands of hours of supervised internship experience, usually taking another two to four years. After the internship hours are compiled, the person becomes eligible to take rigorous written exams and oral exams as the final step in order to gain the professional license.[2]

By the time the counseling professional sees his or her first client as a licensed professional, he or she is often thirty or more years old and has spent tens of thousands of dollars in the quest. For the Christian professional there is the additional necessity of becoming adept at handling the Word of God and effectively integrating a balanced and godly approach to helping people. It is never an easy process, but it does provide the opportunity to gain the expertise, skills, and wisdom in Christ in order to become an effective counselor.

Supporting full-time ministry. The Christian professional charges money for counseling because it is truly a full-time ministry. Fees are necessary so that we can ably focus our time and skills on helping those who are in need. Many pastors will admit that they lack the expertise, time, or objectivity to do quality counseling beyond a few sessions. There is no question that it is costly for the counselor to be available to help, including the provision of office space and other overhead expenses. That counseling is expensive is in large part due to the fact that practice overhead consumes one-quarter to one-half of all fee income.

Traditionally, counselors have argued that people benefit most from counseling if they not only invest their time but their money as well. If you have to pay for something, you are less apt to squander its value. Others, however, assert that this is a myth because there are a variety of other variables which influence client benefit and gain.[3] So, while money may have only a limited role in motivating client gain, it is still important for people to cover the costs of counseling so that qualified helpers can be available. Setting and collecting fees, however, is a difficult boundary issue that so readily exposes the struggles with money in both the client and the counselor.

FEE DISPUTES

Therapists have a long history of fee-related guilt. Charging money for professional counseling is necessary but difficult for most counselors. The "inability to confront payment problems has been correlated with therapist inexperience and difficulty establishing appropriate boundaries."[4] When clients become delinquent in bill-paying, this issue must be addressed in therapy and resolved creatively. Some possible options include reduction of fees, referral to an appropriate helping agency, or seeking financial help to underwrite some of the client's fee.

Lawsuits and disciplinary actions regarding fee issues are on the rise.[5] Clients sue following impasse and conflict over the money spent for counseling. Common client charges include unreasonable payment, fraudulent billing, harassment and infliction of emotional distress regarding delinquent payment collection, and breach of confidentiality and defamation (for unauthorized release of information to collection and credit agencies or lawyers for action on delinquent bills). Lawsuits represent a serious breakdown of counselor-client relations and tend to be far more costly, to both the counselor's pocketbook and reputation, than they are worth.

FEE DISPUTE SAFEGUARDS

In order to protect yourself from unnecessary fee disputes, we recommend that you consistently practice the following safeguards.

1. *Have a clear written policy for all fees and fee-related issues.* These should include fee schedules, client and third-party payment relations, billing procedures and due dates, procedures for handling delinquent fees, and whether and how missed appointments are charged. Include a brief written description of these policies in your contract,[6] and be sure that each client understands it, signs it, and receives a copy prior to rendering services. You must consistently practice what you state your policy to be; any changes of policy must also be written and disclosed to clients.

2. *Be sure that your fees are reasonable.* Fees must be the same or reasonably close to what a comparably trained and certified professional charges in your geographic area. If possible, in order to provide service to more people, develop a fee scale based on client income and family size.

3. *When clients become delinquent, confront the problem early.* The earlier the fee problem is addressed, the easier it can be addressed in a flexible way. Do not wait until a large bill has accumulated, when addressing it is likely to intimidate, embarrass, or anger the client. Consider adopting a policy that suspends counseling for a time after a delinquent bill accrues to three or four sessions payment, to help the client reduce this figure.
4. *Where applicable, collect fees in advance.* Some types of work, such as child custody evaluations and court-ordered treatment, are notoriously likely to lead to payment problems. It is fair and reasonable to require payment in advance, perhaps placing it into an escrow account.
5. *Use great caution if you use a collection agency.* Some writers caution against use of any collection agencies.[7] If you use a collection agency, be careful to apprise the client at intake that such procedure may be used as a last resort. Naturally it is best to resolve the matter without this alternative, but, for those clients who do not take responsibility for their bills, it may be a necessary risk. In extreme cases an attorney may be consulted to aid in collection.
6. *Never sue your client.* They may sue you, and in extreme cases you may countersue, but never, ever sue your client. Biblically, legally, financially, and reputationally, the costs of such action will always outweigh any benefits.
7. *Give away some counseling time.* Both the American Psychological and American Psychiatric Associations require members to do pro bono work. In addition, it is a fundamental element of biblical Christianity to give to the poor; so if a client refuses to pay, you may want to write this off and consider it as part of your contribution.

AVOIDING INSURANCE FRAUD

One of the more frequently cited reasons for licensure suspension and revocation in California is insurance fraud violations.[8] Fraud often occurs simply out of ignorance, but a growing number of cases reveal deliberate misrepresentation. In either case the counseling professional can doubly suffer—fraud is a crime that can yield prosecution, and insurance companies are becoming more aggressive in filing civil suits. Often, the counseling professional is asked to support a client's misrepresentation in order to help them cover counseling costs. Do not yield to this pitfall; instead, commit yourself to a practice guided fully by biblical integrity.

INSURANCE AND THIRD-PARTY BILLING SAFEGUARDS

1. *Never bill for services that have not been provided.* This kind of fraud is indefensible and easily discovered if the insurance company decides to check. Also, in the case of supervision, review your supervisee's work—you are fully liable for any mistakes or misrepresentations. This especially includes signing forms by supervisors without the supervisee's cosignature—both signatures should be present, and the supervisor must be assured of services rendered.

2. *Be careful about billing for missed or cancelled appointments.* Do not assume billing for these appointments is acceptable as the insurer may disallow it or even consider it fraudulent. Make sure of each specific third-party policy on this matter, especially in any contracts with health maintenance groups and other managed health care providers. If you bill for these sessions, make certain they are clearly noted as missed or cancelled.

3. *Maintain integrity with reimbursement limits.* Do not change or alter diagnoses in order to fit third-party reimbursement criteria. Also, do not change or stretch the date of the onset of the client's episode or the beginning of counseling to fit these criteria. Finally, do not bill multiperson sessions (i.e., couples, family, or group services) as individual sessions with each client. While this may satisfy your client's need for covered services, you run the risk of insurance fraud. On the other hand, if individual therapy is being supplied in conjunction with marital or family work, there is usually some clinical justification for noting primary individual diagnoses on Axis I and Axis II.

4. *Maintain staff integrity.* The counselor must be sure that administrative or clerical staff do not revise diagnostic codes in order to ensure insurance reimbursement. A psychologist discovered this was being done, without his knowledge, by the staff of an employing hospital.[9] Ignorance is no excuse before a judge, and pleading in court that you did not know what your staff was doing will only further weaken your professional credibility.

5. *Do not fail to clarify the provider's licensure status.* This should be clear to the client prior to commencing service provision. Again, we recommend a formal agreement reviewed and signed in the

initial session.[10] In addition, the provider must be clear about licensure status to the insurer. If a psychological assistant, intern, or other unlicensed person is providing the service, billing claims must clearly indicate who provided the service and a title indicating licensing status. Do not just list the supervisor, as this implies that the supervisor provided the service.

6. *If you waive client fees, inform the insurer.* Do not waive the client's copayment or in any way manipulate fees against a vendor. If you give the insurance client a fee benefit, you must inform the vendor that you are doing so, passing on the benefit to the insurer. Some practices with sliding fee schedules may bill insurance at the top rate while giving the client a discount rate. This is fraudulent because it causes the insurance company to pay more than they have agreed to pay in their contracts with employers.

CONCLUSION

The charge in Peter's epistle at the beginning of this chapter to serve without greed is an indispensable attribute for the Christian counseling professional. Professional counseling ministry is honorable work, and making money from it should be done without guilt or defensiveness. As Christian professionals we should be committed to making counseling available to as many people as possible by keeping fees as reasonable as possible. Many Christian therapists do this by having a sliding fee scale, billing insurance, applying for provider status in employee benefit and managed health care programs, and seeking contributions from individuals, churches, and foundations. Doing these things with integrity will serve as many in the church as possible and will also be a powerful apologetic to those who will charge greedy or unjust practice.

NOTES

1. This section is a revision of an article by Peter Mosgofian, "Why Pay for Christian Counseling?" in *Parakaleo* 3, no. 1 (1991): 1–2; published quarterly by The Redwood Family Institute, Eureka, California.

2. The authors are using the California licensure experience as an example here.

3. Jeffrey Danco, "The Ethics of Fee Practices: An Analysis of Presuppositions and Accountability," *Journal of Psychology and Theology* 10, no. 1 (1982): 13–21.

4. Robert G. Meyer, E. R. Landis, and J. R. Hays, *Law for the Psychotherapist* (New York: Norton, 1988), 37.

5. See the APA Insurance Trust Study, in S. Fulero, "Insurance Trust Releases Malpractice Statistics," *State Psychological Association Affairs* 19, no. 1 (1987): 4–5.

6. See appendix A for a sample copy of an agreement form. Please remember that the rules may vary from state to state, so check your state statutes for the best way to prepare this form.

7. See Meyer, Landis, and Hays, *Law for the Psychotherapist*, 38.

8. See, for example, "Board of Behavioral Science Examiners Disciplinary Actions," *The California Therapist* 3, no. 6 (1991): 34–35.

9. See Kenneth Pope, "Ethical and Malpractice Issues in Hospital Practice," *American Psychologist* 45, no. 9 (1990): 1066–70.

10. See appendices A, B, and C for copies of the therapy contract forms used in our offices.

PART V

Special Counseling Modes and Controversial Cases

Chapter 16

Marriage, Family, and Child Therapy; Divorce and Group Counseling

You do have to develop a sense of power that the family has and if you can't find your own way for taking over, you are probably not going to be of much use. . . . Think of five or six people who have been living together through thick and thin, and there is a lot of thick in any family—you know, divorces and deaths, fights with neighbors and attacks by the rabbi, financial trouble and financial luck, which is almost as bad—you name it, and they have gone through it. Along comes this character who thinks that by a few extra words he is going to change their way of living, and that is pretty weird. The whole process of assuming that any individual is going to walk into a group of five or six and take over is weird. . . .
It's a major move; it's a massive political group process and you need to get started with some sense of how important it is for you to carry some kind of power, some kind of political know-how. There are . . . ways of doing this.[1]

Carl Whitaker

MOST GENERALIST PRACTITIONERS ENGAGE IN SOME LEVEL of counseling with couples, with families, or in group settings. More and more specialists work exclusively in these areas. There are several important legal issues that impact effective clinical treatment of marriages and families, children and adolescents, divorcing people, and groups.

MARRIAGE AND FAMILY THERAPY

We will consider three primary legal issues in work with couples and families: informed consent, confidentiality and records release, and the development of a standard of care as a basis for marital and family malpractice.

INFORMED CONSENT

At the onset of marital and family therapy, it is wise to discuss boundary issues, expectations, and possible outcomes of the counseling process with the clients. Informed consent must be undertaken with care in order to meet therapeutic goals and adhere to legal standards of care. Therapeutic outcome is enhanced by couples or families joining the treatment plan and not being intimidated by the possible outcomes of the therapeutic process. This is a delicate balance that is difficult to achieve successfully. The counselor must disclose the expected outcomes, including possible negative ones, with clients.[2] This legal dimension adds a potential threat to the process that may discourage some clients from participation in therapy. However, in order to protect your counseling practice, it may be imperative to mention, if not discuss, these potentially negative outcomes.

CONFIDENTIALITY

There are several avenues a therapist can take with regard to confidentiality issues in marital and family therapy. The therapist may choose to require that secrets will not be kept from each other in therapy. On the other hand the therapist may decide to treat each family member's confidences as though that person were an individual client, with no private information divulged to the other family members. Another option is for the therapist to indicate that, in general, no secrets will be kept from the spouse or family, yet the client retains the right to request that any specific information be kept confidential. We recommend that counselor and marital or family client contract together, after discussion and agreement, about which style of confidential relations will be maintained.

Related to this, the therapist may inform the client(s) that they may ask the therapist to help them to go about sharing secret information with other family members. Yet another option is for the therapist to reserve the right to share the information as he or she deems best for the interest of the entire family system. From a clinical standpoint, we think that confidences need to be considered a process item, not solely an item of legal or ethical content. In many dysfunctional families, the keeping of secrets may in fact be the pathology, or a pathological aspect, of the family system. If this is true, then it is even more vital that confidentiality issues are successfully resolved.

TOWARD MARITAL AND FAMILY MALPRACTICE

Recall, from chapter two, that malpractice is the failure to attain to the standard of proper care in any given case, a failure which leads to client harm and the search for money damages. The extension of malpractice standards to new modes of therapy suggests that lawsuits for negligent marital and family therapy will begin to appear by the twenty-first century. This may happen when therapy results in a divorce that is not wanted by one party. Marital therapy that results in sexual relations between the therapist and the wife are already being litigated against counseling and pastoral offenders.[3] The power dynamics in family therapy, alluded to by Carl Whitaker in the opening quote, reflect the struggle for therapeutic control and directive nature of family therapy that suggests increased legal risk. The standard of care for marriage and family therapy is now developing; malpractice lawsuits will give the standard power against those failing to keep its boundaries.

COUNSELING CHILDREN AND ADOLESCENTS

Children and adolescents present unique practice and liability considerations because of their dependency upon parents or legal guardians. Since the parent(s) or guardian(s) must be consulted or related to as an integral part of the treatment process, minors quite possibly represent the foremost reason for family and systems oriented psychotherapies. We will consider the privacy rights of minors and evaluate elements of higher liability risk. *It is vital to verify this general information within your state, because there is wide variance from state to state as to the specific elements of law.*

PRIVACY RIGHTS OF MINORS

Generally, parents have the right to control private information regarding their minor children, including rights to know certain information regarding their children. For example, mental health professionals generally must advise parents when they are treating minors for sexual assault or substance abuse. Most counseling situations with a minor require parental notification and consent for treatment (see appendix G), the failure of which can lead to suit or licensure discipline. In divorced families, consent is necessary from the parent with sole or primary custody.

However, in some situations the parents do not control the child's private information or decisions regarding treatment help. A child over twelve years of age (or thirteen or fourteen depending on your state) can be treated without the parent's consent if, in the opinion of the counselor, he or she is mature enough to participate intelligently in outpatient counseling and meets one or more of three conditions. The minor must (1) present a danger of serious physical harm to self or others, (2) have been the victim of incest, or (3) have been the victim of child abuse. When a child twelve years or older seeks counseling relating to the diagnosis or treatment of drug- or alcohol-related problems, the parents are to be contacted unless the counselor determines that it is not in the best interests of the child. The counselor must note in the clinical record what efforts, if any, were made to involve the parents in counseling and, if none, why it was unnecessary or inappropriate.

There are certain circumstances in which psychotherapists may control privilege. An example is a child under sixteen years of age who the therapist has reasonable cause to believe is the victim of a crime, and the disclosure of this information is in the best interests of the child. Another situation occurs when a therapist believes that the child's emotional state is such that he or she is a danger to self or other persons or property. If the therapist has knowledge or reasonable suspicion that the child is a victim of child abuse, he or she must report it to the proper authorities.[4] The counselor also controls privilege if subpoenaed in criminal proceedings involving an alleged child abuser. If the child is under sixteen and has communicated information relevant to the case, the therapist must determine if disclosure will be in the best interest of the child. If it would not be, the therapist must claim privilege.

ADOLESCENCE: LIABILITY AND PRACTICE ISSUES

Counseling teenagers is challenging due to their rapid development, mistrust of authority, and general unwillingness to be open with therapists about their thoughts and feelings. Perhaps the most common exception is their willingness to be critical of their parents' actions and values. Once the counselor establishes a relationship of trust with a teenager, it is essential to maintain that trust.

Teen suicide. The high suicide rate among the nation's youth is a tragic reality.[5] Clergy and counselors must learn how to effectively handle this important problem because of the increasing trend for teens to choose this option for dealing with their pain and despair. When suicide is an issue with a teenager, a written agreement should be drafted to outline the intervention steps that will be taken. Legally, as we have explained in chapters 9 and 10, the Christian helper has a duty to intervene in cases where a person is suicidal or homicidal. In virtually every case this would mean that serious suicidal or homicidal intent, with a clear sense of lethality and means, requires that the helper inform parents and any intended specified victims. The exceptions might be in cases of abusive parents or if an agreement was signed negating the option of informing parents.

Sexual behavior. A conflict between ethical and legal duties faces the Christian counselor when a minor confides to a counselor that he or she is sexually involved with someone seventeen or older. California law, for example, stipulates that consenting minors over fourteen may be sexually involved, and the counselor is not required to report such activity. However, at this time, any voluntary sexual activity between a minor over fourteen-years-old with a minor under fourteen-years-old is considered a reportable offense for a mandated reporter. We advise each professional to check with his or her state's attorney general's office to determine the limits of confidentiality in this area. This helps resolve the legal issues but does not resolve the ethical dilemma. It is wise to prepare in advance how to treat this delicate problem in a manner that respects confidentiality and trust and adheres to Christ's intent.

The rigid or neglectful home. Some types of counseling situations develop problems of treating children who are from neglectful or overly strict homes but who do not have the need for child protective services intervention. This may involve parents who allow any activity at all or who forbid a child's participation in peer, school, or even Christian events—parents who are far too lenient or too strict and so harm their child in the counselor's judgment. Since the family boundaries are disturbed and inappropriate, the guidelines of ethical counseling are often challenged and legal risk increased. It is essential that counselors keep careful file notes regarding decisions and the basis for them.

Referral practice. Making responsible referrals is a critical dimension of any counseling practice.[6] A counselor is most apt to refer a teenager for help elsewhere when the helper recognizes his or her own limits of competence, the need for medical or other professional help, or the teenager's need for a residential treatment program. In any case it is vital for the helper to carefully attend to the legal and ethical risks of failure to consult, abandonment, and wrongful termination. For example, it is important for any counselor who refers a teenager to a residential treatment program to be very familiar with the treatment methods employed. A poorly considered referral may only result in a disappointed family, but it could also result in a lawsuit based on negligence.

CONSENT FOR TREATMENT OF A MINOR

Since parents generally have access to their child's records, it is best to either inform the child of this status or to have the parent(s) sign a consent to treatment that releases the child to treatment without the concern of disclosure to the parent. In this regard it is important to consider children younger than fourteen as ones with whom the therapist should not presume an ability to maintain confidentiality. This is a general rule and can vary depending on the situation. However, much research supports the concept that many minors older than fourteen are capable of making well-informed treatment decisions.[7]

For those minors fifteen and older, it is often helpful if the therapist provides a pretreatment family meeting in which the parameters of therapy and confidentiality are discussed. Then a written service agreement could be signed, and the therapist and minor would be protected from legal and counseling blunders. The agreement should include full details of the limits and conditions of confidentiality. Also, the extent of family involvement should be discussed and agreed upon prior to treatment. All participating parties should sign the agreement, and it should be placed in the client's file.

If you are going to convince the older child of the therapeutic value of sharing personal information, you need to be able to assure that most of this information will be kept confidential. Written agreements should emphasize to parents that the counselor will give a summary of information and progress but will not give detailed information about what the child shares in the counseling appointment. If a parent should refuse to cooperate with your request for confidentiality, then it would be best to resolve this matter with the child's parent before proceeding with therapy. The parent or guardian may have a valid reason for not wanting to sign such an agreement, and it would be best to explore those reasons in an initial appointment with the parent before continuing with the child.

One can get into awkward legal and ethical dilemmas if the counselor refuses treatment to the child because the parent will not comply with a signed release. Ultimately the parent(s) or legal guardian(s) are responsible for payment—seeing a child without the parent's consent may lead to no payment. When this is the case, the counselor is left with some tough choices. If the counselor is unable to refer the minor to another professional who can treat for no cost, or if he or she simply stops seeing the minor, it may qualify as abandonment.[8] When the counselor is already into a counseling situation that develops into a payment dilemma, then he or she should continue to see the minor until the situation is resolved. The Christian counselor may agree to see the minor for an agreed number of sessions without cost or for what the minor may be able to pay.

DIVORCE COUNSELING AND MEDIATION

The advent of no-fault divorce has significantly altered the legal and social landscape of America.[9] While the perjury, collusion, and adversarial bitterness that exemplified fault-based divorce has abated somewhat, for over a decade now the divorce rate in America has steadily maintained a grievous balance of one divorce for every two marriages. It is important to consider both counseling and mediation by the Christian counselor in issues related to divorce.

Lawsuits against counselors regarding divorce issues are infrequent but rising steadily. Divorce itself, as significant evidence of harmful outcome, is often referenced in suits for sexual misconduct, alienation of (family) affections, and intentional infliction of emotional distress. In divorce and reconciliation counseling, most suits center around issues of undue influence (telling your client *to* or *not to* get a divorce), breach of confidentiality and privilege (releasing records wrongly), and unauthorized practice of law (lawyers are keen to protect their turf).

DIVORCE COUNSELING GUIDELINES

It is essential to accurately assess the client's purposes and goals when divorce is on the horizon. If he or she comes with divorce papers in hand or by referral from an attorney, what is the intent— to divorce without question or to consider the possibility of reconciliation? The fact that the client has seen an attorney and papers have been filed does not mean divorce is inevitable or desirable in the long run. Every state's law requires a pendency period—a six to twelve month wait before the court will grant a dissolution—that is expressly for the purpose of reconciliation. The Christian counselor, on biblical grounds, may be compelled to advocate for reconciliation. When done, however, the counselor must never demand reconciliation or threaten termination, after agreeing to take a case, if the client pursues an action disagreeable to the counselor. The risks of undue influence and client abandonment are significant in these cases.

The Christian counselor is frequently asked to express his or her views about divorce and related issues of separation versus staying together. While it is essential to respect the client's responsibility to make the divorce decision, it is also appropriate, even necessary, to share your values and opinions. Those racing to divorce and viewing it as the quick-fix solution to their troubles may need to be challenged with the sober realities of the multiple spiritual, emotional, familial, social, and financial costs of divorce. In the alternative, the codependent client who hangs on to a failed marriage in the face of unrepentant infidelity or violent abuse may need to be challenged that divorce is not only allowable but also may be necessary to live. Rigid judgments and inflexible positions about divorce are biblically indefensible, clinically inept, and legally risky.

Separation before divorce. Even when reconciliation is agreed upon by a couple, life together may be so explosive or destructive that separation is necessary to save the marriage. We often contract with couples for time-limited separations that (1) set reconciliation as the goal, (2) break destructive and unyielding relationship patterns, (3) establish agreements about faithfulness, fidelity, financial support, spousal and parent-child relations, and (4) define programs of individual and marital therapy intended to restore right relations. In California, the legislature has wisely created a separation statute distinct from divorce actions. Though not well respected by the legal community, the state recognizes that some marriages may be saved by this course of action. While these separations can and do sometimes proceed to divorce, many more are able, through Christ's healing power, to pull back from the brink of divorce and be changed to live marriage as God intends.

The counselor's bind. Many counselors are caught in the middle in divorce counseling. Helpers get pulled between spouses, between lawyers, and between clients and their lawyers. Knowing who your clients are—one person, the couple, or the family—is essential to define your primary clinical interest and legal duty. You are bound to protect and pursue your client's best interest, an interest that will be defined differently if your client is one person or the marital dyad. Actions taken on behalf of a couple for the sake of their marriage could be seen as harmful if your separated client is headed for divorce. For example, if your client is the couple, never release their records without both persons' consent. If just one person is your client, never release records to the spouse without your client's permission.

Avoid hidden agendas and alliances. It is wise to be as explicit as possible in this arena and to work to uncover any hidden agendas. What kind of child custody, support, and asset and debt issues are involved? Does your client want you to act as an advocate or merely support and affirm his or her position? Is the client using you to present a good face to the court or family—not intending real change but needing the veneer of counseling to hide trouble or avoid just consequences? The therapist must also be wary of getting caught up in a position of representing one or the other person in court; have the client consent and sign an agreement not to subpoena you or your records. If hidden agendas come to light that you are not adequately prepared to deal with or can no longer support, discuss this openly and resolve it or carefully refer your client elsewhere.

Develop clear standards that you consistently adhere to in divorce and separation counseling. A therapist's values play an important role in the outcome of therapy, so it is imperative for the therapist to understand his or her biases. Avoid legal trouble by declining your opinion about the best legal course of action or what you think is the law. Encourage clients to bring the legal issues outlined by their lawyers into counseling to discuss the pros and cons of various legal options and choices. In all cases be sure to carefully document your suggestions, your advice, and your counselee's responses.

DIVORCE MEDIATION

Divorce mediation has become a significant alternative to adversarial litigation over the past two decades.[10] Most of the practicing mediators are mental health professionals, primarily clinical social workers (42 percent) and psychologists (22 percent).[11] In

mediation, a divorcing couple uses a mediator to directly negotiate and resolve the legal and interpersonal issues of divorce—child
custody and visitation, spousal and child support, division of
marital assets and debts, and any other relational issues that must
be concluded. In California and a growing number of states, mediation is required by law in matters of child custody. Mediation
is not therapy but a structured process of mediated negotiation
and agreement concerning specific issues.

> Divorce is one of the most stressful experiences life holds.
> An unfortunate consequence of placing these individuals in
> the adversarial system with all other civil litigants is that stress
> and acrimony are exacerbated, often needlessly, to the detriment
> of the entire family. . . . One way of eliminating certain
> stresses from the proceeding is to remove it from the adversarial
> setting. . . . Mediation honors the parties' relationship by
> fostering a cooperative effort to reach agreement. It also em-
> powers the parties, making them responsible for asserting
> their needs and interests, and arriving at a solution. . . . This
> may be of great value to those who will continue to have con-
> tact with one another as parents. . . . Mediation often results
> in saving of attorneys' fees, and may be more closely adhered
> to than court-imposed arrangements.[12]

Mediation practice is not licensed anywhere in the United
States. Individual states requiring child custody mediation have
regulatory standards for their programs that, by their existence,
point toward a mediation standard of care.[13] The public-sector
(court-services) mediator usually practices within a formal structure, the rule boundaries defining liability in the context of job
performance. The private mediator is more at risk for unauthorized law practice allegations.[14] Discerning the boundary of law
and nonlegal intervention in mediation is not easy; most issues
have some legal implications. The mediator who believes that
every situation can and should be mediated is also at risk. Some
cases—those where the marital power imbalance is great enough
to make an unjust settlement likely—require lawyers and sure
courtroom advocacy for justice.

Structured mediation preferred. We recommend the Christian mediator practice with a clear outline of materials that guide the participants
through a structured process of negotiation. We provide a written
agreement of mediation and help clients shape it into a final draft

that may be submitted with court documents. We do not provide services unless the participants agree and sign a contract promising not to subpoena our records or haul us into court to testify against the other party if the mediation fails. We also recommend that participants, at the end of mediation, take their agreement to an attorney to review it, careful to recognize that some lawyers will disparage it and seek to persuade the client to litigate. Some mediators work in lawyer-clinician team structures to better serve the range of interests and increase protection against unauthorized practice charges.

The church, Christian lawyers, and mental health professionals are developing excellent biblical models of nonlitigated dispute resolution around the country.[15] We encourage such efforts to continue and increase as a primary means of Christ-centered dispute resolution (see chapter 24).

GROUP COUNSELING

Group psychotherapy offers many advantages to Christian counselors, especially for those who are concerned with enabling as many people as possible to benefit from therapy. Through group process a larger number of people (usually five to fifteen persons) are able to receive professional help at minimal cost with the additional benefits of group process. The two primary legal issues center on the special challenge of protecting client confidentiality and the requirements of specialized training in order to function properly in the group setting. These issues are similar to the ones that evolve in the practice of family therapy.

GROUP CONFIDENTIALITY

In a group setting, when more than one nontherapist is present for treatment, counselors must be especially careful to protect confidentiality, since the group participants are not bound by a code of professional ethics. Foster has referred to group members as a "pool of legal witnesses," and challenges whether group confidentiality is even achievable.[16] Certainly, each participant in a group process must be advised of this difficulty and ways to manage this problem. Additionally, in most states there is no confidential privilege when more than one person is present, so any group member may be compelled to testify in court. The counselor must take steps to properly inform each group participant of the state's law relative to these limits and problems.

COMPETENCE IN GROUP PRACTICE

Further, if a counselor provides group therapy services, it is important that he or she is competent to provide those services. The counselor should be able to demonstrate the necessary training or be able to defend his or her inability to refer to others because of no other competent referral sources. In the latter case, it *may* be better to provide some treatment to those who are in need rather than to abandon them because of lack of training. However, carefully document in case notes your reasons for such an approach.

We recommend a prescreening interview with each client who is being considered to be part of a therapy group. This interview should include information as to what to expect generally from the group process. One critical element of this group process is the necessity of understanding confidentiality and its limits in a group setting. We recommend that group members review and sign an agreement that defines the rules of confidentiality and binds each group member to honor its provisions (see chapter 7 and appendix C). This written agreement assures the client of what to expect, and it will help to protect you as a group leader from legal grief should a suit ever ensue.

CONCLUSION

Compared to individual therapy, the demands and challenges of counseling with multiple persons, especially in marriage and family relations, are greatly multiplied. With multiple relations also comes multiple and complex legal and ethical risks. As humorized by Carl Whitaker in the opening of this chapter, the powers of resistance, sabotage, and confusion are likewise greater, but so can be the consequences of healing. Helping a wounded family change releases healing powers that are wonderfully multiplied in many people through the loving strength of God.

To be truly helpful in this area, it is essential to know the power and limitations of your helping skills. Using these skills wisely and within your competence makes these forms of counseling and mediation highly rewarding. Working beyond your competence in this intense therapeutic area shows your limitations early and often in glaring manner—dynamics that will increase the risk of suit as this area becomes more litigious. If it is not yet obvious, we repeat a core refrain of this book that is especially pertinent here: get excellent training, know and respect your limits, and consult or refer when those limits are reached. Your clients will be transformed and pleased with your help, and you will avoid the pain of lawsuit.

NOTES

1. From an address by Carl Whitaker honoring Nathan Ackerman, "The Technique of Family Therapy," in *From Psyche to System: The Evolving Therapy of Carl Whitaker*, ed. John Neill and David Kniskern (New York: Guilford Press, 1982).

2. See chapter 11 for more details about the rules and limits of informed consent in counseling.

3. See *Destafano v. Grabian*, 763 P.2d 275 (Colorado 1988); *Strock v. Presnell*, 527 N.E.2d 1235 (Ohio 1988); and *Handley v. Richards*, 518 So.2d 682 (Alabama 1987).

4. See chapters 7 and 8 for more detailed information. In California, for example, the statute is interpreted to mean that consensual sexual involvement between children who are under fourteen years is not abuse or reportable as such as long as it does not appear, by the professional, to have any of the factors of sexual abuse. However, consensual sexual involvement between one who is under fourteen and one who is over fourteen is reportable as sexual abuse.

5. See data and recommendations on suicide in chapter 9.

6. See chapter 14 for a general review of basic elements essential for clinically responsible and legally safe referrals.

7. Note articles reviewed in Kathryn Gustafson and J. Regis McNamara, "Confidentiality With Minor Clients: Issues and Guidelines for Therapists," *Professional Psychology: Research and Practice* 18, no. 5 (1987): 503–8.

8. See chapter 14 for further discussion of this matter.

9. See "The Family Law Act," codified in the *California Civil Code*, sections 4000–5138.

10. See Kenneth Kressel, *The Process of Divorce: How Professionals and Couples Negotiate Settlements* (New York: Basic Books, 1985); O. J. Koogler, *Structure Mediation in Divorce Settlement* (Lexington, Mass.: Lexington Books, 1978); and John Haynes, *Divorce Mediation: A Practical Guide for Therapists and Counselors* (New York: Springer, 1981).

11. Kressel, *Process of Divorce*, 181.

12. Norma Lambert, "Divorce Mediation Comes of Age," *The California Therapist* 2, no. 2 (1990): 40–41.

13. See Jessica Pearson, M. L. Ring, and A. Milne, "A Portrait of Divorce Mediation Services in the Public and Private Sector," *Conciliation Courts Review* 21 (1983): 1–24; and L. Vanderkooi and J. Pearson, "Mediating Divorce Disputes: Mediator Behaviors, Styles, and Rules," *Family Relations* 32 (1983): 557–66.

14. See Ralph Cavanagh and D. Rhode, "The Unauthorized Practice of Law and Pro Se Divorce," *Yale Law Journal* 86 (1976): 103–84.

15. See Lynn Buzzard and Laurence Eck, *Tell It to the Church: A Biblical Approach to Resolving Conflict Out of Court* (Elgin, Ill.: David C. Cook, 1982); and C. Ken Sande, *Christian Conciliation: A Better Way to Settle Conflicts* (Billings, Mont.: Association of Christian Conciliation Services, 1989).

16. L. Foster, "Group Psychotherapy: A Pool of Legal Witnesses," *International Journal of Group Psychotherapy* 25 (1975): 50.

Chapter 17

Psychiatry and Inpatient Hospital Ministry

To psychiatrists it should be made clear that the institutions of law do not function as a scientific inquiry to determine "truth." The law exists to resolve controversies. . . . Thus all that can be hoped for is an approximation of truth. . . . It should further be observed—to both disciplines—that the issues which the law has to decide are not psychiatric but moral. . . . "The law does not allow the psychiatrist to communicate his unique understanding of psychic realities to the Court and Jury. More often the mutual quest for the whole truth cannot get past a barrier of communication which leaves the psychiatrist talking about 'mental illness' and the lawyer talking about 'right and wrong.'" [1]

Richard Allen

PSYCHIATRY IS THE PREEMINENT MENTAL HEALTH profession. Its status as a medical specialty, uniqueness in the drug treatment of mental disorders, and political, economic, and administrative power within the mental health community all reflect this standing. The down side of psychiatry, as the deep-pockets mental health profession, is that it is most often targeted by patients and lawyers for malpractice suits.

LIABILITY IN PSYCHIATRY AND HOSPITAL PRACTICE

The regime of legal liability is most advanced in psychiatry. Not only is it the most well-paid mental health profession, but it has historically served the most disturbed, needy, and legally risky patient populations. This treatise cannot outline all the issues where law and psychiatry intersect. We have chosen key liability issues that apply primarily in an inpatient hospital context. More and more, psychologists and social workers are also working in hospital settings, so many of these issues do and will impact these groups as well.

INVOLUNTARY HOSPITAL COMMITMENT

We addressed involuntary commitment tangentially in our chapters on suicide and third-person protection duties (chapters 9 and 10). Law and public policy are clashing, and psychiatrists, primarily, are caught in the middle. Involuntary commitment laws have developed over the past twenty years to require both evidence of serious mental disorder and active suicidal, homicidal, or assaultive risk before a person can be hospitalized against his or her will. Moreover, the United States Supreme Court has held that the state has the burden of proving, by clear and convincing evidence, that the person committed meets these legal criteria.[2]

Modern commitment law is a paradigm for the triumph of law over psychiatry. Freedom and the language of rights have superseded the historic therapeutic commitment to treatment and improved health. Psychiatrist Seymour Halleck argues that modern commitment laws have transformed a mental health service into a police action "resembling a criminal proceeding." He noted the ironic consequence of these laws—keeping those who are not dangerous but need intensive treatment from receiving it, while dangerous persons who are not clinically ill fill more and more hospital beds.[3] These people, who otherwise are dealt with by the criminal justice system, present serious management and safety problems for hospital personnel. They are largely untreatable and tend to cast the therapist-patient relationship in a destructive, adversarial form. "Modern commitment [laws] suffer from the worst of both worlds: uninformed legal decision-making concerning [mental health] issues and uninformed decision-making by [therapists] concerning legal issues."[4]

Legislative reform. Some states, recognizing that needed treatment is blocked by these laws, are shifting the pendulum back in favor of treatment values. Alaska, Texas, Washington, and North Carolina have adopted revisions of commitment law that define less strict criteria for involuntary admission based on the "need for treatment."[5] These states have used the Model Commitment Statute of the American Psychiatric Association to revise their states' laws. Under this APA Model Code, commitment is appropriate when:

1. The person is suffering from a severe mental disorder; and
2. There is a reasonable prospect that his disorder is treatable at or through the facility to which he is to be committed and such commitment would be consistent with the least restrictive alternative principle; and
3. The person either refuses or is unable to consent to voluntary admission for treatment; and
4. The person lacks capacity to make an informed decision concerning treatment; and
5. As a result of the severe mental disorder, the person is (a) likely to cause harm to himself or to suffer substantial mental or physical deterioration, or (b) likely to cause harm to others.[6]

Ethical and risk-managed practice. Adapted from Meyer and his colleagues, there are six aspects of careful, thorough clinical evaluation for involuntary civil commitment.[7] These evaluations should be written in clear, nontechnical language by the clinical professional with the court in mind as the intended audience.

1. *Assess the nature and severity of the patient's mental disorder.* It is essential to go beyond conclusory statements to document mental status and current behavior supportive of your diagnosis. Severity of the disorder must be stated precisely and be well documented; psychological testing may be appropriate to this determination.
2. *Give evidence of dangerousness.* Show how the patient presents a significant danger to himself or herself or to someone else. Dangerousness, a legal rather than clinical construct, should be approached with great care. Since there is little predictive validity, one should use tentative and probable language when discussing the concept directly. Clear statements of prior dangerous behavior, spoken threats, and supportive factors are essential to this determination.
3. *Outline the specific treatment needs of the patient.* A clear treatment plan will include the need for and nature of inpatient treatment, medication needs, family and social support services, and similar issues. These should be outlined in point-by-point fashion.
4. *Assess the person's capability for self-care.* Carefully document the degree to which the patient can and (especially) cannot provide for his or her own personal needs. Noting the reasons a patient is unable to manage suicidal ideation without help is essential,

for example, to establishing the groundwork for commitment.

5. *Assess alternative resources.* Outline other resources that might be available to the patient that would preclude court intervention. The lack of alternative resources is often a key factor in commitment decisions. Unavailability of a supportive family system or lack of basic food, shelter, and medical care may be dispositive to commitment. Courts appreciate therapists who have considered this factor up front.

6. *Show commitment as the least restrictive means.* Advocate why hospitalization is the least restrictive means of meeting this patient's needs at this particular time. Lay out the argument for the judge so that he or she is able to know that you have taken precautions to protect the patient's civil liberties. This increases the strength of your advocacy for the need for hospitalization and points the way to less restrictive aftercare resources.

NEGLIGENT RELEASE

Liability for negligent release concerns the other end of the process of hospital commitment. Wrongful death lawsuits on grounds of negligent release can follow release of a dangerous patient who then commits suicide or kills someone else. Some of the largest judgments against psychiatrists and hospitals have come following negligent release; two cases from New York and Alabama rendered judgments of over $10 million in each of the cases.[8]

Halleck notes the simple rule of thumb applied to questions of release risk: "When in doubt, don't let 'em out."[9] While wrongful confinement may ensue from keeping a patient too long, the risk here is far less onerous vis-à-vis the risk of negligent release. Proof of negligence requires that the plaintiff show (1) negligence in the decision to release, (2) harm to the plaintiff, and (3) that the defendant's negligence caused the plaintiff's harm. Avoiding negligent release liability requires careful clinical attention to four issues:

1. *Work from a clear, explicit, written policy on release.* A policy approved by medical staff executives, reviewed and revised annually, and developed with expert legal consultation with your state's law in view is the first line of malpractice defense. Showing the court special care in the development and adherence to policy is a tremendous benefit.

2. *Incorporate an explicit assessment device on assessing dangerousness.* Special attention should be given to discharge assessment, and

the patient should be evaluated by these criteria before release. Again, in contrast to digging through the record to find the information, discharge planning that evaluates dangerousness separately and prominently shows the court that special attention is given to this issue.

3. *Engage in peer review of all release decisions.* Having supervisors or colleagues review release decisions as a matter of policy strengthens the decision's clinical and legal import.

4. *Outline the patient's positive characteristics well in release documents.* Build your case in advance for support of release and in anticipation that a plaintiff's attorney will work to show the patient was unstable and dangerous at the time of release. One clinician recommends that hospitals videotape the release interview, expecting patients to present their best behavior. Then end the tape with a discussion of aftercare plans, addressing any concerns about the release.[10]

NEGLIGENT ADMINISTRATION OF MEDICATION

Psychiatrists have a duty to exercise diligence and close patient care in the prescription and administration of medications. Patients must give consent to medication treatment after being informed of the intended benefits, side effects, course of treatment, and alternatives to treatment. (Review chapter 11 concerning informed consent, and see "The Right to Refuse Treatment" below.) Hospitalization greatly enhances the doctor's ability to closely monitor and adjust dosage and course of treatment.

Incredible advances in psychopharmacology in the past quarter-century have been a major factor in the transfer of most chronically mentally ill persons from institutions to the community. Psychiatrists in community settings have additional duties to conduct thorough medical histories and exams, to educate the patient and, sometimes, the patient's family in the use of medication. The psychiatrist should also provide adequate referral resources in the event of emergency. Many of the suits for negligent administration are community-based or follow release from hospitalization.[11]

THE RIGHT TO REFUSE TREATMENT

Historically, a patient hospitalized involuntarily for a psychiatric crisis was presumed incompetent and unable to refuse medication treatment. The modern revolution in patient rights has challenged this presumption across the country. In *Rennie v. Klein*,[12] a federal district court in New Jersey in 1978 upheld the right of an involuntary mental patient to refuse forced drug administration based on constitutional rights to privacy. Two cases that followed from Massachusetts[13] and New York[14] affirmed that due process required a judicial determination that an involuntary patient is incompetent to refuse treatment before enforced administration of medication can take place. This right has placed hospital practitioners in very difficult dilemmas, caught between the acute psychiatric needs of the person and the patient's power, in many cases, to refuse essential treatment. We believe the law should support a consistent policy of humane but enforceable treatment to people, especially violent persons, who are involuntarily committed to a hospital.

Vanguard Issues in Psychiatry and Law

Because of the preeminence of psychiatry, some of the most forward-looking issues for all the mental health professions are being addressed or litigated now against psychiatrists and psychiatric institutions. Below are three current and critical issues that are beginning to affect psychiatry and eventually will affect all the major professional groups, especially those in hospital practice.

Psychiatry: Professional Service or Profit-Making Business?

Money—making it and managing it wisely as a resource—is an integral part of every profession. The professional ideal is always to maintain service obligations over the pursuit of money. The reality of the modern marketplace and the assault on service values make it harder and harder for professionals to maintain this ideal. The ascendancy of profit making and the corruption of greed in law, medicine, and even in the ministry is being widely revealed. The impact of these dynamics on psychiatry and all the mental health professions is becoming a significant moral and legal issue.

Psychiatry makes and controls the bulk of the money involved in the mental health industry. As this industry undergoes major structural and economic change in the 1990s, psychiatry will be both influenced and a major influencer of this change. The conflicting challenges of improving patient care and access to needed services and the drive to control health and mental health care costs is a critical public policy issue throughout the Western world.

As mental health services are increasingly privatized and cost accountability and capitation become normative, patient care values and the human service foundations of the clinical professions are increasingly at risk.

The rise of for-profit hospitals. Consider a recent national study of trends in psychiatric hospital development. While psychiatric beds nationwide have declined from over 500,000 in 1960 to less than 150,000 in 1990, the number of for-profit psychiatric specialty hospitals *has nearly quadrupled in a decade,* from 88 in 1979 to 350 in 1988. Ninety percent of these facilities are investor-owned, multihospital systems and now contain half the private psychiatric beds in America. Compared to public facilities, these for-profit entities serve much smaller populations of chronic and hard-to-manage patients. For-profit proprietary hospitals also restrict access to care by uninsured patients. The national study revealed that over 68 percent of the revenue of for-profit hospitals comes from insurance companies.[15] Aftercare and case management, often crucial follow-up services to assist a patient after discharge, are extremely insurance dependent and therefore are largely not available in for-profit hospitals.

Scandal and legal trouble concerning patient care came to light in late 1991 regarding some for-profit facilities.[16] Hospitals owned by Psychiatric Institutes of America in Texas are being investigated by the Texas Attorney General for widespread patient abuses. Testimony was taken by many patients about unjust punishment, manipulative and abusive threats, refusal of access to telephones and basic services, and coerced treatment decisions and confinement. Investigations of for-profit hospitals were also announced in Florida, Alabama, and New Jersey.

The rise of Christian inpatient programs. In the spring of 1992, *Christianity Today* profiled the growing influence of Christian inpatient psychiatric care.[17] Over the past decade programs have mushroomed throughout the United States, most attached as units of for-profit general, specialty, or psychiatric hospitals. The three largest Christian care providers—Rapha, New Life, and the Minirth-Meier Clinic—all operate as for-profit ministries. When a day in such hospitals easily runs a thousand dollars and more, multiplied by tens of thousands of patient days annually, Christian inpatient care has quickly become a major industry. We have no doubt that this new form of ministry will influence and be influenced by the Western church in major ways in the new millennium.

We hope that the difficult moral, economic, and regulatory pressures we see building against for-profit psychiatric care will not adversely affect our brethren in this field. We applaud the development of Christian inpatient care as an essential form of twenty-first century ministry. With so many lives and so much money at stake, however, it is not difficult to foresee that the values and integrity of these programs could be seriously compromised in times of future stress. It is also possible to imagine that the Christian programs may survive better than any other—precisely because they may be able, in Christ, to better maintain their fundamental values through the difficult times ahead.

Patients or profits first? We do not hold that for-profit hospitals are per se violative of patient care and community service values. We do presume, however, that for-profit corporations put these values at risk and that professionals who choose these structures to practice will have the burden of showing that they do maintain patient service values above profit values. While Hogan's study (see chapter 2) revealed the modern decline in suits for negligent patient care, they could well rise again in the twenty-first century if patients are cut off from services because the money runs out. The fiduciary duty of the professional to always maintain the patient's best interest as paramount will be severely tested in a privatized health and human services regime where profit making becomes the foremost concern. May the leaders of Christian inpatient care fiercely maintain their priority of people over profits, trusting God to provide the resources necessary to fund the high cost of quality professional care.

Duty to Choose the Most Effective Treatment?

In the April 1990 issue of the *American Journal of Psychiatry*, Gerald Klerman and Alan Stone, two of psychiatry's leading lights, debate the case of *Osheroff v. Chestnut Lodge*.[18] Dr. Osheroff, an internist with a successful medical practice, was hospitalized for seven months at Chestnut Lodge, a famous psychoanalytic inpatient facility. He was diagnosed as being depressed and suffering from a narcissistic personality disorder. The Lodge, focusing on the personality disorder, applied intensive psychodynamic therapy, but the doctor's condition deteriorated markedly in seven months with the staff making no changes in the treatment plan.

His family transferred him to the Silver Hill treatment center, and antidepressant medications were administered. "Dr. Osheroff showed improvement within 3 weeks and was discharged . . . within 3 months. In 1982, Dr. Osheroff initiated a lawsuit against Chestnut Lodge. He claimed that as a result of the negligence of Chestnut Lodge in not administering drugs, which would have quickly returned him to normal functioning, in the course of a year he lost a lucrative medical practice, his standing in the medical community, and custody of two of his children."[19]

The case addresses comparative treatment efficacy—whether medication should have been prescribed for depression when, instead, psychodynamic therapy was applied, focusing on the personality disorder. Clinically, it reflects the ongoing debate between psychodynamic and biological therapies in psychiatry. Legally, it raises the question: should liability exist for poor treatment choices—those that do not reflect demonstrably better outcomes shown in the clinical and pharmacological research literature? In other words, is the law creating a duty to choose the most effective treatment?

Klerman's case for biological treatment. Dr. Klerman characterizes the rift in psychiatry not as between biological and psychodynamic treatment but rather between evidence and opinion. He decries the lack of empirical evidence for the efficacy of psychoanalytic treatment and asserts that the data for biological therapies, driven by FDA standards and significant corporate (drug company) investment, show safe and efficacious treatment through randomized, controlled clinical studies. He asserts that growing scientific evidence demands that empirical standards of care be applied in treatment decision-making. He argues for shifting public policy priorities at national levels to engage in systematic studies of the efficacy of various psychotherapies. While he concedes that evidence from clinical experience and case studies is relevant, theoretical models must be submitted to the rigor of controlled studies to prevail as valid treatments. Klerman recommends that clinicians modify their practices to consider and apply the most effective treatment available—regardless of theoretical adherence.

> The psychiatrist has a responsibility to use effective treatment. The patient has the right to the proper treatment. Proper treatment involves those treatments for which there is substantial evidence. . . .
>
> Applied to the treatment of depression, the available evidence indicates that patients should begin to show improvement within 4–8 weeks or with psychotherapy within

12–16 weeks. Failure of the patient to improve on a given treatment program within 3–4 months should prompt a
reevaluation of the treatment plan, including consultation and
consideration of alternative treatment.[20]

Stone's rebuttal to "Klerman's indictment of psychoanalytic psychiatry."
Alan Stone asserts that his primary concern about Klerman's position is that malpractice lawyers will argue his recommendations to
create a heightened, even impossible standard of care for psychiatric practice. He chides Klerman for using the "rights" and "duty"
language of the law when there is no legal basis for his assertions.
Stone argues that Klerman was highly selective in his presentation
of the Osheroff case, using that material that best supported his
advocacy of an empirically based standard of care.

Klerman suggests that Dr. Osheroff's remarkable cure at the
Silver Hill Foundation was a function of his finally being provided [medications]. If all patients . . . had such remarkable
cures with these drugs, psychiatry would be a different profession. But Dr. Osheroff's psychological response . . . as
described in his autobiography, suggests that other, equally
important, psychodynamic factors were involved. He had es-
caped, if not narcissistically triumphed over, Chestnut Lodge
and his therapist. Such psychodynamic conceptions still seem
as relevant to our clinical understanding of such remarkable
cures as does psychopharmacology.[21]

Stone believes that forcing a narrow, albeit scientific standard
of care upon the entire profession would stifle creativity and innovative research. He agrees that scientific evidence is far better
than no evidence, but objects to an enforced conception of science
as Klerman proposes. If the law enforced Klerman's rigid standard
of depressive treatment on the whole profession, even biological
psychiatry would suffer. Stone recounts the history of the biological treatment of schizophrenia, which has gone through
numerous periods of treatment change due to professional debate
and innovation in both science and theory. Had a rigid malpractice standard been imposed at any point in this evolution of
treatment, development of therapies for schizophrenia would have
been aborted with patients the ultimate losers.

It is striking to me how often legal decisions that offend
the psychiatric profession as a whole are based on the expert

opinion of psychiatrists advocating their own partisan positions. . . . We have less reason to fear our litigious patients and their lawyers than our partisan colleagues in this new era of psychiatric malpractice. . . .

Klerman has often been able to speak for the collective wisdom of the psychiatric profession. His own words, in *The New Harvard Guide to Psychiatry* are the best answer in the courtroom to the partisan position he has asserted here: "Individual psychotherapy based on psychodynamic principles remains the most widely used form of psychotherapy. Although systematic, controlled clinical studies do not exist, clinical experience supports the value of this form of treatment."[22]

Toward a flexible standard of treatment efficacy. The mental health professions, like medicine a century ago, are on the crest of a scientific revolution that is reshaping treatment understanding and patient care.[23] While Klerman's advocacy is too narrow and legally immature, he does point the way toward the maturation of standards of care that are grounded in empirical validity and developing toward greater uniformity. Psychotherapy is moving away from adherence to models and theory for theory's sake to the development of a mature professional science.

The mental health professions should pursue and advocate a flexible standard of effective treatment. Such a standard would be grounded in an expansive scientific validity, using and honoring a variety of empirical methodologies. It would not reject theoretical models, recognizing that good science and theory building go hand in hand, unless empirical or legal evidence has demonstrated them ineffectual or harmful. Mental health practice in the twenty-first century will not merely ask: "What is the best treatment?" It will ask: "What is the best treatment (or combination of treatments) for this person with these problems, needs, and goals at this time in life?"

While mental health research is now beginning to link specific problems with the best treatment, we have shown throughout this book how law, culture, and money also drive the pursuit of the most efficacious treatment. We believe the evidence is clear that the most *efficient* treatment, that which saves the most in time and money, is not always the most *efficacious*, that which best serves the patient's interest. It is critical, therefore, that psychiatry and all the mental health professions adhere to a standard rooted in the primacy of patient care values and not those of corporate or economic efficiency. The legal standard of care will always hold patient care values as primary.

HOSTILITY TOWARD PSYCHIATRY

Christian psychiatry is alive and well within the larger profession. Dr. Marc Galanter and his colleagues recently published a study describing the values and work of Christian psychiatrists.[24] Nearly two hundred psychiatrist members of the Christian Medical and Dental Society, a group that showed distinctly evangelical Christian beliefs, were surveyed about the role of religious belief in psychiatric practice. The perceived effectiveness of different treatment regimens was compared. Except for recommending prayer far more to Christian patients, there was no significant difference in the recommendation of other standard treatments (medication, psychotherapy, or Alcoholics Anonymous) to Christian or non-Christian patients.

However, many Christians are skeptical, even hostile toward psychiatry and the use of psychotropic medications. The reactionary assault on psychology and psychiatry by some prominent church leaders strikes a fearful but responsive chord in the hearts of many in the church. In our counseling practice, and we suspect in most in America, we consistently face sincere Christians who recoil and resist the recommendation to consult with a psychiatrist or their doctor about medication. Some believers suffering major depression, manic-depression, panic and acute anxiety, or the psychotic disorders are deaf to the reality of the medical and biochemical dimensions of these problems. Listening instead to their own misbeliefs or the false but well-meaning warnings of their pastor or Christian friends, these sufferers often compound their trouble by searching for more sin to confess, seeking greater faith to overcome, and casting out stubborn and illusory demons.

This dilemma puts the Christian counselor in an uneasy and paradoxical bind. We believe that sin, faith, and spiritual warfare are central issues to the struggle to find peace and grow in grace and knowledge of Christ. We also recognize that the person is a physical, psychosocial, and spiritual being; most problems intersect all these dimensions as do most solutions. Medical and psychiatric issues cannot be denied behind a simplistic and spiritualized malassessment without harming people. We respect and are often compelled to educate and advocate for understanding the physical and medical dimensions of human problems. Counteracting the practice of antimedicine by those in the church who influence others against medicine and psychiatry, the Christian counselor can often push medical practice boundaries in order to help their clients and parishioners get the medical help they need.

This is merely the tip of the iceberg of the myriad issues the Church will face in an astonishing revolution of twenty-first century biology, medicine, and psychiatry. New medical knowledge and technological change make common today what seemed extraordinary or impossible a decade ago. Modern society desperately needs Christians assisting medical decisions made at personal and societal levels.[25] Questions about life and death, abortion and euthanasia, genetic manipulation and disease control, personality and mood control, organ harvesting and transplantation, and the rationing of medical care and resources must not be left to nonbelievers alone. Pastors and informed Christians who can directly serve their friends and parishioners struggling with these issues, sit on hospital ethics committees, and speak to churches, medical groups, government councils, and legislatures will be lights in a sea of darkness and moral confusion.

RECOMMENDATIONS

In order to help the pastor and counselor serve as salt and light in this area, we recommend the following practice and policy guidelines.

- *Educate yourself.* A little knowledge about medicine and psychiatry may well be dangerous. A fund of working knowledge of these disciplines and their spiritual and ethical dimensions makes you a better advocate for medical help and increases your awareness of the boundaries between medicine and ministry.

- *Forge alliances with key psychiatrists and physicians in your area.* Convince medical and psychiatric professionals of your intent to work with and respect their sphere of knowledge and practice, seeking the same in exchange. Mutually respected professional relations will allow you the freedom to advocate for medical consultation. You will also have a solid foundation for close network intervention on behalf of your client or congregant.

- *Be nondirective, giving suggestions, not instructions, about medical decisions.* Pray with your congregants or clients for peace, wisdom, and guidance. Lead them to places in Scripture that give solace and guide decisions and resolutions by God's leading rather than yours. Help them explore both sides of issues, considering pros and cons for each position. As much as possible, serve as a mediator, coordinator, and team member rather than assuming an adversarial role with physicians and hospital staff.

Communications that may be perceived by others as mandates to be obeyed are legally risky. You may be sued by a client or congregant who later regrets a decision they think you pushed them to make. Such action is usually far too presumptuous and tends to put people off as ignorant or arrogant rather than being helpful.

CONCLUSION

Psychiatry, biopsychology, and the neurosciences may well be the most fascinating and revolutionary fields of human study in the twenty-first century. It is critical then, even as we advance good human science, to avoid becoming enslaved to empiricism. After decades of the scientific revolution in medicine, the profession is rediscovering the *person*, including the role of spiritual, attitudinal, and other intangible factors in the healing process. A growing body of research is demonstrating that a healthy faith in God, quality relationships, and belief in good and whole outcomes are forces for healing, living well, and enjoying long lives. Psychiatry must always keep in view the person it treats, even as its science develops toward greater treatment efficacy.

Christian counseling and Christian psychiatry, especially, may have a unique role in calling forth radical adherence to the personal dimension in the clinical sciences—one grounded in the Personhood of God and reflected by men and women made in his image. Since it acknowledges an objective standard of right and wrong grounded in God's revelation in Christ, Christian psychiatry may be able to speak more boldly to the moral concerns inherent to law. Christians practicing as mental health professionals must avoid losing God's revelation about himself, his creation, and his moral order. If we do not, we may not be able to avoid bowing to the gods of money, humanistic morality, and sterile, manipulative scientism. Our primary duty—legally, ethically, and morally—must continue to be godly service that maintains the best interests of the persons we serve.

NOTES

1. Richard Allen, "Interpersonal Communication and the Law," in *Readings in Law and Psychiatry*, ed. Richard Allen, Elyce Ferster, and Jesse Rubin (Baltimore: John Hopkins University Press, 1968).

2. See *Addington v. Texas*, 441 U.S. 418 (1979).

3. See Seymour Halleck, *Law in the Practice of Psychiatry* (New York: Plenum Medical Books, 1980).

4. Joseph Bloom and L. Faulkner, "Competency Decisions in Civil Commitment," *American Journal of Psychiatry* 144, no. 2 (1987): 193.

5. Robert G. Meyer, E. R. Landis, and J. R. Hays, *Law for the Psychotherapist* (New York: Norton, 1988).

6. See Loren Roth, "A Commitment Law for Patients, Doctors, and Lawyers," *American Journal of Psychiatry* 136 (1979): 1121–27; see also C. Stromberg and A. Stone, "A Model State Law on Civil Commitment of the Mentally Ill," *Harvard Journal of Legislation* 20 (1983): 275–77.

7. Meyer, Landis, and Hayes, *Law for the Psychotherapist*.

8. Reported in J. Klein and S. Glover, "Psychiatric Malpractice," *International Journal of Law and Psychiatry* 6 (1983): 131–57.

9. Halleck, *Practice of Psychiatry*.

10. Norman G. Poythress, Jr., "Avoiding Negligent Release: Contemporary Clinical and Risk Management Strategies," *American Journal of Psychiatry* 147, no. 8 (1990): 994–97.

11. See *Watkins v. United States*, 589 F.2d 214 (5th Cir. 1979), in which a doctor was held liable for wrongful death following negligent administration of large amounts of Valium that would not have been given had the patient's recent hospitalization records been consulted.

12. *Rennie v. Klein*, 462 F.Supp. 1131 (Dist. N.J. 1978).

13. *Rogers v. Commissioner of Mental Health*, 390 Mass. 498, 458 N.E. 2d 308 (1982).

14. *Rivers v. Katz*, 67 N.Y.2d 485, 495 N.E. 2d (1986).

15. Robert Dorwart et al., "A National Study of Psychiatric Hospital Care," *American Journal of Psychiatry* 148, no. 2 (1991): 204–10.

16. Barry Shlachter, "Horror Stories from Texas Psychiatric Patients," *San Francisco Chronicle*, 6 November 1991.

17. Tim Stafford, "Franchising Hope," *Christianity Today* 36, no. 6 (1992), 22–26.

18. Gerald Klerman, "The Psychiatric Patient's Right to Effective Treatment: Implications of 'Osheroff v. Chestnut Lodge,'" *American Journal of Psychiatry* 147, no. 4 (1990): 409–18; and Alan Stone, "Law, Science, and Psychiatric Malpractice: A Response to Klerman's Indictment of Psychoanalytic Psychiatry," *American Journal of Psychiatry* 147, no. 4 (1990): 419–27.

19. Klerman, "Right to Effective Treatment," 410.

20. Ibid., 417.

21. Stone, "Psychiatric Malpractice," 423.

22. Ibid., 426.

23. Thomas Kuhn, *The Structure of Scientific Revolutions*, 2d ed. (Chicago: University of Chicago Press, 1970).

24. Marc Galanter, D. Larson, and E. Rubenstone, "Christian Psychiatry: The Impact of Evangelical Belief on Clinical Practice," *American Journal of Psychiatry* 148, no. 1 (1991): 90–95.

25. See Franklin E. Payne, Jr., *Biblical Medical Ethics: The Christian and the Practice of Medicine* (Milford, Mich.: Mott Media, 1985).

Chapter 18

Counseling in Cases of Abortion, AIDS, and Cult Programming

We watched the news of Magic Johnson's horrible announcement of being HIV positive. . . . "They're so happy that he's so upbeat!" I finally burst out . . . "Don't they realize he is going to die? Don't they know that it is going to be the gates of hell opening for him inch by inch?" I was agitated and upset.

Joe looked up at me from his book and glanced at the TV set. . . . We looked at each other across the hospital room and then looked down at our friend Bruce. He was lying on a bed between us, barely conscious. He was dying of AIDS. We were there for a death watch. Bruce wasn't expected to live through the night. . . .

I have no doubts that Magic Johnson has the valiant and generous soul that all of his admirers ascribe to him. But I know he will be tested by AIDS in ways that make the rest of his life seem almost irrelevant. To hint to him that he may have safe passage through this horror because of his courage and his magnanimity seems to me the worst kind of collective selfishness. However Magic Johnson bears this unfair and deadly burden, it will not save him or us from the reality of perhaps the worst disease known by humankind.[1]

Harriet Swift

IN LESS THAN TWENTY YEARS PASTORAL AND PROFESSIONAL counselors have had to come to grips with three new major forces within Western culture. The legalization of abortion and its aftermath and the issues related to cult programming came bursting into American life virtually within moments of one another in the early 1970s. The awful reality of AIDS has been forcing itself into the consciousness of the world since the early 1980s.

The first two forces were readily recognized as threatening to the mission of the church and have elicited a variety of Christian responses. The church was not jubilant nor proud; these social problems were directly affecting their sons and daughters. The AIDS problem was initially judged by the conservative Church as a clear sign of God's judgment upon homosexuals. There was even jubilation from some Christians that this judgment signaled the end of the practice of homosexuality as a serious alternative lifestyle. But homosexuals are becoming monogamous, and the AIDS virus is steadily killing an ever-enlarging group of heterosexuals.

If it is judgment, it is also killing innocent people as well as the guilty. If it is judgment, we are still called to humbly acknowledge that we are all affected by the curse of sin, to compassionately serve the judged, to act by living out the "truth in love" (Eph. 4:15). Combatting the forces of abortion, AIDS, and cult religions while serving those afflicted by these sorrows is a major test of the Western church in the new millennium. In this chapter we will address the legal issues where these three areas intersect with Christian counseling.

Abortion Counseling

Pro-life and pro-choice proponents have been locked in battle over their respective views ever since *Roe vs. Wade* was decided by the United States Supreme Court in 1973. Currently in the United States we are witnessing a steady erosion of a woman's right to abortion on demand. This intense controversy over issues of life itself is the context in which the Christian counselor must advise women and men regarding abortion decisions. The legal issues are in flux so, again, we urge you to be well informed of your state or province laws.

Coercion and Undue Influence

Counselors must be careful about helping women decide how to resolve pregnancy choices, because their intervention may involve undue influence through coercive tactics. There is a fine line between helping a woman work through the possible outcomes of her choice, and imposing coercive measures to enforce an appropriate or Christian decision. There is a difference between strong suggestion and mild coercion, and this difference varies from person to person. Some people are quite compliant, and others are quite defiant. A suggestion to one may be coercion to another.

The counselor should hear and elicit feedback about what the person feels and thinks about the review of options. In some cases the counselor may seek written feedback from the client that summarizes what she or he heard the counselor say regarding abortion options and reasons. In this manner, one may reduce any coercive dynamics, highlight cooperation, and clarify any misunderstanding. An assertive and zealous counselor may successfully persuade someone to not abort, yet another person may persuade that same person that her rights were violated and encourage her to sue for undue influence and coercion.

Abortion Notification

Adults. The Supreme Court's decision in *Webster vs. Reproductive Health Services*[2] in 1989 effectively shifted control of abortion practice from the federal government to the states. The majority opinion stressed the idea that potential human life should not only be protected by the state *after* viability, but the state should also protect this potential *prior* to viability. This opened the door for the pro-life movement to push for state statutes to protect the unborn. One such method of protection has been to advocate laws that require husband or partner notification prior to abortion; numerous states are considering this type of notification. This requirement is based on the state's interest in promoting marital harmony, trust, procreative potential, and consideration of the husband's interest in the unborn baby. Though there has been much resistance to this requirement from pro-choice people, several states have successfully approved such legislation. Naturally, it behooves the well-equipped counselor to be aware of his or her state's statutes in this regard and to practice accordingly.

Adolescents and parents. Legislation similar to adult notification restricts the minor teenager's right to have an abortion without parental consent. Numerous states have passed laws that require some form of parental involvement in the minor's abortion decision. These statutes either require parental consent or notice before an abortion can be performed. Those opposed believe these laws will result in increased birth rates, late abortions, and medical complications and will force minors to leave the state for an abortion. Advocates who ascribe to teenage abortion rights stress the teen's right for individual liberty over the rights of her parents to be involved in the decision. On the other hand, advocates of these laws stress the benefits of promoting teen responsibility, of fostering parent-child communication, and of facilitating mature decision-making.[3]

In those states with laws requiring some form of notification prior to an adolescent's decision to abort, Christian (and all) counselors must comply with the law in order to avoid prosecution. However, in those states where notification is not required, the matter is somewhat more complicated. In either case it is important to note that age of notification will vary from state to state. Previously (chapters 7 and 11) we have discussed the importance of confidentiality and informed consent issues as they impact a broad range of counseling situations. It is vital to discuss the limits of confidentiality with pregnant clients, including adolescent clients seen individually. In those states without notification laws, the counselor does not have a mandate to report to the teen's parent(s) and may be liable for breach of confidentiality if he or she does report. If the counselor believes that parental involvement in the abortion decision is vital, he or she may consider the following steps to resolve this dilemma.

- *Encourage parental involvement.* Frequently, the adolescent is under some pressure to abort—an appointment to have an abortion is already scheduled. Consequently, if she has not consulted with her parents, start by encouraging her to wait to abort until she can consult with them.
- *Be an advocate and supporter.* If a pregnant teen is afraid to consult with her parents or even inform them of her pregnancy, offer to support her by meeting with her and her parents to inform. Listen carefully to her reasons for not informing her parents, and help resolve her inability to do so, if at all possible. Be careful not to coerce parental contact.
- *Maintain helping relations.* If the adolescent is unable to choose to inform her parents, then seek to maintain a helping relationship that intends to help prevent further pregnancies. Do not break confidentiality at this point to attempt to force the teen to comply with your values or what you may presume about parental values. This could be illegal and might lead to lawsuit both for violation of confidentiality and because of undue influence.

AIDS-RELATED COUNSELING

Steve had acknowledged that a key reason for seeking you out as a counselor was because he felt that, as a Christian, you would be sensitive to his needs as a Christian young man. After several sessions that lacked focus, he finally was able to say that his primary reason for coming to counseling was his struggle with homosexuality. He stated that he really wanted to change but had been unable to do so—now he wanted your help. In the next session, Steve was especially depressed, and when quizzed admitted to having just been notified that he tested positive for HIV (human immune-deficiency virus). When you discussed the facts of the danger to others of continued sexual involvement since this discovery, Steve simply admitted that he would find it very hard to stop his homosexual behavior. When you challenged him to disclose his condition to his sexual partners, he yelled, "I thought I could trust you, man!" With that, he stormed out of the office and ran down the street.

BALANCING CHALLENGE WITH MERCY

The counseling needs of people with AIDS (PWA) and their loved ones are becoming an area of increasing demand. If you have not had to deal with one of these situations yet, it is surely only a matter of time before you do so. There are tough challenges in confronting the dangerous behavior of unsafe-sex by persons with AIDS, and we are called as Christ's ambassadors to respond to those in need with genuine mercy. This call and its demand for balance is a mighty challenge indeed.

It is critical for Christian helpers to be aware of their homophobic attitudes toward the primary population who have contracted AIDS. Needless to say, Christians in general are stereotyped as having extreme homophobic responses. Those for whom this is true will not work well in treating those with AIDS. This is not a disease that is restricted to the big cities either. Many men with AIDS are returning to smaller communities and rural areas to live out their last days and die with their families after contracting AIDS in the city. As a result, we can expect to find small-town counselors and pastors having to face this issue more and more frequently in the coming years.

AIDS FACTS

While there is a lot we do not know about AIDS, we do know that it is contagious, incurable, and nearly always fatal. The HIV viruses attack the immune system of the body, eventually leaving it virtually defenseless against any disease that would attack and kill its weakened host. Pneumonia and cancer, for example, are two common diseases that kill the AIDS-weakened person. Though there are some people who have been HIV positive for years without developing full-blown AIDS, that certainly seems to be the exception, not the rule. The AIDS virus itself can destroy brain cells and cause brain disease and eventually death.

Early on, AIDS transmission behavior was almost exclusively by four modes—homosexual promiscuity, intravenous drug use, blood transfusions, and fetal transmission in pregnancy. Currently, blood transfusions are safe, homosexual rates are leveling off, and transmission by IV drug use and heterosexual contact are on the rise. Teenagers and young adult heterosexuals face the most dramatic increase in risk of exposure. Worldwide, heterosexual promiscuity accounts for 80 percent of all HIV cases. Some African countries are already being devastated by AIDS—death and disease are wiping out whole populations of young and midlife adults. The World Health Organization estimates a total of over 30 million AIDS and HIV cases worldwide by the year 2000.

Medical technology is ineffective in meeting the primary goals of AIDS treatment: destroying the AIDS virus in the body, rebuilding the immune system, and immunizing against further infection. So, the necessary treatment of choice is to prevent other individuals from becoming infected. Since as many as 3 million people may be carrying the virus in America, it is imperative that things are done to protect others who may be at risk to contract this dreadful disease. Except those who are seronegative and monogamous or sexually abstinent and do not get a blood transfusion, all humanity is at risk.

So-called *safe-sex* is anything but safe; failure rates of 5 to 10 percent with condoms is normative. Most people who become infected do so because they do not adhere to proper sex practices; that is, they have been unable to control their sexual behavior to the extent of staying healthy. For example, Campbell reports on a study of sexual behavior of gay men in San Francisco who were knowledgeable about AIDS: "69% of the men having three or more sexual partners the previous month agreed with the statement, 'It is hard to change my sexual behavior because being gay means doing what I want sexually.'"[4] Once the person contracts the disease, safe-sex requires avoidance of sexual behavior unless the preventative steps are adhered to scrupulously.[5] Like the cold war, the sexual revolution is over—promiscuous sex is deadly.

THE LEGAL ISSUES SURROUNDING AIDS

The states vary widely in their laws regarding AIDS-infected persons. Infected individuals are normally required to be reported to a state health agency where the person is informed of the implications of the disease and what to do to protect others. The federal Center for Disease Control has drafted regulations which state that every infected person would need to be informed that "they cannot engage in sexual intercourse, kiss someone, or seek medical or dental care without exposing their partner or health care provider to this possibly deadly virus."[6]

The right to privacy. The central issue in law with AIDS reporting is the conflict between the right to privacy versus the need for public disclosure to be protected from persons with contagious diseases. People do have a legally protected right to privacy. The right, though not explicitly guaranteed in the Constitution, has been inferred and applied by the Supreme Court in areas of sexual and reproductive behavior.

One of the most significant issues regarding AIDS is the right for people to preserve from public knowledge who has the AIDS virus. The fear of unwanted disclosure inhibits many from coming forward to be HIV tested. In order to promote disclosure and protect those who come forward to be tested for HIV, federal laws have been established and enforced. However, partly because of the negative prejudice that impacts those who are HIV carriers, most carriers are as yet unidentified.

Confidentiality and the duty to protect. The issue of maintaining confidentiality versus disclosure to protect third persons in the case of AIDS is a moral and legal time bomb waiting to explode. Under *Tarasoff* (see chapter 10), the clinician has a duty to protect others who are at risk to be killed or injured because of a client's dangerous intentions. *Tarasoff* stands for the proposition that confidentiality "must yield to the extent to which disclosure is essential to avert danger to others."[7] The unaware sexual partner of an HIV carrier is an identifiable victim in serious danger. Warning identifiable third persons can protect them from deadly harm and stop further disease transmission. There is a strong argument that *Tarasoff* duties should and eventually will attach in the case of AIDS.

Even if *Tarasoff* duties attach, the issue of privacy in the AIDS arena has been politicized so greatly by activist gay-rights organizations that the counselor may face liability for both reporting and failing to report.[8] The regime of confidentiality around AIDS is very strong against the policy favoring disclosure for purposes of disease control. Michigan legislators, for example, included a clause requiring mental health professionals to take protective action on behalf of sexual partners of AIDS carriers in their *Tarasoff* statute. It was narrowly defeated in the Michigan House, however, following intensive pressure and debate. Physicians in Michigan and many states have the right, but not an affirmative duty, to warn at-risk sexual partners. How many doctors exercise this right in the face of litigation threats and gay-rights pressure not to disclose is another question.

Suicide risk. The risk of suicide increases substantially among men with AIDS. Consequently, the counselor must be prepared to deal with the right to commit suicide, the impact of HIV infection on the ability of the patient to make a rational choice, and the liability factors involved in fostering such thinking. It is also important to realize that many individuals with HIV show signs of progressive dementia similar to Alzheimer's disease. We recommend that you follow the steps outlined in chapter 9 to intervene with any suicidal individual with AIDS or HIV. No one has successfully sued a therapist for breach of confidentiality when the intent was to prevent suicide.

Recordkeeping. Recordkeeping ought to include some consideration as to whom might review the information at some future date and for what purpose it may be used. Because of the potentially damaging impact with employers, insurance companies, peer-review groups, and the courts, information about who has AIDS ought to be carefully guarded. This raises the general issue of the legality and ethical nature of shielding records through incomplete information and by keeping dual records as some would recommend.[9] We think it best to keep accurate records, to assert confidentiality and privilege to those seeking record disclosure, and to join with your client and his or her lawyer to control disclosure.

Taking action with AIDS clients. Reasonable and loving action must be considered to prevent other individuals from becoming infected. One author suggests a three-stage process of dealing with this conflict.[10] First, take some time in counseling to help the PWA be able to share his or her plight with his or her lover(s). The counselor's role may be much more efficacious if he or she helps the PWA resolve the psychological and spiritual complications that may be the root cause restraining a PWA from informing his or her partners. If that fails, then the therapist should seriously encourage the PWA to practice *safer* sex habits while the counselor considers the reporting dilemma.

If the PWA still refuses to act responsibly toward others, the therapist should consult with legal and medical advisers and with colleagues before taking action. If the decision is made to breach confidentiality, the client should be forewarned, including a discussion of the legal constrictions that impact the practice of psychotherapy. This should serve as a reminder of the importance of discussing the limits of confidentiality and gaining signed agreement at the *onset* of therapy. Also, if you choose to not work with AIDS or HIV patients, then it is still imperative that you are adequately prepared to make good referrals to those who are prepared to treat. The beginning of counseling is usually the best time to make that decision. Furthermore, we recommend the Christian counselor:

- *Stay informed.* Keep up-to-date on the latest information on AIDS and be well trained about the issues in treating AIDS and HIV-positive patients and those significant others in their lives.
- *Expose, not impose, your values.* Decisions in the area of AIDS are highly value-laden, so the informed therapist must carefully evaluate his or her values when working with AIDS patients. Respecting values you may disagree with while judiciously sharing your own, especially your hope in the saving work of Christ, is a formidable challenge.
- *Challenge abstinence and safer-sex habits.* Make it a practice to inform any clients who are in higher risk AIDS categories to practice safer-sex habits and/or to abstain from high-risk practices. Naturally, as Christians, people ought to be abstinent if they are not married. However, the reality is that many are not and so need to be informed of the potential hazards.
- *Stay informed of the law on confidentiality versus disclosure.* Therapists and pastors must stay informed of their state's laws regarding AIDS confidentiality and disclosure issues. Discuss and agree to the limits of confidentiality. Review the limits of confidentiality in the first session, and include a written agreement that specifies these limits.

CULT PROGRAMMING

The proliferation of cults and cultic activity in the last two decades has frequently raised some serious questions with regard to religious freedom and religious pluralism in the West. The concept and practice of religious freedom, as vital today as at any time in history, was an essential building block in the foundation upon which this nation was established. Yet, because of abuses of the principle of religious tolerance, some people seriously question whether it is in the best interests of this country to tolerate cultic group activities under the umbrella of religious pluralism. Others stress the harm of all religious groups and argue that religious practice is, ipso facto, a sign of mental illness.[11]

These problems directly impact the Christian counselor whenever he or she encounters a situation that involves attempting to help "free" an individual trapped in a religious cult. To some degree, the conflict between new religious movements and secular psychology represents the struggle between the spiritual and the profane attributes of man. As one author noted prophetically in 1984:

> . . . the current rivalry between new religions and psychotherapy potentiates the loss of authority for our "secular priests," a less critical look at established religions, and, from a religious standpoint, the possible awakening or a new religious spirit. Consequently, we should not be surprised if more "communal" or "spiritual" psychotherapies evolve to counter this trend, as some members of the psychotherapy community seek new ways to compete in what, surprisingly enough, may be a more religious future in our society.[12]

Perhaps the best outline of cults is provided by Ruth Tucker, who summarizes six primary cult categories.[13] While most cults fall into one category, some may fit into two or more categories.

- Eastern mystical (Krishna Consciousness, Transcendental Meditation, etc.);
- Aberrational Christian (Children of God, The Way International, etc.);
- Psychospiritual or self-improvement (est, Scientology, etc.);
- Eclectic-syncretistic (Unification Church, Baha'i, etc.);
- Psychic-occult-astral (New Age Movement, Eckankar, etc.);
- Institutionalized or established (Mormons, Jehovah's Witnesses, Christian Science, etc.).

LEGAL ISSUES IN DEPROGRAMMING

From our perspective the legal issues are few and quite focused. One issue is not so much a matter of what defines a cult as it is a matter of determining the biblical and legal means to deal with freeing a person from a cult. It is important to note that people differ significantly in what they consider a cult, so counseling decisions must be based on a sound understanding of what is cultic and include a clear grasp of applicable state laws. It is important to communicate clearly with people who intend to help a person caught in a cult to determine whether your goals as a helper are synonymous with your client's goals.

As we have previously discussed, religious belief is absolutely protected within the context of the Constitution. However, the actions one takes based on religious belief come under careful scrutiny as to their legality. Within broadly defined limits, the state needs to have the authority to interfere in the religious life of its people when clear abuse is taking place. However, the courts seem to be reticent to become involved with the fine points of religious issues with respect to beliefs, focusing instead on the behavioral violations of law.

The Christian counselor must realize that counseling[14] a person who has been involved in a cult is not a simple matter; the process normally takes considerable time and energy.[15] Since abduction of an adult is illegal, it behooves the counselor to avoid entanglement in such behavior by direct act or by undue influence in advocacy. Naturally, if the deprogramming is successful, the counselor is not at risk. However, if the deprogramming is not successful, then the counselor may be at risk for a variety of civil and criminal charges. If the client is not the one who is in the cult, then your actions are severely limited. The focus of the counseling process must be on those issues that concern the parent or friend's adaptation to the child/friend's predicament.

One way parents may be able to deal with an adult child in a cult, permissible in *some* states, is to establish a temporary conservatorship as a means to rescue and aid such a person. If the cult member is a minor child, then a court order may be obtained in order to rescue the child from the cult. This aspect of the process must be directed to an attorney competent to handle such matters. In advising parents in this respect, avoid counseling in such a manner that would appear to be providing legal advice.

CONCLUSION

We suspect the battle over abortion, AIDS, and cults—the moral, social, medical, legal, political, and spiritual warfare—will likely not abate. In fact, we believe these battles, and many others, may well rage on even more fiercely until Kingdom come. This is not a time for timidity, complacency, or stupidity in the church. Counselors, pastors, and others on the front lines of these battles will need all grace and wisdom to fight them with honor, trusting in God's ultimate victory.

Our obedience to the call to be wise as serpents yet harmless as doves will be proved out in these arenas. God's wisdom demands that we be very well informed of the issues, including our legal and ethical boundaries, in order to fight the good fight. This is a fight, not against the people holding contrary beliefs, but against the beliefs themselves, "against the rulers, against the authorities, against the powers of this dark world and against the spiritual forces of evil in the heavenly realms" (Eph. 6:12b). Our strength comes from the mighty power of God—he will sustain us in the fight and honor our studious preparation for the warfare to come.

NOTES

1. Harriet Swift, "Magic's Future Holds More Pain, Gloom Than His Smile Belies," *Eureka Times-Standard*, 28 November 1991.

2. *Webster v. Reproductive Health Services*, 109 S.Ct. 3040 (1989).

3. For an excellent discussion of this controversy, see Everett L. Worthington, Jr. et al., "The Benefits of Legislation Requiring Parental Involvement Prior to Adolescent Abortion," *American Psychologist* 44, no. 12 (1989): 1542–45.

4. Emily Campbell, "Mandatory AIDS Testing and Privacy: A Psycholegal Perspective," *North Dakota Law Review* 66 (1990): 488–89.

5. Reflect on the demands of being safe with "safe-sex"; in the *British Journal of Venereology* 53, no. 6 (1977), the following means were suggested to protect oneself from sexually transmitted diseases (STDs): "Veneral disease can be prevented if before sexual intercourse the man applies a condom, the woman an antiseptic cream, and if afterwards the man immediately passes water and anoints his genitalia with a prophylactic ointment while the woman has a prophylactic douche: both should then have a bath before spraying each other with an antiseptic lotion, and they should visit a physician to receive 2.4 mega units of procaine penicillin by injection plus 1.0 g of probenecid by mouth—which should prevent gonorrhea and syphilis—plus a 10-day course of oral tetracycline to prevent non-gonococcal urethritis and a one or two-day course of metronidazole or nimorazole against trichomoniasis—even with such commendable caution the risk is not entirely removed of infection from the viruses of condylomata acuminata, molluscum contagiosum, or even that of hepatitis B; neither would it

be beneficial for venerophobia." Quoted in Josh McDowell, *Research Almanac and Statistical Digest,* (Julian, Calif.: Julian Press, 1990), 62.

6. Campbell, "Mandatory AIDS Testing," 456.

7. Douglas Lamb et al., "Applying *Tarasoff* to AIDS-Related Psychotherapy Issues," *Professional Psychology: Research and Practice* 20, no. 1 (1989): 38.

8. Ralph Slovenko, "The Therapist's Duty to Warn or Protect Third Persons," *Journal of Psychiatry and Law* 16, no. 2 (1988): 180.

9. See Constance F. Morrison, "AIDS: Ethical Implications for Psychological Intervention," *Professional Psychology: Research and Practice* 20, no. 3 (1989): 166–71.

10. Ibid. *See* also Greg Albers, *Counseling and AIDS,* (Dallas:Word, 1990).

11. For an excellent discussion of this dynamic, see Brock Kilbourne and James T. Richardson, "Psychotherapy and New Religions in a Pluralistic Society," *American Psychologist* 39, no. 3 (1984): 247–49.

12. Ibid., 249.

13. Ruth A. Tucker, *Another Gospel: Alternative Religions and the New Age Movement* (Grand Rapids, Mich.: Academia Books, 1989), 21.

14. Some people may use the more definitive term *deprogramming,* but that may be too narrow a term for our use here.

15. See Margaret Singer, "Coming Out of the Cults," *Psychology Today* (January 1979): 72–82.

PART VI

Corporate Risks and Counseling Credentials

Chapter 19

The Counseling Pastor: Competent Counseling, Referral, and Leadership

Counseling is often a moral, legal and emotional "minefield." Pastors and lay helpers should not attempt long-term, in-depth counseling and psychotherapy unless they are specifically trained to do so. The subtle but powerful moral conflicts and ego dynamics inherent to counseling have trapped many well-meaning pastors and their counselees in moral compromise and spiritual defeat. . . .

I recommend that pastors develop and seek support from their staff and boards to honor a three-part policy of pastoral counseling and referral. (1) Set clear limits to the time, number of sessions, and kinds and depth of problems that you will work with, referring parishioners when these limits are reached. . . . (2) Develop and train lay ministers for both one-to-one help and, especially, small support group ministry that can be a first source of referral. . . . (3) Finally, refer the more difficult and long-term problems to . . . professional Christian counselors.[1]

Pastor Amos E. Clemmons

EFFECTIVE CHURCH LEADERSHIP REQUIRES A VARIETY OF gifts and talents which the pastor must use to "equip God's people for work in his service, to the building up of the body of Christ" (Eph. 4:12 NEB). It must be clear by now that this task is becoming more difficult to accomplish with the increasing legal regulation of the church by the state. Much of what is involved in effective leadership of the church deals with areas of heightened risk for some form of lawsuit. Church pastoral administration requires counseling, church discipline, supervision of others' work, teaching, preaching, and employment decision-making. Counseling and employment supervision carry the risks of sexual misconduct and abuse, breach of confidentiality, and breach of oral contract. Church discipline and, to a lesser degree, pulpit teaching carry the risk of invasion of privacy, breach of confidentiality, and intentional infliction of emotional distress. The highest risk areas are in the realms of sexual misconduct and abuse, breach of oral contract, and invasion of privacy. Therefore it is imperative that we address these areas and find successful ways to protect the church and the pastor from legal action.

Toward a Legal Duty for Clergy Counselors

As we outlined in chapter 3, a primary reason for the rise in lawsuits against church and clergy is due to the fact that more and more people seek legal action to redress complaints rather than deal with them biblically. It would be too simplistic and inaccurate to lay all the blame on secular society, however, as the church has also contributed to this problem through poorly trained and marginally ethical ministers and by ineffective corporate accountability. There is also increased pressure on the church to provide counseling help as more people become dissatisfied with secular counselors who are not advocates of or sensitive to biblical values.

These pressures help us understand why lawsuits are increasing against pastoral counselors and the church. Some have responded to this challenge by advocating a total separation of church from the mental health system, demanding the right to practice counseling without any interference from state law.[2] They are adamant that, for the Christian, counseling should be done solely within a church setting by ministers who are biblically and not psychologically trained.

Like the zealous Pharisee at the time of Jesus who expected the Messiah to come in a certain well-delineated fashion, this rigid view of separation of counseling ministry from state regulation also misses the mark. Restraining God's power behind a wall of separation, religious legalists supersede the law of love, leading to a blindness akin to the blindness of the first-century religious zealot. May God's Spirit gently open the hearts of our separatist brethren to this problem before the courts force open their ministries to an oppressive state accountability.

We agree with the limited clergy liability that exists for gross negligence, intentional tort, or actual malice.[3] Clergy should not be allowed to hide major failures or evil actions behind the First

Amendment. This was a key point in our analysis of the *Nally* case and support for Justice Kaufman's concurring opinion (see chapter 4). People harmed by grossly negligent or intentionally harmful pastoral behavior, especially if that pastor has trumpeted his or her competence and expertise, do have a valid cause for some form of legal redress. The church must recognize this and work internally to stop its harmful behavior rather than just reactively fight the "enemy" state.

SMITH WILL SUPERSEDE NALLY

The *Nally* case represents a temporary victory against the invasion of secular accountability into the religious arena. However, there are many influential people who disagree with the court's church-protecting decisions—the church should expect vigorous efforts by lawyers, academics, and other policymakers to create an accountability to the state for clergy counseling mishaps. We believe the trends in law and society—especially as seen in the *Smith* case—clearly point to increased state encroachment into the domain of Christian ministry, especially into Christian counseling.

Once the clergy-congregant relationship is legally recognized, a pastoral duty of care will be imposed that will require behavior consistent with that duty. The church, honorably engaged with the state, must be in the vanguard in the definition of that duty. The separatist church would, by default, concede such definition to those members of the secular state who neither know nor respect God's standards. Therefore, it behooves the wise pastor to begin to act consistent with this expected change in law in all counseling ministry. Two standards are fundamental here: genuine competence in counseling and effective referral of those cases beyond the competence of the helper.

COMPETENCE IN PASTORAL COUNSELING

Counseling has been a normal part of pastoral duties as clergy historically have been a key resource for advice on spiritual concerns, personal problems, and marital and family crises. Recent surveys verify that most people who seek counseling help consult with clergy as their first contact.[4] Nevertheless, *unquestioned* public confidence in the pastor as counselor has eroded over the past thirty years, with a steady increase in the number of lawsuits against clergy in the last decade.

The problem of clergy harm in counseling is primarily a question of counseling competence. How well trained and prepared is the pastor to help people successfully in counseling? What percentage of pastors are educated in seminary or, at the very least, in Bible college? Of those so educated, what percentage have had quality education and supervised training as counselors? Of those who do not have education or training in counseling skills, what percentage have gifts that facilitate some level of effective counseling? Even with good training, gifts, or competence, how many clergy are subject to self-defeating and parishioner-harming traits of questionable character and moral misconduct? We recognize, as do many in our society, a very mixed field of pastors, only some of whom are truly competent to counsel.

PASTORAL COUNSELING PROBLEMS

The primary roles of preaching, teaching, discipling, evangelism, administration, and leadership training leave the average pastor with little time to invest in the intensive counseling that many people require today. The average clergy's limited educational investment in counseling skills and relatively poor knowledge about basic psychopathology[5] further limit the clergy's ability to help a broad range of people. Frankly, few clergy can afford the time for in-depth counseling, nor can they justify spending the time to train for extensive counseling ministry.

The net result of the lack of pastoral training for counseling ministry is the provision of inadequate care by growing numbers of clergy and the increasing frequency of lawsuits against clergy. We believe that the majority of these lawsuits are preventable. Needham outlines the following practices and beliefs which the prudent pastor will *avoid* or *correct* in the practice of pastoral counseling.[6]

1. Counseling beyond your competence, ability, or training.
2. Advice against medical or psychological treatment.
3. Advice regarding medications.
4. The administration, interpretation, and scoring of personality and psychological tests.
5. The improper care of records.
6. Inadequately trained and supervised lay and pastoral counselors.
7. The failure to give credence to violent intentions or statements.
8. Misdiagnosing psychotics (or others) as demon-possessed.

9. Misrepresenting one's title, position, degrees, or abilities.
10. Recommending divorce.
11. Sexual involvement with a counselee.
12. Violations of confidentiality (by minister or staff secretaries).
13. The denial of the existence or severity of a psychological or psychosomatic disorder.
14. The belief in simple spiritual solutions for complex emotional and psychological problems.
15. The belief that all problems are spiritual or physical, with denial of the emotional and psychological dimensions.
16. The belief that pastoral and lay counselors need only biblical training to solve such severe problems as neuroses, psychoses, suicide, and the like.
17. The belief that pastors should be all things to all people.

WHO COUNSELS: PASTORS OR THE BODY OF CHRIST?

It is naive to presume that the average pastor with a minimum of counseling training is able to effectively help the broad range of people who need counseling help. Also, becoming a pastor, even an ordained minister, does not imbue that person with a mantle of giftedness in counseling. Many sincere pastors have seriously wounded or inadequately helped needy members of their flocks due to this type of naive and faulty thinking.

However, it is nonsense to conclude that pastors are generally inept and should do little or no counseling. Christians will rightly approach their pastors and priests as the first and usually most effective resource in the myriad problems faced in living. Most ministers have the wisdom and skill to help their flock or know when and to whom to refer when further help is needed. God gives gifts throughout his church in order for the body to function as a unit for benefit of the other members and the world. This benefit seems to be best served by many people with a diversity of gifts working in a complimentary fashion with one another.

This corporate philosophy of counseling ministry stems from 1 Corinthians 12 and Romans 12. "There are different kinds of gifts, . . . there are different kinds of service, . . . there are different kinds of working, but the same God works all of them in all men. . . . The body is a unit . . . in fact God has arranged the parts in the body, *every one of them, just as he wanted them to be.* . . . so that there should be no division in the body, but that its parts should have equal concern for each other" (1 Cor. 12:4–6, 12, 18, 25; italics ours; see also Rom. 12:4–6a). One cannot say "I have no need of you," nor can one say "I am enough in myself." God's way supports the validity of the pastoral gift, but the fulfillment of these godly goals requires the intervention and help of the entire church.

TOWARD EFFECTIVE REFERRAL

Effective referral is the left hand to the right hand of counseling competence for the helping pastor. When the limits of competence are reached, the pastor should refer his or her parishioner to those who are more competent to help the person. Ideally, there will be competent Christian helpers to whom the pastor can refer. As professional Christian counselors become more numerous and diverse in their locale, pastors are better able to refer needy congregants with confidence.

Unfortunately there are some areas where a referral person is not available who is Christian, or at least sympathetic to Christian values. As one lawyer well noted in this regard, "Pastors are under a mandate to protect those in their care from counsel that might undermine their faith (see Ps. 1; 2 Tim. 4:1–4; Titus 1). In any given case, there may not be a psychiatrist, psychologist, or other mental health professional who is supportive of the doctrinal stance of the church. It would seem untenable that a legal duty would be created forcing such churches and their clergy to refer their troubled members to professionals who may, in fact, be hostile to the member's faith."[7]

We believe there is a boundary here that defines pastoral liability. While the secular state is not equipped to determine the competence of Christian counselors, it is assuming the right to determine when a pastor should have referred. This increasingly occurs in cases of suicide, homicidal threats, child abuse, and elder/dependent abuse. The competent pastor will recognize the limits of counseling and develop procedures for effective referral in these situations. While referral has its set of problems, more serious problems occur when a pastor does not make appropriate referrals.

SHOULD PASTORAL COUNSELORS BE LICENSED?

There is a growing argument that clergy must become licensed in order to do counseling, even counseling within the church.

Proponents for clergy licensure assert two major propositions: (1) Counseling is not directly ecclesiastical in nature, but ancillary to such church functions, and therefore does not implicate constitutional protections of religious liberty. (2) Even if counseling cannot be separated from religious ministry, the benefits to the public in imposing licensing standards outweigh the burden on religion. The primary benefit of licensing would be an increase in the number of skilled counselors resulting in a measurably positive effect on the quality of counseling.

The courts have ruled, as a basic constitutional principle, that while the individual has absolute freedom to believe, the freedom to act is subject to regulation and restriction for the protection of society (see chapter 4). In fact, Paul argues in Romans 13:1–5 that it is important for the believer to submit to the authorities, because they are in place as a function of God's order. Since the state licenses mental health professionals, it is argued that religious counselors must also be regulated for the benefit of those who seek help from clergy. Many clergy admit to their lack of expertise in counseling and helping skills and seek greater training in the pastoral counseling area. Therefore, requiring specialized training and a formal standard of pastoral counseling care would better serve the church by protecting many people counseled by incompetent and immoral pastoral counselors.[8]

SHOULD THE STATE SET CHURCH STANDARDS?

Is it proper for the state to require clergy to meet legal standards for competence and referral? This proposition does strain First Amendment protections of ministry, because it requires the state to intrude upon church doctrine and clergy behavior. It views the clergy's counseling function as no different from the professional clinician's and holds him or her to a similar, even if less rigorous, standard of care. The *Nally* court wisely determined that holding clergy liable for negligent counseling would discourage private assistance efforts and have a chilling effect on those who seek help from clergy. The lines between protected pastoral ministry and unprotected pastoral counseling are unclear, however, and licensing proponents have neither a good plan nor a consensus about clear boundaries here.

In addition, licensure laws intended to establish general standards could never fairly apply to the diversity of church expression. We do not believe that states are able to evaluate the church's counseling quality in a way that respects religious freedom or the diversity of the church. Also, licensing proposals require clergy to have some minimal level of training, asserting that training improves the quality of counseling. While we agree that training can have a beneficial effect on the quality of the counseling provided by clergy, it is not clear what training would be required. Even if such standards could be fairly defined, the church, not the state, should set the standard.

State licensure for clergy counseling will not work. It would create government standards that are ill-defined and far too intrusive in the church. Proponents of clergy licensure tend to minimize the chilling effect on those seeking pastoral assistance, the difficulties of fair state administration, and the number of clergy who would be offended by such a policy. Lawsuits for grossly negligent and intentionally harmful clergy behavior are precise, effective, and quite enough state intrusion.

EFFECTIVE CHURCH DISCIPLINE

We learn from Matthew 18:10–20 that Jesus established church discipline as a key means to elicit repentance and restore a fallen or erring member to fellowship. Consistent with this purpose, the Greek word *parakaleo* aptly describes two key elements of church discipline: exhortation and consolation. The intent, like the shepherd who leaves the ninety-nine to rescue the one (vv. 10–14), is to pursue the erring member to save a precious soul (see James 5:19–20). In this regard Paul writes about an erring brother: "The punishment inflicted on him by the majority is sufficient for him. Now instead, you ought to forgive and comfort him, so that he will not be overwhelmed by excessive sorrow. I urge you, therefore, to reaffirm your love for him" (2 Cor. 2:6–8).

This concern for the individual must be balanced by the need to preserve the health of the fellowship. Paul writes to the Thessalonians that they are to carefully watch anyone who does not obey his instructions in this letter, "Do not associate with him, in order that he may feel ashamed. Yet do not regard him as an enemy, but warn him as a brother" (2 Thess. 3:14a–15). To Timothy he states, "Those who sin are to be rebuked publicly, so that the others may take warning" (1 Tim. 5:20). This public rebuke should have the effect of providing guidance to the church community as people see the consequences of persistence in sinful behavior. We rob people of the possibility of forgiveness when we do not confront; we need to see discipline as a gift, an opportunity to love and heal. Discipline gives identity and provides safety to people because it sets clear boundaries and honors them.

Church discipline, which is essential for the health of the Christian community, has no strong counterpart in the world today. Though the church is not of the world, it must operate within the world and so comes under the scrutiny of the state. In addition, societal norms of personal privacy and individual freedom are at odds with the necessity of church discipline, and many church members subscribe to those values as well. This causes real tension with church discipline, because some people are willing to seek solutions outside the church in the secular courts.

As a result, the church is becoming more closely monitored about fairness in the disciplinary treatment of its members, leading to some of the most serious tort claims being brought against the church. Congregants from a growing and diverse number of churches are suing the church for invasion of privacy, outrageous conduct, and intentional infliction of emotional distress. Therefore, if a church disciplines a parishioner and follows the guidelines in Matthew 18:15–17 without consideration of the legal ramifications, that church may be sued with a growing possibility that the plaintiff will win.

THE *GUINN* FIASCO: HOW BAD LAW ISSUED FROM A FAIR CASE

A disturbing lawsuit that illustrates the legal trouble with church discipline is the *Guinn* case.[9] Marian Guinn, a member of the Church of Christ in Collinsville, Oklahoma, became involved in an adulterous relationship. The elders of the church counseled with her several times, encouraging her to break off the affair. She agreed to do so but refused to follow the elders' request that she come before the church and repent. Guinn then wrote a letter to the church elders telling them she was terminating membership and, through her attorney, warned the elders not to tell anyone of her affair and personal matters.

The church would not allow her to withdraw fellowship, a matter based on their doctrinal beliefs. Consequently, the elders announced her disfellowship before the church and sent a letter to four other Church of Christ congregations in the area spelling out the nature of her sin. Marian Guinn sued the church, and the jury found against the Church of Christ, awarding damages totaling over $400,000, including $185,000 in punitive damages! The church was found guilty of publication of private facts, intrusion upon seclusion, and intentional infliction of emotional distress.

Upon appeal, the Oklahoma Supreme Court ruled that, although the church had the right to discipline its members, the church loses that right whenever a member withdraws membership—liability attaches after membership is withdrawn. It upheld the judgment against the church, including award of punitive damages, for acts following Marian Guinn's termination of membership. It remanded (sent back) the case to the trial court for determination of pre- and post-membership liability.

Church discipline and the state. Collinsville Church of Christ argued that, since a church member is a member of the Christian family for life, there is no doctrinal basis for withdrawal from membership. In addition, the right of a church to discipline its members without state interference is firmly grounded in constitutional law. Therefore, the court's distinction between pre- and post-membership liability usurps its religious doctrine and violates its First Amendment religious freedom. This was persuasive to two Oklahoma justices who sharply dissented the majority opinion: "This Court's review of the Church's doctrine of lifetime membership and moral discipline is precisely the kind of action the Constitution forbids."[10]

This was not persuasive to the majority, however, which held that a church can be held liable for wrongful acts after membership is withdrawn. In *Guinn,* the court agreed that the plaintiff's right to privacy was violated because the church acted publicly after she withdrew her membership. Avoidance of invasion of privacy becomes a critical concern for church leaders, then, after withdrawal of membership. The rule against invasion of privacy is based upon any one or more of the following four forms: (1) intrusion upon a person's seclusion or solitude or into his or her private affairs; (2) public disclosure of embarrassing private facts about a person; (3) publicity that places a person in a false light in the public eye; and (4) appropriation of a person's name or likeness.

Errors great and small. Both the Collinsville Church (slightly) and the Oklahoma Supreme Court (greatly) erred in this matter. The church conscientiously followed its own disciplinary rules, and this fact alone makes the court's intrusion all the more offensive. The church, however, seemed to lose the spirit behind the discipline—

the loving restoration of a person to Christ himself. Following the letter but missing the spirit of the law—and we mean God's law here—will increase the risk of the church becoming a lawsuit victim. The Spirit truly does give life; even those who oppose God's way will usually not sue if they are treated with the care and respect that Christ shows all deserve. ·

Even granting that the Collinsville Church erred, the Oklahoma court's ruling is still a travesty. The opinion violated a mass of precedent against finding religious-based torts for anything other than things that violate the state's compelling interest in public safety, peace, and order.[11] To then uphold intentional infliction of emotional distress and punitive damages against the church is truly a judicial case of adding vindictive insult to unjust injury. Marian Guinn herself admitted to the truth of the affair, which was well-known throughout the small town, and stated that the elders were kind to her throughout the proceedings. This ruling may well be the worst example of just and well-reasoned opinion regarding the church by any appellate court in America.

RECOMMENDATIONS FOR CHURCH DISCIPLINE

1. *Distinguish members from nonmembers.* Biblical discipline is directed toward believers (members), not unbelievers (nonmembers) (see Matt.18:15–20 and 1 Cor. 5:9–13). While some churches may not agree, we recommend respect for a member's right to withdraw, with churches agreeing to stop disciplinary matters at that point in time. Clear policies regarding this distinction—even doctrinal revision based on biblical argument—is essential for all churches in this litigious age.
2. *Move from implied to explicit consent.* Churches should consider requiring classes and written agreement to church membership that would include new members being informed of and counseled about the church's policies regarding disciplinary matters. Provide new members with a copy of the church constitution and bylaws, cover these areas closely in new membership classes, counsel prospective members about their concerns, and then have both pastor or church leaders and new members sign clear membership agreements.

   Based on clear communication and understanding of church bylaws *before* a person becomes a new church member, churches that gain explicit, written consent could maintain discipline of the member even after he or she withdraws membership. While this is not entirely risk-free, it is probably an acceptable risk to those churches with doctrines similar to those of the Church of Christ. It would be well to consult an attorney and verify the law in your state, as the Oklahoma decision applies only to that state.

3. *Use a board or leadership group to represent the church.* Many churches use a board or group of elders/leaders to represent the church as the corporate body denoted in Matthew 18:17. The Scriptures do not demand that the entire congregation be told of the sin. Use of a leadership group can better maintain the restorative purpose by respecting the person's privacy while adding authoritative influence to the challenge of the discipline. Such a group should agree to maintain strict confidence within group boundaries. If a person is disenfranchised from membership, that action can be communicated to the whole body without detailing the reasons why it was done.

4. *Maintain love and be flexible in the discipline.* The biblical rule is that churches have the right to withdraw fellowship, but only as a last resort and always with the purpose to restore right fellowship. When churches engage in harsh or rigidly legalistic behavior, especially if that behavior is formalized in a program that harmfully shuns a person, churches will be held liable.[12] When disciplining, the church must be especially wary to avoid defamation, intentional infliction of emotional distress, and violation of privacy rights. It is vital that the church consistently apply disciplinary procedures, following the steps outlined in the church bylaws.

5. *Respect the right to defend, and honor the defense.* Respecting civil law tradition, some church disciplinary processes have also included an opportunity for the accused to defend himself or herself. Two witnesses are required prior to sustaining a charge; this is particularly true for one who is an elder or church leader (see 1 Tim. 5:17–19). This process usually includes the right to confront one's accusers, the right to present a defense, and the right to not be compelled to testify against oneself. Provision should also be made for the accused to have one(s) who will assist as counsel—another member of the church trusted by the accused and respected by the church. The process should be a fair and impartial evaluation of the facts prior to the imposition of any discipline. Be especially careful that the privacy of the individual is protected, and do not allow any unsubstantiated charges to be publicly proclaimed by the church.

Supervision of Pastoral and Counseling Staff

A complex web of state and federal statutes, court decisions, and church rules regulate counseling practices, and each year the web becomes more tightly woven around church and religious organizations. The law of agency or *respondeat superior* (reviewed more fully in chapter 21) makes the pastoral supervisor wholly responsible for the counseling work of his or her subordinates. With this principle in view, we focus on recommendations to pastors and church leaders for effective and risk-managed supervision. The pastor must balance the goal of effective administration of the church (see Rom. 12:4, 8; 1 Cor. 12:27–29) with the biblical and legal mandate to protect the flock from harm (see Matt. 18:10–14). In this context the flock would include both members and nonmembers who participate in the particular pastor's church fellowship.

General Recommendations for Church Supervision

The supervision of pastoral and counseling staff must adhere to the guidelines suggested in chapters 12 and 21 of this text with respect to the prevention of lawsuit through high-risk beliefs and behavior. For example, publicly disclosing the sins of erring members or attempting to coerce and manipulate behavior beyond the norms of biblical freedom to decide tends to cause more harm than good and increasingly leads to lawsuit.

It is important that the pastor is adequately prepared to supervise lay and pastoral counselors and consistently participates in continuing education in order to meet the standards of care expected for such a role. Adequate supervision means more than time spent on a weekly basis in a staff meeting taking care of church business. Part of the process of supervision should include weekly or biweekly meetings with counseling staff to discuss and review cases. Particular attention should be paid to discussion of matters that are problematic or potentially high-risk, especially those cases that involve moral risk, ethical dilemmas, and problems beyond staff competence.

Develop Clear Policies for Helping Ministry

We suggest that the local church develop guidelines for helping ministry and that they adhere closely to those guidelines in a consistent fashion. It is wise to begin with a formal written policy for your church combined with the development of adequate selection, training, and supervision of pastoral and counseling staff. Your policy should define the limits of your competence and work in a practical way, with clear direction for referral and follow-up once those limits are reached. Setting limits as to the time, number of sessions, and types and severity of problems you will work with will help avoid both legal trouble and the black hole of unlimited (and impossible) counseling ministry.

We recommend, to mitigate legal trouble, that churches refer to their counseling ministries as helping or encouragement ministry, unless they have professional counselors on staff. Be especially careful about the use of titles when referring to a Christian helper; for example, do not call a lay helper a *Christian psychiatrist* or *Christian psychologist*. *Lay helper* or *lay minister* is accurate and adequate. In all promotions of the counseling ministry, great care must be taken to avoid misleading claims about expertise, competence, change, or healing prowess.

GUARD CONGREGANT CONFIDENTIALITY

Be sure that staff carefully guard the confidentiality of records and information. Confidentiality is "the act of protecting from disclosure that which one has been told under the assumption that it will not be revealed without permission."[13] Confidentiality can only be breached under certain specific legal requirements (see chapter 7) or if the client gives permission. Suits against the church are rising because breach of confidence in church ministry is common. Many leaders do not respect this principle and do not model confidentiality to their staff and congregations.

It is important to distinguish staff protected by the clergy-penitent privilege from those not protected. Staff who function in nonordained or lay counseling roles will usually not be protected by the privilege. Therefore, some staff would be required to adhere to state regulations (e.g., to report child abuse), while some clergy in his or her priest-penitent role would not have that same requirement. This is a vital consideration for evaluation of adherence to state law in those cases where reporting is an issue.

In order to respect the legal and moral right to privacy of church members and attenders, any preaching or writing based on real-life situations should include the person's written permission. We suggest that a written permission form include: what information is to be used; where and under what conditions it is to be used; how long the permission is granted to use such information; how the person may revoke the permission; and what the pastor will do if he or she desires to use the information in any other way and at any other time.

FAIR EMPLOYMENT POLICIES

As the pastor usually represents the church as an employer, part of his or her job will involve some measure of hiring, job evaluation and discipline, and possible termination of employment. It is vital to attend to three general rules regarding termination: be honest, be fair, and be consistent. Review church employment policies to be sure of clarity and fairness in application to employees. Make sure that no employment policies and personnel practices violate fundamental rights against termination without cause. If certain types of employment are intended to be terminable without cause, be certain that all written materials are consistent with this policy. All employees should understand the policy and sign an agreement to such possibility before they are hired.

It is essential to regularly review the performance of all employees. Be accurate in the evaluations, paying particular attention to areas that require improvement in order to give the employee clear job expectations and opportunities to satisfy the job requirements. These performance reviews should be written, then signed and dated by the employee, and maintained in the employee's permanent record. If the employee disagrees with the conclusions, a written rebuttal can also be included in his or her personnel file.

A procedure for progressive discipline prior to firing should be outlined and adhered to carefully. It should distinguish those situations that must lead to immediate dismissal (abuse, theft, sexual misconduct) versus those less serious situations that require progressive discipline. Any disciplinary conferences with the employee should be well documented. The nature of the problem, the time and date, the opportunity for improvement, and the discipline imposed should all be filed in the employee's personnel file.

CONCLUSION

We need to be careful to not presume that since the *Nally* case concluded as it did that the pastor is protected from liability and can act solely as he or she deems biblically correct. It is difficult to trust that the state will protect the best interests of the church as it gains greater jurisdiction over pastoral counseling. We must recognize that we live in a culture that is hostile to the Christian message and that will demand that the clergy adhere to similar standards of care as the licensed professional. They will be joined by those who are not hostile to Christianity but do not understand why the clergy should not be required to adhere to secular definitions of standards of counseling care. We must therefore prepare ourselves to do battle with all wisdom, being careful to advocate clear standards of pastoral leadership, counseling competence, and committed and effective referral.

NOTES

1. Amos Clemmons, "The Pastor and the Institute," *Parakaleo* 3, no. 3 (1991): 1–2; published quarterly by The Redwood Family Institute, Eureka, California.

2. See, for example, John MacArthur, *Our Sufficiency in Christ* (Dallas: Word, 1991); Martin and Diedre Bobgan, *Psychoheresy: The Psychological Seduction of Christianity* (Santa Barbara, Calif.: Eastgate, 1987).

3. Ibid.

4. George Domino cites statistics from a 1960 study of those who seek counseling help which revealed that 42 percent first went to clergy, 29 percent to physician, and 31 percent to practitioner or agency known as a mental health resource. The follow-up study in 1981 of those who sought help from 1957 to 1976 indicated that: 39 percent to clergy, 21 percent to family physician, 29 percent to psychiatrists and psychologists, and 20 percent to other mental health sources. See George Domino, "Clergy's Knowledge of Psychopathology," *Journal of Psychology and Theology* 18, no. 1 (1990): 32–39.

5. Ibid. The results of his study indicated this about clergy.

6. Adapted from Thomas Needham, "Helping When the Risks Are Great," in *Clergy Malpractice*, ed. H. Newton Malony, Thomas L. Needham, and Samuel Southard (Philadelphia: The Westminster Press, 1986), 89-90.

7. Samuel E. Ericsson, "Clergy Malpractice: Ramifications of a New Theory," *Valparaiso University Law Review* 16 (1981): 163. Ericcson was the defense attorney for Grace Community Church in the *Nally* case.

8. Robert C. Troyer, "Protecting the Flock from the Shepherd: A Duty of Care and Licensing Requirement for Clergy Counselors," *Boston College Law Review* 30, no. 7 (1989): 1179–1220.

9. *Guinn v. Church of Christ of Collinsville,* 775 P.2d 766 (Okla. 1989).

10. Ibid., 795.

11. See *Cantwell v. Connecticut,* 310 U.S. 296, at 303–4, where the U. S. Supreme Court distinguishes "the freedom to believe [from the] freedom to act." While the freedom to believe, by nature, is absolute, the freedom to act cannot be "for conduct must remain subject to regulation for the protection of society."

12. For a case of harmful shunning, see *Paul v. Watchtower Bible and Tract Society of New York, Inc.,* 819 F.2d 875 (9th Cir. 1987).

13. H. Newton Malony, "Confidentiality in the Pastoral Role," *Theology, News and Notes* (October 1986): 12.

Chapter 20

Professional Christian Counselors: Issues in Training and Licensure

Professionals profess. They profess to know better than others the nature of certain matters, and to know better than their clients what ails them or their affairs. This is the essence of the professional idea and the professional claim. . . . The professionals claim the exclusive right to practice, as a vocation, the arts which they profess to know, and to give the kind of advice derived from their special lines of knowledge. This is the basis of the license, both in the narrow sense of legal permission and in the broader sense that the public allows those in a profession a certain leeway in their practice and perhaps in their very way of living and thinking.[1]

E. C. Hughes

THE PROFESSIONAL CHRISTIAN COUNSELOR IS A NEW FORM of helping minister—the product of twentieth-century development of the psychological and social sciences integrated with Christian helping ministry. We define the professional Christian counselor, for purposes of legal analysis, as a Christian who works professionally with state and social sanction as a counselor or clinician. The following attributes are common to this designation:

- Professional work in psychosocial service to clients or patients. One receives a salary or fee-based income and identifies publicly as a professional in one of the major helping disciplines—counseling, psychology, psychiatry, social work, nursing, or marriage and family therapy.
- Licensure by the state wherein one practices, or sanction in some manner by a reputable and recognized national

credentialing group. This is crucial to demonstrate a requisite level of knowledge and applied skill in professional practice Increasingly, state licensure is being recognized and required as the minimum standard of professional practice.

* Attainment of a master's or doctoral degree in the field of one's professional identity. While all of the counseling disciplines grant doctorates, only psychiatry and psychology require the doctorate to practice in their fields.

Considering these elements of professional identity and practice, it is easy to ascertain why issues of training and licensure are so important. The legal implication of these issues are growing and becoming more crucial as the helping professions mature into the twenty-first century.

Legal Issues in Professional Training

Broadly speaking, preparation for professional counseling work falls into four areas: graduate study, personal psychotherapy, internship training, and licensing exams. Getting in and getting out—this describes in a nutshell the challenge and the legal focus of graduate training in the helping professions. Getting in refers to the problems of admission to a graduate training program. Getting out with a bona fide degree, able to begin professional practice and work toward licensure and independent status is the second hurdle. A large body of litigation exists around both of these issues.

Access to Professional Training Programs

Graduate programs operate as front-line gatekeepers for the professions. They function to admit the very best clinicians-to-be while screening out inappropriate and incompetent applicants. Graduate and undergraduate programs must function responsibly to protect the public from people who will not act in ways that are healthy for society as a whole. Educators must be aware of the growing legal liability in admissions and retention decisions and exercise due caution. Liability in admissions usually involves arbitrary decisions, implied and formal contracts, and discrimination issues.[2]

Arbitrary decisions. In order to protect the public and to meet the requirements of responsible admissions requirements for students, schools must spell out objective and specific admissions standards to their programs. Applicants must not be discriminated against in an arbitrary and capricious way in admissions decisions. As one author states, "A federal court reaffirmed . . . that there must be equal opportunity for admission and attendance by qualified persons and that this opportunity is protected by law." Schools must also spell out "disciplinary, scholastic and behavioral standards which are relevant to its lawful mission."[3] This can include an expectation of moral and ethical behavior that is superior to that required of the average population.

Contract theory. Schools must honor, as a matter of contract, the offers of admission spelled out by published catalogs. In *Steinberg v. The Chicago Medical School,*[4] for example, the court found that the plaintiff and the school had entered a contract, and once the application fee was accepted, the school had to fulfill its promise of admission. The school must focus on training and meet the criteria of the programs as advertised in school bulletins. The incoming student expects training and should receive an education similar to what is promoted. If the student does not receive such training, he or she may fail to meet the licensure standards of the state.

Discrimination. No school may establish criteria for admission that discriminates against a person based on race, sex, age, citizenship, or physical handicap. Physical handicaps, however, may be one area where some individuals may not be able to complete tasks required in the profession. If this is so, then the school has an obligation to the profession to disallow admission. This judgment must be sound, nondiscriminatory, and easily defensible. For example, while a school would not be prevented from considering mental illness as a prohibiting factor for admission, they cannot reject a candidate solely because he or she had once been admitted to a mental hospital. If, on the other hand, a person has a recurring problem (e.g., a personality disorder or alcoholism), then the school may be allowed to deny admission.[5]

One area that is only partially protected from discrimination is religious belief. Gartner studied the evaluation of conservative religious applicants by graduate programs in clinical psychology.[6] Nine hundred and eighty graduate professors evaluated mock applications to their programs and rated applicants for graduate school suitability. Among identical applicants, data showed that the nonreligious applicants rated higher on evaluations than applicants indicating religious preference.[7] Graduate psychology programs "were more likely to admit an applicant who made no mention of religion than they were to admit an *otherwise identical applicant* who was identified as an evangelical fundamentalist Christian."[8]

The second author of this book applied to a graduate psychology program in 1975 and was advised by a psychology professor not to emphasize his Christian values in the application process. This type of anti-Christian bias violates the ethical principles of most major professional associations and violates the intent of the laws against discrimination. Beyond that, this discrimination promotes an underrepresentation of qualified conservative religious professionals within the mental health professions. This also fosters a lack of skill within the counseling professions to provide mental health services to those with Christian religious values. In effect, this discrimination is similar to that which discriminates against anyone of another racial or cultural perspective.

GETTING OUT WITH A DEGREE

Graduating with a reputable degree is another factor that the applicant must consider when applying to graduate programs in the counseling professions. It is wise to pursue admission to training programs that are approved by national professional associations; schools approved by the licensing board of the state in which you intend to pursue licensure is a baseline requirement.

Sexual harassment. For women, especially, a significant aspect of graduate study can be the struggle with sexual harassment. Sexual harassment by teachers, tutors, supervisors, and, increasingly, other students is illegal and can lead to firing, expulsion, and lawsuit; nonetheless it goes on. It may be hard for a student to prove harassment, particularly when it is her word against the word of a professor. If the student complains, she may come under further harassment by implied threats of failing a key course or losing a critical recommendation.

Our recommendation to a woman who is harassed is to document her harassment as soon as possible. She should clearly tell the professor that she is not interested. Then find a significant person who will help protect her confidences. She could discuss the matter in the form of an informal complaint to an ombudsperson on campus or in the community. This documentation could be a vital link for dealing with an unethical person.

Fulfilling your contract. Just as a university has contractual obligations to the student (as discussed above), so the student has obligations to the school. If the student fails to make reasonable progress toward educational goals, then the school's contract with the student can be voided. Getting out with a degree means adhering closely to the terms of that contract. In addition, a student of any university, by reason of enrollment, agrees to comply with all rules related to personal conduct and care of university property. Any violation of those rules will lead to suspension, probation, or expulsion. As usual, the rules vary from university to university, and it is essential for the student to be familiar with those standards.

PROFESSIONAL LICENSURE

The state in which a professional Christian counselor resides has the authority to regulate his or her admission and ability to maintain practice in that state. The administrative agency that regulates licensure operates under the statutes of the various civil codes which apply to the particular counseling profession. Legal challenges to the broad, discretionary authority of these agencies to regulate professional practice have uniformly failed.

The general intent of licensing statutes is to protect the consumer from harm. However strongly one might argue that licensure does not guarantee quality, as Christians we are called to adhere to the laws of the land. Licensing laws admittedly can be an annoyance, but they rarely, if ever, fall to the charge of being anti-Christian. While the laws themselves may be static, the interpretation of the laws continues as a dynamic interaction between regulatory boards, professional organizations, consumers, legislatures, courts, and clinicians. Frankly, it can be a real challenge to keep up with the changes, yet it is vital to do so.

INTERNSHIPS

Preparation for licensure usually involves gaining supervised experience in approved internship settings. For those states with internship requirements, there are specific matters which must be carefully considered in order to fulfill those requirements (see chapter 21). Generally, these involve meeting education requirements, completing the required number of supervised hours, working in approved internship sites, the scope of license, and character and fitness.

Stay informed of the rules. Some people have lost valuable hours toward licensure because they did not adequately plan ahead. In the first place, if you are gaining hours for licensure in your state, do not simply rely on your supervisor to keep you informed of your status. Make it a point to keep well informed of the applicable laws yourself. Often those who are gaining hours in one state, which meet the requirements of that state, discover that those hours do not satisfy the licensure requirements in another state. Naturally it is tempting to cheat and adjust your reporting to satisfy the state's requirements without actually meeting the licensing regulations. This opens the counselor to potential fraud charges if he or she is ever discovered, leading to denial of license and possible fines.

Appropriate intern setting. Licensure requires special settings in order to train people to be adequately prepared to provide competent counseling within the scope of the license. It is the intern's responsibility to make sure that his or her supervisor is qualified to supervise and that the setting is an appropriate and valid site for gaining hours. Too many people have tried to gain hours in an inappropriate setting or with a supervisor who did not meet statutory qualifications.

OBTAINING PROFESSIONAL LICENSE

Since a license is becoming the necessary prerequisite to professional practice, obtaining and maintaining one is crucial for the Christian counseling professional. It is devastating to face loss of licensure or the failure to obtain one after years of hard work in preparation for practice. Obviously, for such a critical rite of career passage, there is a significant amount of litigation regarding nearly every aspect of licensure law.

Reciprocity. Practitioner beware! Do not presume, if you are licensed and transferring from one state to another, that your license will be valid in the other state. If you are considering such a move, it is essential to prepare yourself professionally by a careful evaluation of the new state's licensing statutes. There may be substantial differences in the license requirements such that the new state may not accept your license as valid. You may be required to fulfill the new state's prelicense process and take exams in order to obtain a license. Many have failed in their attempts to win a legal case against the state in order to try to procure such licensure.[9]

Character and fitness. Another area of concern for those who wish to transfer to a new state is character and fitness to practice. Traditionally, evidence of alcohol or drug abuse, sex offenses, and fraudulent practice have been the problems in this area. If your reason for changing states is an attempt to evade the full consequences of professional discipline in another state, then be aware that your application will normally include evaluation of practice in other states. If you have been found unfit to practice elsewhere, then be sure that you are transformed, rehabilitated, and can show evidence of change before attempting to become licensed in another state.[10] Lying about or avoiding such disclosures eventually will be discovered to the grief of the practitioner, who can then face both license revocation and prosecution for fraud.

Licensure exams. A growing number of states are requiring an examination as the final hurdle to issuance of a license. Once intern hours are accrued, the applicant may face a written or, as is true in many states, both a written and oral exam procedure. Over the years the examination process has become increasingly rigorous and difficult. In California a hue and cry has arisen about high failure rates and the tests being unfair, arbitrary, and designed to limit new licenses to protect the practices of those already licensed.[11] Since the states require that regulatory agencies merely show a rational relationship between exam content and knowledge required for practice, legal challenges to the exam process have been largely unsuccessful.

LICENSE DISCIPLINARY ACTIONS

State licensing statutes have codified standards of wrongful behavior that have historically been the basis for malpractice lawsuits. While specific statutes of professional misconduct, the basis for disciplinary action, vary slightly from state to state, the following represent common grounds for action.

1. *Fraud in license procurement.* This normally occurs through misrepresentation of one's degree(s) or experience. This could also occur if an individual was convicted of a felony or some other legal or ethical violation and fails to report such on licensure application. This fraud can occur upon license renewal, initial application, or when transferring practice from one state to another.

2. *Unprofessional, immoral, negligent, or dishonorable conduct.* Some of the many ways a license can be revoked under professional misconduct include misrepresentation of qualifications or competence, aiding and abetting unlicensed practice, failure to maintain confidentiality, failure to disclose fees, false advertising, intentional infliction of emotional distress, failure to report child or elder abuse, negligent supervision of staff and subordinates,

or any act of gross negligence.[12] In addition, the state would evaluate such matters as the professional's mental and emotional health and general ability to truly help another person.

3. *Sexual relations with clients.* Though technically a subset of the above heading, sexual misconduct cases are the most frequent basis for loss of license and a key concern of many states regarding client and consumer protection. California, for example, distributes a consumer protection booklet *Professional Therapy Never Includes Sex* (see footnote 9 in chapter 6). This booklet must be given by therapists to clients who report sexual relations with previous therapists or physicians so that they may make an informed choice for action against the offending professional.

4. *Disciplinary actions in another jurisdiction.* This can also include behavior in another state that would likely result in disciplinary action in the state in which the professional currently practices.

EVIDENCE AND REGULATORY DECISION-MAKING

There is significant ferment concerning evidentiary standards and license board decision-making in professional discipline. The professional at risk of losing a license will attack any aspect of the disciplinary process that can reasonably be challenged. These tend to center around issues of the burden of proof, the sufficiency of evidence, and the admission of hearsay testimony.

Burden of proof. This area has been most controversial as the evidentiary standards by which licensing agencies base their judgments are generally less stringent than those required in court. Some states are beginning to require more rigor in the validation of evidence against a professional. New York, for example, is substituting a higher "preponderance of the evidence" standard for the threshold "substantial evidence" standard in some disciplinary cases.[13] In this change, the evidence for revocation must outweigh the evidence against it; the old standard allowed revocation based on evidence which may have been substantially outweighed by evidence to the contrary.

Sufficiency of the evidence. This is closely related to burden of proof issues with conflicting pressures at work. Consumer protection advocates want to relax evidentiary standards, arguing that the disciplinary system operates to protect offending professionals against the victimized client. Professional groups argue that the loss of licensure and all it entails demands that more rigorous standards to protect against unfair and arbitrary decision-making.

This battle is most controversial regarding cases of sexual misconduct. It is difficult to prove sexual misconduct, in court or before licensure boards, when there is but one victim. A my-word-against-yours dilemma will usually be resolved in favor of the professional, giving him the benefit of the doubt. Add the testimony of a second victim, however, and the case shifts dramatically against the professional. Most states are taking strong action against professionals by revoking licenses when two or more witnesses complain.

Hearsay admissions. Hearsay testimony, information not directly witnessed or heard but gained secondhand, is generally inadmissible in court. Certain types of hearsay evidence, however, are not only admissible but are becoming a basis for mandatory action. The California rule noted above requires therapists to give and review the sexual misconduct booklet with clients who report prior offending behavior. The Wyoming Supreme Court recently upheld hearsay evidence by one physician against another where several women had complained of sexual misconduct. The court held that such evidence in a disciplinary action was "the type of evidence commonly relied upon by reasonably prudent men in the conduct of their serious affairs."[14]

PENALTIES AND REINSTATEMENT

License revocation penalties tend to fall into two classes. In most states a license is revoked for a set period of years with reinstatement possible. Licensure boards operate from a body of penalty precedents that are historically based and are usually court tested. A second type does not fix a time frame for revocation, presuming revocation is for life. This presumption may be challenged if the ex-licensee applies for new licensure and can prove he or she is now fit to practice.

A growing number of states are requiring penalized professionals to show evidence of both moral fitness and professional ability to practice by the time of reinstatement. This usually involves evidence of having cured the problem that led to revocation as well as evidence that he or she is still professionally competent. This second element is often met by having to retake exams for licensure. In reinstatement, most states also require a probationary period where the professional practices under close supervision and is required to submit periodic evidence of competent practice to the state board.

CONCLUSION

As Christian counseling becomes ever more professionalized, issues of professional education, intern training, and licensure will ascend as primary concerns. This represents a normalization of (some might say a capitulation to) state influence in the Christian counseling process. So far, this has not been a major offense to the Christian counselor's unique value stance, nor can it be under the First Amendment and antidiscrimination statutes. The fact of discrimination against Christians in professional school admissions should be more vigorously challenged, however. Concern also exists in trends toward rigid and legalistic interpretations in undue influence and dual relations laws that could be used against Christians.

We believe honorable relations between church and state are possible and Christians are not obligated to assume a hostile, adversarial stance to everything connected to government. We are called to be in the world but free of its corruption, to be wise yet harmless in relation to it, and to obey those in authority whenever that authority does not contradict the clear mandate of Scripture. Professional Christian counselors can and must respect the law of the state while we increase our vigilance in the twenty-first century to its power to abuse us. These relations inevitably call us to witness Christ, to be salt and light in state and professional relations with both our believing and nonbelieving colleagues.

NOTES

1. Everett C. Hughes, "Professions," in *The Professions in America*, ed. K. S. Lynn (Boston: Houghton-Mifflin, 1965), 2.

2. This outline is based on Bettie Cole's article, "Legal Issues Related to Social Work Program Admissions," *Journal of Social Work Education* 27, no. 1 (1991): 18–24.

3. Ibid., 19.

4. *Steinberg v. The Chicago Medical School*, 354 N.E.2d 586 (1976).

5. See Cole, regarding *Doe v. New York University* and *Anderson v. University of Wisconsin*, 21–22.

6. John Gartner, "Anti-Religious Prejudice in Admissions to Doctoral Programs in Clinical Psychology," *Professional Psychology: Research and Practice* 17, no. 5 (1986): 473–75.

7. This applicant differed from the evangelicals in that he not only was a Christian, but "hoped to integrate his religious orientation with the practice of psychology." Ibid., 473.

8. Ibid. (italics added).

9. Rudolph Reaves, *The Law of Professional Licensing and Certification: 1987 Supplement* (Charlotte, N. C.: Publications for Professionals, 1987), 7.

10. See Gordon McDonald, *Rebuilding Your Broken World* (Nashville: Oliver-Nelson, 1988), for an excellent book on honest recovery from broken hopes and violated professional and personal practices.

11. Data from *The California Therapist* (September/October 1990): 53, and (May/June 1991): 13.

12. See the *California Business and Professions Code,* section 1881.

13. See *Cerminaro v. Board of Regents, State of New York,* 508 N.Y.S.2d 693 (A.D. 3 Dept. 1986).

14. *Storey v. Wyoming State Board of Medical Examiners,* 721 P.2d 1013 (Wyo. 1986).

Chapter 21

Supervision and Consultation in Private and Agency Practice

. . . if gaining experience at counseling and supervision is like the aging of wines, then this review uncovered two types of wines: counselors and supervisors. One type of wine, the counselor, changes and improves with age. Counselor trainers and supervisors pay attention to the counselor's aging and aid his or her development. The other type of wine, the supervisor, does not clearly improve with age. Supervisors appear to be neglected or given minimal attention by most professional environments, yet are expected to change with age and to age with quality. . . . They are like a fine wine, bottled in sterile glass without a cork. . . . More attention is needed within the profession to the maturing of this wine into fullness.[1]

Everett L. Worthington, Jr.

CHRISTIAN PSYCHOLOGIST EVERETT WORTHINGTON STATED THIS unique conclusion following a comprehensive review of supervisory behavior in the mental health professions. He asserted that, as in counseling, mere experience does not necessarily improve professional competence. Both counselor and supervisor require guided training and close feedback in order to increase professional skill. He calls the clinical professions to a more rigorous and systematic commitment to the development of good supervisors. Considering the growing liability for poor and negligent supervision, such a call comes just in time and must be heeded with all seriousness.

In this chapter we deal with professional risks in supervision and consultation in the context of professional agency and clinic practice. As all fifty states and most Canadian provinces demand an increasingly comprehensive mental health licensure, some type of supervision is required in order for a person to meet the licensing requirements. In addition, it is usually prudent for a counselor to seek and maintain a supervisorial relationship throughout the lifespan of clinical practice in order to continue to grow and meet the challenges of informed clinical practice. The consistent review, evaluation, and assessment of a wide variety of counseling experiences is essential for development into a caring and proficient professional.

LIABILITY IN SUPERVISION AND CONSULTATION

Legal liability for supervision of professional relations can be direct or indirect in nature. Direct liability refers to acts or omissions by a supervisor that are negligent or harmful by themselves, apart from the relationship to client harm. Indirect or vicarious liability follows the legal doctrine of agency or *respondeat superior*— "let the master respond." This doctrine makes an employer, supervisor, or entire supervisory chain of command legally responsible for the employee's or supervisee's work. Since the supervisor is in a position of authority, has the power to choose and define the supervisory relationship, and stands to benefit financially from the relationship, the law has historically held the supervisor accountable.

A supervisor, then, may be doubly liable. He or she can be sued for the harm done to a client by the supervised therapist and can be liable for negligent supervision of the therapist directly. In *Cosgrove v. Lawrence*,[2] a mental health clinic and supervisor were held liable for a clinical social worker who had sex with the plaintiff several times at the clinic offices. Negligent supervision has been found when the supervisor gives poor advice to the client's detriment, performs supervisory tasks in a substandard way, knows or should have known the therapist was not skilled enough for the demands of the client, or has not taken action to protect the client when informed of therapist harm or negligence. Direct client contact is not necessary for a lawsuit against a supervisor. As a psychiatrist who defended four malpractice suits complained:

> I never saw three of the plaintiffs, nor did I talk to the families. In the other case I saw the patient-plaintiff only for 1/2 hour. My associates and partners were not negligent in these cases, but the plaintiff thought so.

The point is that as a senior partner I was considered responsible for the actions of my associates, even though I had never seen the patients. This is an important point to be remembered by every senior physician. The senior officer in every organization is legally responsible for every act of his juniors, both omission and commission.[3]

When a supervisor employs a supervisee (as in private practice), the supervisor's liability is coextensive with that of the employee—he or she is *fully liable* for all actions of the supervisee. In the case where the supervisor is employed by an agency or clinic to supervise, then the agency and the supervisor are fully liable—liability is coextensive up through the entire chain of command. When the supervisor contracts with an agency to exclusively provide supervision, then generally only the supervisor is legally responsible for the quality and appropriateness of the supervision. The key to liability assessment is the agency relationships and degree of control exercised by the supervisor.

LIABILITY FOR PROFESSIONAL CONSULTATION

Consultation has been defined as "a professional method of problem-solving involving a time-limited, purposeful, contractual relationship between a knowledgeable expert, the consultant, and a less knowledgeable professional worker as the consultee."[4] Legal liability for professional consultation is based on contract law. Breach of contract between consultant and consultee is the basis for suit in this arena. Since these relations are more collegial and contractual, liability for consultation is more limited and relative than the coextensive liability of supervision relations. The dilemma for the consultant is that, since the consultee retains control of the clinical relationship, the advice of the consultant may or may not be appropriately applied, if at all. The consultee may apply all or part of the consultant's advice or may choose to forego it altogether. While this reality certainly mitigates liability of the consultant, it does not sever all legal responsibility.

CLINICAL SUPERVISION AND SUPERVISORY RELATIONS

The following principles and guidelines for supervision apply to the employer, whether the employer is the agency or the supervisor. It is vital for each supervisor to be cognizant of the laws of his or her particular state and to apply those laws to the supervision process consistently.

GENERAL GUIDELINES FOR SUPERVISION

Clinical supervision involves the review, evaluation, and assessment of assigned counseling experience on an individual or group basis. A supervisor must meet minimum standards in order to qualify for the role of supervisor. Each state with licensing requirements establishes the standards for supervision. These normally define who may supervise, the responsibilities of the supervisor, the limitations on the supervisor and supervision, the types of professional counseling experience permitted for licensure, and requirements for out-of-state supervision. In addition, the statutes often consider employment settings and other employment considerations, payment parameters, and unprofessional conduct in supervision and supervisee behavior.[5]

The supervisor must be able to meet with his or her supervisees on a consistent basis (usually weekly) in order to ensure that the supervisee properly assesses and treats the client and is acting within the scope of the appropriate license. The quality of counseling provided shall be monitored by the supervisor "by direct observation, audio or video recording, review of progress or process notes or records or by any other means deemed appropriate by the supervisor."[6] The methods of supervision the supervisor intends to utilize should be discussed with the supervisee and agreed to beforehand.

THREE-STAGE SUPERVISION PROCESS

Following is an outline of a three-stage process of clinical supervision that is intended to maximize quality supervisory relations and learning while also minimizing legal risk.

Stage 1: Screening supervisees and supervision preparation. The supervision process begins when the employer interviews a potential intern or trainee. This process must involve a careful evaluation of the supervisee's skill level and provide an explanation of the objectives and goals of supervision. It is also important to assess the intern for the type of clients that he or she can treat and to orient your supervisee to the relevant laws and ethical requirements of your state and profession. Once employed, this process should also include signing appropriate documents to comply with state requirements. Finally, define what manner of supervisee evaluations will occur and how often, and ensure that accurate written records will be made of each evaluation.

The supervisor assumes legal liability for each case of the supervisee as well as for his or her own clinical work. It is imperative that the supervisor become familiar with each of the supervisee's cases and that no major decisions are made without the supervisor's review and possible modification. In a hospital setting, at least, it may be advisable to have the supervising psychiatrist personally evaluate patients prior to any major interventions, since these actions may result in the greatest legal liability.

The supervising clinician must include careful evaluation of his or her own counseling and supervision caseload so as to not overload himself or herself. Be especially careful not to supervise more clients than you can maintain with a full understanding of each of their cases. Be certain to keep malpractice insurance in force (both personally and, when appropriate, with the agency). Finally, make sure that clients are kept informed of each supervisee's licensure status.

Stage 2: Training and monitoring supervisees. The supervised training process is an artful balance of helping the supervisee learn through mistakes while making sure the clients receive quality care without harm. Maintaining this balance takes time, careful planning, and empathetic training. We suggest that intern/trainees be required to fill out an intake evaluation form for each case within a week of the initial interview for supervisor review. In addition, during the supervision hour, whenever possible, use live, video, or audio supervision for best results. Be careful not to overload supervisees with cases, being especially careful about cases at the boundary of their competence.

Each supervision meeting should be regularly scheduled and carefully documented, including those consultations that are not undertaken during the normal supervision hour. It is important for any supervisor to keep clear, precise, and updated case notes on all supervision contacts with careful follow-up on all cases. One goal here is to protect the supervisor from accusations of negligent supervision—accusations which can be refuted through accurate and thorough records. Make sure that supervisees also keep accurate, up-to-date case records.

Avoid dual relationships with the supervisee, including not providing psychotherapy while he or she is under your supervision.

Do not sign insurance forms for clients you have not supervised, which can lead to charges of insurance fraud. Consider utilization of a variety of supervision models in the training process in order to enhance learning and clinical effectiveness for yourself and your supervisees.

Finally, it is critically important to thoroughly investigate all complaints by the supervisee's clients. A physician in *Andrews v. United States*[7] was found liable for not adequately investigating a rumor heard from another patient of sexual contact between an assistant and a patient. The supervisor should guide the trainee in the resolution of the complaint if at all possible. Some complaints are so serious or threatening that the supervisor may be required to make direct intervention. In the worst cases (e.g., sexual relations) supervisee work must be suspended until charges are proven or not, with the supervisor offering to take over the case clinically.

Stage 3: Supervisory evaluations. The best supervision gives *regular verbal and written evaluations* of each supervisee. Trainees should know what style of supervisee evaluations will occur, when they will occur, and how they should present themselves. The supervisee is expected to make reasonable progress; when progress is deficient the supervisor can: (1) recommend a book, article, workshop, conference, or additional coursework; (2) offer direct work with the supervisee to correct deficiencies; (3) remind the supervisee of the contract ground rules and discuss actions that will be taken should the supervisee not comply with the requirements; (4) encourage the supervisee to scale back clinical work and get psychotherapy; or, in the worst case, (5) terminate relations with the supervisee.

It would be wise to have your supervisee(s) evaluate your supervision, using a standard evaluation format which assesses such things as organization, theoretical constructs, general and specific helpfulness of supervision, boundary issues, and the usefulness of various models employed during the supervision process.[8] In addition, various delicate areas of supervision should be evaluated such as dual relationship issues, sexual boundaries, law and ethics, and transference/countertransference issues. Admittedly this is a time-consuming process, but the quality of clinical work produced will have far-reaching, beneficial clinical and legal results. Finally, keep your supervision skills fresh and growing by continued training in supervision. Your supervisory "wine" does not age on its own.

PROPER PROFESSIONAL RELATIONSHIPS

A growing number of clinical professionals are developing practice relationships outside the historic agency model. Partnerships, profit and nonprofit corporations, and private practice office-sharing contractual relationships are becoming more common in the new mental health marketplace. Even when formal agency relations exist, growing numbers of counseling employees are doing private practice outside agency time but often using agency facilities for this work. Although agency as an organizational concept may not apply, the legal doctrine of agency can easily attach liability where these new practice forms are not well defined and fail to properly function.

A psychiatrist, for example, may employ other clinical professionals who may use the medical offices for part-time private practice. Though these relations are not supervised by the psychiatrist, he or she might still be held liable or, at least, joined to a suit as a defendant under apparent (ostensible) agency. The plaintiff may well believe, in this situation, that the psychiatrist is supervising the nonmedical clinician and that psychiatric access is part of the counseling relationship. In order to avoid this type of liability while allowing employees the freedom to practice privately, we recommend the following action be taken.[9]

- *Have all private clients sign disclosure forms.* A form should be signed by the therapist and the client that clearly spells out the exact nature of the service and that the primary clinician is not the supervisor nor is he or she involved in any way with the case. A copy of this disclosure should be kept by the therapist and by the primary clinician or employer.
- *Stay apprised of your employee's status and practice.* Make sure that your associate is properly licensed, has no complaints or legal actions on file, and maintains separate and sufficient malpractice insurance. Also, without being too intrusive, be careful to encourage the associate to practice within competence and only for an agreed number of hours outside of your professional relations.
- *Maintain separate professional communications.* Require that the private practitioner have separate business cards, letterhead, and the like and does not use your professional publicity when seeing clients privately.

Doing Risk-Managed Consultation

Consulting is a voluntary, contractual relationship between a professional helper and a help-needing individual or group. The good consultant is both a competent model and confident teacher. He or she must be able to assist the consultee to solve problems in relation to client service. The goal of the consultation process has been stated by Brown and Schulte:

> The primary goals of consultation are (a) to alter [problem] relationships among the behavior, interpersonal factors, and environmental variables that prevent the consultee from dealing effectively with the client, (b) to alter the relationships among the behavior, interpersonal factors, and environmental variables that prevent the client(s) from functioning appropriately in a particular situation, and (c) to prepare the consultee to deal effectively in the future with problems similar to the one being focused on in the current consultation.[10]

Consulting Contracts and Consultant Behavior

A well-written contract should define all consulting relationships. Any reference to a guaranteed outcome must be strictly avoided. Instead, the problem and goals of the consultation should be clearly and specifically stated. A reasonably specific time frame should be included, with a contingency clause for further work if agreed to by both parties. Fees should be defined clearly (per hour is preferred as it is least disputable), with express agreement about any consultant's time spent researching or writing beyond face-to-face contact. The contract should include a clause for dispute resolution, with both parties agreeing to a process of direct negotiation, mediation, then arbitration before legal action is considered. We encourage consultants to have consultees evaluate their work on a written form at the conclusion of the consultation.

The Consultative Process

As in supervision, a three-stage model outlines the consultation process and is very similar to the therapeutic process—assessment, intervention, and termination. The time-limited, problem-focused nature of consultation lends itself well to a cognitive-behavioral approach.

Stage 1: Assessing problems and defining goals. Problem assessment and goal definition should be done for both the client and the consultee in relation to the client. Helping the consultee help the client is the key to success. Define problems and goals in relation to motivation, skill and behavioral deficits, environmental barriers, self-defeating beliefs, and negative expectations. Clear behavioral outcomes should focus goal-directed behavior for both client and consultee.

Stage 2: Intervention. In this stage the consultant's modeling of effective behavior and teaching new skills reach their apex. It is important to stay consultee-centered to increase the likelihood of success. Use what the consultee already does well, and build upon his or her strengths. Bandura has shown us that self-efficacy is attained as one gains mastery by effective task performance.[11] Modeling mastery of consultee behavior, having the consultee rehearse behavior, imagine, and talk through successful client interventions are all excellent consultant interventions.

A behavioral, task-centered model of consultation also models, for consultees, interventions that will help them resolve their clinical impasse and move forward with their clients. Focused behavioral interventions are useful for a wide variety of clinical problems, including client resistance and lack of motivation, vague goals and poor direction, transference and countertransference issues and deficient clinical skills. We believe such a model is helpful regardless of theoretical orientation.

Stage 3: Termination. Ideal termination comes when consultant and consultee agree that goals have been reached; some consultations, however, terminate before this ideal is reached. Both consultant and consultee should evaluate progress on an ongoing basis. Consultants should help consultees address both what is and what is not going well in their interventions. It is critical, not only to future work but to avoidance of legal action, to avoid leaving the consultee feeling cheated or harmed. When goals are only partially reached, it is important to help consultees find the resources that will further their growth—workshops, books and articles, and classes. It is also valuable to communicate that consultation is an ongoing, periodic function and that you are available for future help.

CONCLUSION

The practice and, inevitably, the malpractice of supervision and consultation is receiving increased scrutiny by the professions, graduate schools, and the regulatory agencies of the state. This scrutiny is long overdue in a sphere of practice so central to professional excellence. Suits and regulatory actions for substandard supervision and consultation are increasing and will definitely influence our field (and all of counseling) into the twenty-first century. The best Christian counselors will be called upon to serve as supervisors and consultants—the teachers of helpers in the church by whatever label they are known. Entrusting this call "to reliable men [and women] who will also be qualified to teach others" (2 Tim. 2:2b) will require that we invest significant resources in the training and certification of these leaders. This will be necessary, not just to avoid suit, but also to fulfill the promise and work of a Christian counseling ministry.

NOTES

1. Everett L. Worthington, Jr., "Changes in Supervision as Counselors and Supervisors Gain Experience: A Review," *Professional Psychology: Research and Practice* 18, no. 3 (1987): 189–208.

2. *Cosgrove v. Lawrence*, 522 A.2d 483 (N.J. Super. App. Div. 1987)

3. G. Robinson, "Discussion," *American Journal Of Psychiatry* 18 (1962): 779–80.

4. Diana Waldfogel, "Supervision of Students and Practitioners," in *Handbook of Clinical Social Work*, ed. A Rosenblatt and D. Waldfogel (San Francisco: Josey-Bass, 1983).

5. See, for example, *California Business and Professions Code*, chapters 13 and 14.

6. Laurel Cox et al., *Practical Applications in Supervision* (San Diego: California Association of Marriage and Family Therapists, 1990), 1–9.

7. *Andrews v. United States*, 732 F.2d 366 (4th cir. 1984).

8. See, for example, "Ethical Principles of Psychologists," Section 7:c., the American Psychological Association, *American Psychologist* 45 (1990): 390–95.

9. Adapted from Gregory J. Firman, "Ostensible Agency: Another Malpractice Hazard," *American Journal of Psychiatry* 145, no. 4 (1988): 510–12.

10. Duane Brown and A. Schulte, "A Social Learning Model of Consultation," *Professional Psychology: Research and Practice* 18 (1987): 283–87.

11. Albert Bandura, "Self-efficacy: Toward a Unifying Theory of Behavioral Change," *Psychological Review* 84 (1977): 191–215; Albert Bandura, "Self-efficacy Mechanism in Human Agency," *American Psychologist* 37 (1982): 122–47.

Chapter 22

Expert Courtroom Testimony by the Christian Counselor

Question (by lawyer on cross-examination): Now doctor, you will have to be a little patient with me. . . . I do not understand just exactly what a psychopathic personality is . . . could you give a . . . concise definition in the language we would all understand of what psychopathic personality means?

Answer (by psychiatrist called as an expert witness): Yes, I think I can. I tried to do that the other day. I said that a psychopathic [now termed a sociopathic] personality was a disorder of character in which the outstanding features . . .

Q (cutting off the witness): No, if you can just define it, doctor. The first was excellent. It is a disorder of the character. Now, without going into the symptoms . . . tell us what pneumonia is.

A (somewhat confused): I will do that. Pneumonia is an infectious disease due to the invasion of the blood stream with the micro-organism called pneumococcus. . . .

Q: And a psychopathic personality—continue from there.

A: I said it was a disorder of the character. My next effort was to tell you what kind of disorder of character it was, and at that point you stopped me.

Q: . . . Can we go further than that without next going into symptoms?
A: I think we can.

Q: All right, if you will.

A: One has to assume that by the word character we include the mental and emotional life of the individual. . . . When I say "character," I mean it is a disorder involving the mental and emotional life.

Q: It is a disorder of character as you have defined the term "character"?
A: Yes.

Q: Anything more concise than that?

A: Well, the next step would naturally be to intimate what kind of disorder of character it was. That gets us into the realm of behavior.

Q: Well, doctor, can we say that as far as you would be willing to go on a concise definition basis, that it is a disorder of character? In other words, you won't go any further than that in your definition, will you doctor, except, of course, explaining the symptoms?
A: I will go further if you will allow me to.
Q: Oh, indeed, yes . . .

Excerpt of trial testimony from *United States v. Hiss* in 1949,
on the veracity and character of a key witness against
Alger Hiss in his famous Soviet spy perjury trial.

Lawyers may smile while mental health professionals shake their heads at the interplay between lawyer and psychiatrist in the *Hiss* case. We include this classic excerpt to make a critical point at the outset of this chapter. The *expert* expert witness is the clinical professional who understands and is prepared for: (1) the knowledge he or she has to offer the court, and (2) the tactics lawyers use to support or impeach the expert testimony. The lawyer above engaged in numerous tactics—literally a textbook presentation— intended to fluster, confuse, and anger the expert and weaken the point he was asserting in his testimony.[1]

The family therapist might recognize in this excerpt similarities to "crazy-making," double-bind communication often seen in pathological family systems. The novice expert, to say nothing of the ordinary mental health witness called to testify in a client's case, may be driven crazy if he or she is not well prepared for the courtroom process. The Christian counseling professional will increasingly be called upon to testify in court as an expert witness. In this chapter, we intend to help you to become as informed as possible about the call and demands of courtroom and expert witness.

THE PURPOSE OF EXPERT TESTIMONY

The central purpose of the expert witness is education—bringing special knowledge to the trier of fact, whether judge or jury, to assist them in resolving the dispute at hand. "The expert witness appears in the midst of adversarial proceedings but is not in an adversarial role. At most it can be said that the expert witness serves as an advocate for his or her expert opinion. He or she is not an advocate for the plaintiff, defendant, or any third party."[2]

The court accepts expert testimony when the knowledge of the expert is essential to assist the trier of fact in their case determination and such information can be obtained in no other way. Expert testimony serves as an exception to the general rule that courts will admit only factual, nonhearsay evidence (that which persons directly involved in the case actually saw, heard, or did themselves). Expert testimony expands the restrictive rules of evidence to allow opinions, hypotheses, and inferences about the evidence to help judge or jury render a proper judgment. Rule 702 of the Federal Rules of Evidence states, "If scientific, technical, or other specialized knowledge will assist the trier of fact to understand the evidence or determine a fact in issue, a witness qualified as an expert by knowledge, skill, experience, training or education, may testify thereto in the form of an opinion or otherwise."[3]

There is a subtle but important difference between helping the court "understand the evidence or determine a fact in issue" and presenting a case in order to help one side win. The expert's opinion is not a judgment about the issues in dispute but instead renders opinion about the factual evidence that affects those issues. Opinion about the alleged facts must be rooted in some objective professional assessment made by the expert who is bound to tell "the truth, the whole truth, and nothing but the truth" regarding his or her assessment. Learning to be nonadversarial but informed and influential in an extremely adversarial forum is the mark of the mature expert witness.

The lawyers, on behalf of their clients, are the adversaries. They will do all they can to present the expert's material in the best (or worst) light for their clients' interests. The lawyer hiring you will make you appear as a competent and prestigious professional—well trained, knowledgeable, and extremely wise and insightful. The opposing attorney, of course, will do quite the opposite on cross-examination. He or she will seek to discredit or minimize your opinion or even twist it to appear to support the opposing position if possible. If your testimony has been especially strong, you may even be attacked as a fraud, an incompetent professional, no more than a hired gun for the other side. Recognizing, even expecting this tactic and not taking it personally, can go a long way to help the mental health professional control anger and maintain professional demeanor and self-esteem.

THE QUALIFICATIONS OF THE EXPERT

A number of personal and professional qualifications are important to anyone who serves as an expert witness. These generally include both technical knowledge and skill in communicating and coping with the courtroom process. We will address courtroom process later in this chapter. Regarding scientific or technical expertise, consider the five aspects of the Federal Rule stated above—education, training, experience, knowledge, and skill.

Education. The expert should hold the highest degree attainable, usually a doctorate, in the field of his or her endeavor.

Training. Specialized training, internships, fellowships, and related honors should be noted. Minimally, holding licensure, certification, or other credentials for independent professional practice are essential.

Experience. Outlining relevant professional work experience establishes a strong basis for expertise. The mental health professional should be able to communicate positions held as well as the nature and problem focus of his or her diagnostic, therapeutic, and supervisory work.

Knowledge. This is established by the evidence on education, training, and experience and is reinforced if the expert has published papers, articles, and books. The value of this knowledge is revealed (or not) throughout the course of testimony. Some knowledge is prepared by written report and submitted to the court for inclusion into the record (although some lawyers dissuade writing reports to protect against their being discovered by opposing counsel). The expert should be thoroughly versed and prepared by attorneys prior to courtroom testimony.

Skill. This final element is the most elusive but often most important with respect to ably handling the process and assisting the court in the pursuit of a fair resolution. In many ways, like practicing therapy or any professional task, there is no substitute for experience. The expert must experience the trial process, especially skilled cross-examiners who artfully belittle the expert and his or her knowledge, to improve his or her skill and increase his or her value to the court.

A skilled expert can hold his or her own with the most aggressive lawyers. The novice or expert who is not skilled or well prepared will be exposed as anything but expert by an aggressive trial lawyer. A favorite story regarding lawyer preparation is the attorney whose case was badly damaged by a good expert. Desperately, the lawyer went on the attack:

> Q: How much are you getting paid to state the opinion we've just heard?
> A: I'm not paid for the opinion; I'm paid for my time.
> Q (with a sneer): And just how much will you be paid for that?
> A: That depends on how long you keep me up here.[4]

PREPARING TO TESTIFY AS AN EXPERT

Effective preparation is the key to excellence in expert testimony. Excellence in preparation can narrow the skill gap for the unexperienced professional, while the lack of preparation will often harm the testimony of highly experienced experts. Moreover, many cases are resolved short of trial, and often the expert may not even appear in court. The quality of his or her written reports or the information gained by pretrial deposition and discovery procedures may be the expert's only contribution to the process of adjudication.

Two rules are paramount throughout the process. First, truly have expertise and skill in the area desired. A good pragmatic test is: Can I handle and remain confident of my expertise in the face of hostile cross-examination? Get a clear answer to this by simulating this challenge with the hiring attorney rather than learning this answer in court. Second, take very thorough notes of your encounter with the client-disputant. These notes are usually more extensive and detailed than those taken in normal clinical practice. You should be able to repeat key material revealed by the client in substantial detail, sometimes verbatim. With the client's and the lawyer's permission, some experts routinely tape record their encounter and evaluative impressions.

The foremost need for the Christian mental health expert is a good professional service contract. The expert should have clear agreement with the calling attorney on fees, work expectations, time frames and deadlines, and contingencies that cannot be pinned down specifically. We recommend the expert be paid on an hourly or daily (including half-day) schedule.

A common pretrial pattern is for the mental health professional to conduct an evaluation and review the findings with the hiring attorney. If the findings coincide with the legal strategy, the expert will be retained for deposition or court testimony. There is a powerful temptation to bend the data in the direction of the client's interest. This should be avoided for two reasons. First, your professional integrity will suffer if you become too partisan, failing to remain objective. Second, the skilled expert learns how to present the facts in the client's interest without bending or distorting them. It is the lawyer's job to direct the questioning in a way that best promotes the client's objective.

DEPOSITION TESTIMONY

Depositions are a pretrial discovery device in which lawyers on both sides learn the evidence to be presented in court. Their value to the administration of justice is their efficiency, fairness, and increased likelihood of a pretrial settlement. Experts are deposed to discover relevant facts, to develop trial content and preserve testimony, to discover the theory underlying the testimony, and to establish the parameters of fair settlement. The expert is under oath, must answer truthfully, and is being recorded by a stenographer. The expert should be fully prepared to expect this data to be revealed and challenged in court. Experts should insist on and contract for a predeposition conference with the hiring lawyer to review the testimony, anticipate opposing questions, and coordinate behavior.

We recommend the following, adapted from Meyer and his colleagues, who suggest this outline regarding deposition practice using the Danner Pattern Deposition Checklist.[5]

1. *Courtesy counts.* Be courteous and polite to all concerned.
2. *Speak clearly.* Speak in a clear voice that can be heard by everyone, but especially by the stenographic reporter.
3. *Think before you speak.* Think about and understand each question before you answer. Your testimony even at this stage can markedly affect the case.
4. *Stick to the facts.* Base your answers only on information you have obtained yourself as part of your study. Be willing to say, "I don't know."
5. *Let the lawyers be in charge.* If the attorney who hired you objects, stop talking. It is best to let the lawyers deal with the point in question.

6. *Realize you are being judged.* Be aware that the opposing attorney will be evaluating you as a witness and may try many things in deposition that will not be used in trial.
7. *Maintain a complete and careful record.* Read the deposition when a copy is sent to you for signature; do not waive your right to sign it. Correct any errors in it as your attorney instructs. Keep a copy of your deposition with your other records pertaining to that case.
8. *Study before you go to court.* Review your copy of the deposition prior to going to court, and take it with you to the witness stand.

COURTROOM TESTIMONY

To outline the court process, we will discuss the two phases of courtroom testimony for the mental health expert.

ESTABLISHING YOUR EXPERTISE

The first phase of testimony involves the establishment of the expert's qualifications in a way that the trier of fact (judge or jury) is sufficiently persuaded that the expert can speak authoritatively on the issue. This process, known as *voir dire* (literally "to speak the truth") involves a careful recitation of the expert's training, degrees, honors, teaching experience, publications, and the like. The generalist practitioner is less influential than the specialist, who will be called more often as an expert. Specialized work in a specific area, with publications, conference presentations, and classes taught on the subject at issue, are highly valued in the qualifications of the expert.

Once your expertise is established before the court, the hiring attorney will then establish that you have been informed about and worked on the case at hand. This second part of establishing your expertise serves to lay the specific factual groundwork for all later testimony. The lawyer will establish that you have conducted an evaluation and have studied background documents and whether you have testified in deposition. This material must be very carefully established as it will be challenged by the opposing attorney. Any evidence that can be excluded or impeached by the opposing camp will help their case. Therefore, it is important to use objective and well-known testing devices and, as much as possible, standardized procedures for interviewing and presentation of data.

PRESENTATION OF OPINION

Direct examination. When the hiring lawyer asks, "And did you form an opinion as to . . . ?" the hard work begins for both you and the lawyers. The hiring attorney will be seeking to present a clear and persuasive case to the trier of fact and will guide you through a precise series of questions. Proper pretrial rehearsal of this phase between attorney and expert will increase the influence of this testimony. This direct examination is the most crucial part of your testimony, and your value to the hiring attorney will be largely judged by the quality of this interaction. Speak directly and clearly to the judge and jury, always remembering that the judge, not the lawyers, controls the courtroom.

The expert must be able to render a concise opinion as well as be prepared to deliver the clinical, theoretical, and empirical data underlying the opinion. Be careful to strike a balance that asserts the authority of your opinion without communicating a rigid posture that implies no other views exist. This must be done in clear, nontechnical language understandable to people who are not expert and who may be barely literate about mental health and psychosocial concepts. Be very careful, however, to avoid simplistic communication and condescending attitudes. The worst outcome for the expert witness is a judge or jury making decisions while aware of their annoyance about the way the expert communicated rather than from a sole focus on what the expert said.

Cross-examination. The opposing lawyer cross-examines the expert following direct examination. His or her primary goal is to discredit or neutralize the expert's testimony. This is the hallmark of the adversarial proceeding, a system that for all its faults has shown a remarkable record of focusing on the crucial evidence upon which fair judgments are made. Mental health professionals, valuing conciliation and trained to mediate disputes, often find this system foreign and distasteful. The skilled expert knows this process and expects to be challenged, learning how to maintain effective communication while managing the assault on his or her opinion.

The tactics of cross-examination focus on the weaknesses and attempt to exaggerate the problems and disagreements about your opinion. You may be asked a question or two about a particular point and be dismissed, just to get you off the stand and out of the jury's mind. At the other extreme, you may be asked a tortuous series of meaningless questions designed to tire the jury into wishing you were done. A common tactic is to force the expert to answer categorically, yes or no, to questions with a range of answers or as a response to two inaccurate choices. If the hiring attorney is not objecting, the expert should be deflecting these forced choices by stating that categorical answers are inappropriate and by asking for question clarification. Other tactics include presenting conflicting opinions by other experts and asserting alternative interpretations and confusing hypothetical scenarios.

If the cross-examining lawyer cannot punch holes in your opinion, he or she may attack your integrity. Challenging the influence of your expertise or asserting that you are nothing more than a hired gun, saying whatever the opposition has paid you to say, are common tactics. These challenges should be expected, especially if your opinion is solid, and should be calmly and directly refuted. If you have not contracted on a strict fee basis and have biased your opinion rather than remain objective, these challenges to your integrity will be more difficult to refute.

Christian counselors may be challenged by opposing lawyers, as was the first author in testimony in a recent child custody dispute, to show evidence of bias in professional opinion due to one's Christian beliefs. While a judge may sustain objections about this line of inquiry, some may not, and the counselor may be compelled to testify to his or her belief in Christ—in itself a good witness in any forum. The critical thing is to be able to assert that such belief does not bias your professional opinion nor that it is the sole or primary basis for your opinion.

Be careful, for example, not to assert the false assumption that the Christian home is always the preferred home in a custody dispute. While this may be true hypothetically (and a lawyer may press you with that hypothetical to push the issue of bias), it is not valid to apply this thought presumptively to all cases. This will be hard for some Christians, but it will be a far more painful lesson if a skilled trial lawyer then shows that the Christian home is abusive and the nonbelieving home is not. While Christian values are preferred, they are only one of many factors that must be respected in the placement decision. The courtroom is an arena where the counselor-witness must know whether the confessing Christian indeed bears the fruits of that confession.

Conclusion

In an increasingly complex and contentious society, many courts are becoming more reliant on the testimony of the expert. The mental health expert is being used with greater frequency to help resolve a myriad range of personal, familial, organizational, and social disputes. "In the absence of solid contributions by psychotherapists, the court must depend on amateurish speculation and simplistic notions of human nature. Consequently, those with special training in [the clinical professions] bear a heavy responsibility to support and assist the legal system."[6]

Christian professionals can bring their professional expertise infused with the values and integrity of their faith to the judicial process. The Christian professional has an opportunity to communicate values and a perspective on human nature that honors the things of God without offending the processes of the state. The Christian mental health expert who testifies in court performs a unique and powerful function of our call to be salt and light in a dying world.

NOTES

1. William Curran, "The Hiss-Chambers Trial," in *Readings in Law and Psychiatry*, ed. R. C. Allen, E. Z. Ferster, and J. G. Rubin (Baltimore: The Johns Hopkins University Press, 1968), 134.

2. Kenneth Pope and Jacqueline Bouhoutos, *Sexual Intimacy Between Therapists and Patients* (New York: Praeger, 1986), 136.

3. Federal Rules of Evidence 702.

4. Adapted from Pope and Bouhoutos, *Sexual Intimacy*, 140.

5. Robert G. Meyer, E. R. Landis, and J. R. Hays, *Law for the Psychotherapist* (New York: Norton, 1988), 227.

6. Ibid., 243.

PART VII

The Maturation of the Christian Counseling Profession

Chapter 23

Protecting the Profession: Defending Christian Counselors

When one comes to trial on any aspect of religious belief or representation, unbelievers among his judges are likely not to understand and are almost certain not to believe him.[1]

Justice Jackson in dissent,
United States v. Ballard, 1944

LITTLE IN LIFE IS MORE DISTASTEFUL THAN BEING on the receiving end of a lawsuit. Even when expected, those words at the top of the notice of suit, "You are being sued!" make most people bristle and cringe. In this litigious age, even the best Christian counselor may be sued, whether or not the suit is valid. While this book has outlined numerous ways to reduce the risk of being sued, it cannot be entirely extinguished. Indeed, it may be quite uncommon in the twenty-first century for a counselor or clinician to practice an entire career without being sued at least once. What is rare, outside of sexual misconduct, is the likelihood of a counselor losing a suit and having large damages awarded against him or her. We should take a certain comfort in the wide discrepancy between suits filed and those lost by the counselor or clinician.

Of course it is unlikely that much comfort will be found while defending a lawsuit. While anger and fear may be unavoidable reactions, maintenance of professional behavior, a good defense strategy, and a positive long-term perspective can mean the difference between a highly painful and a pain-managed litigation journey. This chapter intends to help make the journey as painless as possible for the Christian counselor facing a lawsuit. We review both the necessity of good malpractice insurance coverage, the first line of lawsuit defense, and working principles of good defense behavior.

MALPRACTICE INSURANCE COVERAGE

The professional Christian counselor should maintain adequate malpractice insurance coverage over the course of his or her professional career. Counseling pastors may also want to be covered for their counseling ministries, both individually and as a church ministry.

FERMENT IN PROFESSIONAL INSURANCE COVERAGE

Like the dramatic changes taking place in client health insurance coverage for mental health services, there is also much systemic change in the insurance industry regarding malpractice coverage of mental health professionals. Two countervailing trends are most evident: insurance premiums are beginning to rise (rising dramatically for some professions in certain states) while the scope of coverage of the insurance is being systematically reduced.

Increased premium costs. The rise in the incidence of malpractice suits and the size of damage awards is reflected in the steadily rising costs of insurance. While mental health professionals are in no way facing the cost and coverage crisis of some medical specialties, the trends indicate increasing costs and greater difficulty in coverage. Psychiatry, of course, pays the highest premiums vis-à-vis the other mental health professions. From a low of $1,800 in Arkansas, psychiatrists pay nearly $15,000 annually for malpractice insurance in Dade and Broward counties in Florida.[2] Social work clinicians pay the lowest premiums ($200 to $500 annually). Psychologists have experienced the greatest rise in premium rates, now paying from $500 to as much as $2,000 annually. An agent from the American Professional Agency (AProfA), one of the country's leading professional insurers, recently stated that "no profession has claims as high as psychologists."[3]

Your resident state of practice is a significant factor in your insurance costs. The most costly states are California, New York, and Florida, the states with the highest rates of suits. California is the worst—it is now three times more costly to defend a suit in California than in New York. California is not the most litigious state on a per capita basis—that distinction is held by Michigan. An official of AProfA assserted that "Michigan courts are going crazy with claims—three to four times greater than California."[4] Other states with high and growing rates of litigation are Arizona, Oregon, and Colorado.

Reduced coverage. The reality of reduced coverage is being shown across a number of policy elements. Most insurers are dropping or severely restricting coverage for claims for sexual misconduct (e.g., no more than $25,000 paid per claim). Since these actions comprise nearly 60 percent of all current liability suits, this is an obvious cost control strategy on the part of insurance companies. Some courts, swayed by the unfairness of such policies against the victims of sexual abuse, have denied such exclusions and limitations. Companies are responding to this by dramatically increasing premiums across the board and denying coverage to anyone who has had sexual misconduct trouble in their practice. Failure to control this problem systemically by the professions will surely demand a higher price, reflected in insurance premiums, by all professionals.

The claims-made policy. A second way insurance is reducing coverage is by transfer from *occurrence* to *claims-made* policies. Heretofore, malpractice insurance has been occurrence coverage. In this system, coverage protects the insured for acts that occurred during the policy, no matter how long after the act the legal claim is filed. Practically speaking, this protected the insured long after they dropped their coverage (e.g., following retirement from practice) as long as they were covered when the negligent acts took place. Costs for this coverage tended to be somewhat higher but remained stable over many years, and coverage continued even though the policy might have been dropped.

Claims-made policies require that claims be made against the professional during the life of the policy, or the claims will not be covered. Effectively, this means that you cannot drop the coverage without being at risk for years after an occurrence of negligent practice, thus requiring the retiree to maintain active coverage long after discontinuing practice. Such policies are less expensive initially, but their premium costs increase sharply, and cumulative costs, year after year, are much higher.

These policies also lock you into the company you do business with—switching insurers usually means loss of coverage for prior years. To soften this blow to the professional—implicitly admitting that this change clearly benefits insurers, not subscribers—some insurers are offering purchase of tails. A tail can be bought that, for a set number of years, will provide occurrence-like coverage even though the policy may not be kept active. By the end of 1992 it is predicted that all professional malpractice insurance will be claims-made only.[5]

Coverage for malpractice only. Insurance companies also routinely resist covering costs associated with administrative actions, such as defending oneself in disciplinary actions before state licensing boards and professional associations. These costs are fully borne by the professional. Insurance companies argue that premium costs would more than double for such coverage. They also assert that it would result in many more poor therapists defending themselves and staying in practice when they should instead be driven out thus reducing the harm and overall cost to the profession.

This argument is valid only if you presume that every person called to disciplinary account is guilty as charged. As licensure action becomes more common in the twenty-first century, the lack of coverage for administrative actions will be a serious deficiency for professional practitioners—especially those who are *not* guilty as charged. It is more than a little ironic that insurers, which are increasingly requiring professional license for coverage, will not defend the protection of that license.

Finally, it must be remembered that malpractice insurance is strictly that—coverage for incidents of negligent malpractice only. Not covered are intentional, fraudulent, and criminal acts—behavior that is becoming more frequent. Insurance companies are always seeking to narrow the boundaries of coverage, excluding more and more types of wrongful behavior from coverage. More than a few practitioners are shocked, when filing a defense claim with their insurer, to discover that their malfeasance is not covered.

BUYING INSURANCE

Buying malpractice insurance obligates the insurer to defend you and pay any judgments rendered against you up to the limits of the policy. The general rule of thumb is to buy as much coverage as you can reasonably afford. Certainly purchase enough insurance to cover your personal assets and as much of your professional or corporate assets as possible. Maximizing your coverage should be considered where higher practice risks exist—counseling work with personality (especially borderline) disorders, criminal and sex offenders, sex therapy, and use of nontraditional therapy models and active, physical techniques beyond verbal therapy.

Corporations and agencies should consider separate policies that cover the corporation beyond individual liability. Added coverage should also be considered by supervisors who are liable for their interns' work and for partnership and associational liabilities. AProfA provides automatic coverage for employees and interns, requiring that these people be named and included within the policy.

Most policies will include provision of legal defense costs and services. This can often be a two-edged sword for the practitioner. While a lawyer is hired to defend you, that lawyer is very cognizant of who is paying the bill. Assume that your insurance-chosen lawyer has the insurance company's interests in clear view—that is to save money. The attorney may push for negotiated settlement to pay a small award, even if you believe you can successfully defend the suit. Since you are probably in foreign territory, the insurer's choice of a good trial lawyer and management of legal relations is a benefit that most counselors judge worthy of the costs of giving up some control of their defense. Some insurers will allow some influence by the insured in the choice of lawyers.

A common policy for mental health professionals is $1 million/$3 million coverage. This indicates that the insurer will pay up to $1 million per claim and an aggregate of $3 million for all claims over the life of the policy. The purchaser can, of course, buy more or less coverage. Many practitioners working in hospital settings or contracting as a provider with health maintenance and managed-care providers will usually be required to show evidence of having at least this much malpractice coverage in force.

THE COUNSELOR AS DEFENDANT

Christian counselors will be sued with increasing frequency into the twenty-first century. Even some excellent counselors who will successfully defend suits will not escape this burden. As much as possible, attempts at negotiation and mediation should be continually made right up to legal action. When this fails and the counselor is sued, he or she must retreat into a defensive posture that, while certainly not precluding a nonlitigated solution, must be done to protect both reputation and assets. Once the client becomes a plaintiff with a lawyer bent on extracting a damage award, a new strategy of behavior is required.

Upon receipt of notice of suit being filed, the Christian counselor should immediately contact his or her supervisor, insurer, or denomination. The first task is retaining a good lawyer and meeting for review of the issues and definition of initial action. Until a lawyer has been consulted and initial strategy defined, relations with the client-plaintiff should be temporarily suspended—anything done for or against the client-plaintiff at this point can hurt the counselor legally. Drawing together a support network of colleagues and friends is also recommended as excellent mental and emotional strategy.

LAWYER-CLIENT RELATIONS

Counselors should approach relations with their attorneys in both a collaborative and compliant way. As a defense team member, the counselor is responsible to educate and inform the lawyer on the treatment and clinical decision-making issues that affect the case. As defendant-clients, counselors must acknowledge they are legal laypersons and must defer to the lawyer's expertise in the courtroom and regarding the content and procedure of law. The counselor should not abrogate all responsibility here, however, but should become as informed as possible about procedures and deadlines. Legal malpractice is also a growing epidemic—nearly half of all malpractice actions against lawyers involve failures to meet critical deadlines or some technical procedural requirement.[6]

Absolute candor should be the guiding principle in all relations between counselor and lawyer. The lawyer-client privilege is the most well protected and unassailable of all the professional privileges, and the lawyer is dedicated to protect your confidence against disclosures that would harm your case. The clinician should reveal and discuss all mistakes, doubts, and confusion about the case at issue. Failure to reveal and practice defending the problematic aspects of your case can result in an ill-prepared defense and trouble on the witness stand.

All case records should be reviewed early on by counselor and lawyer together. Of course, these records must not be tampered with or altered in any way as this could result in criminal fraud prosecution. Assessment of benefits and risks from the records should be outlined with agreement as to how to deal with the problem material. All subpoenas and demands for records should be referred to your attorney, who can take action to best manage the flow of information to the plaintiff. Courtroom behavior should be thoroughly discussed and rehearsed beforehand. The counselor who is adept at behavioral rehearsal can assist the lawyer in the appropriate courtroom presentation.

Cohen has noted two paradoxical fallacies under which mental health professionals labor before judge and jury.[7] On one hand, the clinician is expected to have it all together in order to effectively treat troubled people. On the other hand is the notion that one must be a little crazy to enter the field in the first place. No matter the truth of these attributions, it can create unrealistic expectations about the appearance and behavior of the counselor. Coaching and rehearsing proper testimony and professional demeanor is a must.

CLINICAL PRACTICE MAINTENANCE

To assert that defending a malpractice suit can adversely impact your practice may be like saying you will get wet if you fall in the ocean. The counselor embroiled in a malpractice suit may find it difficult to avoid thinking about the suit when working with other clients. Some level of obsessive thinking may be unavoidable and should be expected. Care must be taken, however, to insure that no adverse effects are visited upon other clients as a result. In this case, the Christian counselor should consider a leave of absence or, if able to maintain practice, a reduction of caseload by referral or temporary suspension of new intakes.

For some counselors, clinical practice maintenance may be quite therapeutic. It can serve as a constructive distraction from the temptation to obsessively ruminate on the suit. Clinical practice is a constant reminder that life goes on, challenging the counselor to see beyond the present trauma and keep a long-term perspective in focus. For this reason, as well as avoiding abandoning other clients, a counselor defending a suit should not, as a rule, forsake all clinical and professional activities.

In extraordinary cases, the counselor may be challenged to maintain professional service to the client-plaintiff. Some clients may expect, even demand, continued treatment from the clinician they are suing. This paradoxical dilemma "may reflect, in curious form, the intensity of the patient's involvement with the clinician. Thus, wanting to continue seeing the clinician you are suing is a logical contradiction, but not a clinical one."[8] Gutheil and

Appelbaum wisely recognize that ethical treatment under these circumstances is impossible. The counselor in this case is under no obligation to maintain treatment and should make expeditious referral.

CONCLUSION

While the bulk of this book is geared to lawsuit prevention, lawsuits are a reality in our litigious age and will not be completely avoided by the counseling professional. Solid malpractice insurance coverage and procedures for defensive response are essential strategies in case suit is visited upon the counselor. Our hope is that Christian counselors who are sued will not drift alone but will be able to call upon brothers and sisters in collegial association to assist in carrying the burden. Our final chapter makes specific proposals for such assistance and organization.

NOTES

1. *United States v. Ballard,* 322 U.S. 78, at 93, J. Jackson dissenting (1944).

2. Herbert Dorken, "Malpractice Claims Experience of Psychologists: Policy Issues, Cost Comparisons with Psychiatrists, and Prescription Privilege Implications," *Professional Psychology: Research and Practice* 21, no. 2 (1990): 150–52.

3. Mary Riemersma, "Malpractice Insurance: What the Future Holds," *The California Therapist* 3, no. 6 (1991): 9–14 (quote from 10).

4. Ibid.

5. Ibid.

6. J. E. Horsley, "How to Protect Yourself Against Legal Malpractice," *Medical Economics* 8, no. 7 (1978): 149–58.

7. Ronald J. Cohen, *Malpractice: A Guide for Mental Health Professionals* (New York: The Free Press, 1979).

8. Thomas G. Gutheil and Paul S. Appelbaum, *Clinical Handbook of Psychiatry and the Law* (New York: McGraw-Hill,1982), 202.

Chapter 24

Organizing
the Profession:
A Call to Maturity

The emerging or marginal profession [lacks] on both of the first two attributes of professionalism—generalized knowledge and community orientation. . . . It is typical of the structure of the occupational group that is emerging as a profession that its members are not homogenous with respect to the amount of knowledge and community orientation they possess. . . .

In the attempt to express and strengthen the community orientation of their group, the leaders take pains to construct and publish a code of ethics. . . . The leaders establish or try to strengthen a professional association. In an established profession, such an association effectively carries on the several functions of self-control, socialization and education of the members, communications with the public, and the defense of professional interest against infringement by the public or other occupational groups. The emerging profession's association seeks to increase its effectiveness in all these functions.[1]

Bernard Barber

CHRISTIAN COUNSELING, LIKE PSYCHOLOGY AND SOCIAL WORK a century ago, is an emerging profession. It is not a new movement, yet it is far less developed, understood, and accepted compared to the historic learned professions of law, medicine, and theology. The challenge of a generalized knowledge base—one that is widely accepted and disseminated—is a significant one. With the widely divergent views that exist about psychology, the social sciences, theology, the Bible, and the integration of these disciplines, it may be valid to question whether such a knowledge base will ever coalesce. We believe it is beginning to come together, slowly and with much ferment—a task that will continue long into the new millennium.[2]

This final chapter focuses on the second aspect of an emerging profession—the development of a community orientation. True community is a function of many things that a people share in common—beliefs, purpose, identity, organization, struggle, even suffering. Christian counselors face hostile opposition, even from within the church, in ways that were unprecedented just a few years ago. Dramatically increased litigation and legal regulation, a secularized society, and oppositional powers in the legal, clinical, even ministerial professions press against a nascent and emerging profession. The need to be "wise as serpents" as helping ministers is far more than a personal challenge. We believe the Christian counseling profession must organize itself systemically, as a profession, to defend itself and advocate God's purposes.

TWO SIDES OF THE MALPRACTICE THREAT

We would be remiss if we did not consider that the malpractice crisis and regulatory threat had some potential benefits to Christian counseling. First of all, the threat of malpractice can stimulate Christian counselors to become exemplary in their ethics and excellent in clinical practice. While we might prefer reward incentives to motivate behavior, there is no doubt that the punishing threat of the law checks us at the boundary of harmful wrongdoing. Second, this liability crisis—this dangerous opportunity—could serve to push us to organize professionally so that we can have a collective voice in influencing systemic, legislative, and political change.

The threat of litigation can have the effect of sensitizing the Christian counselor to the entire scope of personal and social responsibility that comes with the right to practice. We can use its force to deal seriously with issues of professional competence, prevention of harm, and effectiveness of treatment. We agree with Hogan's assertion[3] that the intrusion of malpractice into psychotherapy is largely due to the inability or unwillingness of the mental health professions to control the incidence of client harm, whether from incompetent practitioners or ineffective treatments.

If we will deal with these issues biblically,[4] then we will avoid most of the entanglements of malpractice. If we do not, then we deliver to secular society greater power to control counseling ministry by way of law rather than by God's way—working effectively within the boundaries of the church. If we do not, then we simply delegate to law and society's enforcement powers its historic policy function of protecting people from harm.

MORE HARM THAN GOOD

On balance, however, intrusive malpractice liability has more negative effect on both clinical service and professional self-control. It inhibits clinical experimentation and development of effective treatments while delivering too much power to lawyers and judges who, from a clinical perspective, are lay people. This legalization of counseling will continue its excessive encroachment as long as churches, professional associations, and licensing boards continue to fail to ensure professional competence. Christian counseling and the mental health professions must exercise their mandate to sanction harmful practitioners in a timely fashion in order to slow this unwanted encroachment.

The rising tide of malpractice litigation is generally decried as a blight on the helping professions. Halleck asserts that the new legalism has stripped psychiatry of much of its independence and power to treat the mentally ill. The practice of "defensive psychiatry" consumes an ever-growing share of the time the clinician would otherwise have to treat patients. Learning the requirements of defensive treatment has "become an integral part of psychiatric training and practice."[5] Simon asserts that the fear of malpractice paradoxically creates a defensive clinician who, preoccupied with professional survival, is more likely to commit the serious error the law intends to prevent.[6]

As Christians, let us learn wisdom from the experience of our secular colleagues. Let us note carefully the pitfalls they have encountered and push ourselves to avoid those same errors as much as possible. Let's not follow the bad precedent of psychiatry, for example, over the past half-century. That profession failed to use its organizational power and political influence to shape most of the statutory control of psychiatric hospitalization. Its passivity in submitting to an activist mental health bar and the external legalization of psychiatric practice was crucial in the unwanted intrusion of law. Christian counseling can either follow this undesirable precedent, or it can organize and direct its power to create a better future for counseling pastors, clinicians, and clients.

PROFESSIONAL ORGANIZATION AND ADVOCACY

Christian counselors must organize professionally to better advocate our mission, defend our counselors, and maintain

God-honoring, professional self-control. We should not be tying up courts with lawsuits against one another but using alternative dispute resolution methods within the church (see 1 Cor. 6:1–8). We must improve how we police ourselves, or people will be forced to utilize malpractice lawsuits as the only effective means to remedy their grievances. We must become better advocates and peacemakers in defense of counseling ministry, or people will be left with distorted and false perceptions of our unique ministry and its special place in church and society.

Currently, for all the good that is accomplished by Christian professional associations, there is far more that has been left undone. In many respects these organizations remain separated, provincial, and powerless in the face of the legal and political challenges revealed in this book. We should apply ourselves with greater diligence to the task of impacting the world with the beneficial distinctives of Christian counseling ministry. To quote Barabanov, "Today, as never before, a Christian initiative is needed to counter the godless humanism which is destroying mankind, and to prevent humanism from deteriorating into a nonreligious humanism. We are too passive in our attitude to the world."[7]

As Christians we must reclaim our Constitutional heritage and ministry rights guaranteed by the First Amendment. Many fringe and cult organizations have used this amendment and related legal protections to abuse the American public, weakening historic protection of orthodox ministry. We must reclaim our biblical call and constitutional freedom to guarantee that people receive the unique Spirit-empowered help that only a Christian therapist can provide. If small minorities—racists, homosexuals, athiests, the ACLU—can galvanize law and Constitutional rights to advocate for their life-view, then we can certainly stop yielding in timidity and rise up to promote our values. When we do, our culture will benefit, and those we serve will be better served in freedom.

CALL FOR A COMPREHENSIVE NATIONAL ORGANIZATION

We call upon Christian counselors to organize and develop a comprehensive and powerful national professional organization to fulfill the goals and protect the values we have outlined. Nothing in our field yet exists to facilitate our professional mission in this manner. We need an organization that functions with the breadth and power of the primary organizations advancing psychiatry, psychology, and social work. The current transformation taking place within the American Association of Christian Counselors (AACC) holds much promise as the group that could assume this role into the twenty-first century. We believe this organization will thrive if it advances Christian counseling globally, attracts tens of thousands of members from the clinical professions, pastoral ministry, parachurch, and lay ministry, and communicates a bold and biblical mission.

TOWARD LAW-INFORMED ETHICS AND BETTER LAW

A key challenge for an emerging profession is the development of an ethical code. An ethical code performs many functions. It defines the conduct of professional behavior, identifies wrongful or unethical behavior, guides resolution of ethical dilemmas, and communicates to the profession and to society agreed standards that intend to inspire respect and confidence in the profession. All the major mental health professional groups ascribe to an ethical code that serves these functions.

Ethical code development in Christian counseling is being discussed, debated, and pursued in a healthy way. Gary Collins' recent book, *Excellence and Ethics in Counseling*,[8] addresses the multiple issues that the profession must consider. Malony, Beck, and Matthews have called for a code based on distinctly Christian values, built on the person and work of Jesus Christ.[9] Oordt recently published an excellent pilot study indicating areas of agreement, disagreement, and confusion about ethical behavior among Christian counselors.[10]

REFRAMING LAW AS OUR FRIEND

Until recently, little attention has been given to the intrusion of law into counseling ministry and the interaction of law and Christian counseling ethics. Developing ethical codes without reference to law and law-driven behavior is a serious mistake as we approach the twenty-first century. A key principle underlying this challenge requires reframing fundamental conceptions of law. We must understand law as our friend and use it wisely to benefit the church and the mission of our profession. Rather than knowing it only as an external form of control that serves as a despised adversary after the fact, we must see law as a dynamic process that can inform and advise us in ethical practice. This conception sees law as an interactive process by which regulation can positively facilitate acquisition of biblical values and shared goals. This view of law can facilitate active participation in the lawmaking process by Christian counselors across the ministerial spectrum.

Christian counselors must take seriously the need for an ethical code that is informed by the law. This will serve to advance our professional mission as well as protect us and those we serve in so many ways that an ill-informed code cannot. Psychologist-lawyer Robert Woody, tongue in cheek, said it best, "If you rest your practice on ethics and not on law, I'll give you my 800 number."[11] Legal mandates always supercede ethical behavior, and the counselor who is ill-informed about law in this litigious age is indeed a risky practitioner. Woody, only slightly humorously, asserts that graduate programs and the professions as a whole might need to face a national class-action suit to force a harsh but necessary wake-up to the legal realities of professional practice.

A FIDUCIARY TRUST STANDARD

The fiduciary trust is a superior legal framework for defining the duties and understanding the relationship between Christian counselor and client. This is a trust far more consistent with biblical norms than is the law of malpractice or contract. Rapidly evolving from its historic association with financial trust on behalf of clients by lawyers, accountants, and money managers, it is being applied to a broad range of professional services, including those provided by mental health professionals.[12] Rooted in ancient Roman law, the fiduciary is one who holds a special duty to act always in the best interests of the one served, never taking advantage of that trust nor advancing one's own interests.[13] This duty is grounded in the special trust and confidence placed in the professional by the client and in the power of the professional to abuse that trust with devastating consequence.

The *Destafano* case, cited in chapters 2 and 6, is also significant due to the Colorado Supreme Court's recognition of fiduciary law as a cause of action against clergy misconduct. Even though that state had long abolished actions for alienation of affections, and the Court agreed that no malpractice liability existed against the sexually offending priest, under fiduciary law the priest "had a duty, given the nature of the counseling relationship, *to engage in conduct designed to improve the Destafanos' marital relationship.*"[14] Breach of fiduciary trust has been argued in at least one other case against the clergy.[15] It is likely that we will see this cause increasingly argued against the church and its ministers as well as against mental health professionals.

A good standard for both church and state. Frankel asserts that as abuses of the power of professional service providers increase throughout society, reliance on fiduciary law will inevitably increase.[16] For a number of reasons we believe this developing trend in law can bless rather than curse the church and its Christian counseling ministry. First, fiduciary duties are grounded in the fundamental commitment to hold the interests of those served above those who are the designated servants. Jesus asserted that loving God and our neighbor as ourself is the greatest of the commandments (Mark 12:28–31; Luke 10:25–37). Furthermore, in God's kingdom, the one who would rule or be great is the one who most humbly serves the rest, who gives up his or her life for the good of others (Matt. 20:25–28; Luke 22:25–30). Paul's challenge to imitate Christ's humility calls us to "Do nothing out of selfish ambition or vain conceit, but in humility consider others better than yourselves. Each of you should look not only to your own interests, but also to the interests of others" (Phil.2:3–4). Fiduciary law fulfills fundamental ethical duties to hold client interests as primary and bars exploitation of the helping relationship.

For the foreseeable future, fiduciary law will compete for the court's attention with many legal theories of counseling liability. We believe the courts will be increasingly attracted to this standard because it holds client and consumer protection values as primary. If (or when) a fiduciary standard becomes ascendant in law, it will simplify the understanding and application of legal duty to Christian counseling. The fiduciary definition is broad enough conceptually to include the many biblical, ethical, and legal duties that are being attached to Christian counseling. Furthermore this standard is consistent with the actual moral and ethical standards that guide Christian helpers in their day-to-day ministry.

Fiduciary trust and ministry self-control. The pressure on the church of increased liability risk and the imposition of legal standards that inaccurately reflect the nature of true counseling ministry makes the value of a fiduciary standard all the more attractive at the close of the twentieth century. Assuming, as we must following the *Smith* decision, that these liability trends will continue and lawsuits will increase against Christian counselors, a crucial requirement is for informed counselors and the church at large to take control of this standard-defining process. Courts, lawyers, and legal theorists are advancing these standards already, and the church may disagree with their premises and values and be quite displeased with the results.

Fiduciary trust as a unifying concept, and law friendly to biblical standards could allow us to forge the lead in establishing standards and to take action that truly protects those we serve. It might also allow a factional church to overcome some of its historic internal disunity. Such law might also pave the way to agreed standards for Christian counseling ministry and viable twenty-first century relations between church and state that are as nonintrusive as possible for counselors and clients.

ALTERNATIVE DISPUTE RESOLUTION

Christians are enabled by God to adhere to the commands of the Bible as a fundamental call of discipleship. Jesus clearly and simply stated, "You are my friends if you do what I command" (John 15:14; see also John 14:21). This is not selective obedience, but obedience to God's entire word, including the injunctions against taking a brother to court (1 Cor. 6:1–8). Many Christians have failed to adhere to this latter command. However, in recent years the church has been establishing alternative ways to resolve disputes outside of the courts.

The American legal system operates in an adversarial manner, pitting one person or institution against another. The objective of litigation, after a fair hearing of both sides, is for one side to prevail or win, thus resolving the dispute. The intent of alternative dispute resolution is for both sides to win. Mediation asks, "What solution will resolve this dispute in a just way for both parties?" The Apostle Paul challenges us with the query, "Is it possible that there is nobody among you wise enough to judge a dispute between believers?" (1 Cor. 6:5). Going to court to solve problems should be the means of last resort after diligent pursuit of other alternatives is exhausted. However, one author noted that about 20 percent of all civil court cases involve Christians suing Christians.[17]

A call to maturity as Christian professionals must include a serious call to pursue alternative dispute resolution (ADR). In recent years, Christian lawyers have developed ADR models that not only resolve the legal issues but also include reconciliation of persons.[18] In this sense the focus is on all parties winning. This process includes negotiation, mediation, and arbitration with a goal of full reconciliation of the issues and of the persons or institutions involved. Christian counselors who contract for negotiation and mediation with their client or congregant at the outset of counseling are committing to this nonlitigated method of resolving disputes. We call the entire Christian counseling profession to a serious commitment to alternative dispute resolution.

<h2 style="text-align:center">ADVOCATING CHRIST TO THE PROFESSIONS</h2>

Many Christians seeking help to resolve their problems and conflicts within a Christian values framework are mocked and ridiculed. We consistently have clients who comment on the abusive treatment they have received from secular counselors. Apparently, many secular counselors are unable to differentiate between healthy and pathological Christian beliefs and practices. Some appear to reject most, if not all, Christian values, believing Christianity to be inherently pathological.

Furthermore, Gartner's study showed that graduate counseling programs do discriminate against conservative Christians.[19] This discrimination promotes an underrepresentation of qualified Christian professionals within the helping professions. It also fosters a lack of empathy, respect, and skill in work with clients who hold to Christian values, resulting in many within the counseling professions being unprepared to work effectively with clients who hold these beliefs.

Gallup polls, on the other hand, have consistently demonstrated that many people are interested in religious values and want support in living out those values. One of the more recent Gallup polls showed that 71 percent of all baby boomers are members of a church or synagogue, with 34 percent of the nonmembers likely to become members in the next five years.[20] Another study found that clergy are rated highest regarding their warmth, caring, stability, and professionalism when compared with mental health professionals.[21] These studies and many others indicate that religious and Christian values are very important to many people.

We need to carefully, respectfully, and consistently work to challenge secular professionals to grow in their respect toward Christian clients and patients. This is a fundamental challenge which faces a maturing Christian counseling profession. This challenge can be met by (1) demanding an end to religious discrimination in professional training programs, (2) advocating respect for and sensitivity to the unique values and needs of Christian clients, and (3) educating the professions and society about the special beliefs and training necessary to best serve this population within our society.

ADVOCACY TO THE CHURCH

Advocating for Christian counseling in the Christian church may be the biggest challenge of all. The strain of skepticism, even downright hostility by some in the church to the Christian counseling mission is a serious spiritual and professional challenge. We agree with those who caution against uncritical acceptance of the psychological way, cognizant that it can, indeed in some churches has, become an alternative Gospel. Humanistic psychology must be resisted as a substitute for the Gospel of Christ; exchanging our birthright for this unsatisfying meal is foolish.

We reject, however, the hypercritical and unprincipled rejection of everything connected with Christian psychology, psychiatry, and counseling ministry. The witch hunters and heresy hounds in the church must be challenged and exposed for the divisive spirit and deluded understanding they promote. Equating Christian counseling with witchcraft certainly reveals far more about the troubles of the accuser than the accused. However, when voiced by prominent church leaders to naive, uninformed, and troubled members of the flock, serious harm is done and suspicion created toward those possibly most able to help. We believe that the ignorant and unprincipled assault on Christian counseling cannot go unanswered. Christian counselors must tackle this difficult but necessary challenge in an assertive and honorable way.

FINAL CONCLUSION

Christian counseling is a serious call to ministry, one that is demanding in its preparation, often difficult in its practice, but highly rewarding in its fruit to both client or congregant and counselor. We believe in the promise and need for Christian counseling ministry. We have been honored to practice in this emerging profession and to participate deeply in the lives of our clients. The twenty-first century will truly be the best and worst of times in counseling ministry, possibly in all aspects of church life. The counseling ministry is ripe with tremendous challenge as a healing and reconciling vehicle for Christ's supernatural work. It is also fraught with danger, from within and from outside its camp, and could dissipate as a once-promising backwater of Christian ministry in the industrialized West.

CALLED TO GOOD RISK

Risk is inevitable, even normal for those in counseling ministry. Increased legal liability risk is merely one cost that every minister and counseling professional must anticipate in this grave new world. This book has shown ways to minimize the risk of lawsuit and honorably manage the many legal and ethical dilemmas faced in Christian counseling. Furthermore, we have challenged you to consider the necessity of taking godly risks to promote the mission of Christian counseling in our church and culture. We hope this book will serve the best interests of Christian counseling ministry and its legitimate place in both the church and society.

Perhaps we would do well to heed Mordecai's words to Esther. "For if you remain silent at this time, relief and deliverance for the Jews will arise from another place, but you and your father's family will perish. And who knows but that you have come to royal position for such a time as this?" (Esther 4:14). Christian counselors may be called to a special place of ministry "for such a time as this." Let us not settle for the backwaters of Christian ministry or for the American dream of smug self-satisfaction, but let us press on to fulfill all that Christ would have us do. Let us practice his vision as stated in Isaiah 61:1–3.

> The Spirit of the Sovereign Lord is on me,
>   because the Lord has anointed me to preach
>   good news to the poor.
> He has sent me to bind up the brokenhearted,
>   to proclaim freedom for the captives
>   and release for the prisoners,
> to proclaim the year of the Lord's favor
>   and the day of vengeance of our God,
> to comfort all who mourn,
>   and provide for those who grieve in Zion—
> to bestow on them a crown of beauty
>   instead of ashes,

> the oil of gladness
>   instead of mourning,
> and a garment of praise
>   instead of a spirit of despair.
> They will be called oaks of righteousness,
>   a planting of the Lord for the display
>   of his splendor.

Isaiah's vision, owned by Christ in the Nazareth temple and fulfilled in his death and resurrection, can also be fulfilled by Christian helpers who take godly risks and practice under his guidance. Though the legal regime is becoming more intrusive, the counselor who humbly honors Christ, pursues a practical biblical ethic, and respects the boundaries of law need fear nothing in the bold pursuit of counseling ministry. Lawbreakers will reap harsh fruits in this litigious age, but love-givers—those who fulfill the spirit as well as obey the letter of the law—will become the "oaks of righteousness" that are able to "display his splendor" to a world so desperately in need. Counselors who do respect the law, who *do no harm* in their ministry work, will be free to love and give their very best to those they are called to serve.

NOTES

1. Bernard Barber, "The Sociology of the Professions," in *The Professions in America*, ed. K. S. Lynn (Boston: Houghton-Mifflin, 1965), 22–23.

2. See Gary Collins, *Christian Counseling: A Comprehensive Guide*, rev. ed. (Waco, Tex.: Word, 1988); and the thirty-volume series, *Contemporary Christian Counseling* (Dallas: Word).

3. See Daniel B. Hogan, *A Study in the Philosophy and Practice of Professional Regulation*, vol. 1, *The Regulation of Psychotherapists* (Cambridge, Mass.: Ballinger, 1979).

4. For example, see Matt. 18:10–35 and 1 Cor. 3:1–9; 6:1–11.

5. Seymour Halleck, *Law in the Practice of Psychiatry: A Handbook for Clinicians* (New York: Plenum Medical Books, 1980), 9.

6. Robert I. Simon, *Psychiatric Interventions and Malpractice: A Primer for Liability Prevention* (Springfield, Ill.: Thomas, 1982).

7. Evgeny Barabanov, "The Schism Between the Church and the World," in *From Under the Rubble*, ed. Alexander Solzhenitsyn (Boston: Little, Brown and Co., 1974), 192.

8. Gary Collins, *Excellence and Ethics in Counseling* (Dallas: Word, 1991).

9. H. Newton Malony, "Confidentiality in the Pastoral Role," *Theology, News and Notes* (October 1986): 12–21; and "The Future of Ministry in a Changing World," in *Clergy Malpractice*, ed. H. Newton Malony, T. L. Needham, and Samuel

Southard (Philadelphia: The Westminster Press, 1986), 140–47. James R. Beck and R. K. Matthews, "A Code of Ethics for Christian Counselors," *Journal of Psychology and Christianity* 5, no. 3 (1986): 78–84.

10. Mark Oordt, "Ethics of Practice Among Christian Psychologists: A Pilot Study," *Journal of Psychology and Theology* 18, no. 3 (1990): 255–60.

11. Robert Woody, quoted in George Williams, L. Johnson, and P. Diehm, *The Therapist and the Legal System* (North Orange County Psychological Services, 1991).

12. See T. Frankel, "Fiduciary Law," *California Law Review* 71 (1983): 795–836; and Herb Kutchins, "The Fiduciary Relationship: The Legal Basis for Social Workers' Responsibilities to Clients," *Social Work* 36, no. 2 (1991): 106–13.

13. Henry Black, *Black's Law Dictionary*, 5th ed. (St. Paul, Minn.: West Publishing, 1979), 563–64.

14. *Destafano v. Grabrian*, 763 P.2d 275 (Colorado 1988), at 284.

15. *Erickson v. Christenson*, 99 Or.App. 104 (1989).

16. See Frankel.

17. Steve Levicoff, *Christian Counseling and the Law* (Chicago: Moody, 1991), 173.

18. See Lynn Buzzard and Laurence Eck, *Tell It to the Church: A Biblical Approach to Resolving Conflict Out of Court* (Elgin, Ill.: David C. Cook, 1982); and C. Ken Sande, *Christian Conciliation: A Better Way to Settle Conflicts* (Billings, Mont.: Assocation of Christian Conciliation Services, 1989).

19. John D. Gartner, "Antireligious Prejudice in Admissions to Doctoral Programs in Clinical Psychology," *Professional Psychology: Research and Practice* 17, no. 5 (1986): 473–75.

20. George Gallup, Jr., and Frank Newport, "Baby-Boomers Seek More Family Time," *The Gallup Poll Monthly* (April 1991): 31–42.

21. Fred Schindler et al., "How the Public Perceives Psychiatrists, Psychologists, Nonpsychiatric Physicians, and Members of the Clergy," *Professional Psychology: Research and Practice* 18, no. 4 (1987): 375.

APPENDICES

FORMS FOR CHRISTIAN COUNSELING PRACTICE

THE FOLLOWING AGREEMENTS AND FORMS that we have made reference to in the text are those most commonly used in Christian counseling practice. These documents are used in our practice through The Redwood Family Institute in Eureka, California, and are necessarily geared to California law, but they may be adapted to the law of your resident state and your particular practice needs. We have honored the principle of parsimony in the development of our forms—include that which is necessary but no more. Hence, our forms include material required to address the major issues required by law and ethics, but not every conceivable issue and situation is covered—we leave that to ongoing discussion and revision of agreement as we proceed with our clients.

Appendix A

PROFESSIONAL SERVICES AGREEMENT

This agreement for _____ services between [your practice's name] and client(s) _____ shall govern all professional relations between the parties. It is agreed that any disputes or modifications of agreement shall be negotiated directly between the parties; if these negotiations are not satisfactory, then the parties *agree to mediate any differences with a mutually acceptable third-party mediator, considering first either the Executive Director or Associate Director of the practice.*

A. THE STAFF THERAPIST is _____. He or she is a
- ❑ California licensed M.F.C.C., L.C.S.W., or Ph.D. psychologist; or a
- ❑ prelicensed M.F.C.C. intern or trainee, L.C.S.W. associate, or psychological assistant.

B. FEES AND INSURANCE POLICY.

Client fees are to be determined at the first session. Full or partial payment shall be made by the client at the end of each session. Clients agree to pay part of their fee out-of-pocket even if covered by insurance. *As a courtesy to you* we can bill insurance and other vendors on a monthly basis. We will not extend credit or schedule appointments beyond three unpaid sessions until payment is made. Clients understand that a therapist with prelicense status (as checked above) may or may not be able to receive insurance reimbursement. *Clients are fully responsible for all fees if insurance does not pay.*

C. CANCELLATION POLICY.

We agree to and ask that clients maintain responsible relations regarding appointment times. Any appointment *cancelled after 6 PM the day before the appointment or that the client does not show will be charged to the client at (1) half the fee rate for the first incident and (2) the full fee rate for any incidents thereafter.* Most insurance companies will not reimburse you for this charge.

D. CONFIDENTIALITY POLICY.

All therapeutic communications, records, and contacts with professional and support staff will be held in strict confidence. Information may be released, in accordance with state law, only when (1) the client signs a written release of information indicating informed consent to such release; (2) the client expresses serious intent to harm himself/herself or someone else; (3) there is evidence or reasonable suspicion of abuse against a minor child, elder person (sixty-five years or older), or dependent adult; or (4) a subpoena or other court order is received directing the disclosure of information. It is our policy to assert either (a) privileged communication in the event of #4 or (b) the right to consult with clients, if at all possible barring an emergency, before mandated disclosure in the event of #2 or #3. Although we cannot guarantee it, we will endeavor to apprise clients of all mandated disclosures.

Clients with any concerns or questions about this policy agree to raise them with their counselor at the earliest possible time to resolve them in the client's best interest.

E. WORK AGREEMENT.

It is agreed that the client shall make a good-faith effort at personal growth and engage in the counseling process as an important priority at this time in his or her life. Client gain is most important in professional counseling. Suspension, termination, or referral shall be discussed between counselor and client for a pattern of behavior that reveals disinterest or lack of commitment to counseling or for any unresolved conflict or impasse between counselor and client.

[Your practice's name] and client further agree that the following needs or problem issues will be addressed in both counseling sessions and in client homework, with future revisions possible as need arises:

_____

_____

F. FEE AGREEMENT.

The agreed fee *per 50 minute session* is ____ for the base fee rate. If fee scale is elected, fill in the first two categories below:

monthly family gross income _____
number in family _____
fee scale _____ per session.

Service Agreement:

We, the undersigned therapist and client, have read, discussed together, and fully understand this agreement and the stated policies. We agree to honor these policies, including the commitment to negotiate and mediate as stated above, and will respect one another's views and differences in their outworking. We have also agreed to an initial definition of professional work and to the fee to be paid by the client.

Client signature _____ Date _____

Therapist signature _____ Date _____

Appendix B

PASTORAL COUNSELING
SERVICES AGREEMENT

This agreement for pastoral counseling services between [your church or practice's name] and client(s) _____ shall govern all professional relations between the parties. It is agreed that any disputes or modifications of agreement shall be negotiated directly between the parties; if negotiations are not satisfactory, then the parties *agree to mediate any differences with a mutually acceptable third-party mediator, considering first either the Executive Director or Associate Director of the practice.*

A. THE PASTORAL COUNSELOR is _____. He or she is an Ordained Minister and Pastoral Counselor, not a California licensed therapist.

B. PASTORAL COUNSELING AT [YOUR CHURCH OR PRACTICE'S NAME] is confidential, supervised counseling by one trained and experienced in both pastoral and counseling ministry. Pastoral counseling will be limited to 12 sessions overall with an evaluation at the end of this program of counseling. Counseling shall be terminated or referral for further treatment may be made at this time, whichever is in the client's best interest.

C. FEES AND INSURANCE POLICY.
Client fees are to be determined at the first session. Full or partial payment shall be made at the end of each session by the client. Clients understand that a Pastoral Counselor will not be able to receive insurance reimbursement under most policies—clients are responsible to bill their own insurance if they believe a Pastoral Counselor is covered. We will not extend credit or schedule appointments beyond three unpaid sessions until payment is made. *Clients are fully responsible for the payment of all fees.*

D. CANCELLATION POLICY.
We agree to and ask that clients maintain responsible relations regarding appointment times. Any appointment *cancelled after 6 PM the day before the appointment or that the client does not show will be charged to the client at (1) half the fee rate for the first incident and (2) the full fee rate for any incidents thereafter.* Most insurance companies will not reimburse you for this charge.

E. CONFIDENTIALITY POLICY.

All therapeutic communications, records, and contacts with professional and support staff will be held in strict confidence. Information may be released, in accordance with state law, only when (1) the client signs a written release of information indicating informed consent to such release; (2) the client expresses serious intent to harm himself/herself or someone else; (3) there is evidence or reasonable suspicion of abuse against a minor child, elder person (sixty-five years or older), or dependent adult; or (4) a subpoena or other court order is received directing the disclosure of information. It is our policy to assert either (a) privileged communication in the event of #4 or (b) the right to consult with clients, if at all possible barring an emergency, before mandated disclosure in the event of #2 or #3. Although we cannot guarantee it, we will endeavor to apprise clients of all mandated disclosures.

Clients with any concerns or questions about this policy agree to raise them with their counselor at the earliest possible time to resolve them in the client's best interest.

F. WORK AGREEMENT.

It is agreed that the client shall make a good-faith effort at personal growth and engage in the counseling process as an important priority at this time in his or her life. Client gain is most important in pastoral counseling. Suspension, termination, or referral shall be discussed between counselor and client for a pattern of behavior that reveals disinterest or lack of commitment to counseling or for any unresolved conflict or impasse between counselor and client.

[Your practice's name] and client further agree that the following needs or problem issues will be addressed in both counseling sessions and in client homework, with future revisions possible as need arises:

_____

_____

G. FEE AGREEMENT.

The agreed fee *per 50 minute session* is _____ for the base fee rate. If the fee scale is elected, fill in the first two categories below:

monthly family gross income _____
number in family _____
fee scale _____ per session.

Service Agreement:

We, the undersigned pastoral counselor and client, have read, discussed together and fully understand this agreement and the stated policies. We agree to honor these policies, including the commitment to negotiate and mediate as stated above, and will respect one another's views and differences in their outworking. We have also agreed to an initial definition of counseling work and to the fee to be paid by the client.

Client signature _____Date _____

Counselor signature _____Date _____

Appendix C

GROUP SERVICES AGREEMENT

This agreement for group counseling services between [your practice's name] and client(s) _____ shall govern all professional relations between the parties. It is agreed that any disputes or modifications of agreement shall be negotiated directly between the parties; if negotiations are not satisfactory, then the parties *agree to mediate any differences with a mutually acceptable third-party mediator, considering first either the Executive Director or Associate Director of the practice.*

A. THE STAFF THERAPIST(S) is/are _____ and _____. He or she is a

- ❑ California licensed M.F.C.C., L.C.S.W., or Ph.D. psychologist; or a
- ❑ prelicensed M.F.C.C. intern or trainee, L.C.S.W. associate, or psychological assistant.

B. FEES AND INSURANCE POLICY.

Client fees are to be determined at the first session. Full or partial payment shall be made at the end of each session by the client. Clients agree to pay part of their fee out-of-pocket even if covered by insurance. *As a courtesy to you* we can bill insurance and other vendors on a monthly basis. We will not extend credit or schedule appointments beyond three unpaid sessions until payment is made. Clients understand that a therapist with prelicense status (as checked above) may or may not be able to receive insurance reimbursement. *Clients are fully responsible for all fees if insurance does not pay.*

C. CANCELLATION POLICY.

We agree to and ask that clients maintain responsible relations regarding appointment times. Any appointment *cancelled after 6 PM the day before the appointment or that the client does not show will be charged to the client at (1) half the fee rate for the first incident and (2) the full fee rate for any incidents thereafter.* Most insurance companies will not reimburse you for this charge.

D. CONFIDENTIALITY POLICY.

All therapeutic communications, records, and contacts with professional and support staff will be held in strict confidence. Information may be released, in accordance with state law, only when (1) the client signs a written release of information indicating informed consent to such release; (2) the client expresses serious intent to harm himself/herself or someone else; (3) there is evidence or reasonable suspicion of abuse against a minor child, elder person (sixty-five years or older), or dependent adult; or (4) a subpoena or other court order is received directing the disclosure of information. It is our policy to assert either (a) privileged communication in the event of #4 or (b) the right to consult with clients, if at all possible barring an emergency, before mandated disclosure in the event of #2 or #3. Although we cannot guarantee it, we will endeavor to apprise clients of all mandated disclosures.

It is further agreed that the client will maintain the confidence of all group members and not disclose anything outside the group that is shared within it. Clients with any concerns or questions about this policy agree to raise them with their counselor at the earliest possible time to resolve them in the client's best interest.

E. WORK AGREEMENT.

It is agreed that the client shall make a commitment to faithful attendance of the group, recognizing the need for consistent involvement to both gain from the group and give to it as an active participant. Group commitment, termination, or referral may be reviewed after three unexcused absences or a pattern of behavior that suggests disinterest or lack of commitment to the group, or for any unresolved conflict or impasse between the client and the counselor or any other member of the group.

[Your practice's name] and client further agree that the following needs or problem issues will be addressed in both group counseling sessions and in client homework, with future revisions of goals possible as need arises:

_____

_____

F. FEE AGREEMENT.

The agreed fee *per 80 minute session* is $\underline{\ \$\ \ }$ per _____.

Service Agreement:

We, the undersigned therapist(s) and client, have read, discussed together, and fully understand this agreement and the stated policies. We agree to honor these policies, including the commitment to negotiate and mediate as stated above, and will respect one another's views and differences in their outworking. We have also agreed to an initial definition of professional work and to the fee to be paid by the client.

Client signature _____Date _____

Therapist signature _____Date _____

Therapist signature _____Date _____

Appendix D

CLIENT INTAKE FORM

Today's Date _____

A. Client's Name _____ Age _____ Birth date _____
Parent/Guardian's name(s) _____ Age(s) _____
Address _____
          street   city   state   zip
Phone (home) _____ (work) _____ best time to call _____
Marital Status: ❑ single   ❑ engaged
❑   married (how long _____; times married) _____
❑   separated (how long _____) ❑ divorced (how long _____)
Education _____ Occupation _____ Social Security # _____
Spouse's Name _____ Age ____ Birth date _____
Spouse's Education _____ Spouse's Occupation _____

B. List name, birth date, sex, relationship of all children, and whether they live at home with you.

Name	Birth date	Sex	Relationship	At Home?
_____	_____	___	_____	_____
_____	_____	___	_____	_____
_____	_____	___	_____	_____
_____	_____	___	_____	_____
_____	_____	___	_____	_____

C. Who is coming for counseling? _____ Any prior counseling? ❑ Yes ❑ No
If yes, when? _____ Where? _____ With whom? _____
Why? _____
Are you, or another family member, currently seeing a psychiatrist or another counselor?   ❑ Yes ❑ No
If so, what family member? _____ Name of helper _____
For what purpose? _____
Person to contact in emergency (name, relationship, phone, address) _____
_____

PLEASE FILL OUT THE FOLLOWING INFORMATION
AS IT APPLIES TO THE CLIENT

D. State the nature of the problem in your own words: _____

_____

_____

_____

What is your most difficult relationship right now? _____
What is your most difficult emotion right now? _____

E. CRISIS INFORMATION: Any current suicidal thoughts, feelings, or actions?
❏ Yes ❏ No If yes, explain: _____
Any current homicidal or assaultive thoughts or feelings, or anger-control problems? ❏ Yes ❏ No If yes, explain: _____
Any past problems, hospitalizations, or jailings for suicidal or assaultive behavior? ❏ Yes ❏ No If yes, describe: _____
Any current threats of significant loss or harm (illness, divorce, custody, job loss, etc.)? ❏ Yes ❏ No If yes, describe _____

F . MEDICAL INFORMATION: Doctor's name, address, and phone _____

_____

Are you presently taking any medication? ❏ Yes ❏ No If so, what?_____
For what purpose? _____
Any problems with ❏ eating ❏ sleeping ❏ chronic pain ❏ recent weight changes
Describe any answers checked above: _____
Any other medical problems?_____
Have you or a family member ever been hospitalized for mental or emotional illness? ❏ Yes ❏ No If yes, please explain—dates, place, reason:_____

_____

G. Common problem/symptom checklist.
     Fill in: 0 = none, 1 = mild, 2 = moderate, 3 = severe.

___marriage	___divorce/separation	___alcohol/drugs	___God/faith
___premarital	___child custody	___other addictions	___church/ministry
___singleness	___disabled	___grief/loss	___past hurts
___sexual issues	___work/career	___depression	___codependency
___family	___school/learning	___fear/anxiety	___intimacy
___children	___money/budgeting	___anger control	___communication
___parents	___aging/dependency	___loneliness	___self-esteem
___in-laws	___weight control	___mood swings	___stress
			management

     Other (specify): _____

H. Who referred you to us? (name, relationship, and phone number) _____

_____

If a professional referred you to us, may we send them a thank-you, noting your contact? ❏ Yes ❏ No
If yes, we will only send a thank-you, any other contact will require your express written permission.

THANK YOU for taking the time to fill out this information sheet. Your counselor will review this with you in the first session and use it to best assist you in your counseling work. We will maintain your strict confidence regarding this information, subject to the exceptions noted in your service contract. Be sure you review and sign the elements of agreement detailed in your service contract.

[The following section is optional. It can be included in this intake or form the core of a separate sheet detailing financial, insurance, and fee payment information.]

AS A *COURTESY* TO YOU, WE WILL BILL YOUR INSURANCE IF YOU ARE COVERED.

Insured's Name _____ Birth date _____

Social Security Number _____ Relationship to you _____

Insured's Employer (name and address) _____
_____

Insurance Co. Name _____ Phone _____

Insurance Co. Address _____

Group No. _____ Deductible $_____ Deductible satisfied? ___

Percent of coverage after deductible _____

Do you have secondary insurance coverage? ____ Company _____

Address _____ Phone _____

Insured's name _____ Birth date _____

Address (if different) _____ Social Security Number _____

If any other person or agency will be covering the cost of counseling, give their name and address. _____
_____

Appendix E

SERVICE ASSESSMENT FORM

Please take a few minutes to fill out this form. This will help us know how helpful (or not) we were to you and how to improve our services in the future. Please leave this form at the front desk or send it to [your practice's name and address]. We will maintain your strict confidence about this form beyond your therapist and agency administrators. Thank you.

1. Your name _____ 2. Today's date _____
3. Address _____ 4. Phone _____
5. Therapist's name(s) _____
6. Type of service rendered: ❑ marital counseling ❑ family counseling
   ❑ individual counseling/adult ❑ individual counseling/child
   ❑ group counseling/education ❑ psychosocial/custody evaluation
   ❑ separation/divorce mediation ❑ education/training
   ❑ premarital ❑ consultation ❑ other (describe): _____
7. Approximate dates of services (mo/yr to mo/yr) _____
8. Overall, were you satisfied with the help you received from counseling or other services   received at [your practice's name]? ❑ highly satisfied ❑ mostly satisfied
   ❑ somewhat satisfied ❑ somewhat dissatisfied ❑ highly dissatisfied
9. If satisfied, what (one or two things) did you like most? _____
_____
10. If dissatisfied, what is your complaint? _____
_____
11. Did your counselor understand your problem and needs?
   ❑ yes, great understanding ❑ yes, mostly understood
   ❑ no, didn't understand ❑ not sure
12. Did your counselor respect your views and values? ❑ yes, greatly respected
   ❑ yes, mostly respected ❑ no, did not respect ❑ not sure
13. Did your counselor rely on Christian resources—prayer, use of the Bible, respect for God and Christ—in helpful ways? ❑ yes, very helpful
   ❑ yes, somewhat helpful ❑ no, not helpful ❑ no, not wanted or appropriate
   ❑ not sure
14. Were there any problems during counseling with any of the following issues?
   ❑ fee disputes/problems ❑ breach of confidentiality
   ❑ sexual actions or communications ❑ too passive/not enough advice
   ❑ too controlling/not enough listening ❑ lack of timely and adequate phone
     and support   response
   ❑ office staff not friendly/helpful ❑ late/poor preparation for sessions
   ❑ lack of/inaccurate knowledge ❑ improper/incompetent treatment
   ❑ inadequate/poor referral or ❑ lack of competent response to
     consultation with other helping   emergencies
     professionals
15. Explain any issues checked above or not listed: _____
_____

Appendix F

CONSENT FOR RELEASE OF INFORMATION

I, _____, do consent and authorize [your practice's name] and staff member _____ to: (check off and fill in the blanks)

❑ release all records of my (or my dependent's) counseling or other work done by [your practice's name] to _____
(person or organization)
(except for the records of _____).

❑ obtain all records of my (or my dependent's) counseling or other work done by _____
(person or organization)
(except for the records of _____).
These records are to be sent to [your practice's name and address], in care of staff member _____.

❑ exchange all records (except for the records of _____)
as may be necessary between [your practice's name] and staff member _____ and _____
(person or organization)
for the best interests of my (or my dependent's) goals in counseling or other work.

This consent is valid and is to be acted on upon receipt of this form regarding the records of: _____.
(client or patient)
This consent will terminate without express written revocation by the client named herein on or when _____.

Client/Guardian Signature _____ Date _____
Client Address _____
Client Birth Date _____ Client Social Security Number _____
Signature of Staff Member _____ Date _____

NOTE: Federal regulations require ALL blanks to be filled in, including date, event, or condition that terminates consent for release of confidential client information.

335

Appendix G

AUTHORIZATION TO TREAT MINOR CHILDREN

I, _____, give my permission to
     (name of parent or guardian)

_____ to see my son/daughter
     (staff counselor)

_____ for treatment or counseling,
     (name of minor child)

with and/or without me being present in the same session. I/we understand
that we are the holder of confidential privilege—the right to withhold disclosure
of private counseling information about my child. However, in the interest of developing a trust relationship between the counselor and my/our child(ren), I/we
give the counselor permission to reveal or withhold information that in his/her
clinical judgment is necessary to best help and protect my/our child(ren).
The only exception to this discretion would be in the case of _____
_____
_____
_____

Parent/Guardian signature _____ Date _____

Therapist/Witness _____ Date _____

BIBLIOGRAPHY

Books, Articles, and Other Materials

Aharoni, Yair. *The No-Risk Society.* Chatham, N.J.: Chatham House Publishers, 1981.

Albers, Gregg. *Counseling and AIDS.* Dallas: Word, 1990.

Allen, Richard, Elyce Ferster, and Jesse Rubin, eds. *Readings in Law and Psychiatry.* Baltimore: John Hopkins University Press, 1968.

American Association for Marriage and Family Therapy. *AAMFT Code of Ethical Principles for Marriage and Family Therapists.* Washington, D.C.: AAMFT, 1 August 1988.

American Psychiatric Association. *Diagnostic and Statistical Manual of Mental Disorders III-R.* Washington, D.C.: APA, 1987.

American Psychiatric Association. "The Principles of Medical Ethics with Annotations Especially Applicable to Psychiatry." *American Journal of Psychiatry* 130 (1985): 1057.

American Psychological Association. "Ethical Principles of Psychologists." *American Psychologist* 45 (1990): 390–95.

Andreason, Nancy. *The Broken Brain: The Biological Revolution in Psychiatry.* New York: Harper and Row, 1984.

Appelbaum, Paul. "The Right to Refuse Treatment with Antipsychotic Medications: Retrospect and Prospect." *American Journal of Psychiatry* 145, no. 4 (1988): 413–19.

Appelbaum, Paul and A. Rosenbaum. "Tarasoff and the Researcher: Does the Duty to Protect Apply in the Research Setting?" *American Psychologist* 44, no. 6 (1989): 885–94.

Appelbaum, Paul, H. Zonana, R. Bonnie, and L. Roth. "Statutory Approaches to Limiting Psychiatrists' Liability for Their Patients' Violent Acts." *American Journal of Psychiatry* 146, no. 7 (1989): 821–28.

Apter, Alan, M. Kotler, S. Sevy, R. Plutchik, S. L. Brown, H. Foster, M. Hillbrand, M. Korn, and H. van Praag. "Correlates of Risk of Suicide in Violent and Nonviolent Psychiatric Patients." *American Journal of Psychiatry* 148, no. 7 (1991): 883–87.

Aquinas, Thomas. "Treatise on Law." In *Summa Theologica*. Cambridge, England: Blackfriars, 1966.

Association for Specialists in Group Work (ASGW). *Ethical Guidelines for Group Counselors*. Alexandria, Vir.: American Association of Counseling and Development, 1 June 1989.

"Association, Chapter Submit Briefs Supporting Clinical Practice Rights." *NASW News* (April 1981): 12.

Austin, Kenneth M., Mary E. Moline, and George T. Williams. *Confronting Malpractice: Legal and Ethical Dilemmas in Psychotherapy*. Newbury Park, Calif.: Sage Publications, 1990.

Bacigalupi, Ray. "The Last Session." *The California Therapist* 3, no. 4 (July/August 1991): 57–58.

Bandura, Albert. "Self-Efficacy Mechanism in Human Agency." *American Psychologist* 37 (1982): 122–47.

————. "Self-Efficacy: Toward a Unifying Theory of Behavioral Change." *Psychological Review* 84 (1977): 191–215.

Barabanov, Evgeny. "The Schism Between the Church and the World." In *From Under the Rubble*, edited by Alexander Solzhenitsyn. Boston: Little, Brown and Co., 1974.

Barber, Bernard. "Some Problems in the Sociology of the Professions." In *The Professions in America*. Edited by Kenneth Lynn. Boston: Houghton-Mifflin, 1965.

Barclay, Robert. "Apology for the Quakers." In *Documents of the Christian Church*, 2d ed. Edited by Henry Bettenson. London: Oxford University Press, 1963.

Bates, Carolyn M. and Annette M. Brodsky. *Sex In the Therapy Hour: A Case of Professional Incest*. New York: Guilford Press, 1989.

Beck, Aaron, G. Brown, R. Berchick, B. Stewart, and R. Steer. "Relationship Between Hopelessness and Ultimate Suicide." *American Journal of Psychiatry* 147 (1990): 190–95.

Beck, Aaron, H. Resnik, and D. Lettieri, eds. *The Prediction of Suicide*. Bowie, Md.: Charles Press, 1974.

Beck, James C. "The Psychotherapists' Duty to Protect Third Parties from Harm." *Mental Disability Law Reporter* 11 (1987): 141–48.

Beck, James C., ed. *The Potentially Violent Patient and the Tarasoff Decision in Psychiatric Practice*. Washington, D.C.: American Psychiatric Press, 1985.

Beck, James R. and R. K. Matthews. "A Code of Ethics for Christian Counselors." *Journal of Psychology and Christianity* 5, no. 3 (1986): 78–84.

Bednar, Steve. "The Psychotherapist's Calamity: Emerging Trends in the *Tarasoff* Doctrine." *Brigham Young University Law Review* (1989): 261–81.

Belser, E. "BBSE Joint Hearing with the Board of Psychology: Public Input Sought Regarding Dual Relationships." *NASW California News* 17, no. 5 (February 1991): 6.

Benetin, Juanita and M. Wilder. "Sexual Exploitation and Psychotherapy." *Women's Rights Law Reporter* 11, no. 2 (1989): 121–35.

Bergin, Allen E. "Values and Religious Issues in Psychotherapy and Mental Health." *American Psychologist* 46, no. 4 (1991): 394–403.

Bergman, Ben Zion. "Is the Cloth Unraveling? A First Look at Clergy Malpractice." *San Fernando Valley Law Review* 9 (1981): 47–66.

Berlin, Fred and E. W. Krout. "Pedophilia: Diagnostic Concepts, Treatment, and Ethical Considerations." *American Journal of Forensic Psychiatry* 7 (1983): 13–30.

Bernstein, Barton E. "Malpractice: Future Shock of the 1980s." *Social Casework* 62 (1981): 175–81.

Bezanson, Randal, Gilbert Cranberg, and John Soloski. *Libel Law and the Press: Myth and Reality*. New York: The Free Press, 1987.

Black, Henry. *Black's Law Dictionary*. 5th ed. St. Paul: West Publishing, 1979.

Bloom, Joseph and L. Faulkner. "Competency Decisions in Civil Commitment." *American Journal of Psychiatry* 144, no. 2 (1987): 193–96.

"Board of Behavioral Science Examiners Disciplinary Actions." *The California Therapist* 3, no. 6 (1991): 34–35.

Bobgan, Martin and Diedre Bobgan. *Psychoheresy: The Psychological Seduction of Christianity.* Santa Barbara, Calif.: Eastgate, 1987.

Bongar, Bruce. "Clinicians, Microcomputers, and Confidentiality." *Professional Psychology: Research and Practice* 19, no. 3 (1988): 286–89.

Bonynge, Eugene R. and Dave Cozzens. "Opinions Toward Changes in Education, Training and Licensure." *Professional Psychology: Research and Practice* 20, no. 6 (1989): 421–22.

Borys, Debra S. and Kenneth S. Pope. "Dual Relationships Between Therapist and Client: A National Study of Pschololgists, Psychiatrists, and Social Workers." *Professional Psychology: Research and Practice* 20, no. 5 (1989): 283–93.

Bouhoutsos, Jacqueline C., J. Holroyd, H. Lerman, B. R. Forer, and M. Greenberg. "Sexual Intimacy Between Psychotherapists and Patients." *Professional Psychology: Research and Practice* 14, no. 2 (1983): 185–96.

Brooks, A. "Mental Health Law: The Right to Refuse Treatment." *Administration in Mental Health* 4, no. 2 (1977): 90–95.

Brooks, Lew. "Intentional Infliction of Emotional Distress by Spiritual Counselors: Can Outrageous Conduct Be 'Free Exercise'?" *Michigan Law Review* 84 (1986): 1296.

Brown, Duane and A. Schulte. "A Social Learning Model of Consultation." *Professional Psychology: Research and Practice* 18 (1987): 283–87.

Brown, Phil. *The Transfer of Care: Psychiatric Institutionalization and Its Aftermath.* Boston: Routledge and Kegan Paul, 1985.

Bryant, Bruce C. "Red Flags and the Bureaucratization of Therapy." *The California Therapist* 2, no. 4 (1990): 42–44.

Bullis, Ronald K. "Child Abuse Reporting Requirements: Liabilities and Immunities for Clergy." *The Journal of Pastoral Care* 44, no. 3 (Fall 1990):244–48.

Burek, Lawrence M. "Clergy Malpractice: Making Clergy Accountable to a Lower Power." *Pepperdine Law Review* 14 (1986): 137–61.

Burtchaell, James T. "Travesty at Wichita." *Christianity Today,* 11 November 1991, 20–21.

Buzzard, Lynn. "Scarlet Letter Lawsuits: Private Affairs and Public Judgments." *Campbell Law Review* 10, no. 1 (1987): 1–68.

Buzzard, Lynn and Laurence Eck. *Tell It to the Church: A Biblical Approach to Resolving Conflict Out of Court.* Elgin, Ill.: David C. Cook, 1982.

California Association for Marriage and Family Therapists. "Ethical Standards for Marriage and Family Therapists." *The California Therapist* 3, no. 5 (1991): 31–39.

California Department of Consumer Affairs (CDCA). *Professional Therapy NEVER Includes Sex.* Sacramento: CDCA, 1990.

Cameron, Alan S., John P. Galassi, Janice M. Birk, and Natalie Moss Waggener. "Trends in Counseling Psychology Programs: The Council of Counseling Psychology Training Programs Survey, 1975–1987." *The Counseling Psychologist* 17, no. 2 (1989): 301–13.

Campbell, Emily. "Mandatory AIDS Testing and Privacy: A Psycholegal Perspective." *North Dakota Law Review* 66 (1990): 449–90.

Cassidy, Patrick S. "The Liability of Psychiatrists for Malpractice." *University of Pittsburgh Law Review* 36 (1974): 108–37.

Cavanagh, Ralph and D. Rhode. "The Unauthorized Practice of Law and Pro Se Divorce." *Yale Law Journal* 86 (1976): 103–84.

Chamow, Larry. "What to Look for in a Clinical Supervisor." *The California Therapist* 2, no. 3 (1990): 60.

Chase, Steve. "Clergy Malpractice: The Cause of Action that Never Was." *North Carolina Central Law Journal* 18 (1989): 163–85.

Chemtob, Claude, G. Bauer, R. Hamada, S. Pelowski, and M. Muraoka. "Patient Suicide: Occupational Hazard for Psychologists and Psychiatrists." *Professional Psychology: Research and Practice* 20, no. 5 (1989): 294–300.

Chesler, Phyllis. *Women and Madness.* Garden City, N.Y.: Doubleday, 1972.

Chilstrom, Corrine. "Suicide and Pastoral Care." *The Journal of Pastoral Care* 43, no. 3 (1989): 199–208.

Clemmons, Amos. "The Pastor and the Institute." *PARAKALEO* 3, no. 3 (1991): 1–2. Published quarterly by The Redwood Family Institute, Eureka, California.

"Clergy Malpractice: Bad News for the Good Samaritan or a Blessing in Disguise?" *University of Toledo Law Review* 17 (1985): 209.

Cohen, Ronald J. *Malpractice: A Guide for Mental Health Professionals.* New York: The Free Press, 1979.

Cole, Bettie S. "Legal Issues Related to Social Work Program Admissions." *Journal of Social Work Education* 27, no. 1 (Winter 1991): 18–24.

Coleman, Phyllis. "Shrinking the Clergyperson Exemption to Florida's Mandatory Child Abuse Reporting Statute." *Nova Law Review* 12 (1987): 115–45.

Collins, Gary. *Can You Trust Psychology?* Downers Grove, Ill.: InterVarsity, 1988.

————. *Christian Counseling: A Comprehensive Guide.* Rev. ed. Dallas: Word, 1988.

————. *Excellence and Ethics in Counseling.* Dallas: Word, 1991.

Colson, Charles. *Kingdoms in Conflict.* New York: Morrow/Zondervan, 1987.

Conway, Jim. *Men in Mid-Life Crisis.* Elgin, Ill.: David C. Cook, 1978.

Cox, Laurel, Corbett Phibbs, Kathy Wexler, and Mary Reimersma. *Practical Applications in Supervision.* San Diego, Calif.: California Association of Marriage and Family Therapists, 1990.

Cull, J. G. and W. S. Gill. *Suicide Probability Scale Manual.* Los Angeles: Western Psychological Services, 1982.

Curran, William. "The Hiss-Chambers Trial." In *Readings in Law And Psychiatry.* Edited by R. C. Allen, E. Z. Ferster, and J. G. Rubin. Baltimore: Johns Hopkins University Press, 1968.

Danco, Jeffrey C. "The Ethics of Fee Practices: An Analysis of Presuppositions and Accountability." *Journal of Psychology and Theology* 10, no.1 (Spring 1989): 13–21.

Dawidoff, Donald J. *The Malpractice of Psychiatrists: Malpractice in Psychoanalysis, Psychotherapy and Psychiatry.* Springfield, Ill.: Thomas Publishers, 1973.

Denmark, Florence L. "Back to the Future in Education and Training of Psychologists." *American Psychologist* 44, no. 4 (April 1989): 725–30.

Diamond, Bernard. "The Psychiatric Prediction of Dangerousness." *University of Pennsylvania Law Review* 123 (1974): 439.

DiClemente, Ralph J., Mark M. Lanier, Patricia F.Horan, and Mark Lodico. "Comparison of AIDS Knowledge, Attitudes, and Behaviors among Incarcerated Alolescents and a Public School Sample in San Francisco." *American Journal of Public Health* 81, no. 5 (1991): 628–30.

Dobson, James and Gary Bauer. *Children at Risk: The Battle for the Hearts and Minds of Our Kids.* Dallas: Word, 1990.

Domino, George. "Clergy's Knowledge of Psychopathology." *Journal of Psychology and Theology* 18, no. 1(1990): 32–39.

Dorken, Herbert. "Malpractice Claims Experience of Psychologists: Policy Issues, Cost Comparisons with Psychiatrists, and Prescription Privilege Implications." *Professional Psychology: Research and Practice* 21, no. 2 (1990): 150–52.

Dorwart, Robert, M. Schlesinger, H. Davidson, S. Epstein, and C. Hoover. "A National Study of Psychiatric Hospital Care." *American Journal of Psychiatry* 148, no.2 (1991): 204–10.

Egan, Gerard. *The Skilled Helper: A Systematic Approach to Effective Helping.* 4th ed. Pacific Grove, Calif.: Brooks/Cole, 1990.

Elliot, Diana M. "The Impact of Conservative Christian Faith on the Prevalence and Sequelae of Sexual Abuse." Paper presented at CAPS (Christian Association for Psychological Studies) 1991 International Conference, Anaheim, Calif., June 1991.

Ericsson, Samuel. "Clergyman Malpractice: Ramifications of a New Theory." *Valparaiso University Law Review* 16 (1981): 163.

Ethics Committee of the American Psychological Association. "Trends in Ethics Cases, Common Pitfalls, and Published Resources." *American Psychologist* 43, no. 7 (1988): 564–72.

Feldman-Summers, Shirley and G. Jones. "Psychological Impact of Sexual Contact Between Therapists or Other Health Care Practitioners and Their Clients." *Journal of Consulting and Clinical Psychology* 52, no. 6 (1984): 1054–61.

Firman, Gregory J. "Ostensible Agency: Another Malpractice Hazard." *American Journal of Psychiatry* 145, no. 4 (1988): 510–12.

Fischer, J. "State Regulation of Psychologists." *Washington University Law Quarterly* 58 (1980): 639.

Fisher, K. "Charges Catch Clinicians in Cycle of Shame, Slip-ups." *American Psychological Association Monitor* 16 (1985): 6–7.

Foster, L. "Group Psychotherapy: A Pool of Legal Witnesses." *International Journal of Group Psychotherapy* 25 (1975): 50.

Frankel, T. "Fiduciary Law." *California Law Review* 71 (1983): 795–836.

Fremont, Lora. "A Supervisee Looks at Supervision." *The California Therapist* 1, no. 5 (1989): 27–28.

Fulero, S. "Insurance Trust Releases Malpractice Statistics." *State Psychological Association Affairs* 19, no. 1(1987): 4–5.

Furrow, Barry. *Malpractice in Psychotherapy.* Lexington, Mass.: Lexington Books, 1980.

Gaffney, Edward, D. Laycock, and M. W. McConnell. "An Answer to *Smith:* The Religious Freedom Restoration Act." *Christian Legal Society Quarterly* 11, no. 4 (1990): 17–23.

Galanter, Marc. "Charismatic Religious Sects and Psychiatry: An Overview." *American Journal of Psychiatry* 139, no. 12 (1982): 1539–48.

Galanter, Marc, D. Larson, and E. Rubenstone. "Christian Psychiatry: The Impact of Evangelical Belief on Clinical Practice." *American Journal of Psychiatry* 148, no. 1 (1991): 90–95.

Gallup, George, Jr. and Frank Newport. "Baby-Boomers Seek More Family Time." *The Gallup Poll Monthly* (April 1991): 31–42.

—————. "Large Majorities Continue to Back AIDS Testing." *The Gallup Poll Monthly* (May 1991): 25–28.

Gartner, John D. "Antireligious Prejudice in Admissions to Doctoral Programs in Clinical Psychology." *Professional Psychology: Research and Practice* 17, no. 5 (1986): 473–75.

Gartrell, Nanette, J. Herman, S. Olarte, M. Feldstein, and R. Localio. "Psychiatrist-Patient Sexual Contact: Results of a National

Survey, I: Prevalence." *American Journal of Psychiatry* 143, no. 9 (1986): 1126–31.

————. "Reporting Practices of Psychiatrists Who Knew of Sexual Misconduct of Colleagues." *American Journal of Orthopsychiatry* 57 (1987): 287–95.

Gergen, David. "America's Legal Mess." *U.S. News and World Report*, 19 August 1991.

Givelber, Daniel, W. Bowers, and D. Blitch. "Tarasoff, Myth and Reality: An Empirical Study of Private Law in Action." *Wisconsin Law Review* (1984): 443–97.

Gross, Martin. *The Psychological Society.* New York: Random House, 1978.

Gustafson, Kathryn and J. Regis McNamara. "Confidentiality with Minor Clients: Issues and Guidelines for Therapists." *Professional Psychology: Research and Practice* 18, no. 5 (1987): 503–8.

Gutheil, Thomas and P. Appelbaum. *Clinical Handbook of Psychiatry and the Law.* 2d ed. New York: McGraw-Hill, 1991.

Halleck, Seymour. *Law in the Practice of Psychiatry: A Handbook for Clinicians.* New York: Plenum Medical Books, 1980.

Hansen, Mark. "$10 Million Dollar Defamation Award: Evangelist Claimed His Exploits Exaggerated by Rival Preacher." *ABA Journal* 77, no. 2 (1991): 28.

Hardcastle, David. "Certification, Licensure and Other Forms of Regulation." In *Handbook of Clinical Social Work,* edited by Aaron Rosenblatt and Diana Waldfogel. San Francisco: Jossey-Bass, 1983.

Hargrove, David S. "Ethical Issues in Rural Mental Health Practice." *Professional Psychology: Research and Practice* 17, no. 1 (1986): 20–23.

Harkin, Jeff. *Grace Plus Nothing.* Wheaton, Ill.: Tyndale House, 1992.

Harris, M. "Tort Liability of the Psychotherapist." *University of San Francisco Law Review* 8 (1973): 405–36.

Hart, Archibald. "Being Moral Isn't Always Enough." *Leadership* 9, no. 2 (1988): 24–29.

Hashima, Patricia Y. *Child Abuse Prevention Handbook.* Sacramento: Crime Prevention Center, Office of the Attorney General, California Department of Justice, 1982 (revised 1988).

Hayford, Jack. *Restoring Fallen Leaders*. Ventura, Calif.: Regal, 1988.

Haynes, John. *Divorce Mediation: A Practical Guide for Therapists and Counselors*. New York: Springer, 1981.

Herron, William G. and Suzanne Sitkowski. "Effect of Fees on Psychotherapy: What Is the Evidence?" *Professional Psychology: Research and Practice* 17, no. 4 (1986): 347–51.

Hirsh, H. "Will Your Medical Records Get You Into Trouble?" *Legal Aspects of Medical Practice* 6 (1978): 46–51.

Hogan, Daniel. *The Regulation of Psychotherapists. Vol. I: A Study in the Philosophy and Practice of Professional Regulation*. Cambridge, Mass.: Ballinger, 1979.

————. *The Regulation of Psychotherapists. Vol. III: A Review of Malpractice Suits in the United States*. Cambridge, Mass.: Ballinger, 1979.

Holmes, Oliver Wendell. "The Path of the Law." *Harvard Law Review* 10 (1897): 459–64.

Horsley, J. E. "How to Protect Yourself Against Legal Malpractice." *Medical Economics* 8, no. 7 (1978): 149–58.

"How Common Is Pastoral Indiscretion? Results of a Leadership Survey." *Leadership* 9, no. 1 (1988): 12–13.

Hughes, Everett. "Professions." In *The Professions in America*, edited by K. S. Lynn, 1–14. Boston: Houghton-Mifflin, 1965.

Joslin, George. *The Minister's Law Handbook*. Manhasset, N.Y.: Channel Press, 1962.

Kasper, Dennis. *Liability Workshop 1989: Balancing Prevention and Risk for Clergy, Counselors, Administrators and Educators*. Los Angeles: Caldwell and Toms, Inc., 1989.

Kilbourne, Brock and James T. Richardson. "Psychotherapy and New Religions in a Pluralistic Society." *American Psychologist* 39, no. 3 (1984): 237–51.

Kilpatrick, William K. *Psychological Seduction: The Failure of Modern Psychology*. Nashville: Thomas Nelson, 1983.

Kirk, Stuart A. and H. Kutchins. "Deliberate Misdiagnosis in Mental Health Practice." *Social Service Review* 62 (1988): 225–37.

Klein, Joel and S. Glover. "Psychiatric Malpractice." *International Journal of Law and Psychiatry* 6 (1983): 131–57.

Klerman, Gerald. "The Psychiatric Patient's Right to Effective Treatment: Implications of 'Osheroff v. Chestnut Lodge.'" *American Journal of Psychiatry* 147, no. 4 (1990): 409–18.

Knapp, Samuel, L. Vandecreek, and D. Shapiro. "Statutory Remedies to the Duty to Protect: A Reconsideration." *Psychotherapy* 27, no. 2 (1990): 291–96.

Koogler, O. J. *Structured Mediation in Divorce Settlement.* Lexington, Mass.: Lexington Books, 1978.

Kressel, Kenneth. *The Process of Divorce: How Professionals and Couples Negotiate Settlements.* New York: Basic Books, 1985.

Kuhn, Thomas. *The Structure of Scientific Revolutions.* 2d ed. Chicago: University of Chicago Press, 1970.

Kutchins, Herb. "The Fiduciary Relationship: The Legal Basis for Social Workers' Responsibilities to Clients." *Social Work* 36, no. 2 (1991): 106–13.

LaHaye, Tim. *If Ministers Fall, Can They Be Restored?* Grand Rapids, Mich.: Pyranee Books/ Zondervan, 1990.

Lamb, Douglas H., Claudia Clark, Philip Drumheller, Kathleen Frizzell, and Lynn Surrey. "Applying *Tarasoff* to AIDS–Related Psychotherapy Issues." *Professional Psychology: Research and Practice* 20, no. 1 (1989): 37–43.

Lambert, Norma. "Divorce Mediation Comes of Age." *The California Therapist* 2, no. 2 (1990): 40–41.

Lamberton, Henry H., Cheryl R. Azlin, Siang-Yang Tan, John S. Brekke, and David B. Larson. "Religion and Mental Health: Attitudes of Fundamentalist Pastors." Paper presented at CAPS 1991 International Conference, Anaheim, Calif., June 1991.

Lasch, Christopher. *The Culture of Narcissism.* New York: Norton, 1979.

Last, Uriel and Zipora Schutz. "Patient's Reported Initial Reactions to Abrupt Disruption of Psychotherapy: The Aftermath of a Doctors' Strike." *Psychotherapy* 27, no. 3 (Fall 1990): 436–44.

Lawton, Kim. "Uncle Sam v. First Church." *Christianity Today,* 7 October 1991, 38–41.

LeBoeuf, Denise. "Psychiatric Malpractice: Exploitation of Women Patients." *Harvard Women's Law Journal* 11 (1988): 83–116.

Leslie, Richard. "Confidentiality." *The California Therapist* 1, no. 4 (1989): 35–42.

————. "The Dangerous Patient: Tarasoff Revisited." *The California Therapist* 2, no. 2 (1990): 11–14.

————. "Dual Relationships Hearings Held." *The California Therapist* 2, no. 1 (1991): 18–19.

————. "Dual Relationships: The Legal View." *The California Therapist* 1, no. 5 (1989): 9–13.

————. "Should I Keep Clinical Records?" *The California Therapist* 1, no. 5 (1989): 19–20.

Levicoff, Steve. *Christian Counseling and the Law.* Chicago: Moody, 1990.

Lieberman, Jethro K. *The Litigious Society.* New York: Basic Books, 1983.

Luken, Debora. "An Empowerment Model of Supervision: A Guide to the Therapist Within." *The California Therapist* 2, no. 3 (1990): 42–46.

MacArthur, John. *Our Sufficiency in Christ.* Dallas: Word, 1991.

MacDonald, Gordon. *Rebuilding Your Broken World.* Nashville: Oliver-Nelson, 1989.

McDowell, Josh. *Research Almanac and Statistical Digest.* Julian, Calif.: Julian Press, 1990.

Malony, H. Newton. "Confidentiality in the Pastoral Role." *Theology, News and Notes,* October 1986, 12.

Malony, H. Newton, Thomas L. Needham, and Samuel Southard. *Clergy Malpractice.* Philadelphia: The Westminster Press, 1986.

Margenau, Eric A. *The Encyclopedic Handbook of Private Practice.* New York: Gardner Press, 1990.

Marks, Gary, Jean L. Richardson, and Norma Maldonado. "Self-Disclosure of HIV Infection to Sexual Partners." *American Journal of Public Health* 81, no. 10 (1991): 1321–23.

Marmor, Judd. "Some Psychodynamic Aspects of the Seduction of Patients in Psychotherapy." *The American Journal of Psychoanalysis* 36 (1976): 320–21.

Masters, William H. and Virginia E. Johnson. "Principles of the New Sex Therapy." *American Journal of Psychiatry* 133 (1976): 548–54.

Medical Essays. Rochester, Minn.: Mayo Clinic Health Letters, September 1985.

Menendez, C. "Clergy Confidential." *Church & State* 39 (1986): 128.

Mermin, Samuel. *Law and the Legal System: An Introduction*. 2d ed. Boston: Little, Brown and Co., 1982.

Messinger, Steve. "Malpractice Suits—The Psychiatrist's Turn." *Journal of Legal Medicine* 3 (1975): 21–25.

Meyer, Robert G., E. R. Landis, and J. R. Hays. *Law for the Psychotherapist*. New York: Norton, 1988.

Meyers, C. J. "Hard Cases: The 'Duty to Warn' As a Felt Necessity of Our Time." *Journal of Psychiatry and Law* 15 (Summer 1987): 189–204.

Miller, D. J. and M. H. Thelan. "Knowledge and Beliefs About Confidentiality in Psychotherapy." *Professional Psychology* 17 (1986): 12–19.

Mitchell, Mary. "Must Clergy Tell? Child Abuse Reporting Requirements Versus the Clergy Privilege and Free Exercise of Religion." *Minnesota Law Review* 71 (1986): 723–825.

Mithers, Carol. "When Therapists Drive Their Patients Crazy." *California* 13, no. 8 (1988): 76–85, 135–37.

Monahan, John. *The Clinical Prediction of Violent Behavior*. DHHS Publication, No. (ADM) 81-21, Washington, D.C.: Government Printing Office, 1981.

———. "Limiting Therapist Exposure to Tarasoff Liability: Guidelines for Risk Containment." *American Psychologist* (in press).

Morrison, Constance F. "AIDS: Ethical Implications for Psychological Intervention." *Professional Psychology: Research and Practice* 20, no. 3 (1989): 166–71.

Mosgofian, Peter. "Why Pay for Christian Counseling?" *PARAKALEO* 3, no. 1 (1991): 1–2.

Muck, Terry, ed. *Sins of the Body: Ministry in a Sexual Society*. Dallas: Christianity Today Institute and Word, 1988.

National Association of Social Workers. *NASW Code of Ethics*. Washington, D.C.: NASW, 1980.

National Association of Social Workers Task Force on Ethics. "Ethics Analysis—Conduct and Responsibility to Clients." *NASW News* (May 1980): 12.

Neill, John and David Kniskern, eds. *From Psyche to System: The Evolving Therapy of Carl Whitaker.* New York: Guilford Press, 1982.

Nelson, Alan A. and William P. Wilson. "The Ethics of Sharing Religious Faith in Psychotherapy." *Journal of Psychology and Theology* 12, no. 1 (1984): 15–23.

Nietzsche, Frederick W. *Beyond Good and Evil.* New York: Vintage Books, 1966.

Nixon, Mary. "Professional Training in Psychology." *American Psychologist* 45, no. 11(1990): 1257–62.

O'Brien, Raymond C. "Pedophilia: The Legal Predicament of Clergy." *Journal of Contemporary Health Law and Policy* 4 (1988): 91–154.

O'Conner, David F. "Dysfunctional Clergy and Religious." *Human Development* 11, no. 4 (Winter 1990): 43–48.

Ohlschlager, George. "Liability in Christian Counseling: Welcome to the Grave New World." In *Excellence and Ethics in Counseling*, Gary Collins, 41–74. Dallas: Word, 1991.

Oordt, Mark. "Ethics of Practice Among Christian Psychologists: A Pilot Study." *Journal of Psychology and Theology* 18, no. 3 (1990): 255–60.

Ornstein, Robert and David Sobel. *The Healing Brain.* New York: Touchstone, 1987.

Ostling, Richard. "Sins of the Fathers." *Time,* 19 August 1991.

Patten, Christi, Therese Barnett, and Daniel Houlihan. "Ethics in Family Therapy: A Review of the Literature." *Professional Psychology: Research and Practice* 22, no. 2 (1991): 171–75.

Paulsen, Michael and R. K. Smith. "A Luxury . . . We Cannot Afford: Religious Freedom After the Peyote Case." *Christian Legal Society Quarterly* 12, no. 2 (1990): 18.

Payne, Franklin E., Jr. *Biblical Medical Ethics: The Christian and the Practice of Medicine.* Milford, Mich.: Mott Media, 1985.

Pearson, Jessica, M. L. Ring, and A. Milne. "A Portrait of Divorce Mediation Services in the Public and Private Sector." *Conciliation Courts Review* 21 (1983): 1–24.

"Physician Team Studies OB Claims." *Malpractice Digest* 12 (June 1985): 2.

Pope, Kenneth S. "Ethical and Malpractice Issues in Hospital Practice." *American Psychologist* 45, no. 9 (1990): 1066–70.

Pope, Kenneth S. and Jacqueline C. Bouhoutos. *Sexual Intimacy Between Therapists and Patients*. New York: Praeger, 1986.

Pope, Kenneth S., P. Keith-Spiegel, and B. G. Tabachnick. "Sexual Attraction to Clients: The Human Therapist and the (Sometimes) Inhuman Training System." *American Psychologist* 41, no. 2 (1986): 147–58.

Poythress, Norman G., Jr. "Avoiding Negligent Release: Contemporary Clinical and Risk Management Strategies." *American Journal of Psychiatry* 147, no. 8 (1990): 994–97.

Prosser, William L. *Handbook of the Law of Torts*. 4th ed. St. Paul, Minn.: West Publishing, 1971.

Prosser, William and W. Page Keeton. *Prosser and Keeton on the Law of Torts*. 5th ed. St. Paul, Minn.: West Publishing, 1984.

Reaves, Rudolph P. *The Law of Professional Licensing and Certification: 1987 Supplement*. Charlotte, N.C.: Publications for Professionals, 1987.

Rediger, G. Lloyd. *Ministry and Sexuality: Cases, Counseling and Care*. Minneapolis: Fortress Press, 1990.

Reisman, Judith A. and Edward W. Eichel. *Kinsey, Sex and Fraud: The Indoctrination of a People*. Edited by John H. Court and J. Gordon Muir. Lafayette, La.: Huntington House Publishers, 1990.

Richo, David. "Maintaining Personal Boundaries in Relationships." *The California Therapist* 2, no. 4 (1990): 40–41.

Riemersma, Mary. "Malpractice Insurance: What the Future Holds." *The California Therapist* 3, no. 6 (1991): 9–14.

Rinck, Margaret. *Christian Men Who Hate Women: Healing Hurting Relationships*. Grand Rapids, Mich.: Zondervan, 1990.

Robbins, Thomas. "Cults, Converts and Charisma: The Sociology of New Religious Movements." *Current Sociology* 36, no. 1 (Spring 1988): 1–248.

Robinson, G. "Discussion." *American Journal Of Psychiatry* 18 (1962): 779–80.

Robitscher, Jonas. *The Powers of Psychiatry*. Boston: Houghton-Mifflin, 1980.

Roehlkepartain, Jolene. "Saving the Suicidal." *Leadership* 13, no. 1 (1987): 53.

Roetter, Friedrich. *Might is Right*. London: Quality Press, 1939.

Rogers, James L., Robert F. Boruch, George B. Stoms, and Dorothy DeMoya. "The Impact of the Minnesota Parental Notification Law on Abortion and Birth." *American Journal of Public Health* 81, no. 3 (1991): 294–98.

Roth, Loren. "A Commitment Law for Patients, Doctors, and Lawyers." *American Journal of Psychiatry* 136 (1979): 1121–27.

Russell, Diana. "The Incidence and Prevalence of Intrafamilial and Extrafamilial Sexual Abuse of Female Children." *International Journal of Child Abuse and Neglect* 7 (1983): 133–39.

Rutter, Peter. *Sex in the Forbidden Zone*. Los Angeles: Jeremy P. Tarcher, 1989.

Ryan, Barbara and Eric Plutzer. "When Married Women Have Abortions: Spousal Notification and Marital Interaction." *Journal of Marriage and Family* 51 (February 1989): 41–50.

Sande, C. Ken. *Christian Conciliation: A Better Way to Settle Conflicts*. Billings, Mont.: Association of Christian Conciliation Services, 1989.

Schindler, Fred, Michael R. Berren, Mo Therese Hannah, Allan Beigel, and Jose M. Santiago. "How the Public Perceives Psychiatrists, Psychologists, Nonpsychiatric Physicians, and Members of the Clergy." *Professional Psychology: Research and Practice* 18, no. 4 (1987): 371–76.

Schoener, Gary Richard and John Gonsiorek. "Assessment and Development of Rehabilitation Plans for Counselors who have Sexually Exploited their Clients." *The California Therapist* 1, no. 6 (1989): 32–39.

Schoener, Gary, Jannette Milgrom, John Gonsiorek, Ellen Luepker, and Ray Conroe. *Psychotherapists' Sexual Involvement with Clients: Intervention and Prevention*. Minneapolis: Walk-In Counseling Center, 1989.

Schwitzgebel, Robert L. and R. Kirkland Schwitzgebel. *Law and Psychological Practice*. New York: Wiley, 1980.

Shackelford, John F. "Affairs in the Consulting Room: A Review of Literature on Therapist-Patient Sexual Intimacy." *Journal of Psychology and Christianity* 8, no. 4 (1989): 26–43.

Sherman, Rorie. "Legal Spotlight on Priests Who Are Pedophiles." *The National Law Journal* (4 April 1988).

Shlachter, Barry. "Horror Stories from Texas Psychiatric Patients." *San Francisco Chronicle,* 6 November 1991.

Siegel, Carole and S. Fischer, eds. *Psychiatric Records in Mental Health Care.* New York: Brunner/Mazel, 1981.

Simon, Robert I. *Psychiatric Interventions and Malpractice: A Primer for Liability Prevention.* Springfield, Ill.: Thomas Publishers, 1982.

Singer, Margaret T. "Coming Out of the Cults." *Psychology Today* (January 1979): 72–82.

Slater, Greg. "Nally v. Grace Community Church of the Valley: Absolution for ClergyMalpractice?" *Brigham Young University Law Review* (1989): 913–42.

Slawson, P. F. "Psychiatric Malpractice: A Regional Incidence Study." *American Journal of Psychiatry* 126 (1970): 1302–5.

Slovenko, Ralph. "Malpractice in Psychiatry and Related Fields." *Journal of Psychiatry and Law* 9, no. 2 (1981): 5.

—————. "On the Need for Record-Keeping in the Practice of Psychiatry." *Journal of Psychiatry and Law* 7 (1979): 339–440.

—————. "Psychotherapist-Patient Testimonial Privilege: A Picture of Misguided Hope." *Catholic University Law Review* 23 (1974): 649–73.

—————. "The Therapist's Duty to Warn or Protect Third-Persons." *Journal of Psychiatry and Law* 16 (1989): 139–209.

Smith, H. W. and C. Kronauge. "The Politics of Abortion: Husband Notification Legislation, Self-Disclosure, and Marital Bargaining." *The Sociological Quarterly* 31, no. 4 (1990): 585–98.

Smith, R. *Privacy.* Garden City, N.Y.: Anchor Press/Doubleday, 1979.

Sonne, Janet, and Kenneth Pope. "Treating Victims of Therapist-Patient Sexual Involvement." *Psychotherapy* 28, no. 1 (1991): 174–87.

Steinke, Peter L. "Clergy Affairs." *Journal of Psychology and Christianity* 8, no. 4 (1989): 56–62.

Steiny, Nancy. "The Alchemy of Supervision." *The California Therapist* 1, no. 5 (1989): 29–31.

Stone, Alan. "Law, Science, and Psychiatric Malpractice: A Response to Klerman's Indictment of Psychoanalytic Psychiatry." *American Journal of Psychiatry* 147, no. 4 (1990): 419–27.

Strasburger, Larry, Linda Jorgenson, and Rebecca Randles. "Criminalization of Psychotherapist-Patient Sex." *American Journal of Psychiatry* 148, no. 7 (1991): 859–63.

Stromberg, Clifford and A. Stone. "A Model State Law on Civil Commitment of the Mentally Ill." *Harvard Journal of Legislation* 20 (1983): 275–77.

Sullender, R. Scott and H. Newton Malony. "Should Clergy Counsel Suicidal Persons?" *The Journal of Pastoral Care* 44, no. 3 (1990): 203–11.

Swenson, Elizabeth V. "Legal Liability for a Patient's Suicide." *Journal of Psychiatry and Law* 14 (1986): 409–34.

Swift, Harriet. "Magic's Future Holds More Pain, Gloom Than His Smile Belies." *Eureka Times-Standard*, 28 November 1991.

Taub, Sheila. "Psychiatric Malpractice in the 1980's: A Look at Some Areas of Concern." *Law, Medicine and Health Care* (June 1983): 97.

Tjeltveit, Alan C. "Christian Ethics and Psychological Explanations of 'Religious Values' in Therapy: Critical Connections." *Journal of Psychology and Christianity* 10, no. 2 (1991): 101–12.

Troyer, Robert C. "Protecting the Flock from the Shepherd: A Duty of Care and Licensing Requirement for Clergy Counselors." *Boston College Law Review* 30, no. 7 (1989): 1179–1220.

Tucker, Ruth A. *Another Gospel: Alternative Religions and the New Age Movement.* Grand Rapids, Mich.: Academia Books, 1989.

Vanderkooi, L. and J. Pearson. "Mediating Divorce Disputes: Mediator Behaviors, Styles, and Rules." *Family Relations* 32 (1983): 557–66.

Van Hoose, William H. and Jeffrey A. Kottler. *Ethical and Legal Issues in Counseling and Psychotherapy.* 2d ed. San Francisco: Jossey-Bass, 1987.

Vinson, Jane. "Reflections on Dual Relationships: Therapist Beware." *The California Therapist* (September/October 1989): 15–17.

Vitz, Paul. *Psychology as Religion: The Cult of Self-Worship.* Grand Rapids, Mich.: Eerdmans, 1977.

Vogel, Joan and R. Delgado. "To Tell the Truth: Physician's Duty to Disclose Medical Mistakes." *UCLA Law Review* 28 (1980): 52.

Waldfogel, Diana. "Supervision of Students and Practitioners." In *Handbook of Clinical Social Work,* edited by Aaron Rosenblatt and Diana Waldfogel. San Francisco: Jossey-Bass, 1983.

Wapner, John H., Jill G. Klein, Myrna L. Friedlander, and Frank J. Andrasik. "Transferring Psychotherapy Clients: State of the Art." *Professional Psychology: Research and Practice* 17, no. 6 (1986): 492–96.

Watson, Holly and Murray Levine. "Psychotherapy and Mandated Reporting of Child Abuse." *American Journal of Orthopsychiatry* 59, no. 2 (1989): 246–56.

Will, George F. Excerpt from a commencement address at Duke University. In *Reader's Digest,* January 1992, 172.

Williams, George, L. Johnson, and P. Diehm. *The Therapist and the Legal System.* North Orange County Psychological Services, 1991.

Wilson, Susan J. "Confidentiality." In *Handbook of Clinical Social Work,* edited by Aaron Rosenblatt and D. Waldfogel. San Francisco: Jossey-Bass, 1983.

Woody, Robert. *Fifty Ways to Avoid Malpractice: A Guidebook for Mental Health Professionals.* Sarasota, Fla.: Professional Resource Exchange, 1988.

Worthington, Everett L. "Changes in Supervision as Counselors and Supervisors Gain Experience: A Review." *Professional Psychology: Research and Practice* 18, no. 3 (1987): 189–208.

Worthington, Everett L., David Larson, Malvin Brubaker, Cheryl Colecchi, James Berry, and David Morrow. "The Benefits of Legislation Requiring Parental Involvement Prior to Adolescent Abortion." *American Psychologist* 44, no.12 (1989): 1542–45.

Yellin, Jacob. "The History and Current Status of the Clergy-Penitent Privilege." *Santa Clara Law Review* 23 (1983): 95.

Young, Stephanie D. "Sexual Molestation within America's Parishes and Congregations: Should the Church be 'Thy Priest's Keeper'?" *West Virginia Law Review* 91 (1989): 1097–1125.

Yudin, P. "Socialism and Law." In *Soviet Legal Philosophy,* translated by Hugh Babb. Cambridge: Harvard University Press, 1951.

Cases, Constitutions, and Statutes

Abille v. United States, 482 F.Supp. 703 (N.D. Cal. 1980).

Abraham v. Zaslow, Case No. 245862 (Cal. Super. Crt., June 30, 1972).

Addington v. Texas, 441 U.S. 418 (1979).

Anclote Manor Foundation v. Wilkinson, 263 So.2d 256 (Fla.Dist. Ct.App. 1972).

Andrews v. United States, 732 F.2d 366 (4th Cir. 1984).

Baker v. United States, 226 F.Supp. 129 (S.D. Iowa 1964).

Bellah v. Greenson, 146 Cal.Rptr. 535, 81 Cal.App.3d 614 (1978).

Brady v. Hopper, 570 F.Supp. 1333 (D. Colo. 1983), *aff'd*, 751 F.2d 329 (10th Cir. 1984).

California Business and Professions Code, sections 726, 728, & 729 (West Supp. 1989).

California Business and Professions Code, section 1881(f) (West Supp. 1989).

California Business and Professions Code, sections 4982(k) & 4983 (West Supp. 1989).

California Business and Professions Code, section 4996.13 (West Supp. 1989).

California Civil Code, section 43.92 (West Supp. 1989).

California Civil Code ("The Family Law Act"), sections 4000–5138 (West Supp. 1989).

California Evidence Code, sections 1010 & 1033 (West Supp. 1989).

California Penal Code, section 11165.6 (West Supp. 1989).

California Penal Code, section 11172(a) & (e) (West Supp. 1989).

Canterbury v. Spence, 464 F.2d 772 (D.C. Cir. 1972).

Cantwell v. Connecticut, 310 U.S. 296 (1940).

Cerminaro v. Board of Regents, State of New York, 508 N.Y.S.2d 693 (A.D. 3 Dept. 1986).

Colorado Revised Statutes, section 13-21-117 (Supp. 1988).

Colorado Revised Statutes, section 18-3-405.5 (Supp. 1988).

Cosgrove v. Lawrence, 522 A.2d 483 (N.J. Super. App. Div. 1987).

Cotton v. Kambly, 101 Mich.App. 537, 300 N.W.2d 627 (1980).

Currie v. United States, 644 F.Supp. 1074 (M.D.N.C. 1986).

Cutter v. Brownbridge, 228 Cal. Rptr. 545 (Cal. Ct. App. 1986).

Destefano v. Grabrian, 763 P.2d 275 (Colo. 1988).

Employment Division, Dept. of Human Resources of Oregon v. Smith-Black, 763 P.2d 146 (Ore. 1988).

Employment Division, Dept. of Human Resources of Oregon v. Smith, 110 S. Ct. 1595 (1990).

Erickson v. Christenson, 99 Or.App. 104, 781 P.2d 383 (1989).

Florida Statutes Annotated, section X (West 1990).

Florida Statutes Annotated, section 90.505(1)(2) (West 1990).

Funkhouser v. Oklahoma, 763 P.2d 695 (Okla. 1988), cert. denied, 109 S.Ct. 2066 (1989).

Guinn v. Church of Christ of Collinsville, 775 P.2d 766 (Okla. 1989).

Hammer v. Polsky, 36 Misc.2d 482, 233 N.Y.S.2d 110 (N.Y. Sup. Ct. 1962).

Handley v. Richards, 518 So.2d 682 (Ala. 1987).

Hedlund v. Superior Court of Orange County, 34 Cal.3d 695, 194 Cal.Rptr. 805, 669 P.2d 41 (1983).

Hester v. Barnett, 723 S.W.2d 544 (Mo. Ct. App. 1987).

Indiana Statutes Annotated Code, section 34-4-12.4.

In re Daniel v. Daniel, 269 Cal. App. 3d 624 (Cal. App. 6 Dist. 1990).

In re Gregory, 515 N.E.2d 286 (Ill. App. 1987).

In re The Bible Speaks, 73 Bankrup. 848 (D. Mass. 1987).

Jablonski v. United States, 712 F.2d 391 (9th Cir. 1983).

Johnson v. Lincoln Christian College, 501 N.E.2d 1380 (Ill. 1986).

Kaimowitz v. Michigan Department of Mental Health, Case No. 73-19434-AW (Mich. Cir. Ct., July 10, 1973).

Krikorian v. Barry, 196 Cal. App.3d 1211 (Cal. App. 2 Dist. 1987).

Lake v. Cameron, 364 F.2d 657 (D.C. Cir. 1966).

Lessard v. Schmidt, 349 F.Supp. 1078 (E.D. Wis. 1972).

Lipari v. Sears, Roebuck & Co., 497 F.Supp. 185 (D. Neb. 1980).

MacDonald v. Clinger, N.Y.S. 2d 801 (App.Div.1982).

Maine Revised Statutes, title 17-A, section 253(2) (Supp. 1989).

Meier v. Ross General Hospital, 69 Cal.2d 420, 71 Cal. Rptr. 903, 455 P.2d 519 (1968).

Meroni v. Holy Spirit Association (Unification Church), 125 Misc.2d 1061, 480 N.Y.S.2d 706 (N.Y. 1984).

Michigan Compiled Laws Annotated, section 330.1946 (West Supp. 1989).

Minnesota Statutes Annotated, section 609.341 et seq (1987).

Mississippi Code Annotated, section 13-1-22(4).

Mitchell v. Robinson, 334 S.W.2d 11 (Mo. 1960).

Moxon v. County of Kern, 233 Cal.App.2d 393, 43 Cal.Rptr. 481 (1965).

Nally v. Grace Community Church of the Valley, 194 Cal. App. 3d 1147, 240 Cal. Rptr. 215 (Cal. App. 2 Dist. 1987).

Nally v. Grace Community Church of the Valley, 47 Cal.3d 278, 763 P.2d 948, 253 Cal. Rptr. 97 (1988); cert. denied, 109 S. Ct. 1644 (1989).

North Dakota Revised Statutes Annotated, section 12.1-20-06.1 (Michie Supp. 1989).

O'Connor v. Donaldson, 422 U.S. 563 (1975).

Ohio Revised Code Annotated, section 5122.34 (Anderson 1989).

O'Neil v. Schuckardt, 112 Idaho 472, 733 P.2d 693 (Idaho 1986).

Paul v. Watchtower Bible and Tract Society of New York, Inc., 819 F.2d 875 (9th Cir. 1987).

Peck v. Counseling Service of Addison County, 146 Vt. 61, 499 A.2d 422 (1985).

People v. Hodges, Case No. 614153 (Cal. Superior Crt., 1989).

Rennie v. Klein, 462 F.Supp. 1131 (D.N.J. 1978).

Reynolds v. United States, 98 U.S. 145 (1879).

Rivers v. Katz, 67 N.Y.2d 485, 495 N.E.2d 337 (1986).

Roe v. Wade, 410 U.S. 113 (1973).

Rogers v. Commissioner of Mental Health, 390 Mass. 498, 458 N.E.2d 308 (1982).

Roy v. Hartogs, 85 Misc.2d 891, 381 N.Y.S.2d 587 (N.Y. Sup. Ct. 1976).

Runyon v. Reid, 510 P.2d 943 (Okla. 1973).

St. Paul Fire and Marine Insurance Co. v. Love, 447 N.W.2d 5 (Minn. Ct. App. 1989).

Sard v. Hardy, 281 Md. 432, 379 A.2d 1014 (1977).

Schuster v. Altenberg, 144 Wis.2d 223, 424 N.W.2d 159 (1988).

Shaw v. Glickman, 45 Md.App. 718, 415 A.2d. 625 (1980).

Sherbert v. Verner, 374 U.S. 398 (1963).

Simrin v. Simrin, 233 Cal.App.2d 90, 43 Cal.Rptr. 376 (1965).

State v. Brown, 95 Iowa 381, 64 N.W. 277 (1895).

Steinberg v. The Chicago Medical School, 354 N.E.2d 586 (Ill. 1976).

Storey v. Wyoming State Board of Medical Examiners, 721 P.2d 1013 (Wyo. 1986).

Strock v. Presnell, 527 N.E.2d 1235 (Ohio 1988).

Tarasoff v. Regents of the University of California, 13 Cal.3d 117, 118 Cal. Rptr. 129, 529 P.2d 551 (1974).

Tarasoff v. Regents of the University of California, 17 Cal.3d 425, 131 Cal. Rptr. 13, 551 P.2d 334 (1976).

Taylor v. United States, 222 F.2d 398 (D.C. Cir. 1955).

Thompson v. Alameda County, 27 Cal.3d 741, 167 Cal. Rptr. 70, 614 P.2d 728 (1980).

Truman v. Thomas, 165 Cal.Rptr. 308 (1980).

United States v. Ballard, 322 U.S. 78, J. Jackson dissenting, (1944).

United States Code, chptr. 42, sections 2681–87 (1963).

United States Code, chptr. 42, section 1983 (1964).

United States Constitution, amend. I, cl. 1 & 2.

Vistica v. Presbyterian Hospital, 67 Cal.2d 465, 62 Cal. Rptr. 577, 432 P.2d 193 (1967).

Watkins v. United States, 589 F.2d 214 (5th Cir. 1979).

Webster v. Reproductive Health Services, 109 S.Ct. 3040 (1989).

Whitree v. State of New York, 56 Misc. 2d 693, 290 N.Y.S.2d 486 (N.Y. Ct. Cl. 1968).

Wisconsin Statutes Annotated, section 940.22 (1983).

Wisconsin v. Yoder, 406 U.S. 205 (1972).

Wyatt v. Stickney, 325 F.Supp. 781 (M.D. Ala. 1971), 344 F.Supp. 373 (M.D. Ala. 1972),aff'd sub nom *Wyatt v. Aderholt*, 503 F.2d 753 (5th Cir. 1974).

Zipkin v. Freeman, 436 S.W.2d 753 (Mo. 1968).

INDEX

About the Authors

George Ohlschlager is the Associate Director and cofounder of The Redwood Family Institute in Eureka, California. He is a licensed clinical social worker and a member of the American Association of Christian Counselors and the California Chapter of the National Association of Social Workers. Dr. Ohlschlager teaches part-time in the graduate psychology tutorial program of Sierra University.

A psychology graduate of Humboldt State University, Dr. Ohlschlager holds an M.A. in counseling psychology from Trinity Evangelical Divinity School, an M.S.W. from the Graduate School of Social Work, and a J.D. from the College of Law of the University of Iowa.

He and his wife, Lorraine, live in Eureka, California with their three children.

Peter Mosgofian is Executive Director and cofounder of The Redwood Family Institute in Eureka, California. He is a licensed marriage, family, and child counselor and is a member of the American Association of Christian Counselors, the Christian Association for Psychological Studies, and the California Association of Marriage and Family Therapists. Mr. Mosgofian teaches part-time in the graduate psychology tutorial program of Sierra University. He is also an ordained pastor.

A graduate of Humboldt State University, Mr. Mosgofian holds an M.A. in theology and marriage and family therapy from Fuller Theological Seminary.

He and his wife, Gale, live in McKinleyville, California. They have four children.